BUILDING ACCESS
WEB SITES

ISBN 0-13-079830-4

90000

9 780130 798305

PRENTICE HALL PTR

BUILDING A WEB SITE SERIES

Prentice Hall PTR
Building a Web Site Series

BUILDING ORACLE WEB SITES

James J. Hobuss

BUILDING SYBASE WEB SITES

James J. Hobuss

BUILDING ACCESS WEB SITES

James J. Hobuss

BUILDING ACCESS WEB SITES

James J. Hobuss

To join a Prentice Hall PTR Internet mailing list, point to:
http://www.prenhall.com/mail_lists/

Prentice Hall PTR
Upper Saddle River, New Jersey 07458

Library of Congress Cataloging-in-Publication Data

Hobuss, James J., 1955–
    Building Access web sites / James J. Hobuss.
       p. cm.
    Includes index.
    ISBN 0-13-079830-4 (pbk. : alk. paper)
    1. Microsoft Access.   2. Web sites--Design. I. Title.
QA76.9.D3H589   1997
005.75'85--DC21   97-39037
                                   CIP

Editorial/production supervision: *Patti Guerrieri*
Cover design director: *Jerry Votta*
Cover designer: *Design Source*
Manufacturing manager: *Alexis R. Heydt*
Marketing manager: *Miles Williams*
Acquisitions editor: *Jeffrey Pepper*
Editorial assistant: *Christy Schaack*
Compositor/Production services: *Pine Tree Composition, Inc.*

©1998 Prentice Hall PTR
Prentice-Hall, Inc.
A Simon & Schuster Company
Upper Saddle River, NJ 07458

Prentice Hall books are widely used by corporations and government agencies
for training, marketing, and resale.

The publisher offers discounts on this book when ordered in bulk quantities.
For more information, contact: Corporate Sales Department, Phone: 800-382-3419;
Fax: 201-236-7141; E-mail: corpsales@prenhall.com; or write: Prentice Hall PTR,
Corp. Sales Dept., One Lake Street, Upper Saddle River, NJ 07458.

Printed in the United States of America
10 9 8 7 6 5 4 3 2 1

ISBN   0-13-079830-4

Prentice-Hall International (UK) Limited, *London*
Prentice-Hall of Australia Pty. Limited, *Sydney*
Prentice-Hall Canada Inc., *Toronto*
Prentice-Hall Hispanoamericana, S.A., *Mexico*
Prentice-Hall of India Private Limited, *New Delhi*
Prentice-Hall of Japan, Inc., *Tokyo*
Simon & Schuster Asia Pte. Ltd., *Singapore*
Editora Prentice-Hall do Brasil, Ltda., *Rio de Janeiro*

Once again, and always, to my wife, Robin, for being so patient and understanding with who I am as a husband, father, and man. I love you will all of my heart, which is more than I can say, but not as much as I can show. My very good friend while I was a kid growing up in Colorado, Benny Martinez, whose life ended too soon for too stupid of a reason, but whose friendship has remained with me all my life. (Benny, I liked you for our friendship, not to get close to your sister Angie.) My sister, Mari-Beth, for being such a special person in my life now, that it leaves me wondering how you could have ever been so mean and nasty when we were kids. To Laura Poole, the original Development Editor for this book, not only for her abilities in her craft but the skillful way in which she would prod and pursue even higher levels of quality in this manuscript. Finally, to all the kids in Junior and Senior High school who tormented me and contributed so much to making those years brutal for me being a kid, BITE ME.

James J. Hobuss

Contents

Introduction

This book will show you the skills and describe the techniques you need to know to become successful designing, developing, and implementing production Web applications that use Access 97 databases.

I trust you're not surprised to learn that you are not alone in the migration of developers to building Web database applications. Your ability to be successful in large part is determined by your skillset and how you apply those skills to solve business computing problems. Learn what is in these pages and you will have the basis to be successful. How you apply those skills is up to you.

What You'll Need

The book assumes you have a beginners understanding of Access 97. It also assumes you are running Access 97 on a Windows 95 or Windows NT machine. It is designed to introduce Access 97 database design, construction, and incorporation to the Internet application development process. There is emphasis on the latter and the facilities in Access 97 to build and deploy databases for use and access over the Internet. Key topics are the planning, design, and implementation of enterprise-quality Internet/intranet applications that include database connectivity to Microsoft Corporation's Access 97 databases with production-level security and performance. All technical terms used in the book are defined and there are abundant screen images, tips, and callouts. Also included in this book are abundant examples of Web page construction and program code with database access.

How to Read This Book

The layout of this book is designed to be informative and valuable for those who like to read a book from the front cover to the back. If you are the type of person who likes to read only those topics that interest you, then you will be pleased to learn that with 20 chapters and three appendices, you can pick and choose which chapters to read without missing anything. The following paragraphs provide a brief description of each of the chapters in this book.

Section 1: Planning

In this section you will learn about the Internet and Web in general, as well as some of the specifics of the different programming languages and development suites available to help in the construction process. Following this introduction, you will read introductory chapters to HTML, and CGI programs. If you have no interest in any of these topics, I would recommend that you read at least Chapters 6 and 7. The material in these chapters is preparatory to, and referenced in, future chapters.

Chapter 1: The Web Connection. Before you plunge into the issues specific to the design, development, and implementation of Web database applications, it is valuable that you understand a few things about the origins of the Web. That's what this chapter is about. With this as a foundation, hopefully you can make better sense out of all the Web-hype that so pervades the computer industry.

Chapter 2: Web Commerce. This chapter introduces you to some of the reasons why companies are turning to the Web as the production platform of database applications. You will learn the role that the database plays in these applications. Following this is a list of some of the things you should consider, outside of the technical issues that you'll learn about in the remainder of this book, when doing business on the Web.

Chapter 3: Choosing a Programming Language. Choosing a programming language to use to develop a Web database application is becoming increasingly more difficult. Currently, there are a myriad of languages, derivatives of languages, dialects of languages, development suites, programming suites, and various iterations of each of these from which to choose. This chapter focuses on the most popular languages available to build Web database applications

Chapter 4: Overview of Java and Java Script. The release of Java from Sun Microsystems coincided with the release of Java Script. Partly because of this, some people view these two languages as being an either/or decision. This is not the case. Although these two languages share similar syntax and use objects similarly, the languages were developed to solve different sets of problems, as you will learn in this chapter.

Chapter 5: Application Development Suites. This chapter presents information on a number of application development suites. The major features of the products are described along with contact information. Most vendors will supply you with evaluation copies of their products, and in many cases, you can download these evaluation copies directly from the Web.

Chapter 6: Overview of HTML. This chapter is an overview of the HyperText Markup Language (HTML). If you are new to the Web, this chapter gives you a good introduction to what HTML is, how to read it, write it, and use it. If you are an experienced Web developer or user, you, too, will find useful information in this chapter on topics such as the structure of HTML, advanced HTML topics, good HTML coding practices, and the future of HTML.

Chapter 7: Overview of CGI. In this chapter, you'll learn about the Common Gateway Interface (CGI) and the role it has in Web database application development. You'll learn about the CGI standard as it applies to UNIX and Windows operating systems. Simple programs are used to communicate and demonstrate CGI capabilities.

Section 2: Internet Database Design

This section includes chapters that are specific to the process of designing and constructing an Internet database application. You will learn about the facilities in Access 97 that are specific to creating database objects and building queries to an Access 97 database.

Chapter 8: Web Application Design and Development. This chapter takes the fundamental concepts of client/server database application development and applies them to the unique attributes of the Web. It begins by discussing what those concepts are, progresses through describing the architectural components of the Web, and ends with the application of those concepts to the Web architecture.

Chapter 9: Introduction to Access 97. Beginning with this chapter and continuing into chapters 10 and 11, you are introduced to Microsoft Corporations Access 97 product. This chapter provides an overview of the product and some of the features (most of which are new) specific to Web database application development. It continues on with specific information on DDL, SQL, and the facilities in Access 97 to define databases and database objects.

Chapter 10: Access 97 Queries. In this chapter you will learn how to build and execute simple queries in Access 97. You will also learn how to use an external data source, including Open DataBase Connectivity (ODBC), in your Access 97 tables and queries. This information will assist you if you are using a development tool besides Access 97 to build your front-end Web database application.

Chapter 11: Designing Advanced Access 97 Queries. In this chapter you will go deeper into the facilities in Access 97 to create advanced queries. This includes using multiple aggregate functions, applying criteria in the query, parameter queries, nested queries, and optimizing performance of queries.

Section 3: Interfacing with the Internet User

This section includes chapters that describe the process of building a Web database application that incorporates user access and input. This includes not only building the components that provide user access, but also building user interfaces that extend this capability to include database updates. Included in this section is a chapter on how to incorporate multimedia and advanced graphics and images in your Web application. Finally, you will learn things you can do to improve the performance of your Web database applications.

Chapter 12: HTML Forms and Database Access. This chapter gives you a thorough introduction into the markups (controls) available to construct and transmit an HTML form. These markups, and the actions and attributes you code to the controls on the form, are the input mechanism into your Web database application.

Chapter 13: Accessing Web Databases Using CGI Programs. This chapter begins with a review of CGI basics you learned in previous chapters in this book. You will learn about CGI input and output processing, and some of the different ways that exist in which a client can make a request to the server when an HTML form is submitted. Then, you will see how CGI programs can be used to generate HTML. Later in this chapter you will learn among other things, how to write a CGI program to perform whatever type of database access required by your Web database application.

Chapter 14: MIME and Advanced Data Presentation. Earlier chapters include a number of examples of how data can be formatted and displayed throughout many of these chapters. In this chapter, you'll learn how to incorporate multimedia components in your Web database applications.

Chapter 15: Managing Web Database Access and the Application State. The Web is an inherently "stateless" environment—it is non-conversational in nature. This chapter describes three different techniques (hidden fields on forms, database tables, and cookies) that you could use to keep track of where an application is a serial process—the application state.

Chapter 16: Improving the Performance of Web Database Applications. This chapter describes some techniques you can use to build efficiency in your Web database applications. It is segmented into two major sections; Application Optimization and Database Optimization.

Section 4: Advanced Topics in Internet Database Publishing

This section contains chapters that will conclude your understanding of the process of designing and constructing dynamic Web applications that incorporate database access. You will learn about the facilities in Access 97 for migrating data from Access 97 databases from one location to another, as well as how to use security components to protect the data you are making available over the Internet. Following this are two chapters that walk you through the process of designing and developing an actual Web database application.

Chapter 17: Migrating Data from Enterprise Data Stores to Server-based Databases. In this chapter you will learn about some of the techniques used to migrate data from enterprise data stores to server-based Web databases. Specifically you'll learn about the features in Access 97 that facilitate this process, such as replication and synchronization.

Chapter 18: Using Firewalls and Security Components to Protect Your Data. This chapter introduces you to the issues of Web-based security and describes some of the things that you can do to secure your Web applications, including your Web-accessible Access 97 databases. It is not intended to be a primer on the subject. It is intended to introduce you to the issues and components of which you need to be aware to safeguard your investment in your Web site and your data.

Chapter 19: Designing an Internet Course Delivery System. This is the first of two "summation" chapters. In this chapter, you will take what was learned in the previous chapters and see how it is applied to the design of a Web database application. Specifically, you will recall that in Chapter 8 you learned how to design a Web database application to take into account the unique considerations of a Web-based database application. You will have seen how the information contained in that chapter, plus various other pieces of information from the other chapters in this book, are applied to the actual design of a Web database application. Then, in Chapter 20, this will be taken to the next logical step, which is the actual construction of a Web database application.

Chapter 20: Building a Simple Class Registration System. This chapter focuses on how to use HTML and a Web database application development suite to construct a Web database application that includes both Internet and intranet access. The company profiled in this Chapter is A Better Computer (ABC) Company, a fictitious corporation that provides, among other things, computer training. The Web application profiled contains, among other things, a query facility so that Web visitors can see what training classes are held in cities near them. This is the Internet component to the database that is profiled. The intranet component presented is the facility used by ABC employees to update the Access 97 database that maintains the data that describes the course offerings of ABC Company and their availability.

Appendices

Appendix A: CD-ROM Contents. This appendix provides a detailed description of the contents of the CD-ROM that accompanies the book.

Appendix B: Frequently Asked Questions. This is a Frequently Asked Questions (FAQ) that provides answers to many of the most frequently asked questions from people new to the process of Web database application development.

Appendix C: WWW Database Development Resources. This appendix includes a list of the resources available on the Internet that are specific to the process of designing and building Web database applications. This includes Web sites, newsgroups, and forums.

In addition to the content of the book and the material contained in the chapters, this book also includes a companion CD-ROM. Evaluation copies of many products referenced in the book that relate to the topic of the book are included on the enclosed CD-ROM.

Finally, I welcome your comments on the book. Feel free to e-mail me at: jhobuss@teleport.com.

About the Author

Jim Hobuss has been either building computer applications or managing the activities specific to building computer applications since 1977. After leaving a successful career in which he was the Development Center Manager for a major Northwest Bank (soon to be an acquisition of an even larger mid-West Bank) in 1991, he built a successful high technology training and consulting company. From 1991 through 1996, Jim built his company into a successful enterprise, finally disposing of it in 1996 to enter a phase of semi-retirement at the ripe age of 40! Finding himself at least 20 years away from official retirement and pensions, Jim is currently enjoying a more leisurely lifestyle (family, golf, and the hot tub) and spends much of his working time consulting, writing, and speaking at industry events.

Jim has previously written three books. The first, titled *Application Development Center: Implementation and Management*, is popular with IS executives and management who are charged with the responsibility of implementing new technologies in application development departments. The second, titled *Application Development Using PowerBuilder*, is a very successful book written for developers using PowerBuilder to create client/server applications. The third book, titled *Oracle 8 Database Publishing on the Internet* is a best-seller. He has written countless articles that have appeared in magazines ranging from *Systems Builder* to *Journal of Information Systems Management*. He also writes a monthly column for *Exploring Sybase SQL Server* journal. You can e-mail Jim at: jhobuss@tele-port.com.

CHAPTER 1

The Web Connection

Chances are that you bought this book because you have either an interest or a mandate to develop a Web database application. I have the knowledge to help you do that. You and I have forged a *Web Connection*. The Web has brought us together with what started as an exchange of commerce and continues on now as an exchange of information.

Chances are you can't pick up a computer trade magazine without seeing a front-page reference to the Internet. Regardless to what type of magazine you're looking at, you will find a substantial amount of it that is devoted to the Internet. It is not surprising then, that our paths cross, first by me writing this book, and second, by you deciding to purchase it.

Of all the options to consider when building a Web site, this book presents options for incorporating a database using Microsoft Access 97. Of course, this Relational Data-Base Management System (RDBMS) can not be used by itself to create a Web site—other components are required. These additional components are discussed in detail, and you will see how they interface with Access 97.

Before you plunge into the issues specific to the design, development, and implementation of Web database applications, it is valuable that you understand a few things about the origins of the Web.

Internet Background

A few years ago the Web was an unknown—preceded by the Internet. The Internet being preceded by ARPANET.

Definition: Internet—The collection of inter-connected networks that all use the TCP/IP protocols (or gateway facilities) and that evolved from the ARPANET of the late '60s and early '70s.

Definition: ARPANET—A wide-area networking facility developed by the U.S. Department of Defense in the late '60s and early '70s with the intent of providing a communication backbone and architecture that would survive catastrophic calamities.

ARPANET (Advanced Research Projects Agency—NET) was established by the U.S. Department of Defense (DoD), beginning in the late 1960s, as a result of the cold war the United States was engaged in with the USSR. Government officials wanted to create a communications and networking facility whereby governmental and academic computer systems would be able to communicate even in the event of a nuclear strike against the United States.

Thought: The U.S. DoD certainly succeeded in its objective for ARPANET. Did you know that in 1988 a hacker-initiated virus called the "Internet-worm" was unleashed that disabled or negatively affected almost one-half (a little over 6,000) of the total number of servers comprising the Internet? What a nuclear bomb could never do was almost accomplished without so much as a pop from a cap gun.

Having succeeded in accomplishing this objective, the Internet remained a largely academic, scientific, and military communications vehicle until around 1988 when the backbone speed of the communications supporting the Internet was upgraded to 1.544 mbps—thanks in large measure to the commercial availability of T1 data communication facilities.

Thought: The achievement of implementing a backbone Internet communication speed of 1,544,000 bits per second (1.544 mbps) in 1988 was astounding, especially when you consider that currently most analog telephone lines can achieve at best 28,800 bits per second transmission speed of data. Then, in 1990, two events occurred that solidified the commercial application of the Internet. First, a researcher named Tim Berners-Lee published a paper referring (for the first time ever) to the Internet as the World Wide Web, or WWW. Second, and in large measure due to the end of the cold war as seen during the Reagan U.S. Presidential administration, the DoD cancels the ARPANET program and turns the Internet over to commercialization. Regarding the former, in retrospect I think that Mr. Berners-Lee might have done more harm than good by coining the phrase "World Wide Web—or Web" to describe the Internet. The two are often used interchangeably when they should not be. As you will learn later in this chapter, the Web and Internet are not synonymous. The Internet is a global network and the Web is a set of communications applications and software that execute on the Internet.

Even though the computers that attached to the early Internet did so using TCP/IP protocols, computers on non-TCP/IP networks can now access the Internet via gateway computers or systems that perform the necessary protocol translations.

A Chronological History of the Internet

The initial ARPANET configuration linked together the following four sites:

- Stanford Research Institute (SRI)
- University of California at Santa Barbara (UCSB)
- University of California at Los Angeles (UCLA)
- University of Utah (UU)

The following timeline provides a thumbnail overview of the events triggering the growth of the Web up through today.

> **1957** The USSR Launches Sputnik, generally recognized as the beginning of the Cold War between the USSR and the United States.

> **1961** Bay of Pigs occurs, forcing then U.S. President John F. Kennedy to a showdown with then USSR Premier Nikhita Kruschev.

Thought: What we know now as the Internet was created out of a U.S. response to the cold war. The above two events were the catalyst to the U.S. seeking to develop a secure and persistent communications mechanism that would withstand a nuclear war.

> **1969** United States Department of Defense (DoD) commissions the establishment of ARPA, and the communications facility known as ARPANET.

> **1970** ARPANET begins using Network Control Protocol (NCP) for inter-site communications.

> **1972** Telnet specification RFC-318 was proposed to establish a common format for one Internet site to establish communications with another.

> **1973** Bob Metcalfe, now a columnist and founder of 3COM corporation, outlined the facilities of Ethernet networking in his Ph.D. thesis at Harvard University. This is also the year that File Transfer protocol specification number RFC 454 was proposed.

Information: 1973 was also the year that Bill Gates and I were graduating from High School. Bill Gates and I also share a common thread—our birth dates are the same.

> **1974** TCP/IP communications protocol was proposed by Vint Cerf and Bob Kahn which today remains as the defining way in which devices on the Internet communicate with each other.

> **1976** Bell Labs developed the UUCP (Unix-to-Unix CoPy) protocol that allows devices connected to the Internet to share and transfer information in a consistent manner.

> **1982** DoD specifies TCP/IP as the standard ARPANET protocol.

1984   The number of Internet host sites reaches 1,000. This is the year that Domain Name Services is established.

Definition: Domain Name Service is a method by which each site that attaches to the Internet is assigned a unique name.

1987   The number of Internet host sites reaches 10,000.

1988   The Internet worm disables or infects more than ½ of all Internet host sites.

1989   The number of Internet host sites reaches 100,000.

1900   With the end of the Cold War, the DoD terminates the ARPANET initiative and allows the Internet to commercialize.

1991   Brewster Kahle of Thinking Machines develops the first Wide Area Information Server. Paul Lindner and Mark McCahill of the University of Minnesota write Gopher.

Information: You get one guess to come up with the mascot for the University of Minnesota.

Definition: Gopher—A method of making menus of materials available over the Internet. Gopher was the predecessor to Hypertext.

1992   The number of Internet host sites reaches 1,000,000. Researchers at the University of Nevada release Veronica—a frequently updated database of the names of almost every menu item on almost all the Gopher servers. This is also the year that U.S. Vice President Al Gore begins discussing the "Information Superhighway."

Information: One of the researchers at the University of Nevada who created Veronica was a fan of the old Archie cartoons and comic books. What was the name of Archie's girlfriend?

Definition: Veronica—Very Early Rodent Oriented Net-wide Index to Computerized Archives—is a constantly updated database of the names of almost every menu item on almost every Gopher server.

1993   NSF creates InterNIC to facilitate the creation and registration of Internet services. Marc Andreesen, now of Netscape Corporation, releases MOSAIC while employed by NCSA.

Definition: MOSAIC—The first Web browser available for all the major operating systems with the same graphical Interface. MOSAIC was the "killer application" that launched the popularity of the Web.

1994   The first commercial application is developed and delivered over the Internet by Pizza Hut Corporation. With this application, you could order a pizza (and specify the toppings!) from your nearest Pizza Hut franchise and have it delivered to your home—from your Web browser. The term "spam" (not the processed meat product developed and sold by Hormel Corporation) became popular to describe an inappropriate attempt to use a mailing list.

Information: A bit of trivia that you may be quizzed on later: In the 1970s, my father—Orville Hobuss, while working on a contract for the American Can Company, designed the machine that made Spam cans.

1995 Compuserve, America Online, and Prodigy all begin offering Internet connectivity through their online services. They become so successful with this that most of their subscribers think that Compuserve, America Online, and Prodigy are the Internet. This is also the year that Marc Andreesen issues an Initial Public Offering (IPO) for Netscape Communications Corporation that ranks it as the #3 highest initial public offering share price of all time. Also, major software companies (i.e., Microsoft, Lotus, WordPerfect) begin to announce plans to port their applications to the Internet.

Thought: It wasn't but 6 months after Netscape's IPO that Microsoft Chairman Bill Gates stated in a news conference that Microsoft Corporation was going to restructure itself to become a major Internet tools provider.

1996 America Online is swamped with customer complaints about not being able to connect to their service after they begin offering unlimited-access Internet connections. They discovered that many customers were not terminating their connections when done using their computers—presumably waiting for e-mail. Microsoft Corp releases Access 97—an RDBMS product with extensive Web database application development and deployment tools.

1997 Prentice Hall publishes this book. The number of host sites reaches 10,000,000.

The Internet Today

The Internet today is a global information resource accumulation and dissemination facility that dwarves the expectations of its creators. On the Internet today you can find the latest research into AIDS treatments, schedule a vacation including making reservations at restaurants and hotels, view the world's great art works, send a resume to a confidential job search site, and find and communicate with your high school buddies. Web sites that deal with subjects as diverse as the effects of ribonucleic acids on the upper gastrointestinal tract and the current box office smash hit are popping up at an ever-increasing rate. The number of new Web sites and the growth of the Internet are astounding.

Believe it or not, the Internet is not an Al Gore (Vice President of the United States between 1992 and 2000) initiative. Those of you reading this who voted in the 1992 Presidential elections probably remember Al Gore's Democratic National Convention pledge to develop an "information superhighway" during Bill Clinton's first term administration. Did you know that this was a very safe statement for Al Gore to make, considering the momentum had been building for this during the previous 30 years?

An average of 11,000 new sites are added each day, and an estimated 300,000 Web servers (each Web server can host a minimum of one and an unlimited maximum number of Web sites) are expected to be shipped in 1998. It is expected that by 1998 there will be over 22,000,000 Web sites!

With all this information available, one of the critical issues to users becomes finding the information being sought. To help, there are a growing number of tools available, called *search engines*. These search engines browse information stored in various site's Web pages for key words that you supply and display a summary page of the sites containing those key words. Many of these search engines display their results page as hypertext links so all you have to do is click on the link and your browser will automatically go to the site that satisfies your search request.

What Is the Web?

The Web is *not* the Internet, and the Internet is *not* the Web. Although the terms are used synonymously, they are not synonymous. They are closely related and frequently discussed in the same sentence. If you look you will find instances in this book where the two terms *appear* to be used interchangeably.

The Internet is a global network. It is the communications infrastructure by which our computers communicate with other computers attached to it.

The Web is a set of communications applications and software that execute on the Internet. The Internet is to our highway system what the Web is to automobiles, motorcycles, and trucks.

Web applications share some of the following common characteristics with each other:

- They understand and use HTML as their display vehicle.
- They use the bi-directional Client/Server model of data communications and information collection.
- They provide facilities to access a variety of protocols, including HTTP, FTP, Telnet, and Gopher.
- They use Uniform Resource Locators (URLs) for document and resource addressing.

What Are Intranets?

Recently a new word has become popular when describing a segment of the Internet—*intranet*. An intranet is a private network inside a company or organization that uses the same kinds of software that you'd find on the public Internet, with one exception. An intranet is targeted for internal employee use only. Because of their secure nature (they can only be accessed by employees of the company that has the intranet), intranets were the first vehicle for development and deployment of Web database applications.

Intranets, like the Internet, are not defined by physical or geographical boundaries. Anyone with a Web browser can access a corporate intranet site from anywhere in the world—although only those people who have security permissions are allowed to enter. An intranet site is usually identified in the same way that an Internet site is identified—by an URL. For instance, I used to work for a company named XDB Systems, Inc. Its Internet URL is: `http://www.xdb.com`. Its intranet URL is: `http://home.xdb.com`. A PC-based tools provider, they had developed a very extensive intranet facility that employees all over the world could access through their local Internet Service Provider. Here was a company that in a very short time built a large information distribution system that provided the following capabilities:

- Disseminated corporate human resources types of information
- Disseminated sales activities and status of orders
- Collected and disseminated problem tracking information
- Disseminated marketing information

Note: The statistics describing the popularity of the Web are staggering, and I'll add one more to the cauldron. Zona Research estimates that corporate spending on intranet development projects will outpace spending on Internet projects by a factor of 4:1 by 1998—to a whopping $7.8 billion.

Benefits of Intranets

Intranets are expanding the reach and scope of ways in which corporations collect and disseminate information. Because intranets offer many advantages over traditional groupware tools like IBM Notes, their acceptance is expected to continue to escalate.

By using corporate intranets, companies gain many benefits, some of which are discussed in the following paragraphs.

Centralize Information for Dissemination Globally. Because of intranets, employees can go to a single location (the intranet URL) to obtain corporate information. If those employees are located in remote areas and they have access to a local Internet Service Provider, they can attach to their corporate intranet site for the price of a local telephone call.

Provide a Very Productive Application Development Environment. Once the architectural components are in place, the tools have been purchased and employees have been trained, developing an application for deployment over an intranet is a very quick process.

Organize Information. Not only do intranets help to centralize and disseminate internal information, but they can also organize information existing outside the corporation. Via hypertext links, an intranet can provide point-and-click attachment to any external Internet site via that site's URL. This could include directions to home offices, white papers, product descriptions, etc.

Categorize and Analyze Captured Data. Because of the "list" nature of Web pages, data is easy to organize and disseminate in meaningful ways. Lists of one sort or another were one of the very first ways in which data was presented on Web pages and remains to this day the most popular data dissemination format. This is especially true for Web database applications that display the results of queries in tables, which are bi-level lists.

Reduce Network Cost. Once TCP/IP communications are established to a Web site and the user has a Web browser, there are no additional network costs associated with connecting to either the Internet or an intranet. Network cards are not required and Ethernet or Token Ring cabling is not required. The cost to establish and maintain an intranet connection is significantly less than the cost to establish and maintain a connection to a LAN or WAN.

The following items include some of the many documents companies distribute over intranets:

- Programs to install disks for all approved software
- Computer-based training
- Corporate policy manual
- Production status for all current and new products
- Current sick leave and vacation allotments
- EEO guidelines and affirmation statements
- Employee and corporate 401(K) information
- Internal job postings
- Job satisfaction surveys
- New employee orientation manuals
- Corporate financial statements, especially if your company's stock is traded publicly
- Corporate newsletters
- Departmental newsletters
- Merger and acquisition information (a sign of the times—your company is either being bought or is buying)
- Inventory
- Marketing materials
- Pricing policies
- Sales leads
- Sales materials
- White papers
- Project schedules and task breakdowns
- Personnel assignments
- Team meeting scheduling and status reporting
- Goal reporting
- Problem reporting and tracking

- Help desk access
- Service call and history reporting

What Is a Web Database and Why Have One?

Web databases are not too much different from non-Web databases—in fact, in most cases they are the same. A Web database is a collection of data that is accessed via a query language or programming API. Whereas non-Web databases are accessed via front-end interfaces built with tools like Microsoft Access 97, Oracle PowerObjects or Sybase PowerBuilder. Web databases are accessed indirectly from HTML forms.

As you'll learn later, HTML specifications do not provide for direct database access from within an HTML page. Rather, special "tags," or commands, that are embedded within the HTML page trigger another program that actually reads the Web database. The results are then formatted into an HTML page for display back to the person who requested the information.

Most commercial Web database applications today provide at least query-only Web database access capabilities. As companies become more comfortable with commerce transactions over the Internet and as security issues become a thing of the past, more applications will be written that provide update capabilities to the Web databases. The technology certainly exists to provide this capability today.

Web databases are accessed from a Web browser and can have no data components that reside on the user's machine. A Web database is part of an application that is deployed over either the Internet (for external user's access) or a corporate intranet (for internal use only). Web databases come in many different varieties, such as:

- Microsoft Access 97
- Oracle
- Sybase
- Informix
- DB2

In Chapter 20 of this book is a discussion of how one company took an existing customer and accounting database and, with minor changes, deployed that same database in an application that was delivered over the Internet via Web browsers—thus creating a Web database application.

Although the development and deployment of database applications over the Web is still in its infancy, there are a number of recognizable advantages to not only your company and your users, but to you as well. This section will explore those advantages.

Intranet Database Application Benefits

Although the installation of the architectural components to deliver a Web database application are *usually* expensive, there are a number of advantages to the company that undertakes to develop and deliver a Web database application. These are:

- The potential to spend less money by purchasing less expensive client machines as Web applications become more prolific
- The development of skill sets in employees that will usher in the 21st century
- Greater job satisfaction for employees, resulting in decreased turnover
- Increased productivity in the development staff
- The ability to interface with more potential customers at less cost per customer than any other means
- The ability to market products and services globally without having to suffer the burden of establishing overseas offices
- Increased opportunity to develop systems that meet more of the needs of the company due to the rapid application development nature of HTML and GUI development tools
- Easy maintenance of Web database applications due to the smooth integration of HTML and CGI programs

---

Tip: I use the phrase "... *usually* expensive..." with emphasis on the word *usually*. It does not have to be an expensive proposition to develop a Web presence and deliver a Web database application. For the price of a Pentium-based machine, Operating System, modem, RDBMS software, and access to a local Internet Service Provider, you can build a relatively inexpensive Web database application. The other necessary components, such as application development tools, Web server, application server, and CGI programming language are all available as shareware on the Web.

Advantages of Web Database Applications for the User

There are two groups of users of Web database applications: employees who access Web databases deployed over the intranet, and everyone else. The advantages of Web database applications to intranet users are summarized as:

- Access to graphical user interfaces to corporate data
- Access to up-to-date company information
- Greater opportunity to interact with other people, departments, and technologies within the company
- Ability to customize their browsers to meet their specific needs
- Integration of the Web database application with other applications running on their machines

  The advantages to everyone else accessing Web database applications are:

- Ability to reach an automated sales force at all hours
- Access to company information from the comforts of home (or their workplace)
- Ability to interface with the company data without having to purchase expensive equipment or software

Moving On

This chapter introduced you to the Internet, the Web, and intranets. You also read about many of the benefits and advantages available to companies, users, and application developers who build and use Web database applications.

In the next chapter you'll read about why it makes sense in today's environment to build and deploy a Web database application as well as the role of databases and RDBMS products in the whole process. Finally, you'll learn about some of the ways that companies are using the Web database applications they build.

CHAPTER 2

Web Commerce

Web database application development is about "Web Commerce"—that is, making or saving money. Period. In a scene from the movie Jerry Maquire, the character Rod Tidwell, said "Show me the money!" To find a purpose for developing and deploying a Web database application you need do nothing more than follow the money. Companies are building them for one of two purposes:

- To sell more product or services and thus make more money—the primary use of Web database applications deployed over the Internet
- To save money by using a more efficient information collection and delivery mechanism from that which has been available in the past—the primary use of Web database applications deployed over an intranet

This chapter introduces you to reasons why companies are turning to the Web to develop production database applications. Included in this is the role that the database plays in these applications. Following this is a list of some of the things you should consider, outside of the technical issues that you'll learn about in the remainder of this book, when doing business on the Web.

Today's Competitive Business Environment

It has been a very long time since a manager in a business found success in managing a portion of the business by saying, "Well, that's the way we *used* to do it." Sure, Coca Cola is making Coke with the same recipe they have used for eons, and Hormel & Sons are still making Spam, but that's not what this is chapter is about. Even though these companies' products are the same as they have been for years, the way in which both of these companies (and most all others) go about running their businesses is much different now than it has been. If you want proof of this, check out their Web sites at:

Coca Cola Corp: `http://www.cocacola.com`

Hormel & Sons: `http://www.hormel.com`

Even though companies may still be producing the same products or offering the same services that have been available for years, they must have changed the way they do business to remain competitive. Building and deploying Web database applications is an extension of this.

Do you remember when you first started taking notice of the Web? For most (myself included), this did not occur until we were in the 1990s. I still remember a 1995 article written by Jim Seymour of *PC Magazine* that focused on how companies were trying to figure out how to make money on the Web. Mr. Seymour wrote that there existed a deep-rooted sense that it was somehow possible to reap financial benefit by building and deploying a Web presence, but the process of actually doing this was unknown. Static pages of information were expensive to create and tedious (and expensive) to maintain. Most of the organizations that were the pioneers in establishing a Web presence found reasons other than financial to justify the expense.

With the advent of HTML pages being able to access corporate databases via CGI programs and proprietary extensions to HTML specifications, the Web became significantly more viable as a place for businesses to conduct their business. We are just on the cusp of the Web becoming the latest arena where businesses can become gladiators in unabated competition that usually and inevitably results in the death of one of the combatants.

There are a number of factors that precipitate the movement of businesses to build Web database applications.

Changing Marketplace

The rapidly changing marketplace forces companies to respond quickly to business opportunities. One of the quickest ways to build and deploy a database application is over the Internet using the latest generation of application development tools.

Cost Containment

The profit margins guiding companies are continually being squeezed. There are two things that corporate management can do to contain costs and thus maintain their profit margins: reduce costs or increase productivity. Both of these are possible with a database application deployed over the Internet.

Increased Services

Customers are more astute now than in the past, and they demand more from the company from which they purchase their goods. Web database applications provide a means of offering these services in a very cost-efficient and easy-to-deploy manner.

Organizational Change

Changes in the organizational structure of companies are leading to new ways of doing business—business models. As corporations continue a trend that began in the early 1980s of downsizing and removing hierarchical layers, collaborative product development leads to more creative ways of marketing and selling products and services. One of the new ways to do this is with Web database applications accessible by customers.

Shrinking Product Life Cycles

Due primarily to a more competitive marketplace, companies are releasing new products and new versions of existing products on an ever-accelerated schedule. Marketing and customer service activities necessary to sell these products are being accelerated accordingly. Applications developed for deployment over the Internet represent a means to provide this accelerated marketing and sales support.

Why Do Business on the Web?

A few years ago, doing business on the Web meant having a series of very static Web pages that described the company, provided phone numbers and addresses, and perhaps a brief description or two about the company's products and/or services. While businesses were trying to figure out *what* to say on the Web, technology was taking care of figuring out *how* to say it.

With the advent of HTML editors, application development tools and suites, and access to RDBMS, the use of the Web as a place to conduct business is secured.

Definition: RDBMS—A Relational DataBase Management System is a software solution that stores and presents its data in tabular format and provides for the manipulation of data stored in sets of data, as opposed to individual records.

The number one reason why a company should do business on the Web is that if they don't, with all other competitive issues being equal, their competition will outperform them. The following list and sections describe some of the reasons why this is the case:

- Expanded Reach
- Corporate Image Enhancement
- Improved Customer Service
- Lead Generation
- Product/Service Delivery Channel
- Reduced Operating Expenses
- Test Marketing

Expanded Reach

On the Web, you can make a sales presentation or put promotional material in the hands of interested people while all your salespeople are sound asleep in their beds. Orders can be taken and products queued for shipment before your first cup of coffee in the morning.

You no longer have to put up the $3–$4k it costs to send a salesperson around the world to meet with customers—although this is not to say that business travel for sales purposes can be eliminated by the Web.

What this *is* saying is that with the Web, and the Internet, your company has the ability to interact with customers and potential customers in a format where geography and time have no relevance. When you do business on the Web, you have increased your accessibility to customers, and customer's accessibility to you.

For example, I used to own a computer training company. We offered our services to companies in the United States and Canada. We also had a Web page advertising our company and the courses that we offered. One day a company from Denmark contacted us via e-mail. This e-mail resulted in us going over to Denmark to conduct a series of training classes. Although we had never before advertised overseas, we were able to get this business—thanks to the reach of our Web page.

Corporate Image Enhancement

The image that a corporation has with customers is a very valuable asset. On the financial statements of most large corporations (and those of smaller corporations that want to boost their numbers) a line item titled "Goodwill" appears. By deploying a Web database application, a company has a very direct, immediate, inexpensive, and significant opportunity to project and enhance its image.

I used to work for a company named XDB Systems, Inc. From 1986 to 1996 they were a company known as an add-on tool vendor to a much larger software vendor's products. In 1996, XDB began a highly visible marketing campaign to enhance their corporate image by recasting a new image as an Internet tools provider. One of the key tools used in this attempted metamorphosis was their Web page. On their current Web pages you will find very little mention of their earlier technologies—even though they still sell and support those products. What you will see is a lot of attention to their newer technologies. Do you want to see how they're doing this? Check out their Web page at: `http://www.xdb.com`.

In addition to the marketing and sales opportunities of doing business on the Web, there is an opportunity to conduct public relations activities. This image enhancement includes corporate mission statements, goals, philosophies, charities receiving donations, and testimonials.

Improved Customer Service

Customers are demanding more from the companies they do business with, such as more product choices, less expensive products and services, and increased customer service in an inexpensive manner. The Web provides a tremendous opportunity to provide customer service that is not only very responsive but one of the least expensive ways to implement.

Web-based customer service not only means that customers have access to product support over the Web, but also that they can perform the following:

- Receive an on-line and interactive status of past-reported problems
- Browse a support database for similar problems and resolutions
- Submit a question to a company technical support person

- Download patches to software and free utility programs
- Read a Frequently Asked Question (FAQ)
- Submit a request for future enhancements to the product(s)

    The company offering Web-based customer service has the following advantages:

- The ability to track problem areas in product to help determine where to place R&D dollars
- The ability to monitor the performance of product support technicians

Lead Generation

When a person browses your Web site, you can track and extract their login ID. You know they are at least a potential customer—and with their login ID you can send follow-up sales/marketing material. You can then follow-up on that lead. The point is that it has cost you very little to generate this lead.

Product/Service Delivery Channel

Before the Web, companies had a number of choices in terms of how they delivered products and services. How they managed these choices was a big determinant to the success of the company. The careers of many sales executives were made or broken over the way sales and delivery channels were set up and managed.

The Web represents a new delivery channel for products and services. It is not the only one for most companies, but it is one that deserves attention. In the coming years, as companies become more astute at doing business on the Web, you will see the recognition that the Web is a viable and significant ways to increase sales and customer satisfaction.

Note: Increasingly, you can find companies that do business only over the Web. They do not have a store front, and they have no direct face-to-face interaction with their customers. One of these is a company that describes itself as having the largest selection of books in the world. The company's Web page address is: `http://www.online-books.com`. This Web site is the only place you can order a book from its inventory.

Reduced Operating Expenses

Companies are operating with profit margins that are thinner today than ever before. Doing business on the Web allows companies to reduce their operating expenses by:

- Maintaining current sales volumes while decreasing sales staff and expenses, or increasing sales volumes without increasing staff and expenses
- Reducing the number of support staff
- Reducing the cost of marketing by taking advantage of the Web as a communication vehicle for advertising and promotion
- Reducing public relations costs
- Measuring and tracking the profitability of products and services, and culling out the unprofitable ones

Test Marketing

The Web is a great place for a company to test market new products, new services, and new marketing campaigns.

The reason why the Web is a great place to conduct a marketing test for a company is due to its reach and the economics of conducting the test market there. As already discussed in this chapter, doing business on the Web represents an opportunity to reach customers who may never have been contacted before and in a way that is extremely inexpensive. I haven't been able to find a book written specific to this issue, but it won't be long before one appears as more and more companies find that conducting a test marketing campaign on the Web is a good thing to do.

What to Consider When Doing Business on the Web

Establishing a Web presence and publishing a Web database application requires a certain amount of technical expertise. That's what the remainder of this book will teach you. The following notes some of the things you need to consider, outside of the technical details, when doing business on the Web.

Customer Feedback.   Can you find a Web site that does not allow for customer feedback? I don't think so. You too should build adequate interfaces and hot links to a customer feedback form. You should also make sure that someone within your company is promptly reading and addressing those customer feedback forms when they do come in. Don't let them become a black hole in your Web universe.

Easy Navigation.   Make your site not only easy to use but easy to navigate. You want to use abundant links to other pages and sites in a format that is easy to maneuver through.

Maintenance.   Make a commitment to maintain your Web site frequently. Forget about using those "Under Construction" labels. If you do not frequently maintain your Web site or modify its appearance and information, you will find that people stop revisiting it.

Monitor Access.   There are various tools and freeware products available that let you monitor who is accessing your site, which pages on your site, and how long they stay there. There are even products that will extract that person's ID for later follow-up (presumably by the sales department). This information will become invaluable to you in monitoring the effectiveness of your Web site and seeing where people spend the most time.

Security.   I'm quite positive that you've heard and read about some of the concerns about commerce transactions over the Internet and the supposed lack of security in them. Although much of this is hype, some of it is valid. You must recognize and appreciate that if you have a retail concern and expect to take orders over the Web, your customers will want to know that their financial information is secure. Many of them read the same magazines that you do, and watch the same television shows. They have an understanding of some of the dangers in performing financial transactions on the Web.

Select Your Internet Service Provider Carefully.   If you do not establish your own Web site, be very careful of who you use as an Internet Service Provider. Make sure that they will allow you to build and install an application on their servers that requires the components you need.

My first Internet Service Provider (ISP) provided very reasonable rates with unlimited duration on connections. Unfortunately, they would not allow me to place a CGI program in their cgi-bin directory. Without this I could not implement by first Web database application. The solution was to switch service providers. This was not an easy solution as I had invested a lot of resources and time in building a Web presence through this ISP that required even more time and resources to move to the new ISP. I learned then the value of the consideration mentioned above.

Target Marketing.   The Web is often used as a marketing vehicle. As is the case with any product or marketing approach, you must develop a thorough understanding of who your target market is and develop a Web presence to address and interest that market. Merely setting up a Web site and building/deploying a Web database application is no guarantee of success. You must build your site and your Web database application with your customers in mind. In addition to identifying your target market, you also need to have a clear understanding of what your Web site is intended to accomplish. Earlier in this chapter you read about many of the ways you could use a Web database application. When designing and building your Web site and Web database application, you must know what purpose there is for the existence of that entity.

Web Site Life Cycle.   Your Web site and the database applications you deploy over the Web have life cycles. In most cases, these life cycles are much shorter than traditional mainframe or PC-based database applications. Recognize this fact when doing your cost-benefit analysis and resource planning.

The Role of Databases in Web Applications

In the last section you saw some of the things to consider when doing business on the Web. Certainly databases play an important role in all of the items discussed. The following list is a good introduction to some additional ways your company can make use of a Web database:

- Develop inter-business agreements for document processing, such as ordering, purchasing, invoicing, and automated payment processing
- Assess demographics, such as customer, supplier, and business partner profiles that are accumulated and used to improve and customize customer services
- Maintain customer status and account management used to manage past purchase history, and predict future purchase patterns
- Establish and maintain customer profiles for use in finely tailored advertising and sales campaigns
- Manage inventory to reduce cash reserves held in inventory
- Track sales and call management to monitor and increase the effectiveness of the sales force and various marketing campaigns

- Provide technical product specifications that are available to customers and field staff to search for products, parts, troubleshooting information, and pricing.

There are many, many types of Web database applications, with more coming on-line every day. The few listed here are just a sample of the many that exist.

Advertising

Advertising of a company's products and services is one of the traditional types of Web applications. With the advent of the technology that allows database queries, a resurgence exists in this type of application. In addition to companies providing advertising on their own products and services, increasingly companies are setting up on the Internet for the sole purpose of providing advertising for other companies. These electronic bulletin boards (or street signs as I refer to them) are becoming as popular as home shopping networks are on the television.

Customer Services

Companies have learned that it is not only cost-effective to offer customer services via Web database applications, but it also promotes customer goodwill. A Web customer service database application gives the user the ability to interact with the information stored in the database in ways that were unavailable via conventional customer service representatives. As a result of their pioneering efforts, companies such as Federal Express and Microsoft have recently established customer service Web database applications.

Financial Services

Banks and other financial institutions are quickly building Web applications that access corporate databases as a way to provide improved financial services to their customers. One of the companies with a most extensive array of services offered is Charles Schwab & Company. Their URL is: `http://www.schwab.com`. In addition to being one of the first brokerages to offer financial services over the Web, they also did a very good job of leveraging their investment in building order entry and processing applications and databases by building Web interfaces into their existing databases. This allowed them to create a series of Web database applications for a quite modest investment.

Information Collection and Dissemination

Increasingly, companies are providing search capabilities within their Web applications. These search capabilities allow the user to enter a key word, or series of key words, and initiate a search of all known sources of information, including databases, for the supplied parameter(s). The results are displayed for follow-up by the user. In addition to this "information dissemination" capability, some companies are providing the ability to collect information and store it in databases via surveys and on-line questionnaires—an "information collection" function. The information provided by the survey/questionnaire participants is stored in databases for later analysis or follow-up.

Job Recruitment

Another application for Web databases that is becoming increasingly popular is job recruitment. Although smaller companies include this function in their Web applications via static, non-database applications, larger companies have sufficient numbers of openings that it is cost-effective for them to use a database in this Web application. A good example of this type of Web database application is the home page for EDP Markets—a national high technology recruiting firm. Their URL is: `http://www.edpmarkets.com`.

Luxury Products

Do you have the time to fly to Nantucket, Massachusetts to view the yachts for sale in the various marinas? Do you want to invest your money and time in flying to the other side of the country to visit automobile dealerships, looking for the pearl white Rolls Royce that you can now afford? I'm sure if you're in the market for one of these luxury products, you certainly have the money to fly around and find what you're looking for. But, do you have the time? Web database applications allow the selling party (or business) the greatest exposure of their product while also respecting the time of the prospective purchaser.

Real Estate

It is difficult to find a real estate company that does not have a Web database application that shows its listings to customers. A few years ago these same firms were limited to static Web pages giving their contact information and possibly some marketing/sales promotional material. Now, these same companies are deploying database applications that display their listings in dynamic and interactive Web pages.

Specialized Product Sales

Specialized product sales are an increasingly popular form of Web database application. There is virtually (pardon the pun) no limit to the reach that such an application has for the speciality firm. A good example is the Virtual Vineyards company. Their URL is: `http://www.virtualvin.com`.

Virtual Shopping Malls

This is one of the most noteworthy applications of Web database application technology. Virtual shopping malls provide the electronic equivalent of a physical shopping mall by allowing a user to browse through the products of many stores in a virtual mall of stores. This same concept can be downsized to the individual store level, with each department showcasing its goods in a virtual shopping environment. A good example of this is what Sears Roebuck and Company have done with their home page, which is at: `http://www.sears.com`. (Hint: Check out the Craftsman section. It'd make Tim the Toolman envious.)

Moving On

In this chapter you learned some of the reasons why companies are turning to the Web as the production platform of database applications and the role that the database plays in these applications. You also read about some of the things you should consider when doing business on the Web.

Chapter 3 introduces you to some of the options you have available to you when choosing a programming language to use to develop your Web database application. Although your choice for an RDBMS product has been made (the selection you made is in the title of this book), you have a number of options when it comes to programming languages.

CHAPTER 3

Choosing a Programming Language

C hoosing a programming language to develop a Web database application is becoming increasingly more difficult. This chapter focuses on the most popular ones
available.

Which Language to Use?

The decision of which programming language to use to develop your Web application is
not much different from the decision of which programming language to use to develop
any other application (Figure 3–1). It helps to view a Web database application as just another application development project. It has its own unique set of factors that must be
evaluated. For example, consider the following scenarios:

- Your company has told you that you are now responsible for developing an order-
  entry system to replace the one that has been running on the mainframe for 25 years.

- Your boss tells you that you must develop a statistical reporting system to analyze
  the data that the company's automated tele-sales system is generating.

- You need to write an application interface program to transfer the information
  stored in your home inventory application over to the retirement planning system
  that you just purchased.

- You have a brilliant idea for an application that you want to write in your free time
  that will make enough money so you can retire (at the age of 42) in the Caribbean on
  a 45′ sailboat. The application is a replacement for many of the functions on the

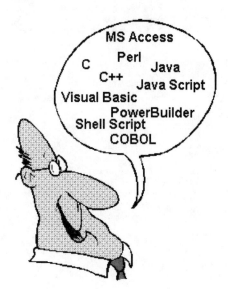

Figure 3–1 Some of the choices of programming language.

Windows Control panel and allows users to adjust many of their system settings by clicking a button without the need of having to reboot the machine to get the changes to take effect.

There are a number of items to consider in each of these scenarios to determine which is the best programming language to use. In the following sections we'll take a look at each of these in greater detail.

Skillset of Developers

The decision to develop a new Web database application does not necessarily mean that a set of skills foreign to current staff is required. To the contrary, you're probably familiar with many of the languages that we'll review in this chapter. For example, COBOL, Visual Basic, PowerBuilder, and of course MS Access can all be used to develop powerful Web database applications.

The following are some skills required for development:

- Language proficiency
- Experience in
  - System and program analysis
  - Database design
  - Database implementation and tuning
  - Graphical User Interface (GUI) design
  - Open DataBase Connectivity (ODBC) or Java DataBase Connectivity (JDBC)
- Knowledge of Web page applications and HTML

Note: ODBC experience is becoming quite common while JDBC is relatively new.

The DataBase Administrator (DBA), programming, and language skills that exist in the team members of your Web database development project are very important in helping you select the correct programming language.

Scope of the Project

Each of the development scenarios presented earlier in this chapter differ in scope. Chances are your projects will too. Some of the factors that should be considered when evaluating the scope of the project are:

- Interfaces to other computer applications (i.e., inventory, accounting, etc.)
- Relationship to new technology (i.e., Voice response system, new operating systems, etc.)
- Project timeframe (i.e., compressed and accelerated, or flexible and adequate)
- Project team member composition (i.e., Are required skills spread among a large number of team members or is each team member expected to have a large number of skills?)
- Existence of data files (i.e., Do data files exist or do they need to be created? If they need to be created, does any of the information currently exist in another format or does it have to be entered?)

An awareness of the scope of the project and the range of functions and capabilities of the various programming languages is vitally important in selecting the correct language for a particular development task.

Application Interfaces

There is a direct relationship between the complexity of a computer system and the number of interfaces that system has with other applications. It is a rare event in today's computing environment when a computer system is built with no interfaces of any kind to other applications. The presence of ODBC and JDBC demonstrates the need to refine and facilitate the interfacing of computer applications with data files.

There is a difference between a computer system interfacing with another computer system, and interfacing with the data files used by another computer system. An example of the former is a computer application which uses the subroutines (header files, copybooks, DLLs, etc.) that were written for another computer system. An example of the latter is a computer application that is a report writer which reads the data files created from another application.

In the case of a Web database application, most of these applications will interface to either existing or newly created databases supplied by another vendor. That vendor could be Microsoft with its Access product, Oracle with its Oracle 8 product, Sybase with its Sybase System 11 product, IBM with its DB2 product, or any of a number of other RDBMSs. A recognition of the nature and scope of interfaces to other systems and data files is critical to selecting a correct language in which to develop a Web database application.

Availability of Support Tools

Programming languages never are the complete toolset used by programmers. A particular language choice is only the first step in determining the complete suite of tools to be used in a Web database application development project. Additionally, once the language is selected and attention turns to what tools to use in support of the language, you must once again assess the skills of the team members in using those other tools. In fact, many would argue that the entire set of tools to be used in a development project, the language as well as support tools, should be considered as a whole before a language decision is made.

Regardless of which approach you use to assess the skills of your developers against the requirements of the task, it is a very valuable investment of time to address the issue of support tool requirements and availability.

Note: Some of the languages included in this chapter could be argued as being development suites, meaning encompassing more support tools than just a programming language. Examples of this are PowerBuilder and Visual Basic. It is my belief that the tools and utilities in neither PowerBuilder nor Visual Basic are comprehensive enough for either to be the only tool used by developers in Web database application development activities. People still have need of functions such as testing tools, source code protection (assuming you don't want to use the facilities shipping in PowerBuilder v5.0), advanced RDBMS capabilities, HTML utilities, etc.

Matching the requirements of the development project to the capabilities and limitations of the language(s) you select to write the code is an important step in determining the nature and type of support tools needed to create a complete set of tools. For example, most RDBMS products have limited data modeling capabilities—which is something from which you derive tremendous benefit, especially when designing and normalizing a new database. Recognizing that the RDBMS product you are using has limited data modeling capabilities and assuming that your project requires data modeling steps allows you to provide for this need by selecting one of the many tools available that do this. For example, EasyCASE, DBArtisan, or ER/1 are all products that allow you to easily perform data modeling functions. Demo copies of the latter two are available on the CD-ROM accompanying this book.

Another example of a support tool you may want to consider is an HTML editor. Although many programming languages have interfaces to HTML, they do not provide the extensive editing and formatting capabilities that you'd need from an HTML editor. Fortunately, support tools provide this function, and one of the best is available on the accompanying CD-ROM—HTML Assistant Pro '97.

Database Interfaces

The type and number of databases your Web database application will access and interface with is an important factor in determining what language you select. For example, if you are accessing a Microsoft Access database, then you may want to consider Microsoft Access as your application development language. A decision to have your Web application access an Oracle 8 database would prompt you to consider using Oracle Developer 2000 as your application development language. Likewise, a Web application that accesses a Sybase System 11 database would cause you to consider using PowerBuilder as your application development language.

However, all of these can be accessed by the programming languages written by any of the other vendors. For example, an MS Access database can be accessed from a PowerBuilder program. In fact, most RDBMS vendors have ODBC interfaces to development languages. This is the benefit ODBC—a database supported by one vendor is accessible by a programming language supported by another vendor.

Although ODBC provides great flexibility in matching RDBMS with programming languages, there is a penalty. As ODBC is actually a set of drivers that translate the SQL commands or response codes from one vendor to equivalents that can be recognized by another vendor, there is a performance degradation in doing so. A Web application written in PowerBuilder that accesses a Microsoft Access database via ODBC will execute those database calls more slowly than if the application was written in Microsoft Access and reading Microsoft Access databases directly, without having to process through ODBC. You need to be aware of the RDBMS your application is accessing to make an informed decision about programming languages. Sometimes, however, it is more advantageous to select a programming language that requires use of ODBC to access a database than to use a language that accesses the database directly.

Platforms on Which Application Will Run

It is very hard to find an Operating System that does not allow Web access. This is one of the major benefits of doing business on the Web—it is pretty much platform independent. However, if you are writing an application where components of that application are distributed to a client's machines, then you must be aware of the platforms that run on those machines.

It is not uncommon to write a Web database application where components of that application are distributed to a client machine. An example of this is a parts manufacturer that maintains a price list of the parts in inventory on its Web site that customers can access and download to feed in to their own inventory systems. You could write a small application and distribute that application to each client that performs the data migration and population activities. An awareness of the operating systems that the various clients use is very important in picking the correct programming language in which to write this application. This is particularly true if the language creates intermediate, or p-code, modules that require an interpreter to execute.

This is especially true in intranet applications, where the Web server is only accessible to (or accessed by) employees or authorized users once they pass a security checkpoint. In such cases, it makes good sense to distribute parts of the application to these client machines as security is much less of a serious concern when an approved person is accessing the intranet. This "distribution" of application components is most often done to improve the overall performance of the application.

Following is a description of some of the major Web programming languages available.

Microsoft Access 97

Microsoft Access v1.0 was one of the first Relational DataBase Management System (RDBMS) products available. In addition to being an outstanding RDBMS product for stand-alone, non-Internet access applications, it is also a comprehensive suite of development tools to assist in building stand-alone applications. With Access 97, developers can create back-end relational databases for Web applications that can be accessed from a number of different 32-bit front-ends.

Note: This section is not an attempt to teach you how to use Microsoft Access 97. Rather, the intent is to show you the capabilities of this product and how it "plugs in" to the Web database application development toolset.

You can read what Microsoft thinks of Access 97 by visiting their Web site at:

```
http://www.microsoft.com/msaccess.
```

If you want to read a good introductory book on how to use Access 97 to build non-Web databases and applications, I'd suggest *Access 97 Unleashed*, a Sams Publishing book written by Dwayne Gifford, et al.

There are a number of new features in Access 97 that are specific to Web application support as shown in Table 3–1.

Access 97 is designed for developers to use the RDBMS features of the product to create databases that are accessible in one of the following ways:

- From Access 97 stand-alone (non-Web) applications
- From stand-alone applications written in third-party languages (i.e., PowerBuilder) via ODBC
- From Visual Basic stand-alone (non-Web) applications directly

---

Table 3–1   Access 97 Features

Feature	Description
Hyperlinks	Users can store hyperlinks in all Microsoft Access databases to connect easily to information no matter where it resides
Save to HTML	Users can publish static views of their data for a workgroup or on the Web
Publish to the Web Wizard	Facilitates publishing by guiding you through the process of publishing information to the Web dynamically
HTML Importing and Linking	Users can import or attach their databases to HTML pages and use this information inside their Microsoft Access applications
Internet Replication	Users can replicate their Access databases over the Internet using FTP

- Published in the form of static HTML pages
- From a number of different Web page tools via ODBC

Database Wizard

Microsoft has enhanced the ease in which databases are built with a revamped Database Wizard, as seen in Figure 3–2. With the Database Wizard, you can create one of more than 20 fully functional database applications without having any database experience. For example, with as little as six clicks of the mouse button and a few keystrokes, you can create a complete database, including tables, indexes, and queries for an address book, an inventory system, a contact manager, or at least 20 other types of databases. This capability, coupled with some of the new point-and-click Web page tools available, enables non-technical people to create and administer a Web application with RDBMS access.

Hyperlink Datatype

Access 97 is one of the first desktop RDBMS products to support the storage of hyperlinks as a datatype. This ability gives the Web architect a number of benefits. For instance, a job applicant's name stored in a database can be a hyperlink to the candidates resume, or, a part supplier's name stored in a database can be a hyperlink to the supplier's Web site.

An example of how easy it is to create a hyperlink in an Access 97 database table is seen in Figure 3–3. In this figure, you are looking at the Query By Example (QBE) grid

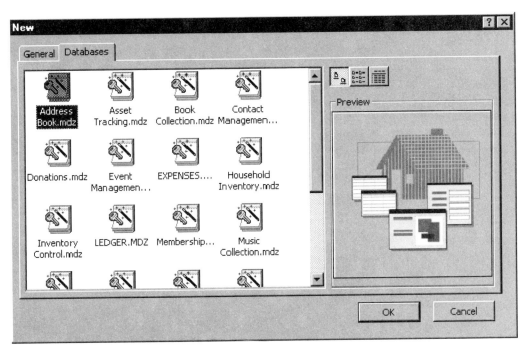

Figure 3–2 The Microsoft Access Database Wizard.

where the Web page address that will serve as the hyperlink is being supplied for a new row being added to a table.

By using the new hyperlink feature in Access 97, developers can create entire databases using hyperlinks as the mechanism to connect objects. A user clicking on an entry that is defined as a hyperlink datatype will cause that person's browser to immediately go to the location specified as the value for the hyperlink.

Save to HTML

With Access 97, you can output tables, query results, or reports directly into HTML format. This is a particularly useful feature to place relatively static data stored in Access 97 database tables directly into a Web page without having to manually type it in. This feature is seen in Figure 3–4. This figure shows the `File|Save To HTML` submenu option

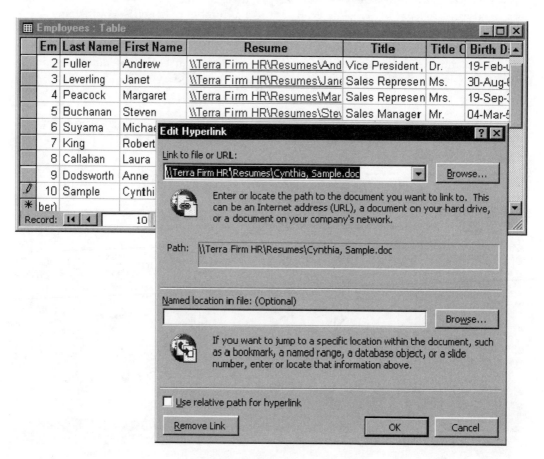

Figure 3–3   Creating a hyperlink location as a datatype in an Access table.

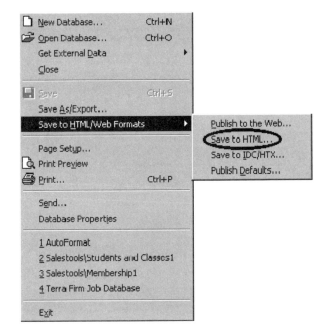

Figure 3–4 Save to HTML option.

that initiates the publication of the database object selected (Tables, Query Results, Forms, or Reports) as a static HTML page.

Publish to the Web Wizard

The Publish to the Web Wizard allows you to publish any object that exists in your database directly to the Web either statically or dynamically. This gives you the capability of customizing HTML forms using templates while retaining all of the settings used to output the objects in the form of a configuration, as shown in Figure 3–5. Specifically, this example shows one of the few screens required to be passed through in the Publish to the Web process. In this screen, the user is being asked to specify which tables to publish.

Using the Publish to the Web Wizard, you can select which database objects to output statically, and which others to output dynamically. You have the flexibility of selecting a different template for each database object.

HTML Importing and Linking

With the HTML Importing and Linking feature in Access 97, you can read and import data from HTML tables directly into Access databases. This is seen in Figure 3–6 where a user is being prompted to supply the name of the table to which data is to be imported. Access 97 creates the candidate list of Tables from what it knows about the database.

To accomplish this, you simply point to an HTML page that contains a table of data. The HTML Import Wizard reads the information in the table and either directly imports it into a new table or appends the new information to an existing table. Once the information is imported, it becomes native Access data.

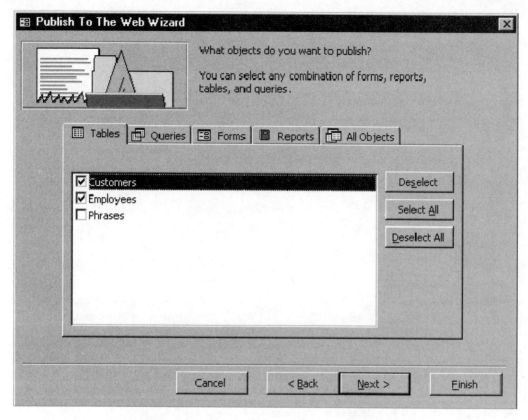

Figure 3–5   The Publish to the Web Wizard.

Internet Replication

Using Internet Replication, as seen in Figure 3–7, the functionality of Briefcase replication introduced in Windows 95 and Windows NT is extended to the Web. In this figure, Access 97 is notifying you that there is a need to replicate the information in one database over to another, and it provides a date/time stamp of the last time each of the objects was updated.

Using Internet replication, changes that are made to either master or replicated databases are transferred through FTP to the appropriate client or server location. The synchronization component of the Briefcase merges the appropriate changes with the database. As with all the other major new enhancements in Access 97, Internet Replication is accomplished with just a few mouse clicks.

Internet Database Connections

Beginning with Access 97, Microsoft has added functionality so that users can access data stored in Access 97 databases over the Internet. This is seen in Figure 3–8, where a user is being asked to indicate for future occurrences the exact location of data that is to be

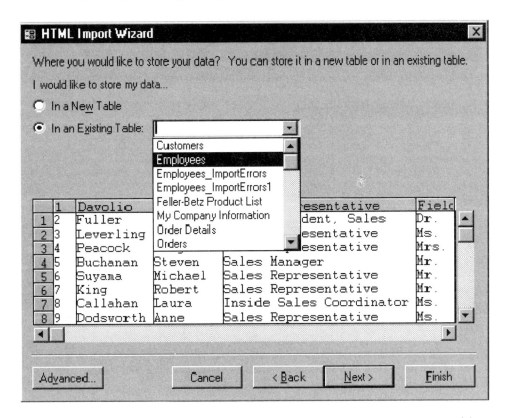

Figure 3–6   Importing HTML table information into an Access 97 table.

accessed by an Access 97 application. In Figure 3–8, the data source happens to be on a database on a Web server. With this feature, you can link Access tables together by selecting the appropriate FTP site from the Link dialog box, and then choose any compatible database object.

The Bottom Line: Microsoft Access 97 is a great tool to develop Web accessible and non-Web accessible databases. These databases can be accessed from a wide range of languages and application development tools. Its developer tools are very convenient and easy to use for building applications accessing Web databases and non-Web databases. The HTML import and hyperlink datatype components, as well as the other features added to version 97 make Microsoft Access a major contender in the Web database arena.

Useful MS Access URLs

Table 3–2 presents a list of useful URLs if you are using MS Access 97 to make your databases accessible over the Web.

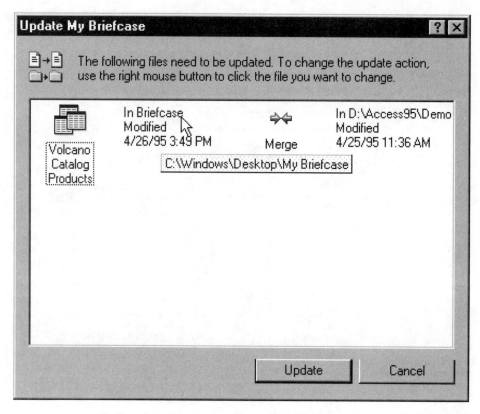

Figure 3–7   Internet Briefcase replication.

Table 3–2   Useful Access 97 URLs

URL	Description
http://www.magnets.com/lists/aolserver~1	A great place to find information on a number of technical issues, not just MS Access.
http://cyber.tec.army.mil/archive_java/programmer	Provides information about connecting to MS Access using JDBC and through Java applets.
http://porthos.phoenixat.com	Contains information about using JDBC to read MS Access 97 databases.
http://www.microsoft.com/msaccess	The Microsoft Access 97 site where you can find information, utilities, sample code, etc.
http://www.clearlight.com	Clearlight Communications is a Web site hosting service. Information is available in their archives on connecting FrontPage applications with Access databases.

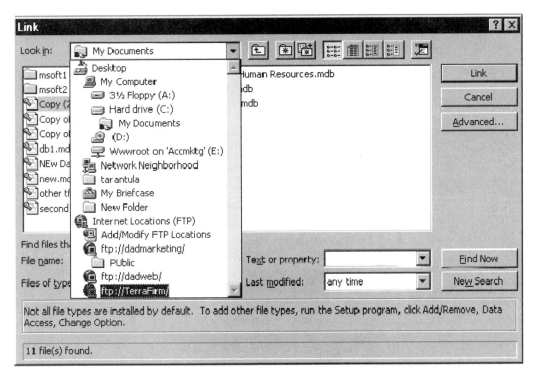

Figure 3–8   Accessing Access 97 data over the Internet.

Note: URLs are supposedly a unique way of identifying an Internet service. The fact is that as the use of the Web explodes, increasingly, duplicate URLs are popping up.

In addition to the URLs listed in Table 3–2, you may find the following books of value.

Access 97 Developers Handbook

By:	Paul Litwin
Publisher:	Sybex, Inc.
ISBN:	0-78-211941-7

Access 97 Unleashed

By:	Dwayne Gifford
Publisher:	Sams Publishing
ISBN:	0-67-230983-1

Interactive Web Publishing with Microsoft Tools

By:	Evangelos Petroutsos
Publisher:	Ventana
ISBN:	1-56-604462-6

Microsoft Access 97 Power Toolkit

By: Michael Groh
Publisher: Ventana
ISBN: 1-56-604609-2

The following languages are all front-end application development languages. By that I mean that they all can be used to write applications that access Microsoft Access 97 databases. As you probably know, Access 97 has its own facility to write non-Web database applications. But, when used in a Web database application environment, it is best used as the back-end RDBMS product.

C

C and C++ are probably the two most common languages for PC application development. It is expected then, that individuals and companies that have invested in building skills in these languages leverage that investment to building Web applications. C compilers are now available on all platforms that support Web browsers, making C as portable a programming language as is needed for Web application development. The limitation of C, as is the limitation with most programming languages, is that the object and execution modules created are platform dependent.

Programs written in C tend to be much larger than other programming languages. The most basic of operations (i.e., writing a line of output) takes many lines of code to write.

At the time of this writing, there was no standard CGI interface to C. As a result, a number of routines and libraries are available offering their idea of how this should be done. These are CGIHTML, LIBCGI, and CGIC.

CGIHTML

This flexible approach provides for the use of a skeleton program in which application specific variables and functions are added. This approach is promoted by Eugene Kim, of Harvard University. His CGIHTML home page, as well as sample program and header files, can be found at: `http://www.eekim.com/software/cgihtml`. A Developers Guide to his approach can be found at: `http://www.eekim.com/pubs/cgibook`.

LIBCGI

LIBCGI is a tool that allows you to link your program with the CGI specifications. The programming interface is fairly simple, and the tools are quite efficient. This efficiency does not come without a price, however. Some of the more complex data handling routines must be written by hand. For Web database applications, this could spell T-R-O-U-B-L-E.

CGIC

CGIC is a library of routines that handle CGI tasks at a very high level. Its author is Tom Boutell. You can find a copy of the library, as well as accompanying documentation at: `http://www.boutell.com/cgic/`.

CGIC is very easy to use and quite powerful. Because it handles CGI tasks at such a high level, working at a very granular level will stretch the utility of this to its limits. One of the most valuable features of this routine is the way in which it provides a means to capture CGI situations that occur for playback in a debugging environment.

Note: If you have a large investment in C skills and a relatively small to medium Web database application to develop, then C is a possible candidate for you. However, the network programming interface, string handling capabilities, and database access components are not nearly as refined and easy to use as many of the other languages. If you can live with the loss in productivity when writing C code, you will appreciate the gain in performance that compiled C code provides over other languages like PERL, Power-Builder, Visual Basic, etc.

Useful C Language URLs

Table 3–3 presents a list of useful URLs if you are using C to build your Web database applications.

The following books should be of value if you want to learn more about the C language.

Advanced C Programming

By:	Steve Oualline
Publisher:	Prentice Hall
ISBN:	0-13-663170-3

Expert C Programming Deep C Secrets

By:	Peter Van Der Linden
Publisher:	Prentice Hall
ISBN:	0-13-177429-8

Table 3–3 Useful C URLs

URL	Description
http://www.tardis.ed.ac.uk	Tardis is a limited-access UNIX service hosted by the University of Edinburgh with extensive information and resources for LibCGI
http://Web site.ora.com	A site with great potential for people looking for CGI tools and libraries.
http://wsk.eit.com	An extensive selection of CGI and C development programs and libraries.
http://www.compusult.nf.ca	C language CGI programmers will want to look at this site and the author's CGIC library.
http://www.camtech.com.au/jemtek/cgi/lib	A set of C development libraries for CGI

Variations in C Programming Techniques for Developers

By: Steve Schustack
Publisher: Microsoft Press
ISBN: 0-91-484548-9

C++

C++ is a very popular programming language that combines much of its syntax and constructs from C while incorporating object-oriented programming capabilities. As a language, it is more difficult than Visual Basic to learn, primarily because of the OO components that are foreign to most people. Of the languages reviewed in this chapter, C++ is the most similar to Java. In fact, the transition from C++ to Java is much easier for most people than from any other language.

One of the positive features of C++ is that most database vendors supply an API library that can be called from C++ programs. This feature improves the performance of database calls from C++ programs. Until the bandwidth of the Web and the processing capabilities of computers accessing the Web are sufficient to make performance a non-issue, the performance of C++ will continue to make it a very popular language to use to develop Web database applications.

There is an abundance of C++ programmers available. Most programmers who have no or very little Web database application experience will be anxious to tackle such a project to build their skills. This means that a high quality C++ programmer with little or no Web experience will probably cost you less (and subsequently earn less) than a seasoned Java, JavaScript, or J++ programmer.

The Bottom Line: C++ is a language to consider when developing your Web database application if you have skills available in the language. Also, if performance is a critical component of your application, then C++ is an ideal candidate for you. Its easy migration to Java makes C++ an ideal platform in which to develop your first (or pilot) application before investing in Java, building Java skills, purchasing Java support tools, and dealing with the issues that inherently come from a new language that is rapidly evolving.

Useful C++ Language URLs

Table 3–4 presents a useful URL if you are using C++ to build your Web database applications.

The following books should be of interest if you want to learn more about the C++ language.

Advanced C++ Programming Styles

By: James Coplien
Publisher: Addison Wesley Publishing Company
ISBN: 0-20-154855-0

Table 3–4   Useful C++ URL

URL	Description
`http://www.internetdatabase.com`	Internet Resources Database is self-billed as being the ultimate guide to all Internet resources for your PC

Apprentice C++ Programmer

By: Peter Lee
Publisher: Wadsworth Publishing Company
ISBN: 0-53-495339-5

How to Program C++

By: H. M. Deitel
Publisher: Prentice Hall
ISBN: 0-13-117334-0

PERL

PERL is a language that has evolved considerably over the last few years. It is a compiled scripting language written by Larry Wall. Programmers with C or PASCAL experience are finding PERL to be an easy transition. This is because expression syntax corresponds quite closely to C expression syntax.

Definition: Practical Extraction and Reporting Language (PERL) is a shell-like language that allows programmers to develop Web server scripts to perform common and repetitive functions.

PERL is an interpreted language optimized for scanning arbitrary text files, extracting information from those text files, and printing reports based on that information. It's also a good language for many system management tasks. It is for this reason that system programmers love PERL.

The language is intended to be practical rather than beautiful. PERL combines some of the best features of C, so people familiar with those languages should have little difficulty with it. PERL is a UNIX utility, but unlike most Unix utilities, PERL does not arbitrarily limit the size of your data unless you have memory constraints on your machine.

PERL is an excellent text scanning and extraction language because it uses sophisticated pattern matching techniques to scan large amounts of data very quickly. Although optimized for scanning text, PERL is also very efficient working with binary data.

The Bottom Line: PERL is gaining in popularity as a scripting language with both system programmers and application programmers. It has the power, speed, and application support to be one of the languages that survives when others wither. PERL is the language of choice if your Web application calls for parsing or manipulating large amounts of text or binary data.

Useful PERL Language URLs

The Table 3–5 presents a list of useful URLs if you are using PERL in the construction of your Web database applications.

The following books should be of value to you if you have an interest in Perl.

60 Minute Guide to CGI Programming with Perl 5

By: Robert Farrell
Publisher: IDG Books
ISBN: 1-56-884780-7

Developing CGI Applications with Perl

By: John Deep
Publisher: John Wiley & Sons
ISBN: 0-47-114158-5

Perl 5 Unleashed

By: Kamran Husain
Publisher: Macmillan Computer Publishing
ISBN: 0-67-230891-6

Teach Yourself CGI Programming in Perl 5, 2nd edition

By: Eric Hermann
Publisher: Macmillan Computer Publishing
ISBN: 1-57-521196-3

Table 3–5   Useful PERL URLs

URL	Description
http://www.cis.ufl.edu/perl	An archive library of useful PERL information maintained by the University of Florida
http://www.perl.com	A mega-site built and maintained by Tom Christiansen that boosts over 14,000 files spanning 300+ megabytes of information specific to PERL.
http://www.eecs.nwu.edu/perl/perl.html	A Web site maintained by Jennifer Myers with a large collection of resource information and links.
http://www.perl.org	The PERL Institute (which manages this site) is dedicated to making PERL more useful for everyone. They are a non-profit organization, established to support the community of people who use PERL and to support the development of PERL as a language.

Shell Script

Shell Scripts are ASCII text files that contain Unix and shell commands. While Unix commands are the equivalent of DOS commands you'd enter at a command line, Shell commands are those commands that are interpreted directly by the shell you specify. Shell commands are commonly used for branching, looping, decision making, etc. They are similar to the commands in various programming languages, particularly C. Currently, the two most popular shells are the Bourne (sh) and C (csh) shells. Other less popular shells are the tcsh and ksh shells.

The following shell script example prints the content-type of the generated document and displays a message to the user that includes the value entered by a user in the lname field on the form:

```
#!/bin/sh
echo 'Content-type: text/html'
echo ''I was given the following last name by the user: $WWW_lname:
```

Shell scripts are very useful for repetitive coding situations. For instance, if you wanted to copy a series of files with separate file extensions from one directory to another, a script could be written that would save you a lot of typing. The commands you enter in a shell script are executed by typing the name of the script instead of each individual command. This causes Shell Scripts to serve the same purpose as EXECs in CMS, CMD files in OS/2, or BAT files in MS/DOS.

The Bottom Line: The biggest problem with Shell Script is that if you want to write code to access any type of database other than UNIX's internal database system, interfaces to these other RDBMSs are hard to find. This makes Shell Script a very poor choice for a Web database application when the demand is to access database data.

Useful Shell Script Language URLs

Table 3–6 presents a list of useful URLs if you are using Shell Script in the construction of your Web database applications.

The following books may be of value if you are interested in learning more about shell scripts.

UNIX Shell Programming, 3rd edition

By:	Lowell Jay Arthur
Publisher:	John Wiley & Sons
ISBN:	0-47-159941-7

UNIX Shells by Example

By:	Ellie Quigley
Publisher:	Prentice Hall
ISBN:	0-13-460866-6

Table 3–6   Shell Script URLs

URL	Description
http://www.hyperion.com/~koreth/ uncgi.html	This is a site built and maintained by Steven Grimm that offers a popular package for using CGI in Shell Scripts.
http://physics.ucsc.edu/tutor/ shell.html	This site presents a tutorial on using Shell Scripts.
http://www.ccpo.odu.edu/ug/ shell_help.html	Another useful site describing how to write a shell script.
http://theory.uwinnipeg.ca/ UNIXhelp/scrpt/	A site maintained by the University of Winnipeg and devoted to dissemination of information specific to Shell Scripts.

Visual Basic

Visual Basic (VB) is fast approaching being the preeminent language in which to develop Web database applications. Its native support for Microsoft Access databases, coupled with its extensive support via ODBC of the most popular RDBMS packages, makes this a preferred language. Additionally, there is an extensive selection of third-party products that compliment and enhance the basic (pardon the pun) capabilities of the product.

If your plans call for building a CGI application for deployment on a Windows NT or 95 platform, this is a language worthy of consideration. Its language is concise, the syntax is familiar, the drag-and-drop programming interface is efficient, and applications developed in VB are easily maintained.

Perhaps the biggest drawback to using VB as a programming language is Microsoft Corporation's reluctance to recognize any other operating system besides Windows (and occasionally one of the Macintosh OS). Applications written in VB will not run natively in a UNIX environment.

The Bottom Line: It is hard to go wrong using Visual Basic as your Web application development tool, especially if you are accessing a Microsoft Access database. It is equally hard to do right using VB as your Web application development tool if your application would ever run on a non-Windows, non-32-bit Operating System.

Useful Visual Basic Language URLs

Table 3–7 presents a list of useful URLs if you are using Visual Basic in the construction of your Web database applications.

The following books should be of value to you if you want to learn more about Visual Basic.

The Visual Basic Programmer's Guide to Java

By: James W. Cooper, Ph.D.
Publisher: Ventana

Beginners Guide to Visual Basic

By: Peter Wright
Publisher: Wrox
ISBN: 1-87-441655-9

Building Internet Applications with Visual Basic

By: Kate Gregory
Publisher: Macmillan Computer Publishing
ISBN: 0-78-970213-4

Table 3–7   Useful Visual Basic URLs

URL	Description
`http://www.microsoft.com/vbasic/`	Microsoft Corporation's Web page to its Visual Basic product.
`http://www.vbonline.com/`	This site is created and supported by VB Online magazine and contains a wide selection of tips, techniques, and free stuff.
`http://www.apexsc.com/vb/`	Carl & Gary's Home Page
`http://www.vbxtras.com/`	The ultimate tools catalog!
`http://www.apexsc.com/vb/clbv-digest/`	CLBV Digest—Archived Issues
`http://coyote.csusm.edu/cwis/winworld/vbasic.html`	California State's Archives of VBXs
`http://www.windx.com`	Visual Basic Programmer's Journal
`http://www.ionet.net/~robinson/vb.shtml`	Visual Basic Resource Index—Robins Company
`http://www.inquiry.com/techtips/thevbpro/`	Ask the VB Pro page
`http://www.vmedia.com/commodity/onlinecompanions/`	A site maintained by Ventana Communications Group with an abundant selection of resources and links.
`http://www.jumbo.com/prog/win/vbasic/`	Jumbo!—Programming: Windows: Windows Visual Basic Programming

Building Windows 95 Applications with Visual Basic

By: Clayton Walnum
Publisher: Macmillan Computer Publishing
ISBN: 0-78-970209-6

Database Developer's Guide with Visual Basic

By: Roger Jennings
Publisher: Macmillan Computer Publishing
ISBN: 0-67-230652-2

PowerBuilder

Sybase Corporations PowerBuilder products are emerging as one of the leading Web database application development tools available. The 1990s have seen PowerBuilder establish itself as a very powerful client/server application development toolkit. When Sybase acquired Powersoft (the original developer of PowerBuilder) in 1994, it saw a movement in the industry to provide tools for Internet application development. Because Sybase is a major RDBMS vendor, as expected, the company combined the development components of PowerBuilder with their RDBMS products to provide a complete Web database application development environment.

The Enterprise edition of PowerBuilder gives you the ability to extend the capabilities of a Web browser to use its DataWindow Viewer. The DataWindow Viewer is a GUI interface to a database. That database can be either a Sybase database, or any other vendor's database that provides an ODBC interface. This includes Microsoft Access, Oracle, Informix, DB2, etc.

PowerBuilder uses a similar metaphor to CGI application development as Visual Basic. The content of an HTML form is retrieved through either the Win CGI specification or a proprietary vendor-supplied library. Then, whatever database operations are required are performed. PowerBuilder takes the output from the database operation, formats it in a manner you describe, and sends it to the browser in a manner that conforms to HTML standards.

A strength of PowerBuilder is that you can develop an application on a Windows 95 (or NT) machine, and deploy that application on either Windows 3.1, NT, Macintosh, 95, or UNIX devices. Sybase is committed to ensuring cross-platform support for PowerBuilder which is good news for building a Web database application.

The Bottom Line: PowerBuilder is a main contender as a tool to use to build a Web database application. InfoWorld has recently given PowerBuilder its Enterprise Development Tool of the Year Award. Its native driver support for Sybase databases and ODBC support for MS Access, Oracle, DB2, Informix, etc. is well known and clean. The product offers a very clean GUI interface for developers and allows for a great deal of application control through its proprietary PowerScript programming language.

Useful PowerBuilder Language URLs

Table 3–8 presents a list of useful URLs if you are using PowerBuilder in the construction of your Web database applications.

The following book references should be of value to you if you want to learn more about PowerBuilder.

Developing Powerbuilder 5 Application, 4th edition

By:	Bill Hatfield
Publisher:	Macmillan Computer Publishing
ISBN:	0-67-230916-5

Powerbuilder 5—A Developer's Guide

By:	David Mcclanahan
Publisher:	M&T Books
ISBN:	1-55-851473-2

Professional Powerbuilder Programming

By:	Paul Bukauskas
Publisher:	Prentice Hall
ISBN:	0-13-508145-9

Teach Yourself Powerbuilder 5

By:	David Mcclanahan
Publisher:	MIS Press
ISBN:	1-55-828474-5

Visual Basic Script

Visual Basic Script (VBScript) is a subset of the Microsoft Visual Basic language. In its current implementation, it is a fast, portable, lightweight interpreter for use in World Wide Web browsers and other applications that use ActiveX Controls, OLE Automation servers, and Java applets.

Definition: Applet—Traditionally, an applet was considered to be a small program written in Java that is included in a Web page and downloaded on demand to be executed on a client machine. The current thought is that applets can also be written in JavaScript.

VBScript, being a subset of Visual Basic, is ideally suited to accessing documents used in Microsoft Excel, Project, Access, and the Visual Basic 4.0 development system. The product is designed to have a very small footprint and to be a lightweight interpreted language. Because of this, it does not use strict types (only Variants). Also, because VBScript is intended to be a safe subset of the language, it does not include file I/O or direct

Table 3–8 Useful PowerBuilder URLs

URL	Description
http://www.powersoft.com	The home page for Powersoft Corporation.
http://www.sybase.com	The home page for Sybase Corporation, the parent company of Powersoft Corporation.
http://computers.science.org/	A site published and maintained by Science.Org, a nonprofit organization devoted to the application development community.
http://www.advisor.com/pa.htm	The home page for the PowerBuilder Advisor magazine.
http://www.powercerv.com	The home page for PowerCerv Corporation, one of Powersoft Corporation's most successful partners and the provider of training, consulting, and add-on products.
http://www.sigsoft.com/	The home page for Signature Software, another of Powersoft Corporation's most successful partners.
http://ntweb.sigsoft.com	Home of the online PowerBuilder and Java Developer journal.
http://world.std.com/~gorsline/kgfram.html	A site maintained by an avid user of PowerBuilder that provides links to other information sources.
http://www.vmedia.com/commodity/onlinecompanions/	A site maintained by Ventana Communications Group with an abundant selection of resources and links.

access to the underlying operating system. It appears as if VBScript is Microsoft's attempt to compete in the JavaScript market.

When used in an enabled Web browser, VBScript is directly comparable to JavaScript (not Java). Like JavaScript, VBScript is a pure interpreter that processes source code embedded directly in the HTML. Also, VBScript code does not produce stand-alone applets but is used to add intelligence and interactivity to HTML documents.

For the millions of programmers who already know Visual Basic, VBScript is a valuable alternative to JavaScript in activating Web pages. Its comparability to Visual Basic syntax and structure will make learning VBScript a smooth proposition.

VBScript is available for Windows 95 and Windows NT (including native versions for Alpha, MIPS, and PowerPC architectures), 16-bit Windows, and Power Macintosh. Microsoft is working with third parties to provide UNIX versions for Sun, HP, Digital, and IBM platforms.

The Bottom Line: VBScript is a valuable language component for people writing Web database applications. Its conformity to Visual Basic syntax makes it a serious language to consider if you have Visual Basic skills. However, because this is a Microsoft product, you should be aware that Windows derivatives will always be the preferred operating system for this product. If portability is of key importance to you and you don't have a huge investment in Visual Basic skills, and if you have the need to write some code in a scripting language, then you may want to continue looking toward JavaScript.

Useful VBScript Language URLs

Table 3–9 presents a list of useful URLs if you are using VBScript in the construction of your Web database applications.

The books listed below should be of value if you want to learn more about Visual Basic Script.

The Comprehensive Guide to VBScript

By:	Richard Mansfield
Publisher:	Ventana
ISBN:	1-56-604470-7

Creating Cool VBScript Web Pages

By:	Bill Hatfield
Publisher:	IDG Books
ISBN:	0-76-453031-3

Teach Yourself VBScript in 21 Days

By:	Keith Brophy
Publisher:	Macmillan Computer Publishing
ISBN:	1-57-521120-3

VBScript Web Page Interactivity

By:	W. Orvis
Publisher:	Prima Publishing/Random House
ISBN:	0-76-150684-5

Table 3–9   Useful VBScript URLs

URL	Description
`http://www.microsoft.com/vbscript`	Microsoft's VBScript site.
`http://www.vbonline.com`	Home page to Visual Basic Online magazine
`http://www.netins.net/showcase/legend/vb/`	A site maintained by Ryan Heldt as a valuable resource for VBScript techniques
`http://www.vmedia.com/commodity/onlinecompanions/`	A site maintained by Ventana Communications Group with an abundant selection of resources and links.
`http://www.vbonline.com/`	This site is created and supported by VB Online magazine and contains a wide selection of tips, techniques, and free stuff.

COBOL

COBOL is a language that just won't die. Much to the chagrin of the nay-sayers in the 1980s and early 1990s, the venerable COBOL is continuing to reinvent itself as a significant application development tool. COBOL is a viable and valuable application maintenance tool not to be underestimated.

Thought: COBOL is enjoying a resurgence as a development language. COBOL programmers are seeing their salaries increase faster than many other programming-language segment. Consulting companies and recruiters can not locate enough COBOL programmers to meet demand. Why, then, has Micro Focus Ltd. seen a flattening recently of its sales for its base COBOL development suite?

Definition: COBOL—This is an acronym that stands for COmmon Business Oriented Language, although many people are trying to modify history and continue the life of COBOL as a development language by claiming that COBOL stands for Common Object Business Oriented Language.

A number of companies are racing to develop products that allow COBOL to be used for either client or server side Web application development. IBM has their VisualAge product, Computer Associates has the CA-Realia product, and Micro Focus has their Object COBOL.

IBM's product (VisualAge) is touted as soon to include a full range of CGI specification support. This is likely to happen as IBM is committed to being a major Internet tools vendor. Micro Focus' product (Object COBOL) is also being positioned as their tool for Internet application development. Micro Focus has announced support for the use of this product to develop Internet applications, but they are not there yet.

Useful COBOL Language URLs

Table 3–10 presents a list of useful URLs if you are using COBOL in the construction of your Web database applications.

The following books should be of value if you want to learn more about COBOL.

Cobol from Micro to Mainframe, 2nd edition

By:	Robert Grauer
Publisher:	Prentice Hall
ISBN:	0-13-310764-7

Table 3–10   Useful COBOL URLs

URL	Description
`http://www.microfocus.com`	MicroFocus Ltd.'s home page.
`http://www.software.hosting.ibm.com/ad/cobol/`	Home page for IBM's COBOL tools
`http://www.cai.com`	Computer Associates's home page

DB2 for the COBOL Programmer, Part 1

By: Steve Eckols
Publisher: Mike Murach Mike & Assoc., Inc.
ISBN: 0-91-162559-3

Object Oriented Cobol

By: Edmund Arranga
Publisher: Prentice Hall
ISBN: 0-13-261140-6

Structured Cobol Programming, 8th edition

By: Nancy Stern
Publisher: John Wiley & Sons
ISBN: 0-47-11388-6

Moving On

Because of the designed standardization benefits from the CGI specification, the choice of which programming language to use to develop a Web database application is not easy. Many languages support this specification. It is not a matter of *what* language is available to use to write a Web application, but more a matter of *which* of the many options is best suited for your needs?

Java is the universally accepted language for Web application development. As you've read in this chapter, that is no longer a *rubber stamp* decision. It will remain a venerable language, but other languages will continue to erode the position that Java has.

The next chapter will introduce you to Java and JavaScript. You will learn about the strengths and weaknesses of each of these languages and how they are used to build Web database applications.

CHAPTER 4

Overview of Java and JavaScript

The release of Java from Sun Microsystems coincided with the release of JavaScript. Despite the similarity in names, the two languages should not be considered related to each other. Despite sharing similar syntax and a similar use of objects, the languages were developed to solve different sets of problems, as you will learn in this chapter. A popular misconception is that most Web applications are written in either Java or JavaScript. In a January 7, 1997 article by Bill Catchings published in *InfoWorld Magazine*, Catchings estimates that, "There are over 200,000 Java developers, and before long every one of them will be writing code to access corporate information databases." If this is an accurate estimate, then only one out of every four developers are using Java to build Web applications. The point to this is that even with all of its popularity, there are many other languages being used to develop Web applications.

This chapter investigates the use of Java and JavaScript as programming languages, and describes how Java and JavaScript programs are used, along with their benefits and shortcomings.

Introduction to Java

The hype over Java primarily cannot be overstated. Over the last two years, *InfoWorld Magazine* has carried a Java-related article in each of its issues.

Perhaps by the time this book is in your hands, much of this hype will have been dispersed. It is not only unfortunate but also unjustified that Java will probably never gain its full potential as a development language.

Note: Java as a programming language was conceived in 1991 and developed by engineers at Sun Microsystems in 1995 to be a common Web application development language. A little known piece of trivia is that the engineers who developed Java did so out of frustration with working with C++.

Certainly, the trend we see today is for the developers of other products, such as Sybase with PowerBuilder and Microsoft with Visual Basic, to build enough functionality into their products so that the momentum toward Java will ebb.

If Java had been developed a few years sooner, or if Sun had been able to standardize the language more quickly, perhaps Java would have been able to hold on to the market it captured. Such is not the case, however. As you will see throughout this book, there are many languages and development suites currently available that provide the majority of the benefits of Java (and sometimes more), but without its limitations. Now that the other software developers have had time to recognize and address the need for Internet/intranet development languages and facilities, we will never again see Java in the same luster. The language will continue to improve and grow, but at the same time, so too will other languages. But the genie is out of the bottle now, and the entire computing industry is able to compare what exists in the Java language with what is needed in a corporate Web application development and database access tool. Java may have been the first robust Web application and database access tool, but it is certainly questionable whether it is the best.

Note: For those of you interested in reading what the developers of Java intended to accomplish with their new language, you can find the *White Paper* they developed at: `http://www.javasoft.com/nav/read/whitepapers`. For those of you who are highly interested in the underpinnings of the Java language specification, you can find this at: `http:http://www.javasoft.com/nav/read/index.html`.

Java is the first programming language that provides a complete solution to Internet application development. The release of Java version 1.0, coupled with the Java-enabled versions of Web browsers currently available, has resulted in new animated sites appearing on the Web at a record pace. An example of this, along with the HTML code that triggers the Java applet, is shown in Figure 4–1. When viewed through a Java-enabled browser, this image shows a ticker tape symbol running across the page displaying a text message.

Figure 4–2 shows the actual HTML code that executes the Java applet in Figure 4.1. In Netscape Navigator, you'd be able to view HTML code by clicking on `View|Document Source`. (You can do this for any Web page.)

Embedded in the HTML code is the text string that displays across the ticker-tape symbol on the Web page. Using this technique, the developer was thinking ahead. He or she decided to write the Java program so that it would dynamically read and display a text string that could be changed at any time without having to recompile the Java program.

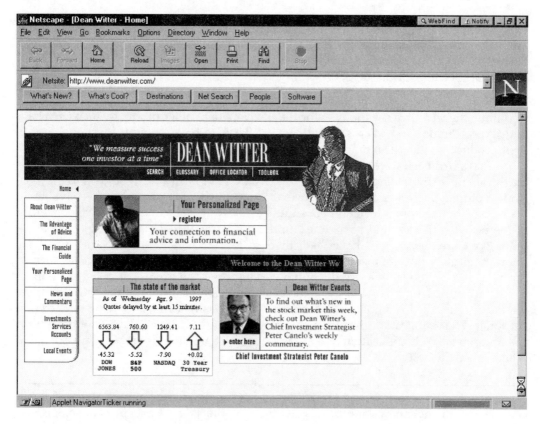

Figure 4–1   A Web site with a running Java program.

Tip: Don't worry if you can't make sense of the HTML code in Figure 4–2. My intention here is to show you how uncomplicated a process it is to cause a Java program to execute from within HTML code. Chapter 6, "Overview of HTML," introduces you to HTML syntax and coding conventions.

Since Java is a full-fledged programming language, it can also be used to write serious, robust, data-aware business-to-business, business-to-employee, and business-to-customer applications. The most critical component to developing these applications is the need to have the ability to perform transaction processing from Java that accesses corporate data stores.

Benefits of Java

Notwithstanding the advent of newer, more powerful, and more comprehensive development tools, the Java developer still receives many benefits. Each of these is described here.

```
Netscape - [Source of: http://www.deanwitter.com/]                    _ 日 X
      <TD ALIGN="RIGHT">
            <applet code="NavigatorTicker.class" codebase="/" width=392 height=26 >
            <H3>Welcome to the Dean Witter World Wide Web Site.</H3>
            <param name=count value=1 >

            <param name=msg0 value="Welcome to the Dean Witter World Wide Web site . . . Disc
  for retirement or for a child's education with The Financial Guide . . . Use the Toolbox to find

            <param name=speed value=5 >
            <param name=bgco value=0,0,0 >
            <param name=txtco value=107,204,20 >
            <param name=linkco value=107,204,20 >

            </applet >
      </TD>
```

Figure 4–2   The HTML code that triggers the Java applet in Figure 4–1.

Platform Independence

Java applications are executable without modification on many different operating systems and platforms (like Windows 95, Windows NT, UNIX, Macintosh, Solaris, OS/2, for instance). In fact, Java was the first programming language that could earnestly make this claim.

Object-Oriented

Since the inception of object-orientation as a development concept in IBM labs in the mid 1960s, the popularity of tools that support Object-Oriented (OO) development is rapidly rising. With the advent of Object-Oriented Programming (OOP) languages such as C++, SmallTalk, and Java, it is hard to imagine a building computer system that does not use tools that support OO concepts. Even the venerable COBOL language is conforming to OO. Micro Focus Ltd., the PC-based application tools development vendor in Palo Alto, California has released a product called OO COBOL which it claims fully supports OO concepts.

Java Is Robust

Whereas JavaScript was developed at the same time as Java with the intent of being a smaller cousin, Java was created to be a development tool for building corporate and enterprise applications. This encompasses Web applications, as well as non-Web applications. Java is well known for its reliance on the early detection and removal of problems before the code is placed in production. Many people think of Java as a newer flavor of C++. Although it is true that Java relies on OO design and construction principles in much the same way as C++, Java uses a process of variable and array management (called a pointer model) that eliminates the possibility of overwriting memory and thereby corrupting data held in memory. Java gives you the comfort of knowing that you can never access a bad pointer within your program and thereby create memory allocation errors.

Distributed

Java has excellent networking capabilities. The Java language and the Java Developers' Kit (JDK) both provide an extensive library of routines for coping with the various TCP/IP protocols like HTTP and FTP. With these easy-to-use routines, a Java programmer can access data files across the world over the Web via URLs with the same ease as traditional programmers would access data files on their local machines.

Definition: TCP/IP—Transmission Control Protocol/Internet Protocol is the common name for a collection of over 100 different protocols that are used to connect computers and networks. Telnet and FTP are two of the most popular of these protocols.

Definition: FTP—File Transfer Protocol is a common name for one of the TCP/IP protocols used to transfer files from one computer or network to the other.

Definition: Telnet—This is a TCP/IP protocol that allows you to establish a terminal session with another computer.

Definition: HTTP—HyperText Transfer Protocol is one of the TCP/IP protocols that facilitates the quick retrieval of information resources located at different remote sites. HTTP also provides support for advanced functions such as document searching, front-end update, and annotation.

Security

With all the hype surrounding firewalls and data security, it is sometimes overlooked that the Java language provides excellent security capabilities. It was designed to be a tool used to build networked and distributed applications. Whereby firewalls and the like provide additional layers of security from that afforded within the Java language, the use of Java as a development language enables the developer to create applications that are fundamentally tamper-resistant and virus-free.

Architecturally Neutral.   As shown in Figure 4–3, Java applications that are compiled are executable on many platforms, under many different operating systems, without modification. This was one of the main objectives of the original developers of the language. The Java compiler accomplishes this architectural neutrality by use of a Java runtime system. Each different operating system requires a Java runtime system which, when installed, provides full architectural neutrality. The magic behind this process is in the type of executable code created from the compile. The Java compiler creates bytecode instructions which have nothing at all to do with a particular operating system or architecture. Although the use of bytecodes does negatively affect performance to a degree, many people believe that the benefits of this architectural interoperability far outweigh the performance considerations.

Portability

Portability refers to the ability to move an application (and the data accessed by that application) from one computing environment to another without the need to make extensive changes. An example of this is a Web database application that is written for the UNIX operating system and is *ported*, or moved, to the Windows NT environment. Such

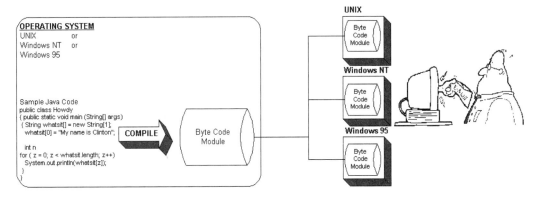

Figure 4–3 Java is architecturally neutral.

an event would occur if a company decides to shelve their UNIX computing environment and implement a Windows NT architecture.

With Java, binary data is stored in a fixed format. Strings are stored in a standard Unicode format. Consequently, writing code in Java represents little of the *implementation-dependent* issues addressed by C++ developers. For example, an int in Java is always a 32-bit integer value, while in C++ an int can be an integer of any size that the manufacturer of the compiler chooses. This portability is not without its problems. For example, Java programmers generally don't have the control over the look and feel of a screen as do non-Java programmers. However, when it comes to a Web application, portability is often much more of a critical component than how pretty the screen appears.

Interpreted

One of the most significant benefits of Java is that the Java interpreter can execute Java bytecodes directly on any machine that the interpreter is running. Although compiled Java code executes much faster than bytecodes, and Java compilers are becoming available, the development process of applications is frequently much more rapid than with other languages such as C++, VB, and Delphi.

Multithreading

Multithreading is very easy to implement in Java. Additionally, Java threads can be written to easily take advantage of devices that use multiprocessors.

Definition: Multithreading—The ability of one program to accomplish more than one task at any one time.

Java Is Dynamic

Java is seeing much more growth and development than any other programming language. Libraries of functions and classes are adding new methods to the language at a record pace.

Java and Object-Orientation

For most of the past 25 years, the dominant programming paradigm has been *structured* programming. (This occurs when all the code in the application that is necessary to be processed together as a unit is combined in a common manner.) OOP is changing this; some would say OOP has *already changed* this. Decidedly, there are many more people using the structural and procedural languages. However, it is also clear that the pace of acceptance of OO-based languages is much higher than that of more traditional languages.

Thought: Some technologists and authors would challenge the use of the phrase "is changing" and would replace it with the phrase "has changed." The deciding factor in determining if the programming paradigm has changed to OOP is identifying the number of people using structural and procedural languages versus those using OO languages. Decidedly, there are many more people using the structural and procedural languages. However, it is also clear that the pace of acceptance of OO-based languages is much higher than that of more traditional languages. Perhaps in five years or so there will be many more OO-based programmers than structural or procedural programmers.

Java is one of the purest OO languages in existence, if not the purest. In fact, it is impossible to write a Java program in a structured or procedural style. There are many compelling benefits of Java being a pure OO language:

- It is much easier to write bug-free code.
- The code that is written is produced much more quickly.
- There is no need to manually allocate memory.
- True arrays are allowable and printer arithmetic is eliminated.
- It eliminates the possibility of confusing an argument with a test for equality in a conditional statement.
- It eliminates multiple inheritance.

The Java/Web Concept

Java programs actually come in a number of varieties. For example, they can be written and executed completely outside of the Web. With the advent of Java compilers and linkers, you can create a Java program that executes without relying on any Web-specific component such as HTTP or CGI.

Definition: CGI—Common Gateway Interface defines how a Web server and an external program (also called a CGI program) communicate.

This book is not concerned with this type of Java program. The type of program you write is a Web-based program that accesses a database. A Web-based Java program is called an applet, regardless of whether or not that program accesses a database.

Figure 4–4 shows the URL for a Web site that is a great source of applets. Take a look at some of the areas that can be accessed from this Web page—you may want to refer to this Web page often as you begin to acquire the tools and develop the techniques of Web database application development.

For people considering writing applets in their Web pages to access databases, the following advantages exist:

- *Responsiveness* is the speed in which a program supplies the user with requested information. A program is said to be responsive if it processes a user's request for information quickly. With Java, it is simply a matter of supplying the correct syntax to make the applet responsive.
- *GUI-Aware.* Java offers Graphical User Interface (GUI) support for all OS's that support a GUI. Applets can include text boxes, command buttons, list boxes, drop down list boxes, etc. Additionally, applets can track the movement of a mouse and can track keystrokes.

Figure 4–4 A great source of applets is www.gamelan.com.

- *Support for Fat Client.* An applet causes the processing contained within the applet to be offloaded to the user's system. This supports the Fat-Client model for client/server architectural design. Today's Web servers are often overloaded with thousands of transactions occurring every minute. Therefore, it makes good sense to isolate as much processing as possible on the user's machine.

Definition: Fat Client—Fat Client is a term used in client/server architecture to describe the amount of the application that processes on the client machine. The more components of an application that process on a client machine, or the more intensive the operations that execute on a client machine are, the fatter the client.

Tip: A common use for applets has traditionally been to display animated images. The applet shown in Figures 4–1 and 4–2 is an example of this. The applet displays a text string that is designed to appear as if it is a ticker tape. Use care in animated applets, however, as the GIF files used in these animations can become quite large. Users will be frustrated if they have to wait for a 1.5 megabyte GIF file to be transferred over a 28.8k modem.

- *HotJava.* In 1995, Sun Microsystems spun off a subsidiary and named it Javasoft. This company is responsible for the development and support of both Java and the HotJava browser. The objective of HotJava was to build a Java-enabled browser that had the ability to dynamically adjust to new types of information coming to it. When a developer needs to send a new type of algorithm or file to the browser, a small content handler is developed that is shipped with the new data to instruct the browser how the data should be processed.

Is It Java or Coffee?

There are many myths about Java. The material in this section is here to dispel these and help you see Java for what it really is . . . and what it is not!

It Is NOT an Extension of HTML

HTML is a page-description language, not a programming language. Java is a programming language, not a page-description language. The only overlap between these two entities is that HTML provides facilities for placing Java applets on the Web page. Java programs can run independently of HTML pages, and HTML pages frequently contain no Java applets.

It Is an Easy Language to Learn

Java is an extremely powerful programming language. In many ways, it is more powerful than C++. Like C++ and unlike COBOL, Java is not an intuitive language to learn—that is, it is not one that is particularly comfortable to learn. I know some people will take exception to the use of the word comfortable. In my case I can say with certainty, though, that Java was a very difficult language to learn.

Java Is an Easy Environment in which to Program

Java is an incomplete programming environment. The Java that you download for free is a very incomplete application development environment. There are an increasingly large number of tools and products coming available that add to the robustness of the base Java compiler. These are tools such as the JDK from Javasoft, Latte from Borland, and Café from Symantec. Barring the use of this type of tool and assuming you still want to use Java to write your code, you will need to acquire a number of additional components to complete your toolset. These include, but are not limited to, an editor, debugger, and design tools. These tools, when combined to form a complete development environment, suffer from the same ease-of-use problems that you'd expect from any computer system where the components are thrown together—not built together.

Java Is a Universal Web Development Tool

This was the hype in 1995 and 1996, but I think few people who are students of the Web industry think this is still the case. There are many reasons for this chamge of attitude, many of which we've already discussed. Perhaps the biggest reason is that Java was not and still is not a complete development environment. It is a language. Tools are built by vendors that are meant to be used with the language. Vendors are coming online with tools that are complete development environments without any Java compiler. These are perhaps the biggest impediment to Java being recognized as a universal Web development tool.

Java Is Too Slow for Serious Applications

This may certainly have been an accurate statement until mid-1996. Until then, Java code was not compiled to machine code. It was converted to Java bytecodes. These bytecodes were then interpreted on the client machine by an interpreter that was appropriate for the operating system on that machine.

In 1996, however, Java compilers appeared and were able to convert the Java bytecodes into native machine code. Although this machine code executes much more quickly, the interoperability that was a hallmark of Java is compromised. It is not possible to take compiled machine code that is generated for a UNIX machine and have it execute unmodified on a Windows NT machine. This, however, is possible with Java bytecodes. The negative consequence to Java bytecodes is performance.

Java Programs Require a Web Page to Run

Java programs *do not* require a Web page to execute. Java applets do, however, require a Web page to run. This, in fact, is the definition of a Java applet: *a Java program that is run from within a Web page*. It is very possible, and certainly probable, that skilled Java programmers are currently called on to write an application for deployment in non-Web environments.

Thought: It is questionable whether the developers of the original Java intended it to be a language so heavily associated with the Web. What the developers perhaps did not see was the explosive growth of the Web and the search for a programming tool that could build applications (applets) that would function as desired across multiple environments.

The use of Java to write applets eclipses the use of Java to write applications presently. As development suites become increasingly popular, the use of Java as a tool to write applets will subside. However, the use of Java as a tool to write stand-alone applications will continue to increase.

Java Eliminates CGI Scripting

As you will see in Chapter 7, "Overview of CGI" and Chapter 13, "Accessing Web Databases Using CGI Programs," CGI scripts handle the communication between a server and an applet. In fact, many argue that CGI is the most popular and easiest communication path between the server and client. This argument is frequently won. Java and CGI can co-exist.

Client/Server Computing Is Dead

Although it is possible that the applications developed for, and deployed on, the Web may significantly modify what you think of when considering what client/server computing is, Java will not be the demise of client/server. As you'll see in Chapter 8, "Web Application Design and Development," application components written in Java to be run in a Web database application are clearly extensions of (not replacements for) client/server architectures and concepts. With the ability to connect to corporate databases through ODBC and JDBC, the use of Java as a programming tool to develop client/server applications over the Web is practical.

Java Allows Me to Use an Inexpensive Internet Appliance

Web *appliances* are chic. People like to talk about them and investors are placing some very large bets that these inexpensive devices will be big. Sun is exploring a micro kernel-based operating system that promises to add intelligence to a new generation of low-cost Internet terminals: a Web appliance.

For those of you with very little or no mainframe development experience, a Web appliance is very similar in capability to the old IBM 3270 mainframe terminal (appropriately called a *dumb terminal*). Both the IBM 3270 terminal and the Web appliance share the following common characteristics:

- Neither one contains local data storage
- Both have an attached keyboard
- Both have limited ability to attach external devices
- Neither one is very powerful

An example of a Web appliance is currently being sold by Motorola Corporation with the name *WebTV*. Perhaps you've seen this advertised. WebTV is a keyboard that attaches to a small box that is plugged into a television set. The television set functions as the monitor for Web access and the keyboard is the input device. There is no local storage and all the memory required to use this setup is contained in the small box into which the keyboard is plugged.

Although it is possible that a market will be found for these devices, I don't see them becoming the mainstream way for people to interact with the Web. For that unique niche, where Web appliances are popular, it is easy to see how Java could be used as a development language, however.

Who Owns Java?

As we have discussed, a team of engineers at Sun Microsystems wrote Java. In 1995, Sun started a subsidiary called Javasoft to continue the support and development of the language. In 1996, Bill Gates announced that although Microsoft had initially missed the Internet market, the company was going to invest huge amounts of capital to make sure that they were a dominant tools provider. To those familiar with how Bill Gates and Steve Ballmer approach a market opportunity, this does not mean that they will be content to simply be in the game. They see the Internet and the tools and applications used by and deployed over the Internet as the next great computing opportunity.

Having learned the lessons of the fallen victims of early Microsoft pursuits, Sun is wary of the Microsoft competitor. To bolster its forces, Sun is teaming with companies like Apple, IBM, Oracle, and Netscape to form a coalition. The thought behind this is that the more broad based support Sun has for its language, the more the likelihood is that developers and third-party providers will support it.

Not to be outdone, Microsoft is tuning the Java and the Java virtual machine support for its Internet Explorer browser for running on Windows 95 and Windows NT. Although Microsoft is committed to delivering a compatible implementation of the Java virtual machine in its browser technology, they have also developed some extensions to the native Java language. These extensions, called "proprietary lock-ins," have the effect of improving the performance of Java applications run in a Windows 95 or Windows NT environment. Unfortunately, many won't run at all in a non-Windows environment.

This lack of portability is at the heart of Sun's initiative to insure and certify that Java becomes the API of the Internet. They understand, as does Microsoft, that the product or company that controls the API to a computing environment controls that environment. Sun's coalition with various other hardware and software vendors, nicknamed Sun's "100% Pure Java" initiative, is the tactical strategy used to confront Microsoft in the marketplace. This initiative calls for a process whereby any company's products that support or work with Java are certified to be 100% compatible with Java.

Definition: API—Application Programming Interface is a programming gateway within a program that provides for another program to communicate with it.

The problem, at least in the short-term, for developers and the Internet community as a whole, is that Microsoft is not a member in this coalition. Therefore, there will ultimately be one initiative that wins. Will it be Sun with its determination to keep the Java platform and operating system independent, or will it be Microsoft with its determination to have Java be another Windows programming language. As of this writing, Sun is winning this battle. Microsoft is gaining ground, however.

Introduction to JavaScript

Unlike Java, which is an interpreted language, JavaScript is a scripting language. It was developed by Sun with the hope that it would be an easier language to learn than Java. JavaScript also includes a suite of powerful tools that add interactivity to your Web pages with very little effort. Because JavaScript is a scripting language and is highly interactive with HTML, it is written directly on the HTML for the Web page with which it is associated.

Note: An interpreted language is one that requires a run-time library to execute on a given machine. The code written in an interpreted language is translated to machine-level instructions for execution by the run-time library. A scripting language like JavaScript offers fewer commands in a simpler syntax that is well-suited for implementing simple, small programs.

The syntax and command structure of JavaScript are very similar to Java. If you know Java, learning JavaScript is greatly simplified. JavaScript also uses many of the same security components and flow constructs as Java.

Uses for JavaScript

If you understand the base structure of the language, you will uncover a plethora of uses for the language. Table 4–1 provides a list and description of some of the more helpful features.

The following is a basic example of JavaScript that demonstrates how it could be used to add interactivity to a form.

```
var y_name=prompt("Enter your first name: ")
var f_name=prompt("Enter a friend's first name: ")
alert("You, " + y_name + & " + f_name + " are friends.")
```

In this snippet, the first line of code is a prompt to enter your first name. The second line of code is a prompt to enter your friend's first name. The last line of code is a message box that displays a friendly message.

Figure 4–5 is the input box that displays as a result of the first line of sample JavaScript executing. Figure 4–6 is the input box that displays as a result of the second line of sample JavaScript executing. Finally, Figure 4–7 is the message box that displays a message to inform you that you and the person named in Figure 4–6 are friends.

Strengths and Weaknesses of JavaScript

It is valuable to you understand the strengths and weaknesses of JavaScript to better determine its suitability to task. These are discussed in this section.

Strengths of JavaScript

Reduced Learning Curve.   JavaScript is easy to learn. Although it borrows much of its syntax and nature from Java, much of the complexity and rules of Java are absent.

Table 4–1   Features of JavaScript

Feature	Description
Dynamic forms	With JavaScript, you can create dynamic forms with built-in error checking.
Frames	As seen in Figure 4–8, frames give the Web page a segregated and partitioned look. In this figure you'll see one large frame plus two smaller frames. With frames, the screen is split into rectangular sections, with each section referencing a different URL. Each frame functions as its own mini-Web page within the larger Web page from which it is viewed. JavaScript includes excellent support for frames.
Spread sheets	JavaScript has functions that allow for simplified creation of spreadsheet-like forms. For example, a real estate company would use JavaScript on their Web page to provide browsers with the capability of calculating a mortgage payment.
User interaction	JavaScript provides excellent user interaction capabilities in the form of warning messages, confirmation messages, and interactive forms. Additionally, JavaScript is ideal for calculating or determining the value of one field based on the changes made to data on another field.
Ease of development	JavaScript eases development and debugging because it is not compiled. Therefore, changes made to JavaScript can be tested interactively and immediately, without having to execute a compile.
Search engines	JavaScript is an ideal language to build database queries that are then sent to a remote database.
Java Mortar	The term *Java Mortar* refers to the process of data created from one Java applet being massaged and passed to another Java applet via a JavaScript program. Because of the high degree of user interaction that is easily programmed into Web pages due to JavaScript, you will be able to transfer data easily between Java applets with JavaScript.
Dynamic URL building	JavaScript is well suited to build customized URLs based on user-specified selections on forms.
Replace CGI	JavaScript is very useful for replacing much of the function that exists in CGI scripts used in client-side processing.

Portability.   Because JavaScript is included in HTML pages, any Web browser that is capable of interpreting JavaScript will execute the code. Currently, this includes all the major Web browsers and the majority of the less well-known ones.

Improved Productivity.   JavaScript is a very productive language. The examples shown in Figures 4–5 through 4–7 were written using three lines of code. To accomplish the same processing in C++ or Java would have entailed more code.

Netscape User Prompt
JavaScript Prompt:
Enter your first name:
Jim
OK
Cancel

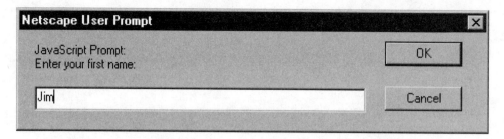

Figure 4–5 The first prompt statement in the JavaScript.

Small Overhead. JavaScript programs are quite a bit smaller than a Java or C++ object module. This reduces storage requirements to contain the code on the server as well as the download time to transfer the JavaScript program or Java/C++ program from the server to the client device.

Weaknesses of JavaScript

Code Is Viewable. Because JavaScript is written directly in the HTML code, and as most commercial browsers include a HTML viewing capability, the JavaScript code you write is viewable. This makes it possible for anyone to copy and thus steal it.

Limited Methods. Although the range of methods supported in the most popular commercial browsers increases with each release, the full range of methods is not yet supported.

Limited Support Tools. As is the case with Java, there is limited availability of support tools to the JavaScript developer.

ODBC

Microsoft's Open Database Connectivity (ODBC) initiative has become a well accepted standard for attaching databases to application programs that access them. Most of the leading DataBase Management System (DBMS) vendors have enabled their applications to support ODBC. To be competitive, a development tool must be ODBC-enabled as well.

Netscape User Prompt
JavaScript Prompt:
Enter a friends first name:
Robin
OK
Cancel

Figure 4–6 The second prompt statement in the JavaScript.

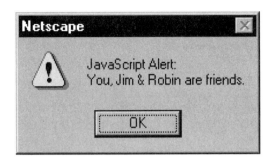

Figure 4–7 The alert statement in the JavaScript.

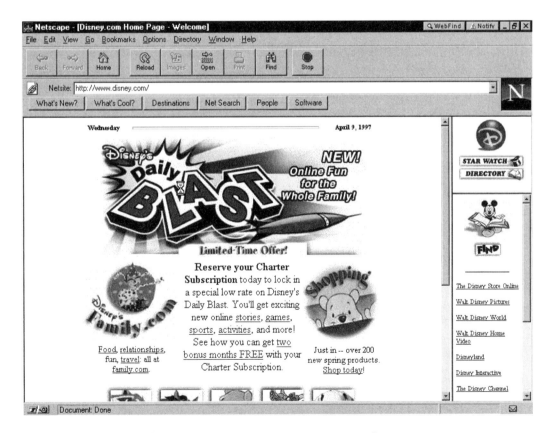

Figure 4–8 The Disney page uses frames.

Most pundits believe that ODBC will continue to be the most commonly used API for heterogeneous RDBMS access for many more years.

The ODBC interface provides for the following features:

- A library of ODBC function calls that allow an application to access a DBMS, execute Structure Query Language (SQL) query statements, and retrieve the results.

- A standard representation of data types.

- A standard set of error codes.

- A standard way to connect to, access, and log off a DBMS.

- Support for DBMS native SQL syntax as well as syntax based on the X/Open and SQL Access Group (SAG) SQL CAE specification, first published in 1992.

A diagram of an ODBC application is shown in Figure 4–9. Here, the ODBC component resides between the application program and the database. Its only purpose is to handle the translation of a database request coming from a program to a format that the

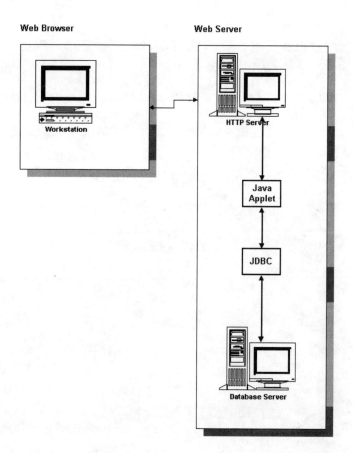

Figure 4–9   Web application with ODBC database access.

database understands. It then accomplishes the translation of the result coming from the database to a format that is recognizable by the program.

JDBC

JDBC is a database connectivity API that provides the necessary means for a Web application to access a database directly, without having the overhead of ODBC. Because JDBC represents a more direct method of communication between a program and a database, it is frequently a quicker form of database access.

There are two fundamental ways to use JDBC. The first way is by an applet making a call to a database. This configuration is seen in Figure 4–10. In this Figure, the Java applet initiates a request for database access which is received and interpreted by the JDBC API into a format that is recognizable by the RDBMS. The results of that database access are then reformatted by the JDBC API into something that the Java applet can process. In the second scenario, a stand-alone Java application has direct access to all available network components directly.

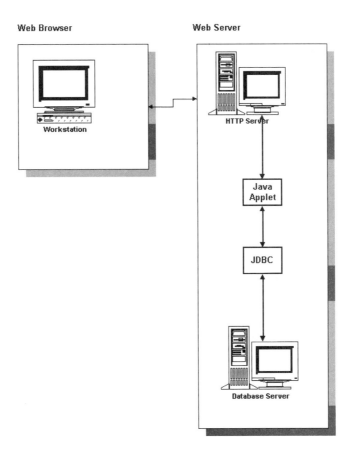

Figure 4–10 Web application with JDBC database access.

There are four primary interfaces described in the JDBC API. These are:

- *Environmental*. The environmental interface provides support for the creation of connections from a device to a database.
- *Connection*. The connection interface provides the connection to a particular database.
- *Statement*. The statement interface encapsulates the SQL statement coming from the program or applet and executes the statements.
- *Result Set*. The result set interface provides the facility to access the result set of the SQL statements executing against the database.

Moving On

Java was the first programming language that provided a complete solution to Internet application development. In just a couple of years, Java has gained in popularity at a pace equal to that of the Web. JavaScript, released soon after Java, is also an increasingly popular language for Web application development.

There are a number of benefits in choosing to develop a Web application that needs database access in either Java, or JavaScript. These pros and cons should be evaluated carefully when deciding what language to use to develop an application.

In the next chapter you will be introduced to Web database application suites and look at several of the most popular ones used to build Web database applications.

CHAPTER 5

Application Development Suites

T oday, application development suites are among the quickest growing segments in the Web market. Companies learned in the early 1990s that a development tool used in isolation and detached from other tools often becomes a little used tool. Application suites remedy this problem by offering a selection of tools used to develop Web applications. For example, HAHTsite IDE, the tool used in this book to create examples, is comprised of the following integrated components:

- WYSIWYG development interface
- An Image Map editor
- Ability to write HAHTtalk Basic or JavaScript scripts
- Basic compiler
- Debugger
- Web publishing tool
- Application server
- 30-day evaluation copy of Quarterdeck WebStar Server

HAHT Software is including the 30-day evaluation copy of the Quarterdeck WebStar Server in its product so that purchasers have all the tools they need to develop and publish sophisticated Web pages on one installation CD-ROM. This is the essence of an application suite.

This chapter presents information on a number of application development suites. The major features of the products are described along with contact information. The information in this chapter was generated by the actual product reviews available from the vendor's Web pages (at time of this writing). If you see a product or range of products that interest you, take a look at the vendor's Web page. You will also find evaluation copies of the majority of the products evaluated on the CD-ROM accompanying this book.

4W Publisher and 4W Publisher Pro

Company Name:	Information Analytics
Address:	PO Box 80266
	Lincoln, NE 68501
Phone:	(402) 489-4411
URL:	`http://www.4w.com/4wpublisher/`

The standard version (2.20) of 4W Publisher is a 16-bit app that generates static Web pages that can be stored on any Web server. Standard 4W Publisher uses MS Access 2.0 (or higher) databases and all records are stored in a predefined data table. User-defined fields can be added to the table as needed. 4W Publisher databases are not directly upwardly compatible with 4W Pro. A 32-bit version is in development and will be available in mid-1997. The 32-bit version will use the MS Access 95 database format.

The Pro version of 4W Publisher is a 32-bit WinCGI application that runs on a Windows NT/95 Web server (we currently support only O'Reilly's Web site). This version supports dynamic queries into any ODBC source, shopping cart and other features. 4W Pro is suitable for development of product catalogs, yellow page applications, online order handling and directories. MS Access 95 is required to develop applications using 4W Pro.

A-XORION Web Database Server

Company Name:	Clark Internet Services
Address:	8970 Oakland Suite I, Route 108
	Columbia, MD 21045
Phone:	(410) 995-0550
URL:	`http://www.clark.net/infouser/`

A-XORION is a PC-Windows/MS Access based database application server to the World Wide Web. It is managed from a Global Management Form, and communicates with a CGI program (AXORION.EXE) written in Visual Basic. The application server A-XORION will execute the requests posted by the CGI program AXORION.EXE. The request can be a login, a query, an insert, a modification, or a deletion, defined by CGI FORMS ELEMENTS such as input, radio buttons, checkboxes, text areas and HTML HIDDEN ELEMENTS in the HTML forms file. After the request is processed, it posts the result (an MS Access report or a customizable action-confirmation) back to the Web Server.

You use easy, standard MS Access reports to develop your output to the Web. Communication between Web Server and A-XORION is accomplished through a unique Message File System: A-XWebFS

A-XORION conforms to the CGI/1.1–1.3 standard. The A-XORION server is built *within* the Microsoft Access environment. It will, therefore, be able to connect to tables from MS Access, Dbase, Foxpro, Paradox. SQL Servers, Sybase and Oracle through

ODBC. A-XORION requires Microsoft Access to be pre-installed. A-XORION does not access data: MS Access does that and therefore, "If MS Access can connect (attach) to a (remote) database, A-XORION can also!"

Amazon

Company Name:	Intelligent Environments
Address:	67 South Bedford Street
	Burlington, MA 01803
Phone:	(617) 272-9700
URL:	`http://www.ieinc.com/`

Amazon, the flagship product from Intelligent Environments, is self-billed as the first open Web development tool for quickly deploying scaleable, interactive Internet applications that leverage legacy systems investments. Amazon supports native connectivity to DB2, Oracle, Sybase, and SQL Server, and ODBC connectivity for Informix, Lotus Notes and other databases.

Using Amazon, developers can build applications that employ an organization's unique business logic using Amazon's Intelligent Rules Language while bridging the gap between legacy data sources and network computer users. Future Amazon cartridges (the vendor's terminology for interfaces) will significantly improve the performance and response time for users running Amazon Web applications that require dynamic data access via Oracle's Web Server.

Amazon is browser independent and so Amazon applications can be accessed from browsers from Netscape, Microsoft, Sun, NCSA, Spry and SpyGlass. Amazon supports advanced features such as HTML 3.0, Netscape and Microsoft extensions to HTML, and support for SSL (Secure Sockets Layer) secure links to Microsoft and Netscape browsers.

Amazon works with Java applets that can be downloaded and executed on any Java-enabled browser, such as Netscape Navigator and Microsoft's Explorer.

Browsers are available for all popular operating systems, including Windows, Mac, Motif, UNIX and OS/2. This means that Amazon applications can be accessed for any of these platforms making it possible to develop a single application that can be used by anyone with a browser on either your intranet or across the Internet.

Amazon works with any server that supports the CGI server interface. CGI is supported by all the major Web servers. Amazon also supports high-performance direct API access to Netscape's servers using Netscape Server Application Programming Interface (NSAPI) and Microsoft Internet Information Server (IIS) using Internet Server Application Programming Interface (ISAPI). Direct API access is about ten times faster than CGI access.

Autobahn

Company Name:	Speedware Toronto
Address:	150 John Street, 10th Floor
	Toronto, Ontario M5V 3E3
Phone:	(416) 408-2880
URL:	`http://www.speedware.com/`

Speedware Autobahn lets you build applications so your WWW server supports dynamic systems. This allows your users to see what they want. Autobahn lets Web users run database applications residing on your WWW server. You can offer custom-tailored forms, live reports and batch jobs. Your old COBOL or C programs can be plugged into the Autobahn server, so you'll leverage your development investment. You can mix both static and dynamic information to create interactive systems.

The package offers many features and benefits. It includes a complete high-level (albeit proprietary) programming language. It can run programs that handle forms, reports, jobs, batch updates, transactions, and subroutine calls.

Autobahn is intended for MIS professionals who don't want to be bothered about networks and interprocess communications. You don't need Internet experts or C language gurus to set up your site. Autobahn lets you control users' access to your information as precisely as you want.

Autobahn applications can mix text, transactions and multimedia content. Your databases can hold images and sound files to enhance the interface. The Autobahn agent, the Open Application Server and the databases can all be on different machines, so large organizations can use their resources as they prefer. For example, if you have a dedicated Web server, you can put the application server on a production machine close to the data. In this way, you can build a firewall and spread the processing load.

Because Autobahn works via the Speedware Open Application Server (OAS), you can run programs on several computers simultaneously. Your Autobahn applications can run locally or across a network. Autobahn can work with Web servers from different vendors such as NCSA and CERN.

Speedware Autobahn works with the Netscape Commerce Server, which supports secure transactions that use credit card numbers or other confidential data. Applications created with Autobahn can run on any Speedware supported platform with almost no changes. The Speedware OAS can access 14 different DBMS and file systems. Autobahn applications can access many databases.

Centura Web Data Publisher

Company Name:	Centura Software
Address:	1060 Marsh Rd.
	Menlo Park, CA 94025
Phone:	(415) 617-4782
URL:	http://www.centurasoft.com/

Centura Web Developer provides all of the programming facilities necessary for building transaction-intensive, database-connected, enterprise business applications for the Web. Centura Web developer helps you deliver business applications for the Web with tremendous efficiency, not only by quickly producing the first application, but by providing for object re-use in subsequent development, by scaling to deal with complex business rules and very large numbers of users, and by easing on-going application maintenance.

All aspects of Web Developer's integrated development environment are designed to enhance productivity. With Centura Web Developer you can navigate easily through application code, move between coding facilities, design WYSIWYG pages, and debug with unparalleled ease.

The applications that you create with Web Developer can encapsulate the most complex business logic into objects that can be used over and over again. It's easy because of the strong object orientation of Web Developer's powerful fourth generation programming language, SAL. In addition, objects created in Java and ActiveX integrate seemlessly into Web Developer applications.

Web Developer applications serve up HTML pages that deliver corporate data and application logic to Internet or intranet clients—with full application security.

dbWeb

Company Name:	Microsoft Corporation
Address:	10500 NE 8th Street, Suite 1300
	Bellevue, WA 98004
Phone:	(800) 426-9400
URL:	http://www.microsoft.com/intdev/dbWeb/

Microsoft Corporation's dbWeb is a gateway between Microsoft Open Database Connectivity (ODBC) data sources and Microsoft IIS. You can use Microsoft dbWeb to publish data from an ODBC data source on the World Wide Web (WWW) or on your internal network without specialized client software.

With dbWeb, you create a schema that contains the specifications for your data and the Web pages. Microsoft dbWeb then produces fully functional Web pages for retrieving and displaying your data. dbWeb supports real-time database queries based on a *client-pull* model, formulating dynamic Web pages as users query your data source over the Internet. Visitors to your Web site can use familiar hypertext-style navigation via standard Web browsers to find information with little or no training.

Using dbWeb, you can publish information from the following client/server and desktop databases: Microsoft SQL Server, Microsoft Access, Microsoft Visual FoxPro, Oracle, and other databases that support 32-bit ODBC.

Delphi

Company Name:	Borland International Inc.
Address:	World Wide Headquarters
	100 Borland Way
	Scotts Valley, CA 95066
Phone:	(408) 431-1000
URL:	http://www.borland.com/delphi/

Delphi Desktop 2.0

Delphi Desktop 2.0 is the easiest way to create the fastest applications for Windows 95 and Windows NT. It combines the most intuitive, object-oriented development environment with over 90 customizable, reusable components for immediate productivity. Drag-and-drop database tools provide an innovative interface for building 32-bit applications.

Delphi Desktop 2.0 applications run up to 300–400% faster than 16-bit Delphi, and up to 15–50 times faster than those built with P-Code interpreters. Delphi 2.0 leverages Windows' 32-bit architecture, adds an Object Repository, and supports the reuse of data modules, once again raising the bar for application development tools. All Delphi 2.0 versions include the 16-bit Delphi 1.0 for Windows 3.1.

Delphi Developer 3.0

Delphi Developer is the fastest way to build 32-bit professional multi-user applications for Windows 95 and NT. It is the next step for Delphi 2.0 owners. Since Delphi 2.0 and Delphi Developer 3.0 are code compatible, no matter where your Windows based applications reside today, Delphi provides a complete solution.

In addition to the features found in Delphi Desktop, Delphi Developer includes: a scaleable Data Dictionary, Multi-Object Grid, complete ODBC support, source code to over 100 native Delphi components, sample OCXs, an expanded Open Tools API, Report-Smith, Local InterBase Server and much more. It also includes 16-bit Delphi 1.0 for free.

Delphi Developer is targeted to professional developers who want to develop high-performance desktop applications accessing local and LAN databases, including: dBASE, Paradox, Local InterBase and ODBC.

Delphi Developer 3.0 includes these additional features for the professional:

- Scaleable Data Dictionary
- Multi Object Grid
- Over 100 VCL components for rapid application development
- 32-bit ReportSmith, for high volume client/server reporting
- BDE low-level API support and Help Files
- ODBC support
- Single User Local InterBase Server
- InstallShield Express for easy installation and deployment
- Winsight 32 for monitoring windows messaging
- Expanded Open Tools API
- Team Development Interface (Requires Intersolv PVCS)
- Visual Component Library Source code and complete manual
- Full documentation of Delphi Desktop plus ReportSmith Creating Reports, Delphi Reference Library Guide, InterBase Server, Getting Started

Delphi Client/Server Suite 2.0

Delphi Client/Server Suite 2.0 contains everything you need to build and deliver high-performance client/server applications. Unmatched performance, data integrity, and code reuse are all contained in a robust object-oriented interface, that maximizes productivity across the enterprise. With a host of tools for optimized client/server development, Delphi Client/Server Suite 2.0 offers a complete solution.

The suite also includes a 2-developer copy of InterBase for Windows NT, a fast and efficient SQL database server; a complete set of database design and analysis tools; integrated team-development support; and native 32-bit SQL Links for royalty-free deployment on Sybase, Oracle, InterBase, and SQL Server.

Delphi Client/Server Suite is targeted to corporate developers, departmental programmers, VARs, system integrators, consultants, and ISVs who want to develop high performance workgroup and client/server applications.

Delphi Client/Server Suite 2.0 includes these additional features for professional client/server developers:

- High performance 32-bit SQL Links native drivers for unlimited deployment
- SQL Database Explorer to browse server meta data
- SQL Monitor for testing, debugging and performance tuning
- 2-user InterBase NT License
- Data Pump Expert for rapid upsizing and application scaling
- Integrated Intersolv PVCS Version Control
- ReportSmith SQL edition
- Visual Query Builder to easily create SQL queries
- Cached Updates
- Client/Server Documentation
- 16-bit Delphi Client/Server 1.0 for Windows 3.1
- Full documentation of Delphi Developer plus Getting Started SQL Links, InterBase Language Reference, InterBase Data Definition Guide

DynaWeb

Company Name:	Inso Corporation
Address:	1 Richmond Square
	Providence, RI 02906
Phone:	(401) 421-9550
URL:	`http://dynabase.ebt.com/dbproduct/index.htm`

The DynaBase Web Management System is an integrated development and publishing system for new media applications. It provides a controlled environment for authoring, developing, and delivering dynamic Web content to multiple audiences simultaneously. It supports Web authors, developers, their clients and end-users.

This product offers the user many benefits. It simplifies the management of Web content. It enables developers to achieve their interactive design goals more quickly. It reduces skill requirements for individuals in Web projects. It eliminates many repetitive tasks, and it allows managers to focus on interaction, design, quality, and consistency.

The DynaBase Web Management System consists of DynaBase Server, DynaBase Web Manager, and DynaBase Web Developer.

The DynaBase Server is a version controlled multimedia repository for all files and scripts used in Web site publishing. The DynaBase Server organizes and manages the links between items in a Web, dramatically reducing the Web administrator's maintenance tasks. Through version control, the DynaBase Server allows items in various stages of development to coexist in the system so that end-users who depend on continued access to specified versions remain unaffected. DynaBase's multiple editions capability provides configuration management over entire Web sites, making publishing large sets of interrelated content a snap. The DynaBase Server is designed to plug into either the Netscape or Microsoft Web Servers. DynaBase Server is the only version controlled repository for professional online publishing.

The DynaBaseWeb Manager is a file manager for Web sites. It provides access to, and control over, the files and programs used in a Web site. Using an intuitive graphical user interface that resembles a file system browser, Web masters and contributing authors may edit, organize, test, and manage content with drag-and-drop ease. The Web Manager provides a launching pad for HTML, graphic, and multimedia applications from vendors like Netscape, Adobe, and Macromedia. DynaBase Web Manager is the only open authoring environment for professional on-line publishers.

The DynaBaseWeb Developer is a full featured interactive development environment for Web Basic. Web Basic is a BASIC language which has been designed to be both compatible with Microsoft's Visual Basic syntax yet remain portable across platforms. Within the Developer, Web Basic can be used to develop both CGI scripts and HTML methods in industry standard BASIC syntax.

Edify Electronic Workforce

Company Name:	Edify Corporation
Address:	2840 San Tomas Expressway
	Santa Clara, CA 95051
Phone:	(408) 982-2000
URL:	`http://www.edify.com/`

The Electronic Workforce software bridges the gap between customers and traditional information systems. With this tool you can create and deliver complete interactive service applications through whatever medium is best: phone, fax, e-mail, PC clients, or the World Wide Web. All of your back-office systems, whether host, client-server, or PC based, are easily accessed from a single delivery platform—one that schedules and manages interactive applications and coordinates phone, host and network resources. With the award-winning Agent Trainer visual development environment, there's no need to write code. Now you can focus on developing new applications faster and more cost-effectively.

The Edify Electronic Workforce has three main components: Edify software agents, the Agent Trainer development environment, and the Agent Supervisor run-time environment. Together these components comprise the most comprehensive, fully integrated software platform available for interactive service solutions.

At the heart of the Electronic Workforce are the *agents*, advanced software that provides interactive services on behalf of an organization. Edify software agents have the widest range of skills possible so they can perform tasks such as answering a phone, operating a host application or exchanging information through online PCs. By defining the sequence of tasks agents will perform, you can quickly create robust interactive service applications that span across various media and back-office systems.

Because software agents are so flexible and multi-skilled, you can concentrate on creative valuable services, without the hassles of hard-coded system integration.

Edify's Agent Trainer is a powerful, object-oriented visual development environment where you define and customize interactive service applications. Agent Trainer's unique point and click interface lets you quickly build interactive services that agents will provide. Because all of the agent skills are represented in Agent Trainer as visual objects, you can create sophisticated applications without writing a single line of code. And to make development even easier, there's an integrated set of graphical tools, giving you everything you need to create services unique to your organization.

The Agent Supervisor is a robust run-time environment that schedules software agents and assigns them to service applications built with Agent Trainer. Once agents and service applications are paired, Agent Supervisor manages all of the phone, fax, PC, host and network resources necessary for interactive service delivery. All of these resources are managed through an architecture that ensures reliability and security. With Agent Supervisor, you can deploy multiple interactive services, confident that they will be delivered through a secure run-time environment whose capacity scales to your needs.

FoxWeb

Company Name:	EON Technologies
Address:	3211 Encinal Ave., Suite D
	Alameda, CA 94501
Phone:	(510) 523-6794
URL:	`http://www.foxWeb.com/`

FoxWeb is a Web application development tool for Windows NT and Windows 95 servers. You can use it to quickly and easily integrate your FoxPro and SQL databases with the Web and to build interactive Web applications for intranets or the Internet. Take advantage of the fastest PC-based database engine and ease of use of Visual FoxPro to create dynamic Web content. Whether you are a seasoned developer or a *newbie*, FoxWeb provides the tools and resources to help you create interactive applications in less time and with less effort.

FoxWeb achieves its speed by pre-installing several FoxPro channels that wait in the background for Web requests. As requests come in, FoxWeb distributes them to the open channels for parallel processing. All data transfers are done in memory so there is no overhead associated with hard-drive activity. No ODBC or temporary files are needed. FoxWeb is scalable and can grow with your business. Just pop in some more memory or an additional CPU and FoxWeb will take advantage of it, by allowing you to open additional channels to improve performance.

Being the first Web application development environment for FoxPro, and having been tested on hundreds of servers word-wide since 1994, FoxWeb has evolved into an extremely stable product that will function under the most adverse conditions. FoxWeb's unique Channel Monitor technology ensures that your mission-critical application will stay up even if your programs contain bugs that would cause other products to crash.

HAHTsite IDE

Company Name:	HAHT Software, Inc.
Address:	4200 Six Forks Road
	Raleigh, NC 27609
Phone:	(888) Get-HAHT
URL:	`http://www.haht.com/`

The HAHTsite Integrated Internet Development System merges content creation, client- and server-side logic development, data access (ODBC or native API), automated distributed deployment to multiple sites, team development, and application lifecycle management into one seamlessly integrated software system.

Extending far beyond point products, such as an authoring tool or database utility, HAHTsite combines hundreds of features into an end-to-end solution designed specifically to address the unique technology and life cycle requirements of complex Internet or intranet applications.

The HAHTsite system is made up of three components: The HAHTsite Integrated Development Environment (IDE), the HAHTsite Application Server, and the HAHTsite Software Developers Kit (SDK).

The HAHTsite IDE is the main interface to the HAHTsite System for all members of the Internet/intranet development team, allowing them to work in a single, drag-and-drop oriented environment for content creation, application logic development and data access, site deployment/publishing, and project life cycle management and maintenance.

The IDE features a WYSIWYG, drag-and-drop interface that provides a visual workspace to accommodate both content creators and professional developers, and has been carefully designed to utilize familiar wizards, toolbars, metaphors and visual cues, while providing powerful, object-oriented capabilities and project management features, as well as full server-side application debugging.

The HAHTsite Application Server is a secure, scalable multi-process, multithreaded deployment engine used to run compiled HAHTsite applications in conjunction with any CGI 1.0 compliant Web server software, and can also take advantage of NSAPI and ISAPI interfaces.

Server-side application logic developed in the IDE using HAHTtalk Basic (a VB syntax-compatible programming language) is compiled at publish time into machine independent P-Code which is executed by the HAHTsite Application Server. The Application server also manages *state* or session information, maintains database connections across multiple pages, and handles accessing any server-based service (like API, DLL, OLE/OCX/ActiveX, shared library, shell, DDE, etc.).

The HAHTsite Software Developers Kit turns HAHTsite into a platform for internal and third party development, and exposes HAHTsite as an ActiveX server.

As an add-in to the IDE, the SDK allows IS/IT professionals to extend the power of HAHTsite with custom, enterprise-wide Widgets (reusable encapsulated code objects) programmed in HAHTtalk Basic, a VB syntax-compatible programming language. Widgets can be used, for example, to control access to corporate resources and simplify complex tasks for other members of the team.

IQ/Live Web

Company Name:	IQ Software, Inc.
Address:	3295 River Exchange Drive, Suite 550
	Norcross, GA 30092
Phone:	(770) 446-8880
URL:	`http://www.iqsc.com/`

IQ/LiveWeb

IQ Software answers the challenge of providing corporate database content to intranets with IQ/LiveWeb, a complete Web-enabled decision support solution. IQ/LiveWeb can be implemented in a matter of days and provides everything a company needs to automatically disseminate database information on an intranet.

IQ/LiveWeb takes advantage of existing intranet infrastructure and standard Internet browsers to provide a complete solution for database reporting on an intranet. IQ/LiveWeb combines IQ/Objects, an award winning object-based reporting tool, and IQ/SmartServer for comprehensive server publishing capabilities for UNIX and Windows NT.

IQ/Objects and IQ/SmartServer, generally recognized as the leading technology for sophisticated client/server reporting, are real world tested, mission critical tools. Today, these tools are in use in thousands of companies worldwide and serve as the technological foundation for IQ/LiveWeb. Extending these tools with Internet features provides several unique capabilities that set IQ/LiveWeb apart:

- Powerful, object-oriented technology enables reuse of previously developed reports and report components which makes it easy to build reports from the simplest to the most sophisticated, all without any programming or scripting.
- Support for a wide variety of report types including multi-dimensional crosstabs, tables, charts, and bitmaps.
- Server-based processing and robust scheduling and administrative facilities support automatic report publishing to an intranet.
- Users can request on-demand execution of reports, taking advantage of high performance, server-based processing to initiate a database query and generate a report containing up-to-the-minute information *on-the-fly*.

IQ/LiveWeb supports server-based processing and report publishing for both UNIX and Windows NT environments.

IQ/LiveWeb's object-based reporting tool lets users create simple columnar reports, multidimensional cross tabulations and charts and even sophisticated reports that combine previously created reports and information from multiple databases into one report.

IQ/LiveWeb has a familiar Microsoft Office look and feel. It offers a customizable work environment with floating toolbars and palettes, and consistent tabbed dialogs. IQ/LiveWeb is available for Windows 3.1, Windows 95, and Windows NT.

Objects can be dragged and dropped into a visual report designer to create an unlimited variety of reports. Standard templates make it easy to create professional-looking reports. Business views give users access to database tables, columns and calculated objects. URLs also can be stored as objects in the Object Directory.

IQ/LiveWeb provides a selection of chart and graph styles as well as several styles for presenting cross-tab information.

IQ/LiveWeb provides comprehensive server-based processing capabilities that make it possible to completely automate and manage the process of publishing reports. Since IQ/LiveWeb supports server-based processing in both UNIX and Windows NT environments, using servers to access databases and perform all the processing required for publishing reports is a very efficient architecture. In addition, server-based processing allows IQ/LiveWeb to support on-demand server execution of reports by end-users with access to a standard Web browser.

You can control execution schedules and decide whether existing reports are overwritten each time a new report is generated, saved for future use, or kept for some specified period then purged. Once the schedule is established, reports will continue to execute automatically until the schedule is changed.

IQ/LiveWeb reports are published in an HTML format. All that users need to view them is a standard Internet browser.

IQ/LiveWeb provides complete status information for every report scheduled to be published. Comprehensive task monitoring, tracking and error handling capabilities reduce support requirements.

IQ/LiveWeb supports multiple UNIX and NT application servers, allowing scalability from dozens to hundreds or even thousands of users.

To request and view IQ/LiveWeb reports, all users need is a standard Internet browser such as Netscape Navigator or Microsoft Internet Explorer. A simple point and click is all it takes to display the desired report. In addition, users who need up-to-the-minute data can run reports in real-time with just a point and a click and see the results immediately.

Using a standard Internet browser, any user can:

- Select a specific report
- View a report
- Specify a report to be executed on-demand
- Pass specific parameters to customize an on-demand report
- Drill down to linked reports for additional detail

By taking advantage of the existing Internet backbone, IQ/LiveWeb makes it possible for companies to give their users the ability to access scheduled and on-demand database information when they need it from virtually anywhere in the world. IQ/LiveWeb is a total Web-enabled reporting solution that removes the barrier between corporate information sources and the Internet, providing flexibility and robust capabilities to meet the needs of users from novice to expert.

Krakatoa

Company Name:	CADIS, Incorporated
Address:	1909 26th Street
	Boulder, CO 80302
Phone:	(303) 440-4363
URL:	`http://www.cadis.com/`

Delivered in either SUN's Java programming language or HTML/JavaScript, Krakatoa allows Web users to search through structured content by interactively refining their search criteria with attributes of interest. At each mouse-click selection, the count of qualifying items is instantly updated, allowing the user to quickly locate the products or documents of interest. Once a desired product is identified, Krakatoa enables the user to request additional product or ordering information, or request a sales contact.

National Semiconductor Corporation is using Krakatoa to publish their extensive product line of over 30,000 component parts over the Web. National's Home Page implementation is the first site of its kind that enables online interactive access to a manufacturer's product information based on attributes of interest to the user. Other customers, including Hitachi, Philips Semiconductors, Burr-Brown, Perceptive Scientific Imaging, and the CMP Group will be using Krakatoa for similar applications.

Krakatoa is an object-oriented client/server system implemented for the Web. The server software consists of the Krakatoa knowledge base management system, schema authoring tool and an API (C++ and Perl). The Java-based client is a Java applet that is downloaded from the Web browser and will run natively on PCs using MS Windows 95, MACs and Motif client systems. The HTML client has been implemented using the latest in Netscape Frames/JavaScript technology.

LivePAGE WebMaster

Company Name:	Netscape Communications Corp
Address:	501 E. Middlefield Rd.
	Mountain View, CA 94043
Phone:	(415) 937-2555
URL:	`http://www.netscape.com/comprod/products/`
	`tools/`

Our product family, known as LivePAGE, is a system of open, non-proprietary text and information management software products that takes full advantage of SGML and SQL relational database technology. LivePAGE was developed based on commonly used and generally accepted standards. It stores SGML documents in an SQL relational database, on Microsoft Windows platforms, using client/server architecture. The suite of products has been designed using component architecture so that there is a seamless integration with other commonly used software products.

When a LivePAGE document is published, all of the generated HTML files and extracted graphics are saved in one directory. You can save your non-HTML files, such as sound and video, in another directory. It is unlikely that you would store these files in your LivePAGE database. The URL reference in your document would be similar to:

`<img src='video/vidfile.avi'>`. In this example, the "video" subdirectory must exist and contain the file vidfile.avi.

LiveWire and LiveWire Pro

Company Name:	Netscape Communications Corp
Address:	501 E. Middlefield Rd.
	Mountain View, CA 94043
Phone:	(415) 937-2555
URL:	`http://www.netscape.com/comprod/products/`
	`tools/`

Netscape LiveWire and LiveWire Pro provide an online development environment that enables novice users to create and manage Web content, Web sites, and live online Web applications for intranets and the Internet, while offering experienced application developers the power to manage highly complex Web sites and scalable client-server applications.

Netscape LiveWire consists of: Netscape Navigator Gold, LiveWire Site Manager, LiveWire JavaScript Compiler, and LiveWire Database Connectivity Library. Netscape LiveWire Pro includes the above, plus Informix-OnLine Workgroup high-performance SQL database and Crystal Software's Crystal Reports Professional Version 4.5 (Windows NT version only).

Netscape Navigator Gold is the premium version of Netscape Navigator, the latest version of the world's most popular Web client. In addition to all the features of Netscape Navigator, Netscape Navigator Gold enables easy navigation, creation, and editing of live online documents. With Netscape Navigator Gold, millions of Netscape Navigator users can immediately begin creating and editing sophisticated hypermedia content, including inline plug-ins, Java applets, and JavaScripts, in a WYSIWYG environment.

Experienced Webmasters know the difficulties of maintaining a large Web site with many pages, images, media types, and links. A single page can contain dozens of links to other pages and files. The process of managing a Web site is a challenging one. Links between pages and content can be broken easily. Universal Resource Locators (URLs) can be changed without the Webmaster's knowledge, often leading unwary users into *dead ends* and *cul-de-sacs* when they link to a page that no longer exists. To solve these problems and to simplify Web site management for novice and experienced Webmasters, Netscape has developed LiveWire Site Manager, a visual site-management tool for creating and managing Web sites with drag-and-drop ease.

For rapid development of client- and server-side applications without requiring extensive programming experience, Netscape and Sun Microsystems developed JavaScript. Today, JavaScript has been widely adopted as the standard scripting language for adding intelligence to Web pages. With LiveWire, Netscape brings JavaScript to Web servers.

Netscape's FastTrack 2.0 and Enterprise 2.0 Web Servers both include the capability to run compiled JavaScript applications. The LiveWire JavaScript Compiler enables application developers to quickly and easily convert JavaScript applications and HTML pages incorporating JavaScript code into platform-independent byte codes ready to run on any Netscape 2.0 Server. A simplified version of the JavaScript Compiler is also built into the LiveWire Site Manager for one-button compiling.

LiveWire helps application developers create server-side programs that enable Netscape Navigator and other Web clients to browse, search, and update relational databases on intranets and the Internet. The LiveWire Database Connectivity Library enables direct SQL connections to databases from Oracle, Sybase, and Informix, and ODBC connections to dozens of other databases, from desktop to mainframe.

High-performance Web applications need a high-performance database, so Netscape LiveWire Pro includes a developer version of Informix-OnLine Workgroup, the entry-level version of Informix's OnLine Dynamic Server. OnLine Workgroup is designed for quick configuration and maintenance, yet maintains full compatibility with Informix's scalable database architecture that supports multiprocessor and parallel processing systems. The copy of OnLine Workgroup bundled with LiveWire Pro is licensed for a single developer on a single Web server, with unlimited users.

The Windows NT version of LiveWire Pro includes a copy of Crystal Reports Professional Version 4.5, the most popular report-design and data-analysis tool for Windows systems. Crystal Reports adds versatile reporting to your Web-based database applications while cutting application development time and expanding report design options. A simple, visual user interface makes report design—including cross-tabs, sophisticated graphs, and drilldown capability—just a few clicks away.

Microsoft FrontPage 97

Company Name:	Microsoft Corporation
Address:	10500 NE 8th Street, Suite 1300
	Bellevue, WA 98004
Phone:	(800) 426-9400
URL:	`http://www.microsoft.com/frontpage/`

FrontPage 97 with Bonus Pack makes creating professional-quality Web sites effortless. Powerful new functionality, support for the latest Web technologies, and seamless integration with Microsoft Office. Microsoft FrontPage 97 with Bonus Pack is the ideal way to get professional-quality Internet or intranet sites up and running fast. It offers all the best new Web technologies, plus powerful tools for all your creation and management tasks.

Microsoft FrontPage 97 with Bonus Pack can quickly turn you into a Webmaster. Use more than 30 built-in templates and wizards to build entire Web sites and individual pages easily. And with the WYSIWYG FrontPage Editor, there's no need to know HTML! Insert hyperlinks and add information from Microsoft Office and other sources with drag-and-drop simplicity. And manage your Web sites easily with the graphical tools in the FrontPage Explorer.

The latest Web technologies are at your fingertips. Drop WebBotTM components onto your pages to add such advanced functionality as full-text searching and forms. Customize your Web sites with JavaScript and Microsoft Visual Basic Scripting Edition, using an intuitive user interface. Or easily connect to databases or add ActiveXTM controls, Java applets, Netscape plug-ins for interactive, compelling Web pages.

FrontPage 97 with Bonus Pack gives you powerful tools to create rich content and manage your Web sites effectively. Enliven your Web pages with images designed in Microsoft Image Composer, included in FrontPage 97 with Bonus Pack, or incorporate professional photographs from the Microsoft Image Composer stock photo library. Edit

HTML code directly in the FrontPage Editor and preview your Web pages in any browser—without leaving FrontPage. And use advanced tools to remotely author and edit your Web sites.

FrontPage 97 with Bonus Pack has a familiar environment that allows you to use any document created with Microsoft Office 97 easily because it works like other Office 97 applications. Use the shared spelling checker, global Find and Replace, and the Microsoft Thesaurus to guarantee your Web remain accurate and compelling.

Personal Web Site (PWS) Toolbox

Company Name:	W3.COM, Incorporated
Address:	444 Castro Street #431
	Mountain View, CA 94041
Phone:	(415) 969-6760
URL:	http://www.w3.com/

The W3 Toolbox is a collection of four software tools that greatly reduce the time it takes to create a monster Web site. The W3 Toolbox is bundled with the Personal Web Site but can be purchased independently!

WebSpin lets you generate HTML pages automatically, from any simple flat file database, using a number of intuitive templates. WebSpin is the ideal solution for online publishing involving massive collections of identically formatted record-based documents. Update your site as often as you need without having to manually edit your HTML files or program macros.

WebScan is a Web site search engine that creates search functions for a Web site. Search for one specific field or any combination of fields on flat databases and WebScan will work in conjunction with WebSpin to return customized HTML pages of matched records. Your users will be able to handle the information displayed on your site more efficiently by focusing on what's important to them.

WebForm simplifies online form handling by generating custom responses to standard HTML fill-out forms without CGI scripting. WebForm automatically saves submitted input to a text file, sends customized e-mail to any address based on the input and returns an HTML response to the user.

WebSweep allows the quick updating of bodies of text, which are common to multiple HTML Web pages by simply replacing common data with macros.

PowerBuilder 5.0

Company Name:	Sybase, Inc.
Address:	6475 Christie Avenue
	Emeryville, CA 94608
Phone:	(510) 922-3500
URL:	http://www.powersoft.com/products/devtools/ pb50/

Build a new breed of dynamic Web server applications! Or extend your PowerBuilder applications all the way out to the Web! Powersoft's new Internet Developer Toolkit is packed with the Internet components, libraries, and productivity tools you need to turn PowerBuilder into a powerful Internet development environment.

If you're puzzled by HTML, or struggling with CGI programming, the Internet Developer Toolkit offers a fast and thorough solution for quickly *Web-izing* your development capabilities. For developers already familiar with the basics, the Internet Developer Toolkit offers the high productivity of point-and-click wizards, HTML controls, sample Plug-ins, and controls for ActiveXs. Leverage your distributed PowerBuilder applications to the Web with standard extensions all in a highly affordable package.

The Internet Developer Toolkit includes everything you need to build a range of Internet and intranet applications, including: PowerBuilder Web.pb, PowerBuilder Window Plug-in, DataWindow Plug-in and Control for ActiveX, Internet Class Library, Personal Web Server, and the Web.pb Wizard.

Distributed PowerBuilder makes a powerful and sophisticated application server environment for the Web. Now, Web.pb, serves as the glue to bind Distributed PowerBuilder applications to Web servers. This means developers can build high-performance database applications on the Web and take advantage of the robustness and flexibility of PowerScript and the patented DataWindow technology to generate dynamic HTML. PowerBuilder supports a true *thin client* architecture. In fact, a Web browser is all you need to run a distributed PowerBuilder application. In addition, you can access Distributed PowerBuilder applications from Web and PowerBuilder clients simultaneously, eliminating the need for multiple coding of business logic.

The PowerBuilder Window Plug-in allows developers to run existing PowerBuilder applications in a Web browser. PowerBuilder 5.0 child windows may be embedded in HTML pages and sent to Plug-in-enabled browsers when the pages are referenced. This enables you to dynamically deliver applications as needed to your users, eliminating the costly cycle of upgrade and maintenance installations. Users will be amazed to work with sophisticated presentation objects (such as Windows 95 tab controls and tree lists) inside a Web browser.

The PowerBuilder DataWindow is Powersoft's patented technology for manipulating and presenting database information. As a Plug-in or ActiveX control used to extend your browser, the DataWindow adds richly formatted presentation of query results to an otherwise bland HTML document.

Now your Web applications will benefit from a class library designed to enable *state management*—the maintenance of session or state information across HTML pages—critical to application server development. The Internet Developer Toolkit also provides PowerBuilder objects that create advanced HTML forms, such as a form with a dropdown list box or radio set, from a DataWindow result set.

The Internet Developer Toolkit includes WebSite 1.1 from O'Reilly and Associates, a 32-bit multithreaded World Wide Web server for Windows NT 3.5 (or higher) and Windows 95 platforms. WebSite 1.1 provides a tree-like display of all the documents and links on your server with an easy-to-use facility for locating and repairing broken links.

Using CGI, you can run a desktop application within a Web document on WebSite. It also features access security to the different areas of your Web server.

A major productivity tool for connecting your distributed PowerBuilder applications to the Web, Web.pb Wizard will automatically generate the HTML forms you need to make appropriate calls to your distributed applications. For example, this wizard helps locate the server, then helps you pick which non-visual user object (NVO) to use, which function within the NVO, and which arguments to pass to the NVO. Then, it creates the HTML form and code required to send the request.

The Internet Developer Toolkit also includes samples and examples for Plug-ins, libraries, Web.pb, and ActiveX controls.

Sapphire/Web

Company Name:	Bluestone Software
Address:	1000 Briggs Road
	Mount Laurel, NJ 08054
Phone:	(609) 727-4600
URL:	http://www.bluestone.com/

For developers creating network computing applications, Sapphire/Web is the *Web-and-Java-to-database* development tool that makes it easy to create high-performance Internet/intranet applications. Unlike other tools that deliver server-side only solutions and technology look-in, Sapphire/Web offers Interactive Java client and server-side business logic in an open approach giving you the choice of Java, ActiveX, and the security and scalability to meet the needs of Enterprise-Wide and World-Wide applications.

Sapphire/Web is designed to work in a manner similar to other application builders for Windows and Motif.

Sapphire/Web also provides for testing and loading of the application program in the specified http server.

SiteBase

Company Name:	Cykic Software
Address:	123 Camino De La Reina
	San Diego, CA 92108
Phone:	(619) 220-7970
URL:	http://www.cykic.com/

Hype-It 3000 is a Web server with built-in relational database and developer's tools. It is a complete Web program development environment allowing you to create any full-blown database application accessible to Web clients through CGI (Common Gateway Interface). This is a developer's server and tool set. To make use of Hype-It 3000, xBase programming skills are necessary. If you or your clients require the full power of Hype-It 3000, you must provide the programming, or at your option, we can contract to provide custom programming, to your specifications.

The development environment of Hype-It 3000 is the MultiBase operating system/database language. This environment offers the following features:

- Supports a multi-user, multi-tasking program development (dBASE-like dot prompt) environment.
- Allows the programmer to create CGI programs to function with HTML documents.

- Supports native xBASE language; a composite of FoxPro, dBASE, Clipper, and over 150 function extensions.
- Gives Hype-It a developer's environment for writing code to interface to the Web server.
- Supports a relational database for Web applications.
- Supports powerful search functions for text or data search requirements.
- Includes graphics library for image manipulation and graphic image database types.
- Includes fax functions to tie into the Web application (fax-back abilities).
- Supports programmer's tools for debugging; cross-reference; text editing.
- Supports multiple workstations for program development across a LAN.
- Gives programmers TCP/IP functions for direct access to the Internet: ping a site, send e-mail, reverse name look-up, etc.

Software Engine

Company Name:	Software Engines, Inc.
Address:	129 Washington Street
	Hoboken, NJ 07030
Phone:	(201) 963-7731
URL:	http://www.engine.com/

SOFTWARE ENGINE is a fifth generation language-less application development system for SYBASE users on SUN Microsystems Workstations. Web database gateway applications for Java and HTML alike, as well as X/Motif.GUI applications are created in an integrated single attribute-based meta-data environment, where the designer describes the application from a functional schema perspective without programming.

It is an open system, and is intensely data driven. Software Engine builds fully functional applications directly from your database design and object attributes.

It builds screens as well as the databases, and bridges the two, with query building facilities, direct database operations and real-time updates from the database.

It understands object relationships, at the GUI level, to incorporate data validation, integrity checking and selection lists for data entry values. You write code only in exceptional cases such as business calculations.

One of the key advantages is that it does not generate source code and does not use a 4GL. Instead, it uses the database to store your application attributes. HTML is only generated on the fly on an as-needed basis.

It only takes a few minutes to create your first simple table object, by using a straight forward intuitive graphical user interface to name the object and its field names and datatypes. This automatically creates a GUI screen, a database table, and provides query building and data browsing and editing capabilities. In the X server environment, a highly interactive graphical user interface is automatically generated with the engbrowse-program. In the WEB environment, the HTML generator provides a complete gateway to the database with the same data browsing and editing facilities. Open interface capabilities are integrated with eng_htcmd.

The Software Engine QuickDive walks you through this process when you get your feet wet with Software Engine. The Create Table Demo lets you go through the same process directly through the Web without having the software around. This will immediately create a table of your choice on our data server, and provide the Web data browsing capabilities.

Software Engine applications range from catalog management and ordering, to risk management in trading environments, to transaction processing, accounting systems, payrolls, inventory tracking, pre-sales and customer support, source control, and many others.

Software Engine excels in its ability to understand and automatically create functionality for intricate database relationships and complex application logic. Software Engine's ability to easily integrate the rarely needed developer code, without the loss of its automatically provided functionally, without generating code, and with an intuitive interface, provides the powerful means to create sophisticated applications in a fraction of the time it would otherwise take.

Tango

Company Name:	Everyware Development Corporation
Address:	6733 Mississauga Rd., 7th Floor
	Mississauga, Ontario L5N 6J5
Phone:	(905) 819-1173
URL:	`http://www.everyware.com/products/tango/`

Tango allows developers to create dynamic Web applications that are integrated with databases. Tango allows you to integrate data from any ODBC database including Oracle, Sybase, Informix, SQL Server, FoxPro, and Microsoft Access. Tango's versatility lets you easily create Web applications on Windows NT, Windows 95 or Macintosh and deploy your solutions on your Web servers running on Windows NT, Macintosh, or Solaris.

WebHub

Company Name:	HREF Tools Corporation
Address:	316 Occidental Avenue South, Suite 406
	Seattle, WA 98104
Phone:	(206) 812-0177
URL:	`http://www.href.com/`

WebHub technology provides a complete object oriented framework for industrial strength Web application development.

WebHub is fast! The apps you build with WebHub components will compile to native Intel machine code. Screamin' fast. Typical non-db page requests take 15 to 50 milliseconds. With a strong database server, you can easily serve a million new surfers a day. With just a P90 and 32meg RAM on NT, you can serve three dynamic pages per second.

WebHub is proven technology. WebHub has been chosen by MCI, Lockheed-Martin, Conoco, the States of California, Utah, Georgia, and Massachusetts, SecureTax, and many other organizations that needed to write applications for the Web. Our portfolio has the whole story.

WebHub is reliable. Compared to writing your own Web interface for ISAPI or CGI, you'll find that it's much easier to use a fully tested, 60k-byte, WebHub "runner" and stay focused on your real goal! WebHub has been tested by thousands of developers.

WebHub saves you development time. Re-use your existing code and skills. WebHub's architecture promotes re-use in every way—of HTML as well as program logic. By using the WebHub framework, you save weeks of work. A complete, extensible save-state mechanism is built-in to the system.

WebHub is flexible. No brick walls. No limits. WebHub is solid OOP for Delphi and C++Builder. It's designed to give you maximum development speed with plenty of room to be creative.

Webinator

Company Name:	Thunderstone Corporation
Address:	11115 Edgewater Drive
	Cleveland, OH 44102
Phone:	(216) 631-8544
URL:	`http://www.thunderstone.com/`

Webinator is a Web walking and indexing package that will allow a Website administrator to create and provide a high quality retrieval interface to collections of HTML documents. Webinator serves as an example of the type of applications that can be built around Thunderstone's Texis RDBMS.

We believe the Webinator is the finest system of its kind in existence on the Web and we would like organizations to try it out and see if they feel the same way.

From the Administrator's perspective Webinator offers the following benefits:

- Indexes multiple sites into one common index.
- Provides detailed verification and logging of document linkages.
- Will index/update documents while database is in use.
- Allows multiple databases at a site.
- Provides an SQL query interface to the database for maintenance and reports.
- Allows remote sites to be copied to the local file system.
- Multiple index engines may run concurrently against a common database.
- Adobe Acrobat/PDF file support (commercial version option only)

From the User's perspective Webinator offers:

- Simple navigation
- Powerful and easy to use queries for:
  - Natural language

- Set logic
- Special pattern matchers (regular expressions, quantities, fuzzy patterns)
- Relevance ranking
- Proximity controls
- Document similarity searches (Doc Surfing)
- Link reference reports
- In Context result listings

WebObjects

Company Name:	NeXT Software, Inc.
Address:	900 Chesapeake Drive
	Redwood City, CA 94063
Phone:	(415) 366-0900
URL:	`http://www.next.com/Webobjects/`

WebObjects is an environment for developing and deploying World Wide Web applications. For development, it provides a scripting language and objects that you use to create Web applications. For deployment, it provides a system of interrelated components that connect your WebObjects applications to the Web.

WebObjects gives you all the benefits of object technology. At the same time, it scales to accommodate the complexity of your programming tasks. You can create simple applications without having to compile anything; just implement the logic in scripts.

Scripted applications can even access your corporate database. For more complex tasks, you can easily combine WebObjects with your own compiled objects.

WebObjects is designed to help corporations create dynamic, server-based applications for the World Wide Web. These applications can be deployed on a company's internal network or externally to the general public.

WebObjects is especially suited to sophisticated applications that need to serve large numbers of clients. WebObjects is also designed to leverage a company's current investments in technology, data, and training.

Many companies are trying to build sophisticated Web applications in order to improve productivity, better respond to customers' needs and generate new business opportunities. Delivering on these goals has proven to be a difficult, if not impossible task. Robust Web applications are often difficult to create because existing Web development tools prevent companies from:

- Leveraging their investments in existing applications and data
- Integrating with complimentary technologies—Web-based and others
- Deploying robust Web solutions in a timely fashion

WebObjects is designed to preserve investments in existing computing resources. Using this technology, Web applications can be easily integrated with legacy technology and data.

Companies can leverage their existing investment in the following areas:

- Windows Applications
- Mainframe Applications
- Hardware
- Databases
- CORBA 2.0 Objects

For example, a WebObjects application can be designed to extend an existing order management system to the World Wide Web. By extending the application in this fashion, the public can place orders directly via the World Wide Web.

The Web application can add value, coexist, and share information with the existing order management system. In this case, WebObjects brings the company closer to its customers by allowing them to use the World Wide Web. It also minimizes the costs of doing so by seamlessly integrating the Web application with their existing order management system.

Protect your investments in hardware, software, data storage, and other IT investments across your enterprise. WebObjects supports all major Web standards with the flexibility to embrace new technologies as they evolve. WebObjects supports the creation of Web applications implemented with Sun Microsystems' Java language. Within a WebObjects application, Java can execute as both client-side applets and server-side business engines. WebObjects offers browser and HTTP server independence.

WebObjects supports native HTTP server APIs. WebObjects provides a scripting framework for application creation, allowing developers to use the language of their choice such as Perl or JavaScript.

WebObjects applications are portable across a wide variety of operating systems and hardware platforms. These include Solaris, Windows NT, and HP-UX .

Industry-standard databases from Oracle, Sybase, and Informix can be accessed from a WebObjects application without writing database specific code.

WebObjects provides the foundation for the development of robust Web applications. With WebObjects, developers need only focus on implementing relevant business logic. Developers are isolated from the complexities of combining their business logic with HTML and data access to form a complete Web application. This segmentation accelerates the development of Web applications.

Moving On

The realm of Web database application development suites is rapidly evolving. If it is true that the vendors of PC software products have abandoned the yearly cycle of major product upgrades, it is particularly true that Web database tool vendors are on a more aggressive release schedule. By the time you read these words, there no doubt will be new versions of some of the products listed, as well as some completely new ones.

Beginning with Chapter 6, "Overview of HTML," I will lay the foundation for designing, building, and maintaining a Web database application. Chapter 6 also introduces you to the command syntax you would use to create your Web pages.

CHAPTER 6

Overview of HTML

I f you are new to the Web, this chapter gives you a good introduction to what Hyper-Text Markup Language (HTML) is, how to read it, write it, and use it. If you are an experienced Web developer or user, you too will find useful information in this chapter on topics such as the structure of HTML, advanced HTML topics, good HTML coding practices, and the future of HTML.

HTML is a specific type of programming language (just as Java and C are other types of programming languages) used by Web browsers to display text, images, graphics, hyperlinks, and play audio or video files. It describes how the data is to be displayed, not how it should be laid out. HTML lets you describe pieces of information such as headers, lists, and inline images. It does not let you describe a header as being 32-point Arial, or a bulleted list with a checkmark (✓) for a bullet. In the future, HTML will support such page layout and presentation functions, but the future is not here now.

HTML is a wonderful facility for defining how data appears on a Web page, but it is not very good at describing how it is to be laid out. For example, it is very easy to describe a text string as appearing in bold typeface, but it is very difficult to position that same text string 1.275" from the top border and 3.250" from the left border. HTML is not a desktop publisher—yet.

As you'll see later in this chapter, HTML specifications are evolving to include more page layout capabilities. This trend is certainly expected to continue. Much the same as PC-based word processing tools are evolving so that the distinction between word processors and page layout packages are becoming blurred, so too will HTML specifications evolve to include more page layout control.

The information in this chapter is important to you to fully understand Chapter 12, "HTML Forms and Database Access." Whereas HTML used by itself to display static information drawn from non-database sources has been its traditional use, tools and technologies recently developed and currently being developed extend its core functions to database access and dynamic page presentation. With WYSIWYG editors and generators, these new tools have the effect of moving the user further and further away from writing hard HTML code. I do believe, though, that it will be a very long time before Web page designers and developers do not need to know and understand HTML.

Introduction to HTML

Creating a Web page using HTML is actually quite easy. As you'll see in this chapter, there are a limited number of commands (called *tags* and *tag pairs*) that you'll need to remember. Although a large selection of tools exist to facilitate and expedite HTML editing, if you have access to a text editor or word processor, you have the tools necessary to write HTML.

HyperText Markup means the character strings that are embedded in a text file and are designed to cause text to display in a specified format in a Web browser. HTML uses tags and tag pairs to accomplish this formatting. As you'll see, HTML documents consist of the following:

- The data that is to be displayed on a Web page that is either included directly in the file that contains the HTML code (called *static*), or is retrieved from an external source such as a database query (called *dynamic*).

- The structure of the data, such as headings and paragraphs, which are the tags and tag pairs.

  HTML supports the following features:

- Structure of a document
- Text formatting
- Style of lists
- Format and layout of tables
- Inline graphics images and the placement of text around those images
- Hypertext anchors
- Image Maps, a feature in HTML that allows a user to click in different portions of a graphic image to link to different HTML documents
- E-mail
- Forms to transmit user supplied data to the server

The following snippet is a sample of HTML code that formats data on a Web page. Figure 6–1 is a screen print of that page as seen in a browser.

```
<HTML>
<HEAD>
<TITLE>ABC MOVIES INTERNAL WEB SITE</TITLE>
```

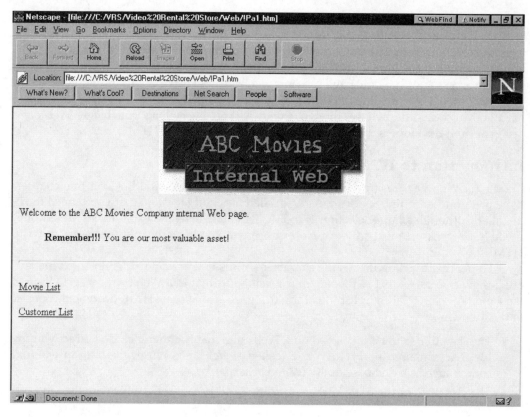

Figure 6-1   The WEB page of the HTML code in the above code.

```
<META NAME="GENERATOR" CONTENT="HAHTsite 2.0"></HEAD>
<P ALIGN=CENTER><IMG SRC="SimpFold/Images/INT_WEB.jpg" WIDTH=322
HEIGHT=117></P>
<P>Welcome to the ABC Movies Company internal Web page. </P>
<BLOCKQUOTE><P><STRONG><FONT SIZE="+0">Remember!!!</FONT></STRONG> You
are our most valuable asset!</P></BLOCKQUOTE>
<P><HR></P>
<P><A HREF="Page2.html">Movie List</A></P>
<P><A HREF="CustList.htm">Customer List</A></P>
<P> </P>
</BODY>
</HTML>
```

Benefits of HTML

Although you really don't have much of a choice when deciding to build a Web database application (you *really should* use HTML), you should be aware of some of the benefits available by using HTML. One is the rapid development environment, especially with the crop of HTML editors and Web application development suites coming available. Another benefit of HTML is its extensive cross-platform support that is so important when deploying an application over the Internet. Also, a key benefit of HTML is its support for multiple types of media to be included in the page, such as audio, video, images, and text.

Limitations of HTML

Like everything else in the world of computing, HTML is not free from limitations. Although the standard is rapidly evolving to remove many of these limitations, the day will probably never come when this tool is totally free from limitations.

The limitations of HTML as a Web page development tool are:

- Limited user-input capabilities
- Inability to specifically locate an object (for example, place a text box in row 12, column 25)
- Limited programmatic capabilities (for example, HTML relies on interfaces to modules developed in other languages to execute complex logic)

Tags

Tags are ASCII characters or an ASCII character string delimited by angle brackets (<>) that contain an HTML formatting command.

HTML uses tags and tag pairs to instruct the browser how to format the document sent to it. Tags and tag pairs also instruct the HTTP browser what to do with audio clips, video files, and graphic image files. Additionally, tags and tag pairs are used to specify hypertext links, accept user input, and launch programs via the Common Gateway Interface (CGI). You'll learn more about tags and tag pairs later in this chapter.

HTML is termed a markup language in that the HTML codes, what are called tags in HTML terminology, are embedded in the text itself. For example, in the previous HTML code snippet is the following line:

```
<P>Movie List</P>
```

The HTML code in this example is everything to the left and right of the words, Movie List.

HTML tags that format a block of text always come in pairs. However, not all tag-pairs are formatting commands for text. There are a number of HTML tags that are independent of text and include no text. For example, the <HTML> and </HTML> tags identify the information contained between this tag pair as an HTML-formatted document.

HTML Conformance

Although the previous are a very simple rendition, it does give you an idea of the structure and syntax of HTML. You can see that the HTML snippet consists of special formatting tags included to describe the layout and presentation of the page. HTML documents are based on the Standard Generalized Markup Language (SGML, of which HMTL is a subset), with generalized formatting tags used to present information on the screen in a wide range of domains.

Table 6–1   HTML Level Specifications

Level	Description
0	This level describes HTML structure and comment elements, as well as headings. Also included in this level are header, list, and image specifications.
1	This level describes image-handling and character formatting and display specifications.
2	This level describes forms and character definition specifications.
3.2	This level describes tables, figures, and graphical backdrops (backdrops are synonymous with wallpaper in a Windows environment) specifications.
4	This level is not yet ratified but describes the formatting and use of mathematical specifications.

SGML is an internationally recognized standard to document exchange over the internet. HTML documents are SGML documents with an important distinction—HTML documents use generic semantics to form and present information. Together with URLs and HTTP, HTML forms the foundation of the World Wide Web.

There are five levels of specifications to the HTML language. The HTML code that you write should conform to a standard that is no higher than the standard supported by the HTML specification, which is supported by the browsers the people accessing your application are using. For example, Netscape Navigator and Microsoft Internet Explorer browsers both support up through level 3.2, but do not support level 4 specifications yet. Table 6–1 describes the various HTML specification levels and what each provides.

Now that you've been introduced to the basic concepts and features of HTML, the following section introduces you to the structure of HTML tags. You will see how easy it is to use the HTML tags and tag pairs to accomplish a wide variety of data display styles.

Structure of HTML

HTML specifications impose no restrictions on using upper or lower case characters when writing tags and tag pairs. I know of no browser that cares about it. Most of the code examples in this book are written in upper case for readability purposes only.

Header and Document Tags

There is usually a pair of tags that officially mark the beginning and ending of the HTML document. These are <html> and </html>. Most browsers do not require this tag pair to work, but you should include it if for no other reason than it has been a part of every HTML standard published. Included within this tag pair are two major components: the header and the body.

The HTML code shown earlier used the <HEAD> and <BODY> tag pairs. Specifically, these are:

```
<HTML>
  <HEAD>
  </HEAD>
```

```
 <BODY>
 </BODY>
</HTML>
```

In addition to the document, header, and body tag pairs, you'll notice one more tag pair. This is the Document Title tag, which reads:

```
<TITLE>ABC MOVIES INTERNAL WEB SITE</TITLE>
```

The document title tag is used inside the `<HEAD>` tag pair to identify the content of the current HTML document. The text you supply inside the `<TITLE>...</TITLE>` tag pair appears centered on the title bar in a user's browser. Although this is not a required tag, it is good practice to include it.

Tip: Many search engines use the text contained in the `<Title>` tag as a search index. Bear this in mind when creating your `<Title>` tag line.

Body Tags

Body tags are the formatting codes used within the `<BODY>` tag pairs. These tags can be placed in the following groupings:

- Headings
- Block Elements
- Lists
- Text
- Anchors
- Images

Headings. HTML specifications provide for six levels of headings (all shown in the following sample), although you will probably never use more than two or three. The code below would be written to produce the Web page as seen in Figure 6–2.

```
<HTML>
<HEAD>
<TITLE>Demo</TITLE>
</HEAD><BODY>
<H1>This is an example of Heading 1</H1>
<H2>This is an example of Heading 2</H2>
<H3>This is an example of Heading 3</H3>
<H4>This is an example of Heading 4</H4>
<H5>This is an example of Heading 5</H5>
<H6>This is an example of Heading 6</H6>
</BODY>
</HTML>
```

Headings `<H1></H1>` through `<H6></H6>` are not to be confused with a header tag pair `<HEAD></HEAD>`. The information contained within the header tag pair does not

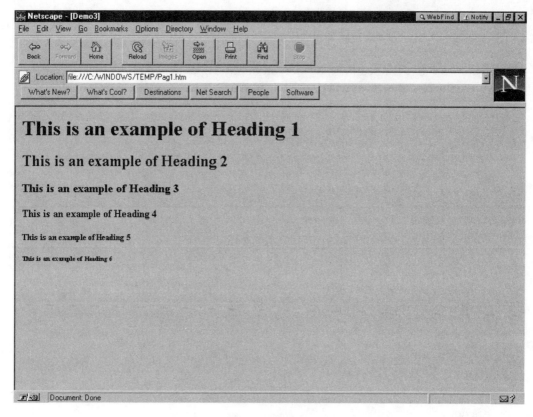

Figure 6–2   Generated HTML header levels as seen in a browser.

display on a Web page and is intended to identify a section of the HTML document. However, headings do display on the Web page.

Tip: Because Web browsers handle formatting differently, you should experiment with headings to pick the one best suited for your page(s). There is no requirement that a <H2> tag follow a <H1> tag. To the contrary, think of each of the six heading levels as completely independent of each other—they are formatting styles.

Block Elements.   When text information is formatted into paragraphs in HTML pages, the formatting of these paragraphs and the type of formatting between the paragraphs are called *block elements*. The following code snippet is an example of the most used block elements, while Figure 6–3 is a screen print of these block elements.

```
<HTML>
<HEAD>
<TITLE>Miscellaneous Stuff</TITLE>
```

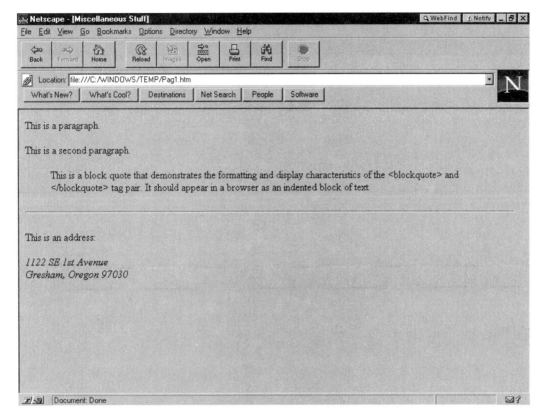

Figure 6–3   Generated HTML block elements as seen in a browser.

```
<BODY>
<P>This is a paragraph.</P>
<P>This is a second paragraph.</P>
<BLOCKQUOTE>This is a block quote that demonstrates the formatting and
display characteristics of the &lt;blockquote&gt; and &lt;/blockquote&gt;
tag pair.
It should appear in a browser as an indented block of text.</BLOCKQUOTE>
<P><HR></P>
<P>This is an address:</P>
<ADDRESS>1122 SE 1st Avenue</ADDRESS>
<ADDRESS>Gresham, Oregon 97030</ADDRESS>
</BODY>
</HTML>
```

Paragraph tags (`<p>` and `</p>`) are used to format the text between the tag pair into a consistent looking paragraph, separated from other paragraphs and objects by a blank line.

Tip: To insert a blank line in a Web page, you could use the <P> tag without a closing </P>. If you use the <P><P> combination, this inserts two blank lines.

Blockquote tags (<BLOCKQUOTE> and </BLOCKQUOTE>) are used to indent text, such as you'd see in a cited quotation.

The Horizontal rule tag (<HR>) is used to draw a straight line horizontally across the page, the full width of the page. You'll notice that this tag does not have a matching </HR> because the <HR> tag extends the full width of the Web page.

Address tags (<ADDRESS> and </ADDRESS>) are used to contain address-type information in a formatted and indented manner on a Web page.

Note: Since all document formatting is accomplished by tag pairs, then blank lines, indentations, and white space that you might add in the HTML source is ignored by Web browsers. There are special tags that handle indentation and blank lines which are presented later in this chapter.

Lists. Lists are a common feature in most Web pages. HTML specifications provide for four types of lists: Unordered, Ordered, Menu, and Definition. The following HTML code snippet used to create these various lists is simple. Depending on the type of list you define, the output will vary, as seen in Figure 6–4.

```
<HTML>
<HEAD>
<TITLE>Demo</TITLE>
</HEAD>
<BODY>
<UL>
<LI>Unordered item 1</LI>
<LI>Unordered item 2</LI>
<LI>Unordered item 3</LI>
</UL>
<OL>
<LI>Numbered item 1</LI>
<LI>Numbered item 2</LI>
<LI>Numbered item 3</LI>
</OL>
<MENU>
<LI>Menu List item 1</LI>
<LI>Menu List item 2</LI>
<LI>Menu List item 3</LI>
</MENU>
<DL>
<DT>Definition Term 1</DT>
<DT>Definition Term 2</DT>
<DT>Definition Term 3</DT>
</DL>
</BODY>
</HTML>
```

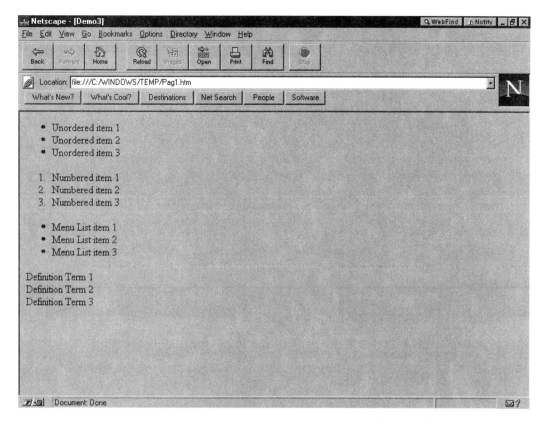

Figure 6–4 Generated HTML lists as seen in a browser.

The first list, the unordered item list, is identified by the `<UL>...</UL>` tag pair and is used to identify list items that should be grouped together, but without a number preceding each item in the list.

The second list, the numbered item list, is identified by the `<OL>...</OL>` tag pair and is used to identify list items that should be grouped together and preceded by a number.

The third list, the menu item list, is identified by the `<MENU>...</MENU>` tag pair. It is used in much the same way as the unordered item list in that it identifies list items that should be grouped together without a preceding number. However, some browsers present the items in a menu list in a more compact format than unordered list items.

The fourth list, the definition list, is identified by the `<DL>...</DL>` tag pair. It is used occasionally to separate a word or word-string from its definition in a consistent manner. However, as seen in Figure 6–4 it can also be used to present a list of items without a preceding bullet or number.

Text. Text characters can be one of four styles, and these styles can be mixed in any configuration. The following snippet shows the HTML code used to define a number of different text styles, while Figure 6–5 shows what the HTML code looks like in a browser.

```
<HTML>
<HEAD>
<TITLE>Demo</TITLE>
</HEAD>
<BODY>
<P>Normal Text</P>
<P><STRONG>Bold (Strong) Text</STRONG></P>
<P><EM>Italicized Text</EM></P>
<P><U>Underline Text</U></P>
<P><STRONG><EM>Bold/Italicized Text</EM></STRONG></P>
<P><STRONG><EM><U>Bold, Italicized, and Underlined
Text</U></EM></STRONG></P>
</BODY>
</HTML>
```

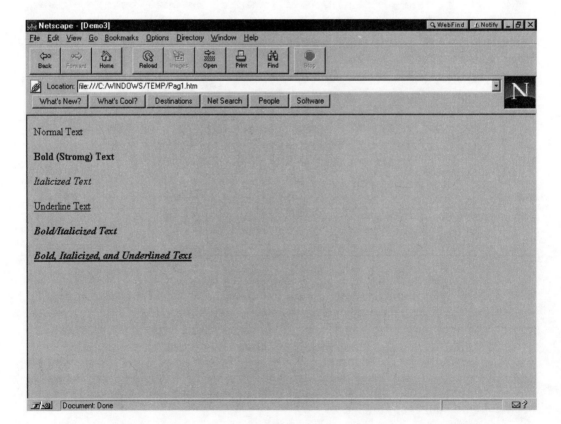

Figure 6–5   Generated HTML formatted text as seen in a browser.

There is an additional tag called emphasis (<EM> and </EM>). This was a tag developed primarily for text-only Web browsers and usually translates in GUI browsers to an italicized font. You should probably avoid the emphasis tag (<EM>) and use the italics tag pair <I> and </I> if you want your text to appear italicized.

You'll notice in the last snippet that highlighted (bold) text is written using the <STRONG>...</STRONG> tag pair. Most people prefer to use the <B>...</B> tag pair. Also, where I have used the <EM>...</EM> tag pair, most people prefer to use the <I>... </I> tag pair. In a GUI-based Web browser, each of these are interchangeable with the other—it makes no difference. However, in a text based browser the <B>...</B> and <I> ...</I> tag pairs do nothing to control the format of text. I've developed the habit of using the more universally consistent tag pairs to avoid problems in certain Web browsers.

You can combine tag pairs for some interesting effects. For example, you can write a line of HTML code as: <EM><U><H1>Scruples—The Movie</H1></U></EM>. This creates a Heading 1 that is underlined and italicized.

Anchor Tags.   Anchor tags are mechanisms in HTML to create links to other Web documents or sites. The syntax for anchor tags is <A>...</A>. You can include optional attributes inside the <A> anchor tag. This is frequently referred to as a *hyperlink*, or *hypertext link* and allows you to build a link from the current location in the Web page to one of the following:

- Another section in the same Web page
- Another Web page
- Images
- Audio files
- Application programs

A hyperlink originates from a graphic element that the user clicks on, while a hypertext link originates from a text string that the user clicks on.

Note: The anchor tag is one of the few HTML tags that requires a parameter. When used, it requires the URL for the linked Web document as well as a text string that is displayed in the Web browser.

```
<HTML>
<HEAD>
</HEAD>
<P ALIGN=CENTER><IMG SRC="SimpFold/Images/INT_WEB.jpg" WIDTH=322
HEIGHT=117></P>
<P>Welcome to the ABC Movies Company internal Web page. </P>
<BLOCKQUOTE><P><STRONG><FONT SIZE="+0">Remember!!!</FONT></STRONG> You
are our most valuable asset!</P></BLOCKQUOTE>
<P> <A HREF="Page2.html">Movie List</A></P>
<P> <A HREF="CustList.htm">Customer List</A> </P>
</BODY>
</HTML>
```

To use an anchor tag pair, you specify the attribute name, followed by an equal sign, followed by its "value"—the "value" being the linked reference. In the following line of code, a link is made to the Page2.html document when a user clicks on the line of text on the page that reads "Movie List."

```
<A HREF="Page2.html">Movie List</A>
```

Figure 6–6 shows the correct formatting of the anchor pairs in a Web browser.

Images. There are two basic types of images recognized by HTML, *inline images* and *image maps*. Inline images are usually graphic pictures used in the following manner:

- To provide smaller (*thumbnail*) images that are hyperlinked to a larger version of the same image
- As window selection buttons
- To block off an area on the page (with a clear image) so that text can flow around the graphic
- To add color and enhancements to an otherwise dull page

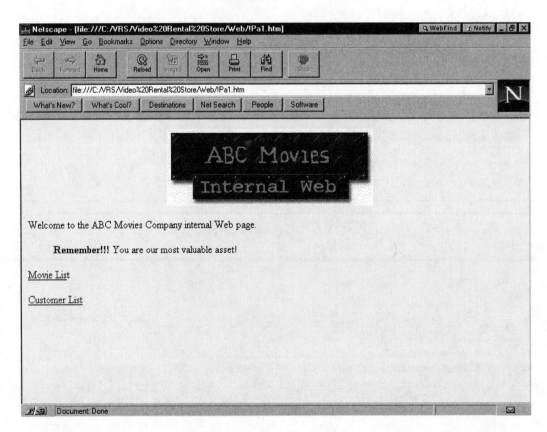

Figure 6–6   Generated HTML code for anchors as seen in a browser.

Image maps are graphic objects that allow the Web client to identify specific locations within an image that has been clicked on by a user. Image maps are a great resource for Web database applications. For example, an image map of the United States could be created so that as a user clicked on a region or state within the image map a customized query would run against a database extracting statistical information specific to the selected region or state.

There are a number of formats for the graphic files used as inline images and image maps, the most popular being GIF and JPEG.

Multimedia and graphics are fast becoming the most popular component on Web pages. With the release of HTML specification 0—the very first one issued—these were supported. The tag for including images in an HTML page is `<img src="`*filename* `(specifications …)">`.

In the following line of code, the browser is instructed to first retrieve a graphics file named int_web.jpg from the SimpFold/Images subdirectory on the current machine. Then display this image at the location on the Web page that this line of HTML code was encountered where the image dimensions are 322 × 117.

```
<IMG SRC="SimpFold/Images/INT_WEB.jpg" WIDTH=322 HEIGHT=117>
```

The result of this line of HTML code is seen in the top-most graphic in Figure 6–6.

Because of the interest in extending the graphic aspects of Web pages and browsers, the format and syntax of the `<img src>` tag is changing rapidly. It is prudent to spend a little time investigating the support provided by the tools in your development environment for the `<img src>` tag. Also, don't forget to consider the types and release levels of browsers that the people accessing your Web pages are using.

Netscape Communications has developed extensions to the IMG tag. Not to be outdone in the quest to make something that is magnificently scalable regrettably unscalable, Microsoft Corporation has released a series of their own HTML extensions.

To learn more about image maps, you should visit the following site:

```
http://hoohoo.ncsa.uiuc.edu/docs/tutorials/imagemapping.html.
```

Comments and Special Characters.   Comments are specified in HTML code by enclosing them in a special tag pair, as follows:

```
<!-- comment goes here -->.
```

Additionally, if you want to have a left arrow (<) or right arrow (>) display on a page, you have to format the source HTML code with the special characters shown in Table 6–2.

Tip: Any ASCII character can be displayed on an HTML page by preceding the ASCII code for the character by an ampersand (&).

The following sample shows what the HTML code using the special characters from Table 6–2, while Figure 6–7 shows what this code looks like in a Web browser.

Table 6–2   Special Characters in HTML

Character String	Character Displayed
&lt	<
&gt	>
&amp	&
&quot	"
&copy	©

```
<HTML>
<HEAD>
<TITLE>Demo</TITLE>
</HEAD>
<BODY>
<P>Less than sign: &lt;</P>
<P>Greater than sign: &gt;</P>
<P>Ampersand sign: &amp;</P>
<P>Double quote sign: &quot;</P>
<P>At sign: @</P>
<P>Copyright symbol: &copy;</P>
</BODY>
</HTML>
```

Tables.   The ability to define tables was added to HTML with the level 3 specifications. Remember, though, that not all browsers support this level, so depending on the format used, some users may not be able to view certain tables. Internet Explorer and Netscape Navigator can, however.

There are a number of tag pairs that you can use to define the specification of a table. These are seen in Table 6–3.

The following sample shows the HTML markups used to define a simple four-row-by-two-column table. Figure 6–8 shows what this table looks like in an HTTP browser.

```
<HTML>
<HEAD>
<TITLE>Demo</TITLE>
</HEAD>
<BODY>
<TABLE BORDER=1><CAPTION ALIGN=TOP>This is a Table.</CAPTION>
<TR>
<TD><STRONG>Car Manufacturer</STRONG></TD>
<TD><STRONG>Car Model</STRONG></TD>
</TR>
<TR>
<TD>Chevrolet</TD>
<TD>Camaro</TD>
</TR>
```

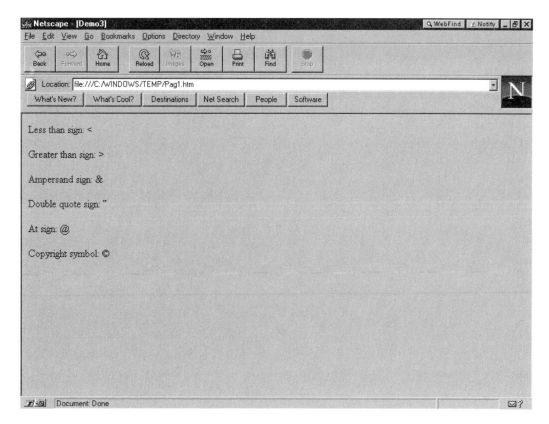

Figure 6–7 The Web browser display of HTML codes.

Table 6–3 Table Related Tag Pairs

Tag	Description
`<TABLE> . . . </TABLE>`	Marks the beginning and end of a table definition.
`<TR> . . . </TR>`	Specifies the number of rows and the vertical/horizontal alignment of the data that appears in the rows.
`<TD> . . . </TD>`	Defines a table cell that appears in a row as well as the alignment and other text attributes of the data that appears in the cells.
`<TH> . . . </TH>`	Defines the table header. Header cells are identical to data cells in all respects except that header cells text appears in boldface and is centered in the cell.
`<CAPTION> . . . </CAPTION>`	Defines and describes the caption for a table, if one exists.

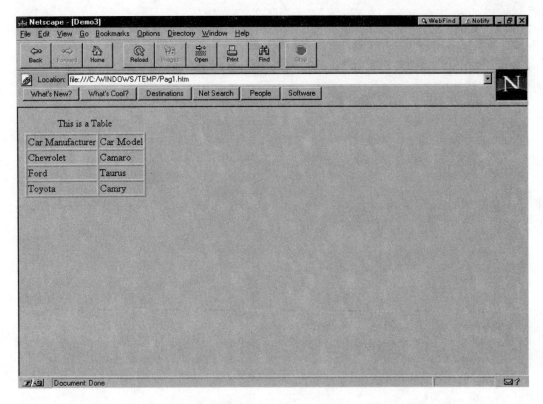

Figure 6–8   The Web browser display of a table.

```
<TR>
<TD>Ford</TD>
<TD>Taurus</TD>
</TR>
<TR>
<TD>Toyota</TD>
<TD>Camry</TD>
</TR>
</TABLE>
</BODY>
</HTML>
```

URLs

Uniform Resource Locators (URLs) are used by HTTP servers to identify and locate documents. Many people believe that each document or site must have its own unique URL, but this is not the case. As the Web continues to expand, the instances of duplicated URLs increases.

The structure of an URL is fairly specific, and includes an identification of the type of resource, the address of the HTTP server the resource is located on, and the location of the document. The syntax for an URL is:

```
resource://host.domain[:port]/path/filename [cgi parameters]
```

The following URLs range from the most simple to the most complex:

- `http://www.microsoft.com`
- `file://c:\temp\demo.html`
- `http://teleport:80.mysimple/page1.html`
- `http://www.haht.com/cgi-bin/hsrun.hse/MultiThread/StateId/`
  `AevayQAnv_QmLcvX-xGcLj6CLu/HAHTpage/LinkMain?N=HS_ProdSideNav&D=`
  `HS_Product`

Note: The second URL listed above (file://c:\temp\demo.html) points the browser to a file on a computer, not a Web site.

Additional Resources

Refer to the following resources for additional information on HTML specifications and coding.

HTML Publishing on the Internet for Macintosh

Author: Brent Heslop
Publisher: Ventana Communications
ISBN: 1-56-604228-3

HTML Publishing on the Internet for Windows

Author: Brent Heslop, Larry Budnick
Publisher: Ventana Communications
ISBN: 1-56-604229-1

HTML Publishing with Internet Assistant

Author: Gayle Kidder, Stuart Harris
Publisher: Ventana Communications
ISBN: 1-56-604273-9

The HTML Programmer's Reference

Author: Robert Mullen
Publisher: Ventana Communications
ISBN: 1-56-604597-5

Advanced HTML & CGI Writer's Companion

Author: K. Schengili-Roberts
Publisher: Academic Press, Inc.
ISBN: 0-12-623540-6

Advanced HTML Topics

Now that you've learned some of the basics of formatting HTML code, it's time to peel back another layer and learn some of the advanced topics relevant to HTML.

Incorporating JavaScript into HTML

JavaScript scripts are incorporated directly into HTML code, using the extensions to HTML specification 3.2 added by Netscape in its browsers (`<SCRIPT>...</SCRIPT>`).

The <SCRIPT> . . . </SCRIPT> Tag Pair

To incorporate JavaScript into an HTML script is a very simple process. First, insert the `<SCRIPT>` tag to the location in the code that you want to begin adding JavaScript. Next, write the JavaScript code. Then end the JavaScript code by including the `</SCRIPT>` tag.

The following sample shows a simple snippet of JavaScript embedded in some HTML code. This sample asks for the user's first name in a message box. Once this is provided and the user presses `<Enter>`, the code formats and displays a greeting line on the page displayed in the user's HTTP browser, as seen in Figure 6–9.

```
<HTML>
<HEAD>
<TITLE>Demo</TITLE>
</HEAD>
```

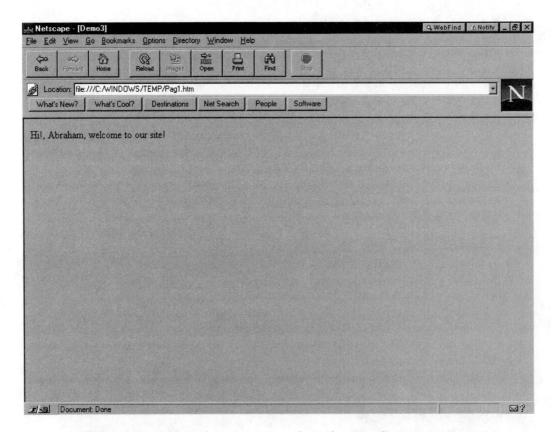

Figure 6–9 What the user sees when the JavaScript executes.

```
<BODY>
<P><FONT SIZE="+0"><SCRIPT LANGUAGE=JavaScript><!--
var fname=prompt("What is your first name: ","fname");
document.writeln("Hi!, " + fname + ", welcome to our site!");
//--></SCRIPT></FONT></P>
<P></P>
</BODY>
</HTML>
```

Tip: You can also reference a file containing JavaScript code (as discussed in Chapter 4, "Overview of Java and JavaScript") from your HTML code, thus separating the JavaScript code from the HTML code. Reusable code: What a concept!!! The tag pair to accomplish this is <SRC> ... </SRC> which is an optional attribute of the <SCRIPT> tag.

You know that a comment in HTML code takes the format:

```
<!-- comments here -->
```

A comment included in JavaScript code starts with a double-dash (--). Also, you can use C-style multiline comments as long as the first line of comment begins with a slash-asterisk pair (/*) and the last line of comment ends with a asterisk-slash pair (*/).

Inline Images in HTML Files

There are a number of tag pairs used to define the source, layout, and presentation of GIF and JPEG format image files in HTML code.

It wasn't until HTML specifications provided support for inline images, and browsers were developed to efficiently present these images, that the World Wide Web became predominantly a text-based environment. The support for inline images is thought by many (including me) to be a substantial determining factor in the increasing popularity of the Web.

There are a number of parameters you should use in conjunction with the <IMG>... </IMG> tag pair to help you define the layout and format of inline images. These are shown in Table 6–4.

Most of these attributes, along with the <SRC> ... </SRC> definitions are seen in the next HTML code snippet. The results of this definition are seen in Figure 6–10.

```
<P ALIGN=CENTER>
<A HREF="z100.map">
<IMG LOWSRC="t_open.gif" SRC="openpage.gif" HEIGHT=256 WIDTH=500 BORDER=0
 USEMAP="#mainmap" ISMAP ALT="Z100 Studio Image Map">
</A>
</P>
```

Considerations with Inline Images. There's no doubt about it, inline images add pizzazz to your Web pages. However, the overuse, or misuse, of inline images will render your pages and applications ineffective and troublesome. Bear in mind that many Web users access the Internet over a 14.4 mbps connection. That translates roughly to 1,800 characters per second. A single GIF image that is 75,000 bytes will take about 41 seconds

Table 6–4   IMG Tag Parameters

Parameter	Description
SRC	The URL of the graphics file
ALIGN=	Describes how text flows around an image
ALT=	Specifies a text message that displays in place of the image for users that have non-graphical HTTP Browsers
ISMAP	Identifies the image as an image map
WIDTH=	Specifies the width of the image/image map in pixel units
HEIGHT=	Specifies the height of the image/image map in pixel units
BORDER=	Specifies the width of the line surrounding the image
HSPACE=	Specifies the amount of horizontal space between the image and any floating text
VSCAPE=	Specifies the amount of vertical space between the image and any floating text

to download to the user's machine. That means that the user will wait 41 seconds before seeing the image.

Now figure that your work-of-art contains six inline images, comprising a total of 450,000 bytes. These images would take over four minutes to transfer over that 14.4 mbps phone connection. When you design and build your Web database application, you should take into account several factors. For example, consider the number of graphics used on your Web pages; the fewer the better, but use enough to make your page appealing to look at. Also, the size of the graphics files is a consideration; the smaller the better, but provide enough clarity and content to make the graphic meaningful. Finally, consider the speed of the connection that people will be using when accessing your page; the slower the connection, the longer it will take to transmit the graphics from your server to their browser.

Tip: Generally, a graphics file saved in JPEG format requires less disk space than if it were saved in GIF format. This means a quicker download for users. Even though there is a slight degradation in the quality of a JPEG image from a GIF image, this probably won't be a viable factor unless precision in the images viewed is vitally important.

Advanced Hypertext and Hypergraphics

As previously discussed, hypertext and hypergraphics are references in HTML code that, when clicked on by a user, causes a browser to jump to another section in the same document, or another document altogether. To create a hypertext or hypergraphic link, you use the tag pair: <A> . . . </A>.

The specific syntax for this tag pair is:

Hypertext link	**<A HREF=**_URL_**>**text**</A>**
Hypergraphic link	**<A HREF=**_URL_**><IMG SRC=**"Image URL"**></A>**

Figure 6–10 The inline image map as seen through a browser.

where URL equals the destination where the user will go when she or he clicks on the text (for a hypertext link) or image (for a hypergraphic link).

The following sample provides an example of the HTML code used to accomplish both a hypertext and a hypergraphic link. Figure 6–11 shows what this HTML code would look like in an HTTP browser.

```
<HTML>
<HEAD>
<HEAD>
<P ALIGN=CENTER><IMG SRC="SimpFold/Images/INT_WEB.jpg" WIDTH=322
HEIGHT=117></P>
<P>Welcome to the ABC Movies Company internal Web page. </P>
<BLOCKQUOTE><P><STRONG><FONT SIZE="+0">Remember!!!</FONT></STRONG> You
are our most valuable asset!</P></BLOCKQUOTE>
<P> <A HREF="Page2.html">Movie List</A><A HREF="Page2.html"><IMG
SRC="MOV_LISTs.JPG" WIDTH=100 HEIGHT=45></A></P>
```

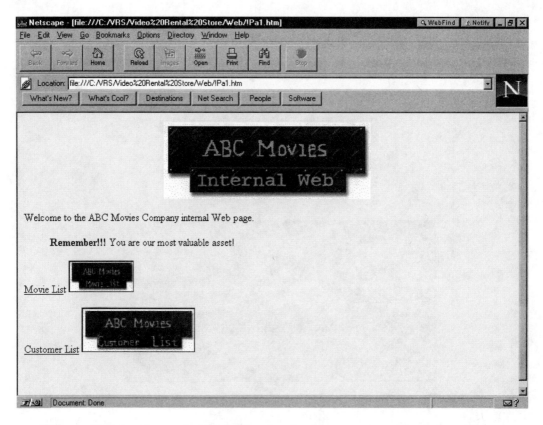

Figure 6–11   Example HTML display for hypertext and hypergraphics.

```
<P> <A HREF="CustList.htm">Customer List</A> <A HREF="CustList.htm"><IMG
SRC="CUSTLISTs.JPG" WIDTH=177 HEIGHT=65></A></P>
</BODY>
</HTML>
```

Good HTML Practices

Now that you have the basics of HTML under your belt, here are some things to keep in mind when writing your own HTML. The Web has been, is, and will largely remain an unrestricted information collection and dissemination vehicle. Companies such as Sun Microsystems seek desperately to have the Web remain as open and unrestricted in terms of architecture as possible. Other companies, such as Netscape and Microsoft, make this same claim, but fail to supply extensions in their browsers written to current HTML specifications. An extension supplied by Netscape and used by a developer will render a troublesome HTML page to a user who views this page using a browser that does not support Netscape extensions.

With that said, the following are considered to be good HTML practices, each of which are discussed in detail.

- Use standard HTML
- Sign and date pages.
- Make your pages printable.
- Use hypertext and hypergraphic links.
- Avoid unnecessary and meaningless links.
- Organize headings and page sequence.
- Consider page size.

Use Standard HTML

If you write your HTML code to the 2.0 specification, you can be fairly sure that *all* the browsers accessing your pages will see what you intend for them to see. Currently, not all browsers support HTML specifications beyond version 2.0, although the majority support HTML specification 3.2. In addition, people may encounter problems using Netscape Navigator to view a page that was built using Microsoft extensions to HTML specifications. Therefore, you should have an understanding of what elements of HTML are specified in each version of the HTML specifications. You should also take into consideration what browsers will be used and what HTML specifications they support. By understanding these components, you can be assured that the HTML code you write will work as intended.

Sign and Date Pages

Authoritativeness is a problem faced by anyone trying to find information on the Internet. Frequently people develop and publish a Web site or page with an intent to update it frequently, only to let it grow stale while other interests are pursued.

To do your share to fix this problem, you should get in the habit of signing and dating all documents on your site. This is done so that people viewing your pages will have some data they can use to determine how authoritative the information on the pages really is. For example:

```
<HR>
<!-- Originally written: October 30, 1995 -->
<!-- Last modified: March 27, 1997 -->
<ADDRESS>
<A HREF="http://www.teleport.com/~jhobuss/">Jim Hobuss</A><BR>
<A HREF="mailto:jhobuss@teleport.com">jhobuss@teleport.com</A>
</ADDRESS>
```

In this code sample, notice the information contained on the second and third lines that are comments only (they will not appear in a user's browser). This gives those people who work on the pages some documented history of their age and last modification date. You could even carry this one step forward by maintaining a *change log,* thereby recording the date and nature of every change made to a page.

Make Your Pages Printable

We have tried for years to become a paper-less society. My eight-year-old son Andrew, complete with 10 green fingers (okay, 8 green fingers and 2 green thumbs), is very environmentally conscious (thus the green digits) and believes we are moving too slowly in that direction. I have to agree with his insight. As much as computers, the Web, and e-mail facilitate the electronic dissemination of information, we are still bound by paper.

As you design your Web page, you must recognize and provide for this. Give people the ability to print what they see on your Web page. Help them out and format the information in a way that will print well, and therefore increase the likelihood that it actually *will be* read at a later time. If you're going to create a Web page, make sure you format the page in a way that people will be able to read later.

Use Hypertext and Hypergraphic Links

One of the advantages to reading information on a Web page over reading the same information in a book is the ability it gives you to drill down on any topics that you read which interest you.

This is done with hyperlinks. When Bill Gates' book, *The Road Ahead*, was published, it included a CD-ROM that contained the complete text of the book. I tried reading the CD-ROM version of the book and found it to be a sterile activity. It was hard to feel nearly as comfortable reading sitting up in a chair at a desk staring at a computer screen as it is curled up on the couch with some good mood music playing and a fire roaring in the fireplace.

When I started to click on some of the hypertext links in the CD-ROM version of the book, things became much more interesting. When Gates was writing about his activities as a Harvard student, I was able to click on a hypertext link of the word Harvard and read some detailed information about the university that included a hypergraphics link to a picture of the Gates' former dorm. With a couple of clicks on the <Back> button, I was back to the main body of the book at the point where I left. This experience was much more exciting and informative that any experience I could have reading the hard copy version of the book.

Avoid Unnecessary and Meaningless Links

If you are convinced that hypertext and hypergraphic links add depth to your Web pages, then you need to understand that these features can be overdone. It is distracting for someone to read 1,000 words of text in a Web page if every other word is a hypertext link. Just because you have the ability and information at your disposal to include a hypertext link on a page, only include it if it adds enough value to the reader to warrant their time to link to it.

You should also carefully consider the wording you use in your link. For example:

Example 1: <u>[Figure 3.2: Click Here To Read About Dogs]</u>

Example 2: <u>[Figure 3.3: A Dog Demonstrating His Ability To Herd Sheep.]</u>

There are two problems with Example 1. The first problem is the phrase "Click Here". This is redundant and wastes the reader's time. In their browsers they will see that this is a hypertext link and know what to do, you don't have to tell them. The second problem is that there is nothing to entice the reader to click on the hypertext link. Example 2 resolves both of these problems nicely.

Organize Headings and Page Sequence

Remember I wrote earlier that it was possible to structure your headings so that a heading level H2 was used for a section heading that was actually a subsection of something that used the heading level H3? Although it is possible to do this, for maintenance reasons, you should avoid doing so. Structure your pages so that they are hierarchical. Headings used on a page should be in sequence. This means that an H3 heading should follow an H2 heading, and an H2 heading should follow an H1 heading.

Organizing your Web pages so they flow smoothly requires forethought and planning. Laying out a series of Web pages before construction begins is much akin to the way cartoonists lay out a story on storyboards before they ever begin to draw the first frame of a cartoon.

On a site that has been available for a long time and seen frequent changes, this may mean a re-write of the pages to put them back into a logical and hierarchical sequence. On an old yet dynamic Web site it will become increasingly more difficult to maintain the links between the pages.

Consider Page Size

Providing several pages where the information on each of the pages is easily viewable without having to scroll is much more attractive than making the user scroll though a seemingly endless document. Recognizing that this is not always possible, try to break your pages into smaller units to make them more aesthetic.

The Future of HTML

HTML will never go away. It will continue to be embellished and enhanced with new tags and tag pairs. You will be able to have more and more control over sophisticated page layouts. As this evolution continues, the language will become increasingly more complex. To handle this complexity and insulate you from it, HTML editors and Web application development suites will evolve to become more graphical. As was noted in the beginning of this chapter, though, your ability to read and write HTML is, and will continue to be, an important component in your Web database application development tools.

VRML

Another exciting evolutionary component of HTML is Virtual Reality Markup Language (VRML). This utility extension to HTML allows the user to explore scenes in three dimensions. For example, a prospective customer could select an automobile from a list of automobiles and take a virtual tour of the inside of the automobile, or even take the automobile for a virtual test drive through the scenery of their choice. Another application would allow you to see what landscaping looks like by virtually walking through the landscaped area. The current release of Netscape Navigator supports VRML although the sites that provide this are limited.

Tip: If you are using Netscape Navigator version 3.0 and want to see what VRML technology looks like, check out URL http://www.kgw.com. This is the site for a television station in Portland that distinguishes itself from the other stations by its extensive use of a helicopter. On this site you can take a virtual tour of the inside of this helicopter using VRML technology.

Moving On

This chapter is an introduction and overview of HTML. Not all the HTML commands were covered in this chapter—this is not an HTML coding book. You should, however, know enough now to build useful HTML pages using most of the available HTML commands.

In the next chapter, you will learn what CGI is, how to incorporate it in your Web database application development project, how to read user data into a CGI program, and learn a few principles of good CGI programming.

CHAPTER 7

Overview
of CGI

I n this chapter, you'll learn about the Common Gateway Interface (CGI) and the role it has in Web database application development. CGI is a means by which Web servers interface to other application programs and thereby extend the services provided by the Web server. By way of CGI scripts, users gain program access to Web servers, and extend the capability of HTML.

Being one of the most important links that connect Web pages to databases, CGI plays a critical role in Web database design and use. You'll learn about the CGI standard as it applies to UNIX and Windows operating systems. Simple programs are used to communicate and demonstrate CGI capabilities.

CGI Introduction

CGI scripts are executable files—programs written, compiled, and linked in one of a number of different languages. The most common language for a CGI program is Perl, although C, C++, Java, JavaScript, Visual Basic, and PowerBuilder remain popular as well. Perl's dominance as a CGI development language has recently been challenged not only by many of these other languages but also by Web development tools. For example, all of the capabilities traditionally provided by CGI programming languages are built into HAHTsite IDE.

As you know, HTML has no facilities to directly query a database. Through CGI, this capability exists. By utilizing CGI scripts, a request can be sent from within HTML, and processed by the HTTP server, to query the database for specific information, and then display the result set in dynamically built HTML code. With this capability, there is no need to manually change a Web page whenever data on that page changes. Simply place the data in a database, and build a CGI script to access the data and display it dynamically. Whenever a request is made to view the page that contains the CGI script, the Web server initiates a request to the database and formats the most current data into a dynamic Web page.

CGI is one of the facilities that make the Web a true client/server environment. Without CGI and Java applets, the Web would be what it was just a few short years ago, an architecture to collect and display static information in a very static format and style.

Although the CGI script is written on and received from a client-side device, it is executed on the server, thereby becoming a server-side process that functions as an interface to other application programs and databases. These programs can reside on the same device as the HTTP server, or on a machine distant from the HTTP server.

The CGI Expanded

CGI programs, CGI scripts, and Gateway programs are synonymous. They are the code that accepts a request initiated by an HTTP browser which is interpreted by an HTTP Server, accepts passed data from the HTTP server, and takes an action predefined and described by the programmer.

This action can be any of the following individually or a combination of two or more:

- Accessing of data either locally or remotely
- Processing of data
- Accessing available resources that are either local or remotely attached
- Creating output

Because of CGI, the Web database application has the ability to extend its reach beyond the confines of the HTTP server. A user in Thailand could provide input on an HTML form that is transmitted from their HTTP browser to the company's HTTP server in New York, where that server processes the HTML code and the request to initiate an external program. That external program could access a regional database located in Charlotte, North Carolina, receive the result set, and format that result set into an HTML form that is then transmitted back to the HTTP browser that initiated the request in Thailand.

CGI Architecture

To fully understand CGI you must understand its architecture and how it works. Once this is understood, you can use whatever language with which you are most comfortable to write the actual CGI code. Without a grasp of the CGI architecture, you won't be able to fully utilize CGI.

CGI Process Flow

The CGI process flow is a matter of taking HTML code as passed to the CGI program from the Web server, taking whatever action is required based on the design of the pro-

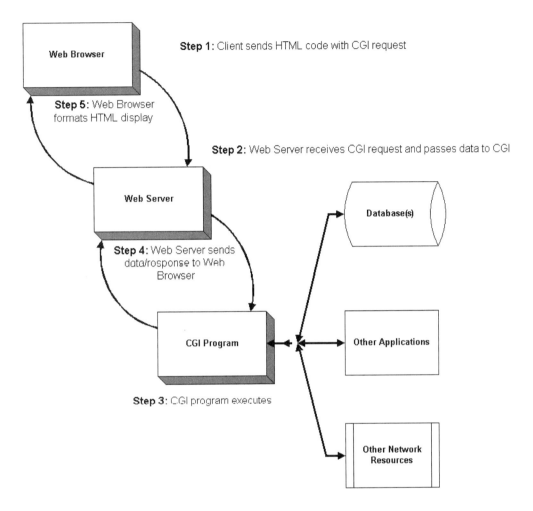

Figure 7–1   The CGI process flow.

gram, and then sending data and/or HTML code back to the Web server. Figure 7–1 is an example of the normal CGI process flow.

This process is described in the following five steps.

- **Step 1:** A user, accessing an HTTP browser, sends a request to an HTTP server via HTML. This HTML includes a request to execute a CGI program, and any parameters the CGI program might need.

- **Step 2:** The HTTP server receives the request from the HTTP browser, processes the HTML, and encounters the request to execute a CGI program. The HTTP server initiates the CGI program's execution by calling it and passing it any parameters that were received from the HTTP browser.

- **Step 3:** The CGI program executes. In its execution, it may:
  Access no other resources
  Access databases either locally or remotely
  Access other applications or initiate the execution of other programs
  Access other network resources
- **Step 4:** The HTTP server receives a result set from the CGI program if one is returned, and sends the data and/or response back to the HTTP browser via HTML
- **Step 5:** The HTTP browser receives the HTML sent to it from the HTTP server and formats and displays the data received

HTTP Server and CGI Program Communication Methods

Step 2 in Figure 7–1 is the process of the HTTP server initiating the execution of the CGI program. Although a CGI program could execute with no parameter input, such an event would be an exception. Generally, the CGI program's execution path is determined by parameter data that it receives.

This parameter data is passed to the CGI program, and the CGI program subsequently passes information back to the HTTP server, in one of the following four ways.

Command Line. By far the most common method, command line input passes the data the program needs in the same command string that is used to initiate the execution of the CGI program. The following is an example of a command line query string:

```
http://www.jackaroo.com/cgi-bin/acctlist.exe?Sydney+Australia
```

Note that the string `Sydney+Australia` is passed to a CGI program named `acctlist.exe` that is in a directory named `cgi-bin` on a server named `www.jackaroo.com`.

Environmental Variables. CGI programs can read the values of environmental variables on the HTTP server, act accordingly, and can even set environmental variables on the HTTP server.

Standard Input. This is the system's standard input file descriptor and can be a terminal device or the output from another CGI program.

Standard Output. This is the system's standard output file descriptor and can be a terminal device or the input to another CGI program.

CGI Input Data

CGI input data is passed to the HTTP server from the HTTP browser, with the intent that the HTTP server will pass it to the CGI program. The CGI program uses this data to determine its logical execution path and to (potentially) format a query to a database.

Additionally, the HTTP server can format and pass information to the CGI program that describes the type of data that was passed. This is what happens when data is passed to a CGI program via standard input. By providing this type of information, the CGI program can determine how to process the data it receives.

CGI Output Data

There is only one way that CGI programs return output. That is by standard output. Even in the rare situation when a CGI program returns no data it still formats and generates a response via standard output that indicates there was no data sent.

CGI standard output data is returned in one of two formats: *parsed header output* and *non-parsed header output*. With parsed header output the data created by the CGI program is received and interpreted by the HTTP server and then sent to the HTTP browser. With non-parsed header output, the HTTP server has the responsibility (and overhead) of generating the header information and sending it, along with the rest of the response, to the HTTP browser.

CGI Environmental Variables

CGI scripts use environmental variables for a number of reasons—not the least of which is to pass data between the HTTP server and the CGI program. There are two types of CGI environmental variables, *request-specific* and *not-request-specific.*

Request-specific variables are those environmental variables that are specific to the client request that the CGI program is fulfilling. Not-request-specific variables are those environmental variables that are set during all client requests. Request-specific variables are very specific to the type of request received from the HTTP browser while not request-specific are very generic to any or all types of requests received from the HTTP browser.

CGI environmental variables, regardless of their type, are used by CGI programs to specify the type of processing and database request the CGI program must perform. They are also used to indicate the type of browser the client is using, and to maintain and pass state information.

Note: The Web is a *stateless* environment. This means that after an HTTP client formats and sends a request to an HTTP server, or after the HTTP server formats and sends a response to an HTTP client, all knowledge of the transaction is lost. This is because the connection between the HTTP server and HTTP client is dropped. It is sometimes advantageous to maintain state; that is, to know what processing has occurred when a request for follow-up processing is received.

There are CGI environmental variables that are assigned in a variety of means, each dependent on the operating system and type of HTTP server. Although most are request-specific, some are not-request-specific. To achieve a sense of how these variables are used, a few are presented here.

CONTENT-LENGTH—The length in bytes of the buffer sent by the HTTP browser to the HTTP server to accommodate the data transferred between the two devices. An example is:

```
CONTENT_LENGTH=256
```

GATEWAY_INTERFACE—This specifies the version of the CGI specification with which the HTTP server is expected to comply. An example is:

```
GATEWAY_INTERFACE=CGI/1.1
```

QUERY_STRING—An URL-encoded string that is appended to an URL referencing a CGI program following a question mark (?) character. An example is:

```
http://microfocus.com/cgi-bin/prod-info?&pname=COBOL&
version=4.0
```

REMOTE_ADDR—The IP address for the requesting HTTP browser. An example is:

```
REMOTE_ADDR=63.628.528.777
```

SERVER_NAME—The HTTP server name, Domain Name Server (DNS), or IP address of the HTTP server. An example is:

```
SERVER_NAME=haht.com
```

Definition: Domain Name Server (DNS) is software that converts host names to IP addresses. IP addresses are what are actually used to contact a computer. The DNS can be thought of as a telephone book where a number used to contact something is identified from a given name.

SERVER_SOFTWARE—The name and version of the HTTP server software that is responding to HTTP browser requests and initiating the execution of CGI programs. An example is:

```
SERVER_SOFTWARE=WebSTAR/2.1
```

Windows CGI Variables.   The environmental variable examples listed in this section are in the format in which they would appear on a UNIX server. If the HTTP server were on a Windows machine the format would be slightly different, although the way they are used is the same.

On a Windows NT/95 machine, these environmental variables are placed in a *.INI file. Inside this file, each environmental variable is identified with an associated variable. Windows provides two APIs (*GetProfileString()* and *PutProfileString()*) to create and retrieve entries in INI files.

Table 7–1 lists some of the UNIX CGI environmental variables and their Windows CGI counterparts.

Passing CGI Data Streams

There are several ways that an HTTP client can transmit data strings to a CGI program, the most popular three being GET, ISINDEX, and POST.

GET Method to Transmit CGI Data Streams.   The GET method is used when passing data provided by users via HTML forms to CGI programs. Because of the limitation on the amount of data that can be passed (usually 256 characters) to a CGI program, the GET method is the least desirable of the three ways listed to transfer data to the CGI program. Its strength is in its ease of use when passing only a few data fields.

Table 7-1 UNIX versus Windows CGI Variables

UNIX CGI	Windows CGI
CONTENT-LENGTH	Content Length
GATEWAY_INTERFACE	CGI Version
QUERY_STRING	Query String
REMOTE_ADDR	Remote Address
SERVER_NAME	Server Name
SERVER_SOFTWARE	Server Software

The GET method causes a query string to append to the action URL when the user presses the <Submit> button on a form. The complete string passed to the HTTP server may look like:

```
GET /cgi-bin/processform.pl?action=READ&screen=QUERY HTTP/1.1
```

ISINDEX Method to Transmit CGI Data Streams. The ISINDEX method is used to perform database queries. The latest HTML specifications allow for the addition of the <ISINDEX> tag to your HTML code. This tag allows the HREF URL to perform a query based on data input by a user. The syntax for this is:

```
<HEAD>
<ISINDEX HREF="URL-CGI Program">
</HEAD>
```

In this example, URL-CGI Program is the URL for the CGI program to execute. Therefore, assuming an URL for a CGI executable as http://teleport.com/cgi-bin/processit.exe, and passed parameters to this program of ?lastname+tax year, the HTML code would be as follows:

```
<HEAD>
<ISINDEX HREF="http://teleport.com/cgi-bin/processit.exe?lastname+
taxyear">
</HEAD>
```

Following this example, the HTTP browser would pass this next string to the HTTP server:

```
http://teleport.com/cgi-bin/processit.exe?lastname+taxyear
```

The HTTP Server receives this string, and causes the processit.exe CGI program to a passed command string of lastname taxyear.

POST Method to Transmit CGI Data Streams. The POST method is conceptually similar to the GET method, with a much broader application. The POST method is formatted and sent to the server in a stream of data of varying length which is passed to the CGI program.

A specific example of using the POST method to receive CGI data streams follows.

```
POST /cgi-bin/processit.exe HTTP/1.1
Accept: text/plain
Accept: text/html
Accept: */*
Content-type: application/x-www-form-urlencoded
Content-length: 42
state=OR&politics=Republican&Minimum=25000
```

When this data stream is received by the HTTP Server, it passes it directly to the CGI program named processit.exe.

Tip: The Content-Length environmental variable is not required, but it is a very good idea to include it—and to be accurate when using it. The reason you should use it is that some servers do not send an end of file marker to CGI programs. Without the Content-Length variable, the CGI program may not receive the correct data. It is important to establish the correct parameter to signify the passed string length to avoid truncating the data or sending extraneous data to the CGI program in the passed string.

Reading User Data into CGI Programs

You've seen in the previous section three ways to get user-supplied data streams to a CGI program. In this section you'll see how to read and process that data in a CGI program.

As you know, CGI programs can be written in a number of different languages. Therefore, the basic steps to read user data into a CGI program are described below in *pseudo-code*:

```
IF the GET method was used to transmit data THEN
  Parse the QUERY_STRING environmental variable name-value pairs into
their respective components
ELSEIF the ISINDEX method was used to transmit data THEN
  Parse the QUERY_STRING environmental variable into its component parts
ELSE
  Read the value of the passed string from the CONTENT_LENGTH
environmental variable and parse this number of characters from the
string in the QUERY_STRING environmental variable.
END
```

Once the passed string is either separated into its component parts or parsed appropriately, it can be processed by the CGI program accordingly.

CGI Generation of HTML

One of the frequently used benefits of CGI programming is the ability it gives to generate HTML code at run-time. This means that one set of HTML code could be generated based upon the results of data input supplied by a user while another set of HTML code would be generated for another user.

In using this feature, you are advised to remember that output from CGI programs is always to the standard output device. For the HTTP server to know that the output is HTML code, the following format is required:

```
Content-type: text/html
<HTML>
...
</HTML>
```

Given this structure, the following example, written in Bourne shell script (a CGI programming language), dynamically builds an HTML page based on the value of the environmental variable REMOTE_USER.

```
#!/bin/progs
echo Content-type: text/html
echo "<HTML>"
echo "<HEAD><TITLE>CGI HTML CODE GENERATION</TITLE></HEAD>
echo "<BODY>"
echo "<H2>Main Menu</H2>"
echo "<HR>"
echo "<P>"
IF $REMOTE_USER = "AL" THEN
  echo Press <F1> For Help "<BR>"
  echo Press <F2> For Employee Listing "<BR>"
  echo Press <F3> For Department Listing "<BR>"
  echo Press <F4> For Vendor Listing "<BR>"
  echo Press <F5> For Parts Listing "<BR>"
ELSE
  echo Press <F1> For Help "<BR>"
  echo Press <F2> For Account Input "<BR>"
  echo Press <F3> For Account Inquiry "<BR>"
  echo Press <F4> For Status Update "<BR>"
  echo Press <F5> For Message Log "<BR>"
END IF
echo "</P>"
echo "<HR>"
echo "</BODY>"
echo "</HTML>"
```

This code relies on the POST method to place a value in the $REMOTE_USER environmental variable, which is evaluated to determine the HTML code to format and send.

CGI Programming Principles

Assuming you are already a programmer, well schooled in sound programming techniques, there are a few issues unique to CGI programming of which you need to be aware. These are described in this section.

Although many HTTP servers allow you to control where you place CGI programs, it is common practice to place CGI programs in a directory named cgi-bin. Without security software installed to protect the contents of this directory, you are at risk of hacker intrusions.

Application Performance

Applications delivered over the Web run more slowly than most applications delivered over the desktop. Be aware of the fact that users will already be waiting while graphics load or huge files transfer over a 14.4 bps modem and code your CGI programs as efficiently as possible.

Comments

All CGI programming languages include self-documentation syntax. Use these language comment facilities extensively. Just because you, the developer, know what you meant by naming a function the way you did, will a programmer working on the CGI program six months from now recognize it as a function? Or, would they initially view it as a variable?

HTTP Protocol

Learn about HTTP protocol. The time invested will be more than returned if you plan on using CGI programming in your Web database application. The more you understand about the type of browsers your users will be using, and the level of HTML support provided in their browsers, the more compatible your application will be.

Language Choice

Because of the nature of the Web, choose a CGI programming language that is at least as portable as it needs to be based on the scope of the complete application. If your completed application is deployed over the Web for execution on all operating systems, you need to make sure that your CGI programming language provides at least this level of support.

Naming Conventions

When writing a CGI program, follow the naming conventions for that program, as well as your company's standards. For example, Perl naming conventions are different from those for Visual Basic or C++. Following the conventions will make maintenance much easier.

Separate Development Site

Use your test Web site as the initial execution environment for any new CGI program. CGI programs can sometimes produce erratic and unexpected results and you don't want your product HTTP server brought down because of a buggy CGI program.

Standards

If your company has standards on the language to use for CGI programs, follow the standards. It will make maintenance easier and save your company money in consultant fees. If your company has no standards on CGI programming languages, use the language with which you are the most comfortable, and stick with it.

Use Libraries

When possible, find code that has already been written for routine CGI program tasks. Newsgroups and Web sites are excellent places to find already-written CGI programs that read data, format data into HTML, and perform database access.

CGI Program Architectures

Figure 7–2 displays the most typical form of CGI program architecture—sometimes referred to as *Straight CGI Program*.

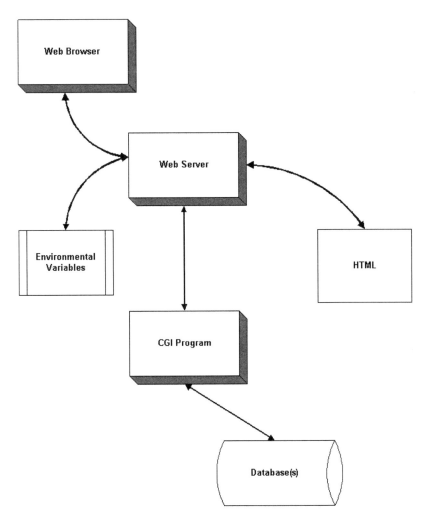

Figure 7–2   Straight CGI program architecture.

The straight CGI Program architecture was the first, and remains the most popular, CGI architecture on the Web. This is the architecture that has been discussed throughout this chapter. In this architecture, an HTTP browser sends a request via URL to an HTTP server. The HTTP server recognizes that the URL contains a reference to a CGI program. It optionally retrieves user-supplied input data from either environmental variables or the URL that it receives. The HTTP server then passes control to the CGI program that performs its processing—in the case of Figure 7–2, that processing performs a database access.

Figure 7–3 is a representation of the hybrid CGI program architecture. In this architecture, two components, a *thin* CGI program and a much larger CGI partner program, produce much better performance than the straight CGI program. This increased perfor-

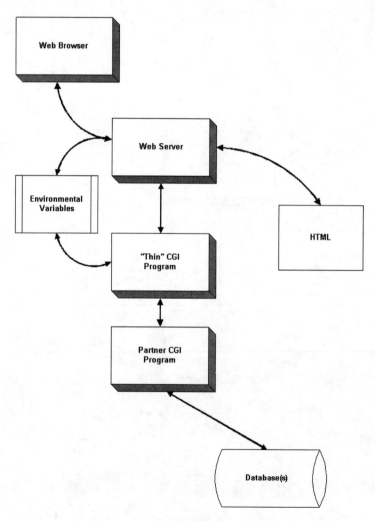

Figure 7–3   Hybrid CGI program architecture.

mance is attributable to the CGI partner program being loaded only once and always being available for CGI requests sent to it from the thin CGI program. Because the majority of the required functions from the CGI process are performed within the CGI partner program, the thin CGI program can be very small. This causes it to load more quickly and execute faster. Additionally, because database processing is requested by the CGI partner program, which stays resident in memory, database connections (which are time-expensive to establish and terminate) stay active. This is another efficiency gain.

Note: The HAHTsite IDE that is used throughout this book for demonstration purposes uses this architecture.

Figure 7–4 displays the API extension architecture, which is what Microsoft and Netscape are trying to establish as Web standards. Microsoft is promoting its ISAPI standard while Netscape is pushing its own standard, called NSAPI.

In this architecture, the server extension program is implemented as a DLL (for Windows NT/95) or a shared object (for UNIX). These server extension programs replace

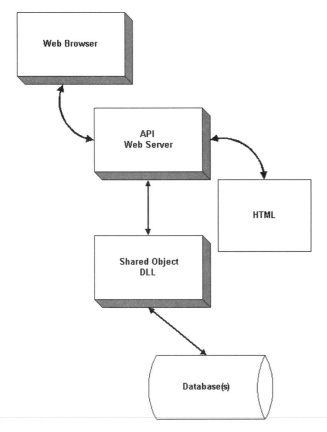

Figure 7–4 API extension architecture.

the functions performed by CGI programs. Server extension programs extend the base functions of HTTP servers via libraries of routines that perform predefined functions. These libraries extend the base functions of HRRP servers by the functions in the libraries. Because this increased functionality is provided by libraries, these libraries can be added, altered, or deleted as demand necessitates.

The main problem with both Microsoft's and Netscape's architectures is that they are competing, and therefore non-standard. Microsoft's ISAPI and Netscape's NSAPI can not co-exist.

The potential for API extension architecture is in providing a very responsive environment that is truly dynamic. The capabilities of the network can be expanded by adding libraries without necessarily having to write program code.

Tip: As already discussed, CGI programs in a straight CGI program architecture represent a potential security risk. This risk is that confidential user-supplied data that is passed from the HTTP browser to the HTTP server night be compromised. A web site with a substantial amount of information on this subject is available at: `http://www.cerf.net/~paulp/cgi_security/`

Moving On

This chapter provided an overview of CGI and discussed the various architectures comprising CGI. It also showed you methods you can use to incorporate CGI in your application in one of three different ways.

The following chapter goes deeper into the process of Web database application development and design by presenting relevant architectural issues. You will learn about the parallels that exist between Web database application development and client/server application development.

Section II: Internet Database Design

CHAPTER 8

Web Application Design and Development

As I've already stated in earlier chapters, the analysis, design, development, and implementation of a Web database application is very much similar to the same functions of a client/server project. If you are familiar with client/server concepts, then you will find the application of those concepts to Web database application development a very easy transition.

Advantages of Deploying an Application on Your Chosen Platform

There are a number of advantages to a company building and deploying an application in a Web database application environment. The items listed below should be self-evident. If they are a bit fuzzy, everything will be made crystal clear as you read through this chapter.

- Enhanced data sharing
- Integrated services
- Sharing of resources
- Data interchangeability
- Masked physical data access
- Location independence of data and processing
- Maximization of workstation resources

Absent from this list, and probably the greatest single strength of building a Web database application, is its "reach." Reach, a marketing term, is defined as the number of entities that will be exposed to your message. By an order of magnitude that is so great it is almost incomprehensible, a Web database application has much greater reach than a similar application deployed in any other type of architecture.

Characteristics of a Web Database Application

All Web database applications share the following characteristics:

- *Service*—They provide a service via either display of information, acceptance of input, provision of a service, or processing of data.
- *Shared Resources*—Web database applications share at least some of the resources on which components execute. Perhaps the most easily recognized shared component in a Web database application is the database.
- *Platform Independence*—The foremost underlying strength of the Web is its platform and operating system independence.
- *Message-Based Interface*—The role of the server, as you will see later in this chapter, is to translate the messages received from Web browsers into something meaningful and actionable.
- *Server Transparency*—The promise of Web applications is to allow you to build and deliver an application to users without revealing where the physical data resides. Tell me, what is the name of the server that is physically attached to the URL http://www.microsoft.com? This is server transparency!
- *Scalability*—Web database applications are very scalable. This means it is a very easy process to add more disk space to accommodate a larger database, add a few more modems to increase the number of concurrent users to your Web, etc.
- *Separate Responsibilities*—In a Web database application, the functions of the application performed within a Web browser are separate and distinct from those executed on the HTTP server, or on the database server.
- *Many-to-one Relationship*—In a Web database application there are many more Web browsers accessing the application via the HTTP server than there will be HTTP servers.

Keys to Successfully Implementing a System

There are as many opinions about what the critical success factors are to building and installing a Web database application as there are people having those opinions. The following four items are consistent throughout all the literature.

- *Management Commitment*—It has taken a few years, but corporate MIS managers are now beginning to see the value in building and deploying Web database applications.
- *Tool Integration*—As you saw in Chapter 3, the capabilities of the tools required to build a Web database application are becoming increasingly recognized in the soft-

ware community. This is evidenced by the frequency in which new integrated tools are coming to market.

- *Environmental and Architectural Support*—The planning of every application, regardless of whether it is a Web database application, a client/server application, or a 3270 application, should include serious consideration to the amount of support that application requires.
- *Training*—Many MIS executives underestimate the amount of training required to successfully build a client/server application. Training on the tools and architecture behind client/server applications is a key, and very critical, component to a development effort. This is certainly true for a Web database application development project.

The four items here are not a comprehensive list. However, if you get 100 people together to compare their lists of critical success factors in developing and implementing a Web database application, you will find these four items on every list.

The Process

The following are steps for the development of a Web database application. They are diagrammed in Figure 8–1.

- **Step *n*:** Build new systems by taking advantage of what was learned and the information present from the previous systems.
- **Step *n* + 1:** Reuse as much of the existing applications as possible.

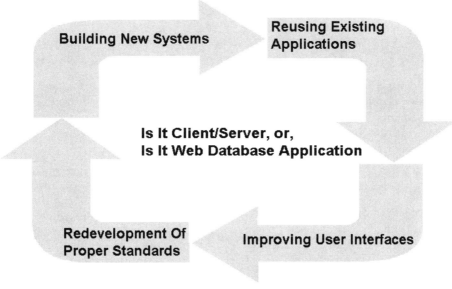

Figure 8–1 What development cycle is it?

- **Step** *n* + **2:** Improve the user interfaces in the newly designed systems.
- **Step** *n* + **3:** Redevelop the proper standards to support the development process.

A Wish List for Development Tools

The list below was culled from a training manual that I was given in 1994 when I attended a Client/Server Analysis and Design course. Even though the list was targeted to a client/server project, the items are just as valid today for a Web database application.

- Operating system interoperability
- Support team development
- Highly interactive debugger
- Good object orientation capabilities
- Easy to use documentation
- Portability
- Highly responsive and intuitive help system
- Vendor commitment for added features
- Support of popular GUIs
- Support of SQL specifications
- Support of class libraries
- Integration with other tools when and where necessary
- Vendor financial stability

I think you can agree that the items listed above are significant to a Web database application. In the following section, you'll see a thorough description of the design process of a Web database application.

The Design Process Described

In this section we will take a look at some of the design issues specific to a Web database application development project. This lays the foundation to go deeper into the process in succeeding sections. This section is not meant to be "tell-all" by any means. Rather, the intention is to describe the people, events, and processes at a sufficiently high level so you can begin to ask the questions you need to ask to tailor this information to your unique environment.

The Process of Design

The design of a Web database application is a process that is as dynamic as the variety of companies building Web database applications. This process is flexible by necessity as the tools and standards are evolving so rapidly. It is adaptable and malleable to each requirement or environment in which it is used. As flexible as it is, though, there are still components that share commonality.

One of these similar components is the *participants*. Each Web database application development project requires one or more of a number of different skillsets. Often, one person will be responsible for more than one of the following sets of skills. This is acceptable for the smaller, less complex projects. As the application and the application interfaces become larger, it is generally more desirable to spread the required skillsets among more individuals. These roles are described below.

Project Leader—This person has the same responsibility as a project leader for any other type of computer application development project. The issues may be somewhat unique for a Web database application, but the responsibilities are very similar.

Webmaster—Whereas a Webmaster's responsibilities used to be that of primary developer and maintainer of a Web site, the role is changing to be more of a system engineer. In many companies, the Webmaster is also the project leader.

End-Users/Audience—The people who use the computer applications that others build are the ultimate authority on the validity of the computer system. Web database applications are no different. One of the lessons learned in the 1980s regarding computer application development is that it is important to involve the users of the system in the early stages of the project. This is particularly true for Web database applications. What many companies are doing to accomplish this is to use focus groups of users during each stage of the development process.

Web Page Developers—In the early days (about 3 years ago!), the Webmaster was also the Web page developer. As the ways in which companies are using the Web to deploy applications become more sophisticated, there is an effectual split in these two roles. Web page developers have responsibility for the development of the more static components of a Web site. Consequently, these people are very skilled in either HTML or HTML authoring tools.

Programmers—As the sophistication of Web database applications increases, the reliance on highly skilled programmers increases as well. It is the responsibility of programmers in a Web database application project to extend the range and capability of the server-side services as well as to write code to implement client-side services.

Graphic Artists—Let's face it, the Web is a wealth of graphical wonder. Companies spend huge sums of money on bitmaps, image maps, and graphics displayed on Web pages in an effort to make the pages more attractive. Skilled graphic artists are as necessary to a medium or large size Web database application project as they are to the development of marketing collateral material.

System Administrator—The System Administrator is the technician responsible for the system hardware, initial troubleshooting of networking difficulties, system backup and security, and maintenance of system software. This person does not need to know a lot about Web database applications, but he or she should be very knowledgeable about the hardware, software and network components used to create and deliver the system.

Database Administrator—The DBA is the person responsible for setting up, maintaining, tuning, and supporting the RDBMS. In addition, this person is responsible for the security of the data contained within the database.

Network Engineers—Network engineers are responsible for the setup, support, maintenance, and tuning of the communication components of the system. As is the case with system administrators, the network engineer needs to know very little about the Web database application to do his or her job in supporting the network that it is developed and/or delivered on.

Tip: The focus of this chapter is on Web database application design. By the nature of this there is little information dealing with Web "page" design standards or approaches. You may read and download one of the most definitive works on this subject. *The Web Manual of Style*, written by Patrick Lynch, can be found at:

`http://info.med.yale.edu/caim/StyleManual_Top.html`

The Design in Progress

There is no single approach to the process of designing a Web database application. The technology and standards are evolving too rapidly to do this.

A typical first step is for one of the team members to identify the business requirements for the system. Another first step in the design of a Web database application might be to model the database. Still another first step might be to design the user interface. The point is that what works for one project probably will not be the correct approach for the next project, or next company for that matter.

If you understand the architecture of a Web database application, the roles of the participants, the business need precipitating the development of the Web database application, and the capabilities of the tools you are considering using in the construction of the application, then the approach that makes the most sense for your project will become clear.

Web Database Application Components

There are five major components in a Web database application environment. You need to understand what these components are and what their functions are before you can develop either a front-end user interface or an efficient back-end database.

Tip: The terms "browser," "Web browser," and "HTTP client" are used synonymously throughout this book, and are generally recognized to mean the same thing.

This section discusses these five components to give you an understanding of their roles in the development process. The components are:

- Server
- Application server
- Web client
- CGI program
- RDBMS

The Server

The server, also known as the Web server, is the software component that reacts to and interfaces with browsers. It has no ability to create or update Web pages or documents. Rather, it reads a request for information coming to it from a browser, usually in the form of an URL, locates the requested page, and sends the requested page back to the browser.

You are probably well aware of what an URL that accesses an HTML page looks like. The receipt of an URL and then processing of that address to retrieve the request for a Web document, finding the document, and then formating it and sending it back to the user is an example of the most widely used feature of servers—*document mapping*.

If you've provided an incorrect URL, or if the server which stores the requested file is not accessible by your server, the server issues an error message which tells you the URL you requested was not found (accessible) by your server. This is seen in Figure 8–2.

Additionally, a server can function as a gateway to external programs and processes when it receives a request for information via the execution of an external program or script. This type of interaction between the server and an external program occurs

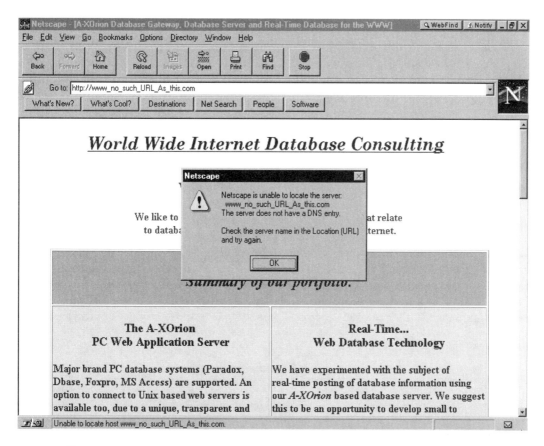

Figure 8–2 Server response when URL requested was not found.

Figure 8–3   A URL with a CGI execution string.

through a standard interface called Common Gateway Interface (CGI) and is commonly referred to as *CGI mapping*. An example of an URL with a CGI execution string is seen in Figure 8–3.

Another key function of a server is to redirect one URL (usually supplied by a user) to another URL. The target URL is usually on another server. This is called *redirect mapping*. Generally when this occurs the user is unaware that the redirection has occurred. Upon reflection, you probably have been the victim of this HTTP server function. Have you ever input an URL such as `http://www.worldinfo.com`, and have the page displayed in the browser with a translated URL of something like `http://www2.worldinfo.com`? If so, then this was redirect mapping.

The final main function for a server is to perform *content mapping*. When content mapping occurs, a specific file extension (i.e., `*.DOC`, `*.TXT`, `*.HTM`) is associated with a content type. A content type is a form of document classification and is defined using Multipurpose Internet Mail Extensions (MIME) format. MIME is a standard for attaching non-text files to standard Internet mail messages. Non-text files include graphics, audio and video files, spreadsheets, word-processed documents, etc. This is discussed in greater detail in Chapter 16.

Application Server

As seen in Figure 8–4, the role of the application server is to sit between the server and RDBMS. It is responsible for maintaining an open connection between the server and the RDBMS at all times.

In this architecture, a CGI program or script that uses the HTTP server API communicates with the application server. The application server takes this request and actually processes the query against the database, retrieves the result, and passes the result set to the program requesting the information. With a Web architecture that relies on an application server, the design of the application is not constricted by the availability of the various components. Rather, the designer is allowed to concentrate on the application.

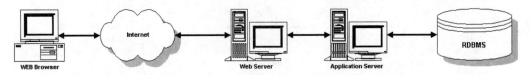

Figure 8–4   A browser, a server, an application server, and an RDBMS system.

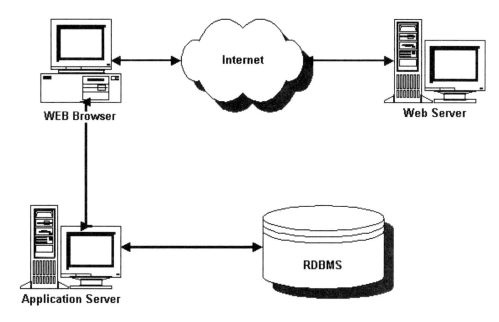

Figure 8–5   A browser, a server, an application server, and a RDBMS system with applets.

A variation of this architecture, as seen in Figure 8–5, is becoming increasingly popular. In this architecture, the server sends an applet to the browser. The browser, via the applet, establishes the connection with the RDBMS and retrieves the data needed directly. The main advantage to this architecture is that more of the processing is done on the browser, thus freeing cycles and resources on the server.

Web Client

The Web client is the software that runs on a client machine and performs necessary communication functions. The main functions performed by Web clients are:

- Establishing and maintaining communications with a server
- Passing user requests to the server
- Passing user data to the server
- Displaying information received from a server
- Viewing files not originating from a server

The three most popular Web client packages are:

- Netscape Navigator (used in the preparation of this book)
- Microsoft Internet Explorer
- Mosaic

A user does not require a server to make effective use of a Web client. You can use a Web client to view the contents of a range of file types, regardless of whether that file is on a server, a shared data server, or in a directory on your machine. Figure 8–6 is a screen print of such an event.

CGI Program

The CGI program, an optional component, is intended mainly to interact with the server by using one of a number of different standards. Its primary method of server interaction in a Web database application is to connect the server to external programs. CGI is discussed in detail in Chapters 7 and 14.

A graphic (albeit simplistic) representation of how a CGI program fits into the mix of components is seen in Figure 8–7. Unlike a server or client, the CGI program remains resident on the server only as long as it takes to accomplish its intended task. Once it finishes this task, it terminates.

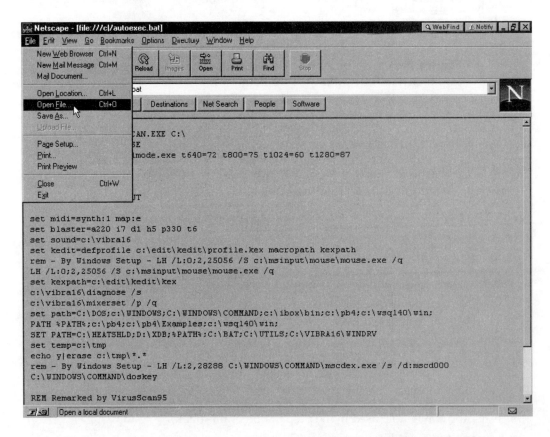

Figure 8–6   Using the Web client to view the contents of a text file.

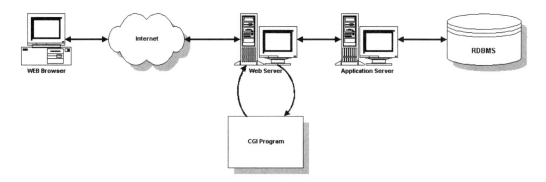

Figure 8–7   Web architecture with a CGI program.

In a Web architecture where CGI programs are used, it is possible for a server to receive concurrent requests from separate clients to execute the same CGI program. Such occurrences are acceptable and allowed, especially in multitasking operating systems such as Windows NT and Windows 95. However, you should be aware of the possibility of this in the design of your application.

You can usually recognize the data that is passed to a CGI program from a client by looking at the URL. Figure 8–3 is an example of this. The person who develops the CGI program controls how data is to be received into it from the client in the form of the command string displayed in the URL. For example, programmer A could develop his CGI program to accept a parameter string that looks like `"?StateCd=OR"` while programmer B could develop her CGI program to accept the same parameter in a string that looks like `"#State_Code=OR"`. For this reason, the person developing the CGI program needs to be in communication with the person developing the HTML pages.

RDBMS

The Web database application that you develop needs (obviously) a database to make it whole. These databases could be of the following types:

- Local, tab delimited text file
- Sophisticated RDBMS system such as MS Access 97 (your database of choice), Oracle 8, Sybase, Informix, DB/2, etc.
- Mainframe DB2, CICS VSAM, IMS

The RDBMS system you choose is based on factors that are outside the scope of this book. But, obviously you (or your employer) have made that choice to get to the point that you are at now. The point is to recognize that the power and capability exists in most programming languages and tools to perform whatever type of data access and manipulation that is required in a Web database application.

With the previous sections as an introduction, the remaining sections in this chapter discuss the details specific to designing Web database applications. Let's begin this material with a discussion of some of the steps to designing a Web database application.

Web Application Design Primer

Designing your Web database application is an intricate activity. There is much to consider and many items to correlate, especially if you incorporate audio/video clips or applets. Consequently, it is best to view the design of your application in terms of four distinct components:

- Database
- Function
- User interface
- Implementation

In this section, I'll guide you through the process of identifying the various issues of concern in each of these four areas.

Database

In this section, let's consider the four basic types of databases available to you. These are:

- Flat-file database
- Relational database
- Object-oriented database
- Hybrid database

Function

When you design a Web database application, you must begin to consider the functions desired in the application from a very high level. Gradually break the high-level functions (think of these in terms of *groups*) into more discrete and granular functions.

For example, consider a class registration system. Some of the high-level functions might be:

- Information collecting
- Registration processing
- Invoice and payment processing
- Certification

Once these groups are identified, you can then dissect them into smaller, more discrete chunks. Some of the tools you use in the course of modeling the data used by your application also would be useful when you isolate the application functions. Specifically, consider a CRUD diagram. CRUD stands for Create, Read, Update, and Delete. This is a device used by system and data architects to help collect and classify the relationships in a business system between the entities that exist in that system and the functions used by those entities.

If we look at a CRUD diagram that could be produced for one of the above groups, the Process Registration group, we could develop the following CRUD diagram.

Entity → Function ∨	Web Master	Student	Training Manager	Training Developer	Sales	Shipping	Exec's
Register/Take Course		C					
Sell/Record Learning Credits					CRUD	CRUD	
Ship Learning Credit Coupons					CRUD	CRUD	
Adjust Course List	CRUD		CRUD	CRU			
Produce/View Status		C	R	R	CR	CRU	R
Adjust Learning Credits			CRUD		CRUD	CRU	

C = Create   U = Update

R = Read   D = Delete

Note: The CRUD Diagram presented here has been simplified for the sake of brevity.

Once we have the CRUD to help us identify the required functions in the new system, we can begin to partition the application into meaningful pieces.

User Interface

The User interface of a GUI-based application, such as the one you are going to deploy after reading this book, is often considered to be the most important component in a Web database application. For example, if your application has a single purpose (such as displaying an account balance on your credit card), then the appearance of the interface that you create is a significant component of your application.

There are a number of books available that discuss effective GUI design techniques. Although the authors of most of these had Windows-based environments in mind when the books were written, the principles are the same regardless of platform. Most HTTP browsers are based on the Microsoft Windows metaphor.

If you decide to use a CRUD to begin to dissect your application, you can use the CRUD to begin to consider how the user interface to your application should look. However, this process should *not* be completed until you have a firm handle on the data location and dependency issues (which we will discuss in detail later in this chapter).

> The process of designing and developing a Web database application is an iterative-based work activity. *When done right*, you will proceed through multiple cycles of analysis, design, construction, and testing. The operative phrase is, "When done right." An effective MIS or business manager recognizes that the process of developing this type of an application is repetitious in nature and will resist the temptation to plunge the first iteration of the system into production.

Implementation

In this context, implementation does not mean slamming the programs, pages, etc. into production. Rather, implementation refers to the placement of functions, events, and processes in the application directly below the user interface layer. This is the level where you define the subroutines needed by your application, the number of programs, the need to access external libraries, and other specifications.

The techniques and processes that you use to implement a Web database application are very similar to the processes you would use in a mainframe application development project, or a client/server application development project. There are some important distinctions, however. These are discussed below but listed here as:

- Open Architecture
- Client Program Components
- Statelessness

Open Architecture.   The Web has a much more open architecture than the one you would probably ever consider in a client/server environment. In a client/server environment you have a fairly good idea what is available on the server and on the client. In a Web environment, you don't have this luxury. As a result, you need to plan for and accommodate this.

It is important that you maintain separate development and production environments. This is for reliability reasons, as well as for security reasons. Regarding reliability, the consequences of a CGI program failing when you move it into production are often more significant than when you move a client/server program into production. The nature of the Web is such that its reach far extends anything you would encounter in most client/server applications. Regarding security, the open architecture of the Web means that anyone can access your server. Whether they get past the server is a function of how much security you've implemented and how determined they are to gain entry. A development environment created and supported separately from the production environment addresses both of these considerations.

Client Program Components.   In a client/server application, the placement of program function (on the server or on the client) is largely based on which location makes the most sense. In a Web database application, your choice of where to place program function is a bit more complicated. If you are using CGI, there is very little program function that you can place on the client. The CGI program executes on the server. If you are using JavaScript or one of a number of new tools, then your choice is made a bit easier. JavaScript and these other tools give you the ability to perform logical operations on the data *after* it is sent to the client from the server.

Statelessness. Another important consideration when designing and building Web database applications is the inherent stateless environment of the Web. Consider the following example which is quite easy to implement in a non-Web application.

1. A user initiates a query of all the employees in a given department.
2. Seeing an employee name that is of interest, he selects to pull up a screen of information specific to that employee.
3. After reviewing this screen, he sees that one of the pieces of information on the screen is a field named Dependents. In this field is the number 3. He clicks on this field to see a list of the names and birth dates of the children for the selected employee.

In a Web database application, the above scenario presents some problems. Without maintaining the state of the application, when Step 2 is executed, the HTTP server or program has lost its knowledge of what department was used for the query executed in Step 1. As if this were not enough, the stateless Web application forgets the name of the employee that the user selected in Step 2 in order to display the names of the dependents in Step 3.

The good news is that statelessness is quickly becoming a thing of the past in terms of Web database applications. Most of the new development suites coming available, and a lot of the existing languages have facilities for maintaining state. If you are planning on using a development suite or programming language that has no facility to handle state (this includes Oracle 8), then consider doing what most people do, include a hidden text field in the form which includes a transaction identification number. This is seen below:

```
<input type = hidden  name = state_cd  value = state_cd>
```

In this example, a CGI program can distinguish one form from another based on the hidden fields and perform the required processing accordingly.

All right, you know a bit more now about the steps and processes of designing a Web application. So, let's peel back one more layer and look at some of the issues specific to designing a Web *database* application.

Web Database Application Design

In this section, you'll move down another layer and learn more of the details surrounding the design of a Web database application. It is a process that becomes complicated due *only* to the immature state of the tools and evolving architectures. Regarding the immature state of tools, the processes and activities described here are pertinent and relevant regardless of the state of the tools or even to a lesser degree which tools are used. Specific to the evolving architectures of the Web, it is also true that the processes and issues described here are relatively immune to the types of architectural changes occurring.

The Web Database Application Development Methodology

The Web database application development process is a 9-step process that is usually an iterative activity. In other words, as soon as step 9 is complete, the process begins again on the same application with step 1. Although some companies prefer to combine these nine steps into a 3-step Rapid Application Development (RAD) approach, or a 4-step prototyping approach, each of the listed activities still occurs. These nine steps are:

1. Systems planning
2. Project initiation
3. Architecture definition
4. Analysis
5. Design (Optionally create, update, or reference a system encyclopedia)
6. Development
7. Facilities engineering
8. Implementation
9. Post implementation support

In the analysis phase, work flows are broken down into detailed Object, ERD, and CRUD matrices. These diagrams then become the basic deliverables into the next phase of the cycle; data modeling, user interface prototyping, and process modeling, collectively known as execution architecture. In this phase, the requirements of the application are matched against the current architecture and new tools and data-process distributions are identified.

Once the technology architecture is determined, the application release is designed via the network design, database design, and process design. When this design work is complete, actual component construction is conducted.

Remember, in a Web database application development project, each activity or phase should produce a formal deliverable that documents, for user signoff, the understanding gained at that stage. It is unfortunate, but the trend in Web database application development is to be sloppy during most of the phases of the project. If history is any predictor of the future, I don't think that this "sloppiness" will be allowed to continue much longer.

The Web Database Application Environment

The Web database application development environment is the mix of hardware, software, interfaces, standards, procedures, and training that are used by an enterprise to optimize its information systems professionals' abilities to support business objectives. A Web database application development environment should include the following:

* Built-in navigation from one process and/or tool to another
* Standardized screen design
* Integrated and uniformly consistent help and hypertext facilities
* Integrated table maintenance in program modules

- Comprehensive security that permits easy navigation for the authorized and barriers to entry for the unauthorized
- Standard skeleton templates

I want to comment on a couple of the items listed above. The first being *standardized screen design* and the second being *standard skeleton templates*. Regarding *standardized screen design*, this is a process of combining good Graphical User Interface (GUI) design principles with the facilities available to accommodate these principles in HTML specifications. Chapter 6 of this book listed references for HTML style guides. Regarding *standard skeleton templates*, you will define your standard skeleton template based on the unique requirements of your site. The objective of this step in the environment is to construct a framework whereby all the visual components in an application have a consistent look and feel and the processing components take advantage of as much reusable code as possible.

The following section is an introduction to some of the issues specific to security in your Web database application. Although the entire Chapter 19 of this book is devoted to this subject, the material introduced here should help you to understand how security is accommodated in and supplied to a Web database application.

Web Database Application Security

Access 97, like other major RDBMS products, includes a number of features that are designed to safeguard access to data, and the data itself. These features work the same in a Web database environment as they do in a non-Web database environment. If a user is granted access to a database, then as far as Access 97 is concerned, that permission is granted regardless of whether the user is accessing the data from the Web or from a non-Web application. In this section, we'll take a look at some of the issues specific to the security of a Web database that are *outside* of the features built in to the Access 97 product.

The perils of Web commerce have been discussed at length in the media. As a result of all the attention paid to the subject historically, the development and deployment of commercial Web sites is much less dangerous. There are four primary areas where you must ensure that proper security safeguards are in place to protect your data and resources. These four areas are:

- *Physical*—This is perhaps the easiest component area to ensure safety in that the physical security of computers and computing devices has been an issue of concern to MIS managers for a number of years.

How many of you remember when you could walk into the mainframe computer operations room with a tape, mount it on the drive, and execute your program from the console? I do, and I don't think I'm that old. Conversely, I also remember the year I was told I could no longer have this type of direct access to the mainframe. It was 1978. That was almost 20 years ago (and I was 24 years old!!!), which means companies have been serious about physical security for at least that long.

- *Software*—Your software is much more vulnerable on a Web site than in almost any other type of delivery method. The Web is a very "open" environment. If you see a graphic on a Web page, or an applet that you'd like, it's easy (albeit illegal) to snag it. Because of this, you must be keenly aware of the security issues prevalent as you design your application.

- *System Hacker!*—The meaning of this name is clearly understood by even the most neophyte computer user. The consequence of a hacker breaching your system and causing damage of some sort could range in severity from annoyance to catastrophic. Even the variety of breach that is merely annoying will cause you great embarrassment when your boss asks you how someone was able to break through the security layers and gain access to your system. Be warned, making your system too secure from hacker attack is something that would be very hard to do, provided you don't make it cumbersome or difficult for the good people to access.

- *Data*—"Protect your data!" As much as "Protect Yourself" was a slogan for the 1980s and 1990s, "Protect Your Data" will become an identifying phrase for the 1990s and beyond. An easy argument could be made for paying more attention to protecting the integrity and confidentiality of the data accessed by your Web database application than to the security of the system as a whole.

For additional information on security of your Web database application, check out the following Web sites:

```
http://www.netscape.com/newsref/std/ssl.html
http://www.nortel.com/entrust/certificates/primer.html
http://www.w3.org/hypertext/www/security/overview.html
http://www.primus.com/staff/paulp/cgi-security
```

The following books are listed here as well as in Chapter 19 as references if you want to learn more about Web application security.

Title:	Internet Commerce
Author:	Andrew Dahl and Leslie Lesnick
Publisher:	Simon & Schuster
ISBN:	1-56-205496-1

Title:	Special Edition: Using Microsoft Commercial Internet System
Author:	Peter Butler, Roy Cales, and Judy Petersen
Publisher:	Que Books
ISBN:	0-78-971016-1

Title:	Web Site Administrator's Survival Guide
Author:	Jerry Ablan
Publisher:	Sams Net Publishing
ISBN:	1-57-521018-5

Title:	Special Edition: Using CGI
Author:	Jeffry Dwight, Michael Erwin
Publisher:	Que Books
ISBN:	0-78-970740-3

Problem Management

In a Web database application environment, effective problem management is at least as critical as a company's internal applications. Effective problem management means that plans are in place and tools necessary to support the following three areas are acquired or developed:

- Troubleshooting
- Debugging and problem tracking
- Vendor management

Troubleshooting problem management systems are critical elements to gain productivity and reliability in your applications. Fortunately, features specific to this area appear frequently in Web database application development suites.

Debugging and problem tracking tools facilitate the identification and removal of problems and bugs in the Web application while it is being developed and after it is in production. It is amazing to me, even now, how ineffective most Web applications currently being written really are. In a random, non-scientific survey that I conducted in preparing to write this chapter, I developed the following statistics:

- Number of Web sites visited where I initiated a bogus problem report with a request for a verification contact . . . 46
- Number of Web sites where I reported (with a request for a verification contact) a bug via an e-mail interface to someone identified as SUPPORT@, or WEBMASTER @ . . . 45
- Number of Web sites that had a 1-800 number provided to call in problems . . . 1
- Number of responses received from the 45 companies where I initiated a bogus e-mail problem report on their Web site . . . 0

That's right . . . out of 45 e-mail messages that I sent out reporting a bogus problem with a company's Web site, not one person got in touch with me, even though I specifically asked for a direct contact. OK, so you could argue that the person receiving the e-mail investigated the reported problem found nothing wrong and dismissed the whole thing. If you offered this argument, I'd respond, "How do they know that the problem I reported either will not happen again or is a problem specific to my HTTP browser?" Don't you think they should know this?

Six Principles of Function Placement

A Web database application is in some ways more complex than a client/server application development project. One of those complexities involves determining where (on which device) to place system functions. You no longer are limited to having to place all of an application's functions on the HTTP server or application server. In this section we'll look at what I call the Six Principles of Function Placement, which are:

- Frequency and Scope
- Application Concurrency
- Location of Data
- Code Reusability
- Processor Allocation
- Application Development Tool

Frequency and Scope.   In this context, frequency refers to how often a particular function is needed while scope refers to the diverse ways in which a function is used. Frequency and scope are often at odds with each other in the design stages of a development project. This does not need to be the case. Intuition tells you that if a function is used frequently, it should be placed as close to the calling source as possible to eliminate network degradation. If that happens to be on the HTTP client, then you can do that through an applet. Generally, the greater the number of calls to a function, the greater is that function's scope. A function that is called by many other functions is said to have "broad scope."

Application Concurrency.   Applications deployed over the Web in the form of Web database applications have the opportunity to execute many functions at the same time—in parallel. A sound Web database application design will recognize this and support it.

There are a number of ways to accomplish application concurrency. First, the application can be deployed on a multi-tasking operating system such as Windows NT or Windows 95 so that multiple instances of the application can be running concurrently. Second, data that the application accesses can be partitioned across multiple database servers. In this way, access to the different servers can be controlled programmatically. Third, *cookies* can be placed on a client to keep track of the state of the application. A *cookie* is a small packet of information that a server stores on a client machine to keep track of certain application specific information. The interaction between the cookie and the program accessing the cookie allows for application concurrency.

Location of Data.   The location of data is often a more complex issue than most people initially believe. There are choices. It no longer is required that all the data that an application accesses be located on the server. The following are some of the locations that should be considered as places to locate data accessed by the Web database application: Web servers, database servers, application server, client, file server(s).

Code Reusability.   Code reusability allows you to more quickly deploy Web database applications that are more reliable than similar applications built without taking advantage of code reusability. When building a Web database application, code reusability is certainly a component to be considered.

There are two ways to achieve code reusability; first, by use of Remote Procedure Calls (RPCs), and second by providing a linked library of subroutines. Remote Procedure

Calls are programs that intercept calls to subroutines, convert those calls to messages, send the messages to the computer where the subroutine really is, and then invoke the subroutine on that computer. In a Microsoft Windows environment, this is via Dynamic Link Libraries (DLLs). Regardless of which method you use, and you could use both simultaneously, you should achieve a higher degree of productivity and reliability in your application when you are able to take advantage of code reusability.

Processor Allocation. If your Web application consists of two components only, the server and the client, and the client does no more than display HTML pages, then you don't have much of an opportunity to allocate the workload of the application across multiple processors. If this is not the case in your environment, you need to consider processor allocation in the design and construction of your application.

For example, you may have an architectural environment where you have the following components: client, server, application server, and a database server.

Each of these components has a processor. Recognition of each of these processors in the design of your Web database application is important to effectively place functions. An example (albeit extremely simplistic) of this is a scenario in which a user asks for a single record to be displayed on his or her machine from a database of 100,000 rows. Does it make more sense to search the database for the one record requested on the database server before sending it to the client or to transmit all the rows on the database server across the Web to the client, and then have the client search out the one row requested? It makes more sense and is definitely more time efficient to search the database for the one record requested and then send that one record to the client.

Application Development Tool. The choice of tools you make to develop the Web database application has an effect on where application functions are placed. For example, a program written in C++ handles concurrent requests much more efficiently than one written in SmallTalk or COBOL.

Be careful though! As seen in Figure 8–8, there is a balance that should be achieved between designing the application within the bounds of the toolset used to construct it and retooling to meet the needs of a new application.

On the one hand, a development environment that continually retools to develop each new application is inefficient and not nearly as productive as it could and should be. On the other hand, a development environment that spends excessive resources designing an application to arbitrarily fit the constraints of an existing toolset may be better off using a new set of tools and spending the time getting the new system to "fit." A development environment that is balanced most efficiently utilizes all of its available resources.

Application Partitioning

Many application partition models exist today. They range from a 7-layer model that tends to be overly complex for Web database applications to a 3-layer model. The 3-layer model is the simplest, the most widely recognized, and the one that I prefer. This model is comprised of the following layers:

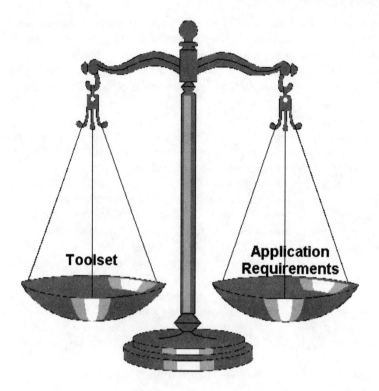

Figure 8–8   Balance the toolset with application requirements.

- Presentation
- Function
- Data Management

Using the 3-layer model, there are five different ways in which you can partition the tiers on the different platforms that comprise the Web database application. Each of the following are examined in detail on the subsequent pages.

- Distributed Presentation
- Remote Presentation
- Distributed Function
- Remote Data Management
- Distributed Database

Distributed Presentation

Figure 8–9 displays a little used but still valid partition type called distributed presentation. In the distributed presentation architecture, the presentation components of the application are split between two or more different platforms. For example, a customer inquiry application may have certain components that display on the HTTP client machine while other components display on the machine located on the desk of the accounting supervisor. In this model, the *Function* and *Data Management* components reside on the same device as the *Presentation* services.

Remote Presentation

As seen in Figure 8–10, in the remote presentation architecture, the *Presentation* components of the application reside on one device type while the other two application tiers reside on another device type. For example, an inventory application for an automobile dealership would provide *Presentation* services on the devices of the people accessing the Web application while all application *Function* and *Data Management* services are handled by a server device in a separate location.

Distributed Function

In the distributed function architecture, the *Presentation* and *Function* components of the application reside on the HTTP client device while other portions of the *Function* components of the application and the *Data Management* components reside on another device. For example, a customer service application for a bank may have the *Presentation* and some of the *Function* components of an account inquiry application on the HTTP client device while the other *Function* components and *Data Management* services are provided on an HTTP server and database server.

Remote Data Management

In the remote data management architecture, the *Presentation* and *Function* components of the application reside on the HTTP client while the *Data Management* components reside on another device, either the HTTP server or the database server. For example, a medical records application would have the *Presentation* and *Function* components of the application processing on a Web browser while the *Data Management* components reside exclusively on a separate device type.

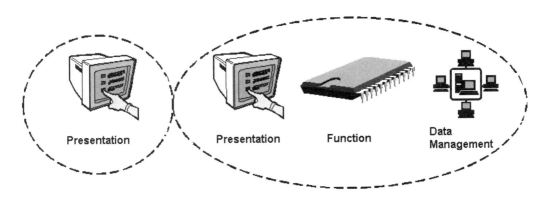

Figure 8–9   Distributed presentation partition type.

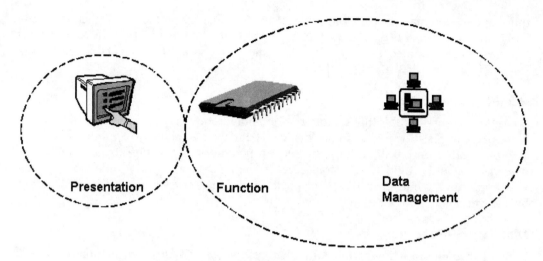

Figure 8–10   Remote presentation partition type.

Distributed Database

In the distributed database architecture, the *Presentation*, *Function*, and some of the *Data Management* components of the application reside on the HTTP client device while other features of the *Data Management* component reside on either the HTTP server or the database server. For example, consider a remote order entry system. This system may have the *Presentation*, *Function*, and some of the *Data Management* components of an application residing on the HTTP client devices. At the same time, at a remote sales office other aspects of the *Data Management* component, such as historical data storage, reside on the HTTP server or database server.

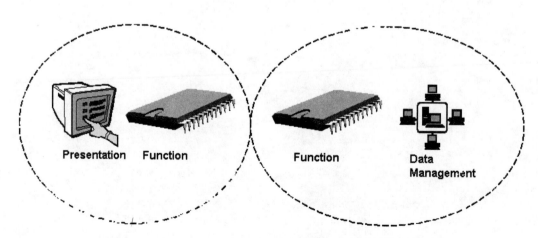

Figure 8–11   Distributed function partition type.

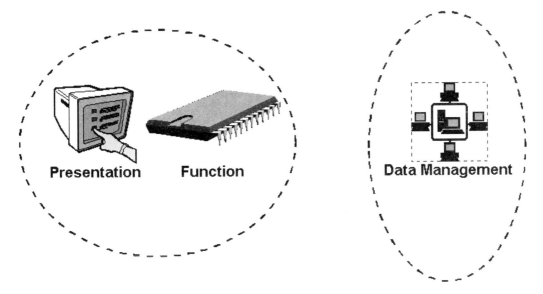

Figure 8–12   Remote data management partition type.

In the research I did prior to writing this book, I found a number of books available that described the process of building Web database applications. By my count, and as of the time I'm writing these words, there are seven. In all cases, the authors presented one application partition strategy—remote presentation!

This presentation not only is overly simplistic, but it does not recognize the other strategies you could use to develop and deploy an application to take advantage of the unique combination of the architecture of the Web and the architecture of your company. When you begin to think of the Web, from an application architecture perspective, as little more than an extension of a client/server architecture, then you will subsequently begin to grasp the full potential of this environment for deployment of database applications.

Application Partitioning Summary

There are many issues that determine the method used to partition the application. As the number of Web database applications installed by a company increases, and as organizations implement strategic, mission-critical applications, companies are looking more closely at the way they allocate the application components that comprise the three tiers. In the early days of client/server (initially) and Web database applications (secondarily), the server was used for data management services while presentation and function services were allocated to the client. As technology evolves, a shift of some of the application functions from one device to the other will occur.

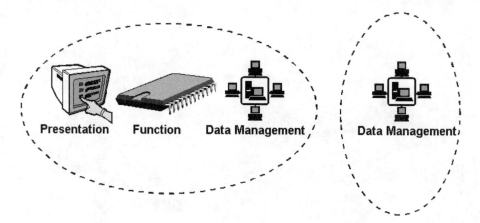

Figure 8–13 Distributed database partition type.

If you want to learn more about application partitioning, I suggest the following sources:

Application Prototyping

Author: Bernard H. Boar
Publisher: John Wiley & Sons
ISBN: 0-47-18931-7

Implementing Application Solutions in a Client/Server Environment

Author: Robert L. Koelmel
Publisher: Wiley-QED
ISBN: 0-47-106068-2

Moving On

In Chapter 9, we peel back one more layer and look at the features in Access 97 that are specific to creating database objects such as databases, tables, indexes, queries. You will learn about table relationships, and how to establish and modify them. We also investigate ODBC in greater depth than we have so far.

CHAPTER 9

Introduction to Access 97

I n earlier chapters we discussed some of the peripheral issues related to the development of Web database applications.

Beginning here and continuing into the next two chapters you are introduced to Microsoft Access 97. This chapter provides an overview of the product and some of the features (most of which are new) specific to Web database application development. It continues on with specific information on DDL, SQL, and the facilities in Access 97 to define databases and database objects.

What Is Access 97?

I could describe for you what Microsoft Access 97 is, but perhaps it would be more meaningful if I show you what Microsoft Corporation has to say about Access 97. The following text is taken off Microsoft Corporation's Web site.

> Corporate Web pages. Sales figures and invoices. Customer names and addresses. Today, data is everywhere—on your PC, on local networks, and on the Internet. But how do you make sense of it all? The Microsoft Access 97 relational database management system structures your data so you can find answers easily, share timely information, and build faster solutions that help you make better business decisions.
>
> Microsoft Access 97 makes it easy to turn data into answers and includes tools that help even first-time users get up and running quickly. The Database Wizard automatically builds any one of more than 20 custom databases in minutes to help you get started fast. And the Table Analyzer Wizard intelligently finds the underlying structure in a flat-file list and

transforms it into related tables so you can immediately harness the power of a relational database—even if you don't understand relational database systems.

Microsoft Access 97 makes it easy to share up-to-date information with others, regardless of where they are. The Publish to the Web Wizard lets you share dynamic or static database information across the Internet or your company's intranet—without writing any code. That means you can place your data on a Web site and let people search it from across your workgroup or the world. And the Import/Export Wizard walks you step-by-step through the process of converting data to and from a variety of popular data formats.

Microsoft Access 97 offers greatly enhanced 32-bit performance, including smaller forms, more efficient compilation, and better data manipulation technology. Other improvements substantially reduce the technical know-how you need to build fast, flexible business solutions. The Performance Analyzer Wizard automatically recommends the best way to create a well-organized, more responsive database. And the intuitive, integrated development environment (IDE) in Microsoft Visual Basic for Applications with ActiveX support makes it easy to develop a powerful database and integrate it with other Microsoft Office programs to create a comprehensive business solution.

As you know, this book introduces you to the process of designing and building Web applications that use Microsoft Access 97 databases. In this chapter you will learn how to use the Web-specific features in Access 97. In subsequent chapters you will learn how to build the application components that allow you to access an Access 97 database in a Web application. If you want to learn how to use Access 97 to build non-Web database applications, I'd recommend the following books:

Title:	Microsoft Access 97 Power Toolkit
Author:	Michael Groh
Publisher:	Ventana Communications Group
ISBN:	1-56-604609-2

Title:	Access 97 Developer's Handbook
Author:	Paul Litwin, Ken Getz, Mike Gilbert
Publisher:	Sybex
ISBN:	0-78-211941-7

Title:	Access 97 Power Programming
Author:	F. Scott Barker
Publisher:	Que Corp
ISBN:	0-78-970915-5

What's New in Access 97?

Microsoft Corporation has been criticized for being a bit slow in the early 1990s to realize the shift that was occurring in Web applications. Recently, though, the company has made up lost ground in its quest for world dominance in the computing world and released a new version of its flagship database application development environment—Access 97. This new release includes many new features and functions specific to Web database application development. These new features that are specific to Web database application development are discussed in this section.

Without a doubt, the biggest areas of improvement that Microsoft made in their Access RDBMS, moving from Access 95 to Access 97, have been in the area of Web support. This is in direct response to Bill Gates' announcement in August 1995 that Microsoft had missed the initial Internet bandwagon, but would invest whatever resources were available to make up for lost time and dominate the market in the following areas:

- The Internet client market with Internet Explorer
- The Operating System market with Internet extensions in the Windows OS
- The tools market with enhancements to their development languages (i.e., Access, Visual Basic, etc.) to support Web application development
- The office applications market with enhancements made to their Office 97 applications (of which Access 97 is a component) that place emphasis on Internet support

In Access 97, Microsoft added the following Internet and Web database application development support:

- Hyperlink Datatype—Stores hyperlinks in database tables as a valid datatype
- Publish to the Web Wizard—An added `File|Save As HTML` submenu item allows you to save an Access 97 object as an HTML file, or as an optional IDC/HTX file. IDC and HTX are extensions used by the Microsoft Internet Information Server to identify files that include data source information and mapped returned data in field merge codes, respectively.
- HTML Import Wizard—Allows you to efficiently import HTML files
- Internet Replication—Features in Access 95 have been enhanced to allow replication of databases over the Web via FTP.

Recall in Chapter 8, "Web Application Design and Development," that the line between RDBMS and OODBMS products was beginning to blur. One of the less significant but nevertheless noteworthy differences between RDBMS and OODBMS products is the support for non-standard data types in OODBMS products. Access 97 storing a hyperlink link as a valid datatype is an example of this.

In the sections that follow, I'll not only introduce you to the features in Access 97 that help you to build a Web database application, but show you how to use them as well.

Hyperlink Datatype

As implemented by Microsoft, a hyperlink datatype can be a link to either an URL, or a Word document on either the client machine or an attached machine. In my opinion, Microsoft did a very good job of implementing this feature and making it easy to use, as seen in Figure 9–1. In Access 97, there are two new properties used to specify a link: *Link to file or URL*, which has an Access 97 property name of HyperLinkAddress, and *Named location in file*, which has an Access 97 property name of HyperLinkSubAddress.

Although only the *Link to file or URL* is required to properly identify the linked location, the second (optional) text box is very useful to position the browser at a specific

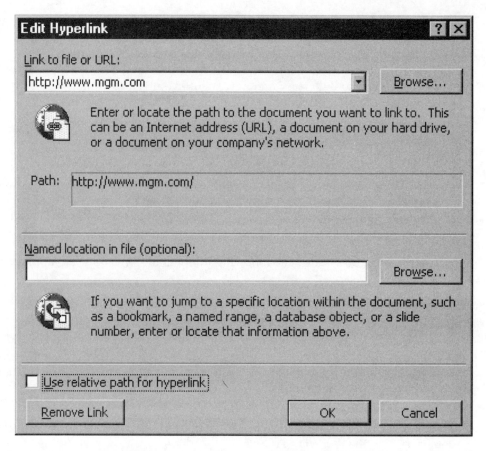

Figure 9–1   Specifying a hyperlink datatype.

sublocation within the document of a file or link. This sublocation can be an object in an Access 97 database, a bookmark in a Word document, a named range in an MS Excel spreadsheet, a slide in a PowerPoint presentation, or a specific location on an HTML document.

Table 9–1 describes how you might use the combination of HyperLinkAddress and HyperLinkSubAddress.

Inserting a column in a table where the datatype is Hyperlink is a simple two-step process as seen in Figure 9–2 and described here.

1. Select the HyperLink Column submenu item from the Insert menu item on the toolbar. The new Hyperlink column is inserted prior to the currently selected column.

2. Once the column is inserted or identified in a table, you can specify the specific HyperLink for each row in the same way that you'd normally provide the values for any row-column combination in an Access table.

Table 9–1   Uses of HyperLinkAddress and HyperLinkSubAddress

HyperLinkAddress	HyperLinkSubAddress	Comments
`http://home.micro soft.com/access 97`		The Access 97 home page on the Microsoft Web site
G:\CORPDOCS\REVIEW. DOT		A Word template named REVIEW that is located on the G:\CORPDOC drive/path
G:\CORPDOC\REVIEW. DOT	SALARY	The SALARY bookmark in the Word template named REVIEW that is located on the G:\CORPDOC drive/path
G:\CORPXLS\97BUDGET. XLS	Cashflow!Expense	The Cashflow!Expense range in the 97BUDGET.xls spreadsheet located on the G:\CORPXLS drive/path
G:\CORPPPT\ PRODDEMO.PPT	15	The 15th slide on the PRODDEMO.ppt PowerPoint slide document that is located on the G:\CORPXLS drive/path

Publish to the Web Wizard

The new Publish to the Web Wizard (PW Wizard) allows you to quickly publish the information in Access 97 databases in either static or dynamic format. You can use the PW Wizard to create HTML pages from tables, queries, reports, and forms. There is a facility to create the HTML pages using a predefined template to ensure you get a consistent look-and-feel from one iteration (generation of HTML pages) to the next. The PW Wizard has the ability to publish a home page that lets users locate and browse through all the pages you develop from a single URL.

The following discussion describes how to use the PW Wizard.

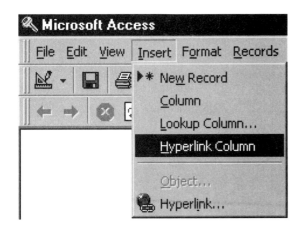

Figure 9–2   Creating a Hyperlink datatype.

1. From the Access 97 main menu, select `File|Save As HTML`, as seen in Figure 9–3.

2. You will see the introductory screen to the Publish to the Web Wizard, shown in Figure 9–4. If you have a defined profile that you wish to use to create the HTML pages, click on the checkbox and select one of the options listed in the list box.

3. The next screen, Figure 9–5, allows you to specify which database objects you want to publish in the form of HTML pages. You can select any combination of objects by choosing the appropriate tab and then selecting (or deselecting) the objects within that tab that you want to include (or exclude).

4. The screens in Figures 9–6 and 9–7, allow you to select a template file to be used to create the new HTML pages. Template files are useful to consistently create HTML pages with the same look-and-feel, even though the content may change. Figure 9–6 is the screen used to *specify* the name of a template file. By clicking the `<Browse>` button, you are presented with the screen shown in Figure 9–7, which allows you to *search* for a template file. If neither of these options suits you, click on the `<Next>` button to proceed to the next phase in this process.

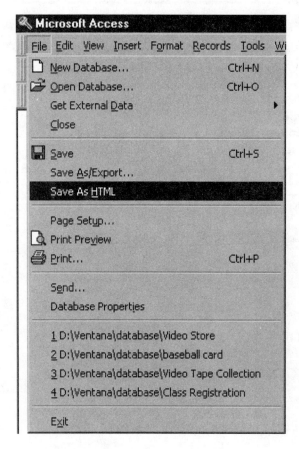

Figure 9–3   The first step in using the Publish to the Web Wizard.

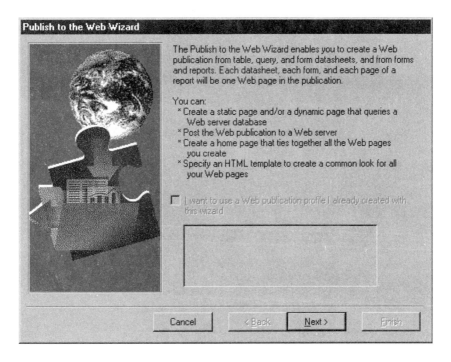

Figure 9–4 The Access 97 Publish to the Web Wizard introductory screen.

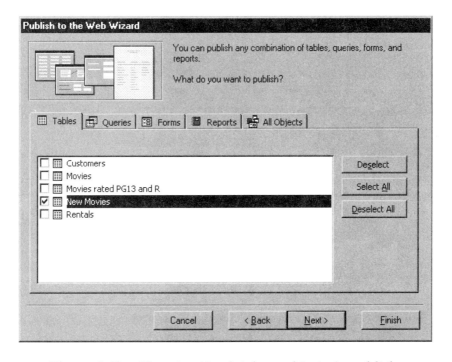

Figure 9–5 Choosing the database objects to publish.

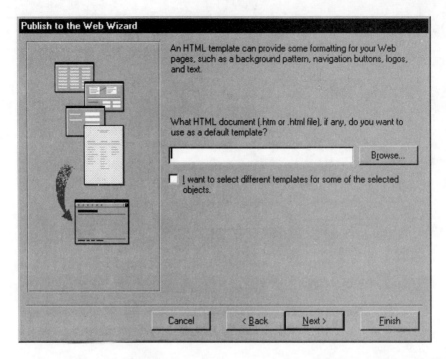

Figure 9–6 Specifying a template to use to create the HTML pages.

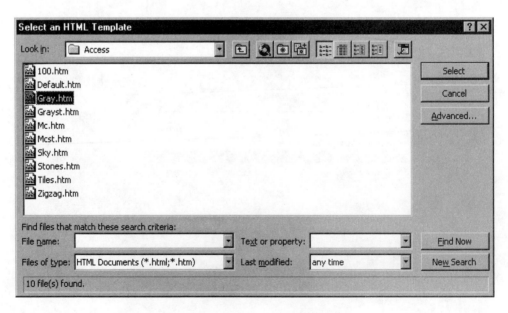

Figure 9–7 Browsing for a template to use.

5. You are next prompted to select the type of page to publish, as shown in Figure 9–8. Once there, you are given three choices. Select one of the following:
   - Static HTML (the default)
   - Dynamic HTX/IDC (requires Microsoft Internet Information Server)
   - Dynamic ASP (requires an ActiveX Server)

6. The next window in the PW Wizard series asks you to specify the location where the wizard will publish the files that it generates. The first selection, as seen in Figure 9–9, allows you to publish the pages in a directory on your machine. If you've installed the ValuPack, you can identify and specify a new Web publishing specification. The ValuPack is a set of utilities and programs that are on the installation CD-ROM and are used to augment the functions in the base Access 97 product.

7. You are then prompted to indicate whether you want the PW Wizard to create a home page for your Web publication. This is shown in Figure 9–10. Creating a home page is generally a good idea if you have a large number of pages that are to be generated and you want to tie them all together.

8. In Figure 9–11, you are then prompted to provide a name for the specifications you have just provided. This then becomes a template and appears on a list of templates (Figure 9–7) that you can select at a later time to generate new HTML pages with the same look and feel as the one you just created. Once you click on `<Finish>`,

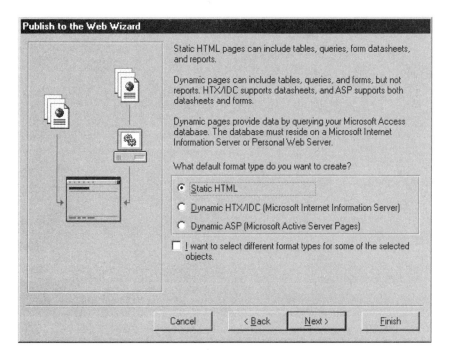

Figure 9–8   Selecting the type of page to publish.

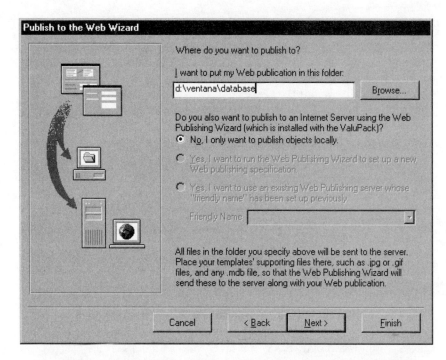

Figure 9–9   Specifying the location for the pages generated.

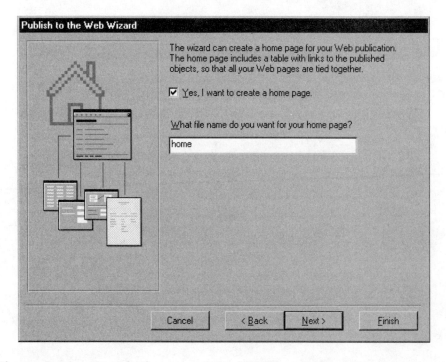

Figure 9–10   Specify if you want the PW Wizard to create a home page.

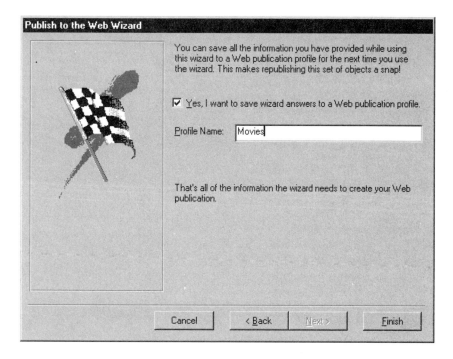

Figure 9–11   Specifying a template name to save your specifications.

Access 97 will create the Web pages as specified. The HTML page created for this section of the book is seen in Figure 9–12.

HTML Import Wizard

Using the HTML Import Wizard, you can import and link (read-only) to a data file on an FTP or Web server. This effectively allows you to copy data through the Internet without requiring a connection to a Local Area Network (LAN) or Wide Area Network (WAN) file server.

The process described here results in data from an external data source being used to populate an Access 97 table. Another use of the HTML Import Wizard is to link to an external table. A linked table is a *snapshot* of the original remote data source at the time you linked. You will not see updates to the data made at the remote location while the table is open. The next time you open it though, Access 97 will refresh the local copy in the cache folder.

To use the HTML Import Wizard, follow this procedure.

- From the Access 97 main menu, select `File|Get External Data`, as seen in Figure 9–13. You will then be prompted to provide the location and name of an HTML file that contains data you want to import (Figure 9–14). Select the HTML file name and click on <Import>.

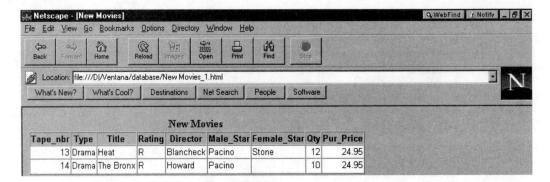

Figure 9–12   The completed static HTML page from an Access 97 table.

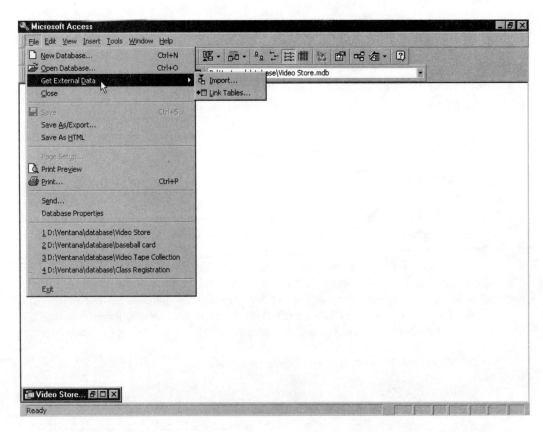

Figure 9–13   The first step in using the HTML Import Wizard.

- If the HTML file you specify contains more than one table or list, you are presented with a dialog box that allows you to specify which table(s) or list(s) you want to import.

- To import data from or link to an FTP server, either type the Internet address in the `File Name` box, or click the arrow to the right of the `Look In` box. Click `Internet Locations` (FTP).

- In the list of FTP locations, double-click the location of the item you want, and then double-click the item.

Internet Replication

Replication is a valuable component in a RDBMS in the following situations:

- *When a database is required to be available 24 hours per day, 7 days a week.* This is a fairly common requirement for Web database applications. To accomplish this in a replicated environment, the replicated database can be defined as read-only and refreshed at scheduled times.

- *When users are located in different offices and required to work across a Wide Area Network (WAN).* This is also a common need in a Web database application. To accomplish this, replicate each required database at each site, thus enabling users to run from the new database.

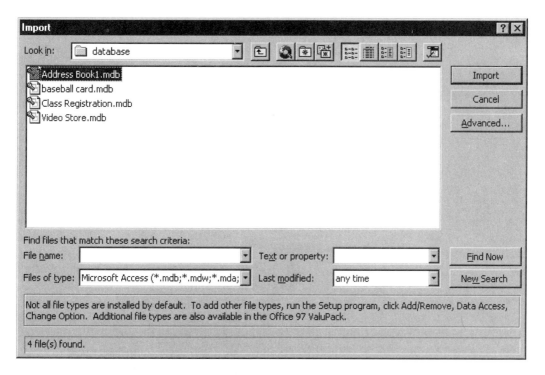

Figure 9–14   Selecting the HTML file from which to import data.

- *When all the databases in an application have some sort of reports that must be run.* When an Access 97 database has reports running against it, the report usually causes record locks to be placed on the table data. This degrades performance. To keep performance optimized, a special replicated report database will isolate report processes to a single, non-critical, replicated database.

The process of making a database replicable and actually replicating a database is outside the scope of this book. This book is concerned with the facilities in Access 97 to replicate and synchronize a database across the Web.

To synchronize a database over the Internet, the database must first be set up on the Internet server. Once this is done, issue the following call to perform the bidirectional synchronization from your database to a database that in this example is called: `http://www.mysite.com/files/accounts.mdb`.

```
db.Sybcnronize "http://www.mysite.com/files/accounts.mdb",
dbRepImpExpChanges + dbRepSyncInternet
```

In the previous sections you've seen the features in Access 97 that are new and which are also specific to Web database application development. The following sections show you how to use Access 97 to manipulate database objects.

DDL, DML, and Access 97

The Data Access Objects (DAO) component in Access 97 provides a set of objects and collections that enable an Access 97 application developer to create and manipulate database components programmatically with Visual Basic (VB). Data Definition Language (DDL) is one of two parts comprising the DAO component in Access 97. The other component is Data Manipulation Language (DML). Whereas DML is the portion of DAO that manipulates database objects and data, DDL is responsible for defining database objects and data.

DAO is outside of the scope of this book (this book is not intended to teach you Visual Basic) and it is mentioned here only as an introduction. The books cited at the beginning of this chapter give excellent coverage of this topic. The point to recognize, however, is that all of the functions described in the following sections and demonstrated via the graphical Access 97 interface can be accomplished programmatically and outside of Access 97 in Visual Basic. Therefore, if you are using Visual Basic as your CGI programming language, you have the ability to create a CGI program accessible from a Web server that adds, modifies, and deletes database objects. How you use this capability is up to you and depends on the requirements of your application.

Although the syntax for creating database objects and data in DDL, and manipulating those objects and data in DML are easy to master, they are outside the scope of this book. This book will cover some of the issues and describe the process of defining database objects, then populating those objects with data, using the graphical interface provided within the Access 97 shell. These topics occupy the remaining pages of this chapter. Chapter 10 begins to discuss the process of defining queries and working with data.

Creating Databases and Database Objects

In Access 95, the Database Wizard was introduced. With Access 97, this feature was embellished to make it a whole lot easier to use. Microsoft also included a number of templates. These templates can be used to create all the objects (including tables, forms, and reports) that you'd need to do a pretty thorough job of identifying a new database.

With Access 97, you can change, view, and define the properties of databases via the standard windows interface. You can create a base hyperlink path that is appended to the beginning of the relative HyperLinkAddress property settings. The Startup properties that follow allow you to specify a customized set of initialization options that are unique for each application.

- Customized toolbar
- Customized status bar
- Customized database window display
- Preselected form to display when a database is opened

The following sections show you how to create some of the database objects you'd need for your Web database application (which happens to be the same process as creating a database object for a non-Web database application).

Creating a Database

Many people new to RDBMS terminology confuse the terms *Table* and *Database*. Even some people who are not new to this technology use the two words interchangeably. A database is a collection of objects such as tables used to store data and table indices in order to keep and maintain relationships between data stored in the tables. A table is a collection of rows of data in which each row is comprised of multiple fields, or columns.

When you choose to create a database, there are two ways to do this. Both are accessible from the File|New Database as seen in Figure 9–15. The two options are to either create a blank database (Figure 9–16), or to create a database using one of the predefined templates (Figure 9–17). The next few sections describe these two methods in detail.

Creating a Blank Database

When you first start Access 97, you are prompted to either create a new database or open an existing one. If you choose to create a new database, or if you select the File|New Database menu item after you've been working with the product, you will go through the following process.

As you can see in Figure 9–16, once you let Access 97 know that you want to create a new database without using a template, there are just a couple more pieces of information needed to complete this definition. This process is seen in Figure 9–17, and the information required is described in the following three steps:

1. Give it a database name, as shown in Figure 9–18.
2. Provide a location (drive/path), also shown in Figure 9–18.
3. Click on <OK>.

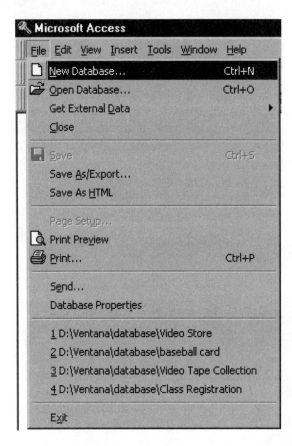

Figure 9–15 `File|New Database`
menu item.

Once this is done, the structure for a new (albeit empty) database is created.

Creating a Database from a Template

The process of creating a database from a template involves a few more steps, but could potentially save you a great deal of time in creating and defining database objects. By creating a database from a template, you don't have to create tables, indexes, forms, or load a sample of *dummy* test data, which is usually about 10 to 15 rows in each of the automatically-generated tables; the database create process does this for you. I personally don't like to create a database using templates. I have found that the template creates so many database objects that end up taking so much of my time to delete that I am usually better off just creating the individual database objects as I need them.

All of this is not without some overhead though. For example, the templates come predefined with table names, table structures, column specifications, etc. If the template is fairly close to what you want in terms of a finished database structure, then use the template. However, as the number of database objects that you need to add, delete, or change increases, the value of using the template decreases. There is no hard and fast rule as to

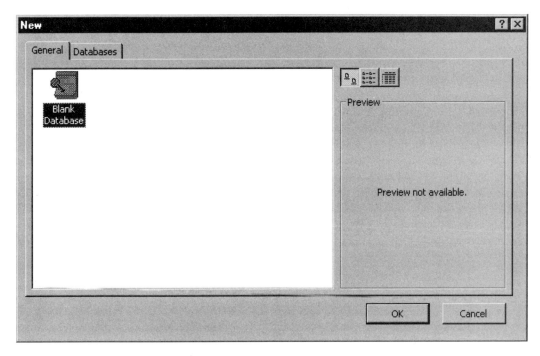

Figure 9–16 Creating a blank database.

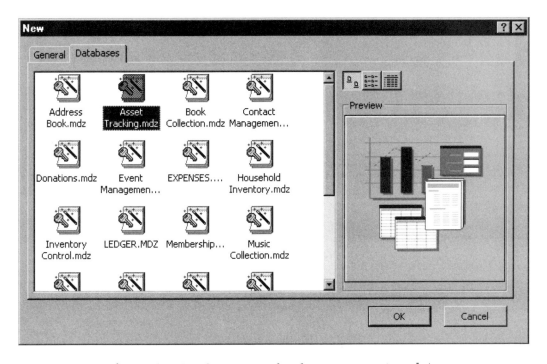

Figure 9–17 Creating a database using a template.

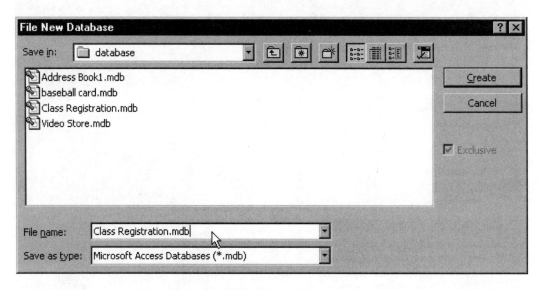

Figure 9–18   Specifying a database name and drive/path combination.

where the breakeven point is—this varies and is highly dependent on your situation. However, using templates to create a new database has the potential for saving you a lot of time.

When you first start Access 97, you see a screen that prompts you for a number of different alternate paths. One of the paths is to create a new database. If you respond that you want to create a new database, or if you select the File|New Database menu item after you've been working with the product, you will go through the following process.

- Click on the tab labeled <Database> to have Access 97 present you with a list of templates. Each template creates a suite of database objects that the developers at Microsoft think you'd be most likely to need in that type of database. Select the template that most closely matches the database structure that you need and click on <OK>.
- You will then see a window that looks like Figure 9–18 where you specify the name and drive/path combination for the database. Provide this information and press <Create>.

As seen in Figure 9–19, Access 97 displays a screen that discloses the types of information this database template maintains. This is provided so you can decide if you want to use this template or not before any database objects are actually created. If you want to continue on, click <Next>, otherwise click <Cancel>.

The next screen, (Figure 9–20) allows you to selectively choose which of the predefined database objects for the template you want to use to create your database. There are three areas on this screen that give you the opportunity to control the types of database objects that will be automatically generated.

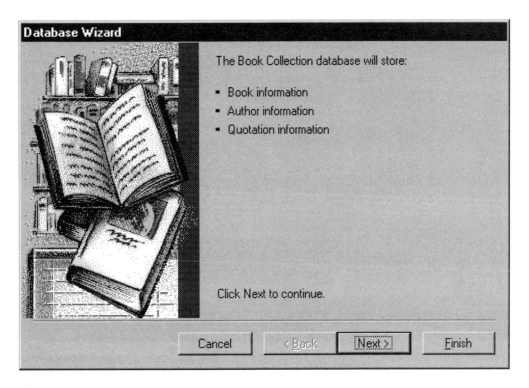

Figure 9–19 A disclosure of the type of information in the selected template.

- Tables in the database—This is a list of all the tables that are defined for the selected database template that will be automatically created as part of the template. This is your opportunity to provide input as to the number and types of database objects created.
- Fields in the table—This is a list of all the fields in the table that is selected in the tables in the database section of the window and is your opportunity to provide input on the number and types of columns that will be automatically generated in your tables.
- Include sample data checkbox—This checkbox, if checked, populates the tables with test data.

Any field names appearing in the `Fields in the table list` box that are italicized can be selected at your discretion. Any field names that are not italicized must be selected.

Once you have chosen the table structure you want, click on the <Next> button to go to the screen display type window, as seen in Figure 9–21. This window is used to select the way information is displayed on forms. Once you select a screen display format

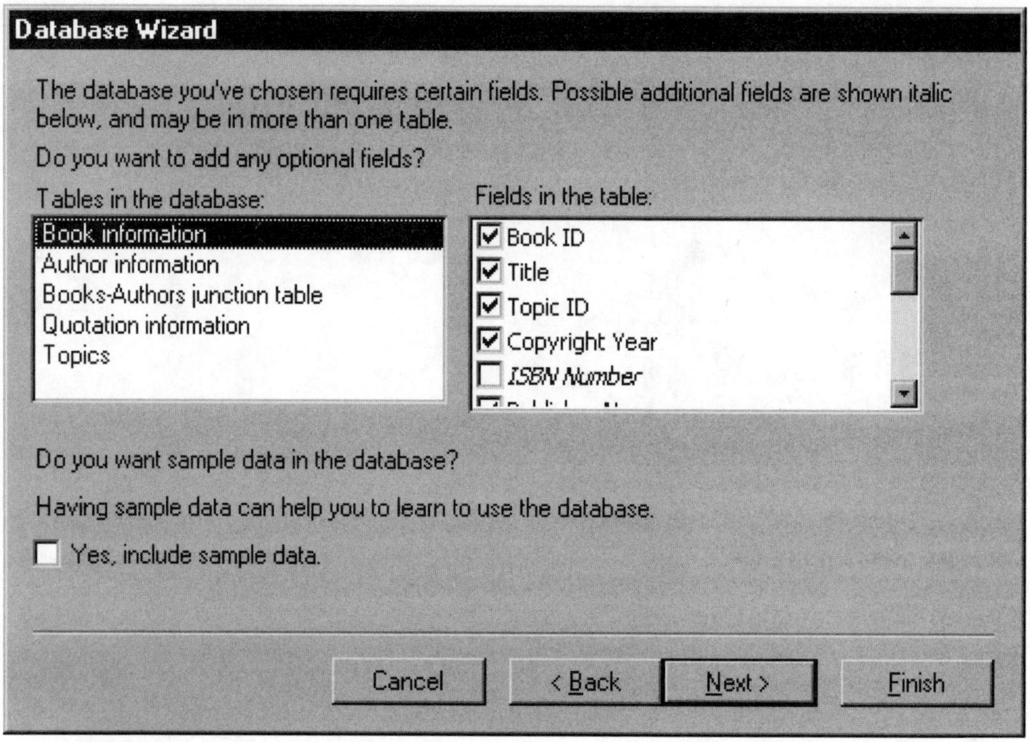

Figure 9-20   Selection window for tables, columns, and test data.

for online forms, click on <Next> to go to the printed report type selection window, as seen in Figure 9–22.

Forms in an Access 97 application are the screens users see to either allow user input to tables or show the results of a query. Reports are the method by which data can be presented in a meaningful and easily understood way. Access 97 reports can be viewed online, printed, or exported to another format. Reports are similar to forms, but reports are only used to display data—they can not accept data.

The report type selection window is used to define a basic structure and layout for a series of reports that are predefined and available to use within the specification of the template. Once you select the report type and click on <Next>, you will go to a screen (Figure 9–23) where you can specify the title for the database as it appears on reports and whether or not you want to include a bitmap picture as an icon on reports. If you want a bitmap picture, you can provide the qualified name of the picture object.

When you have provided a title (not the name) for the database and identified a picture to display on reports, click on <Next> or <Finish>. Access 97 takes a few moments to generate the database objects. As seen in Figure 9–24, this includes a number of tables, that, since we specified we wanted test data generated, are populated with data.

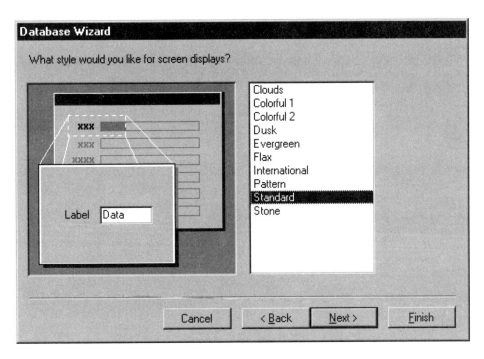

Figure 9–21 Screen display selection window.

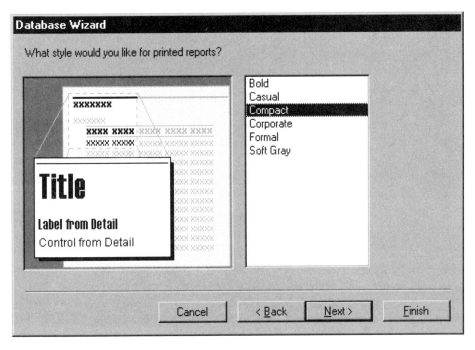

Figure 9–22 Report type selection window.

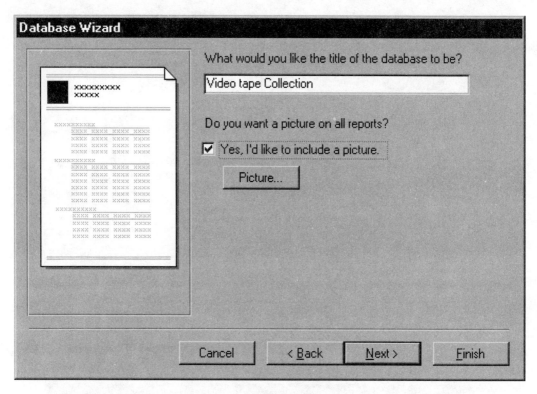

Figure 9–23   Specifying the database title and picture for reports.

Creating a Table

There are two ways to create a table in Access 97: the *basic* method and the *template* method. As you learned earlier in this chapter, when you use the template method to create a database, it automatically creates a suite of tables that are germane to the database. You can then modify these tables by adding, modifying, or deleting columns. Here, you will learn the various methods to create a table in Access 97.

There are two additional methods which are not covered in this book. The first is the Import Table method, which adds a table by importing its structure and contents from an external file, such as another Access 97 table, a spreadsheet, or a delimited text file. The second is the Link Table method, which creates a table by adding a link to another database either on your computer or a computer you are attached to. If you want to learn more about these additional methods, I recommend one of the books listed at the beginning of this chapter.

Creating a Table Manually

The best time to generate a table manually is when there is not a table definition close enough to one that you need in the Database or Table Wizards or when you are more

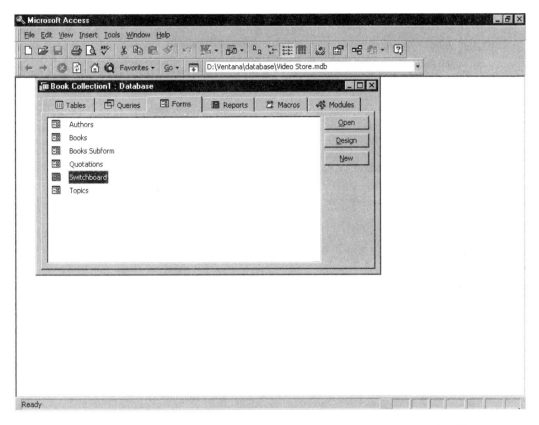

Figure 9–24   The completed database, including populated tables.

adept at creating a table manually and want the control this gives you in the definition of the attributes for the table and columns in the table.

For instance, assume that your boss comes to you with a request to add a table of dependents to an existing Access 97 employee database. After reviewing the types of database objects automatically created using the Database and Table Wizards, you decide that the best approach to satisfy your boss's request is to create the dependent table manually.

There are two ways to create a table manually in Access 97; using the Table Datasheet view (Figure 9–25) or the Table Design view (Figure 9–26).

The Table Datasheet view is a great way to define a simple table but gives you limited direct control on the attributes or properties of the columns in that table. The Table Design view gives you much more control over the attributes and properties assigned to the columns in the new table.

Create a Table Using the Table Datasheet Method.   The advantage to using the Table Datasheet method is that you can create the basic table structure and populate the table at the same time.

Tape_nbr	Type	Title	Rating	Director	Male_Star	Female_Star	Qty	P
1	Drama	Somewhere In Time	PG 13	Blancheck	Reeves	Seymour	12	
2	Drama	Apollo 13	PG 13	Howard	Hanks		10	
3	Comedy	Beverly Hills Cop	PG 13	Purvis	Murphy		4	
4	Romance	Bridges Of Madison Cc	PG 13	Rodman	Eastwood	Streep	29	
5	Comedy	Beverly Hills Cop II	PG 13	Purvis	Murphy		3	
6	Animated	Beauty And The Beast	PG 13	Disney	Beast	Beauty	19	
7	Animated	Lion King	PG 13	Disney	Muphasa		18	
8	Animated	Cinderella	PG 13	Disney	Prince	Cinderella	17	
9	Suspense	Speed	PG 13	Bosworth	Reeves	Bullock	8	
10	Romance	Somewhere In Time	PG 13	Rachins	Reeves	Seymour	9	
11	Action	Tornado	PG 13	Crossword		Hunt	4	
12	Action	Best Of The WWF	PG 13	McMahon	Hogan		10	

Figure 9–25   Looking at a table in the Table Datasheet view.

To do so, click on the <New> button while in the Database window, with the Table tab clicked, as seen in Figure 9–27.

You will then see the New Table window shown in Figure 9–28, which is where you select one of the five methods (Datasheet View, Design View, Table Wizard, Import Table, Link Table). Select Datasheet View and click on <OK>.

A blank Table Datasheet view table displays as seen in Figure 9–29.

The first thing you should do from the blank Table Datasheet view is to change some of the column names. To do this, double-click on any of the column names (currently, they are Field1, Field2, Fieldn, etc.).

Although Figure 9–30 is black and white, the column title changes color and the cursor is in this column heading. Don't look too hard for it though, it really is there. You can type any valid column heading you want at this point and press <Enter>.

Access 97 is much more lenient in the types of column names it accepts than other languages you might be using to access data. For example, even though Access 97 allows you to use a space in a column heading, Visual Basic requires you to enclose the field in

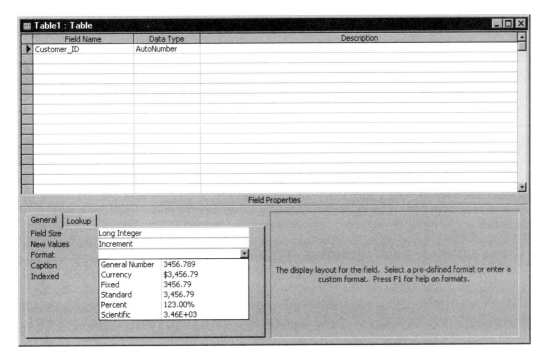

Figure 9–26   Looking at a table in the Table Design view.

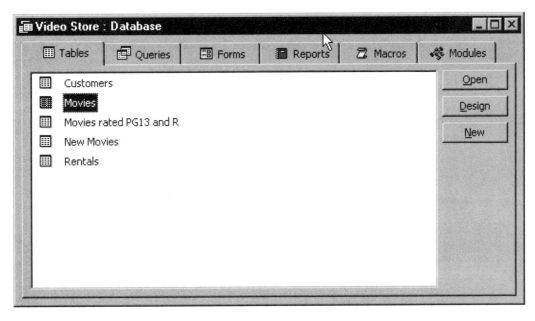

Figure 9–27   The database window with the Table tab active.

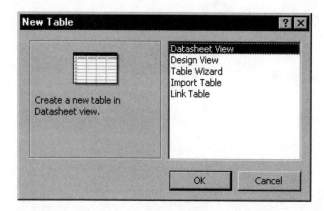

Figure 9–28 The New Table window.

square brackets ([ ]) before you refer to it in an expression. The bottom line is this, don't use spaces in your column names, and keep them short and meaningful.

Once you've changed the column headings to a more meaningful word, you can begin to insert test data. Let's say that you mess up and decide that you really want to insert a column between two existing columns. To do this, follow the directions:

1. Click once on the column heading located directly after the location where you want the new column inserted.

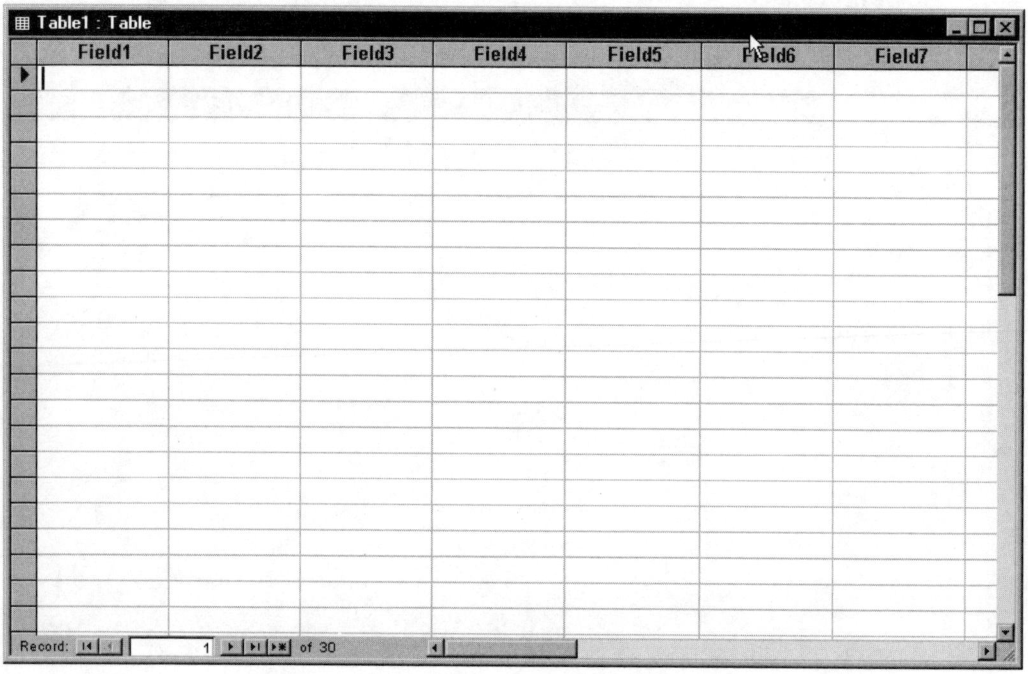

Figure 9–29 Blank Table Datasheet view.

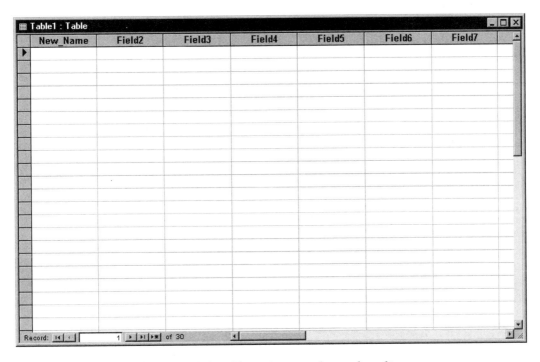

Figure 9–30   Changing a column heading.

2. The entire column will change colors.

3. Click the right mouse button and you will see a column attributes window pop up (Figure 9–31). At this point you could click on the <Delete Column> or <Rename Column> to accomplish either of those actions.

4. Click on <Insert Column> to insert the empty column.

5. Access 97 inserts this column with a column name of Field*n*.

6. As we just discussed, you could then change the column name by double-clicking on the column heading, typing a new name for the column, and pressing <Enter>.

The process of changing a column name or moving a column is the same regardless of the method used to create the table. Also, these processes can be done even when the table is populated with data.

Let's say you want to move, or change the position of a column in the table. To do this you'd follow the next four steps:

1. Single click with the left mouse button on the column heading of the column you want to move. The entire column displays in reverse-video mode.

2. Position your cursor over any area in the selected column and press and hold down the left mouse button.

Figure 9–31   The column attributes window.

3. Without releasing the left mouse button, move (drag) the selected column to its new location. This is indicated by a slight color change in the left side of the column that will appear directly after where the column is moved.
4. Release the left mouse button to effect the move.

With the table initially defined and meaningful column headings assigned, you can begin to enter data. Just start typing data directly into the form. Not all columns require data—they may be defined as Nulls. It is important to input data in the columns in a consistent manner. For example, if you enter a social security number in the format 555-55-5555 in one row and 7777777 in another row, Access 97 will not know which is the correct format for this column. Also, if you want to enter data that is primarily numeric in a column that you want to include alphanumeric datatype, include alphabetic characters in the data string. For example, entering a social security number of 555-55-5555 will cause this column to be defined as a character string. However, a social security number typed is as 777777777 will cause the column to be defined as an integer.

If you save a table where there are no entries in any of the rows in a column, Access 97 will not save that column. So, before you try to save a table that you just defined, be sure there is some data in every column.

When you've finished inputting data, click on File|Save. A message box displays in which you can provide a name for the table just created (Figure 9–32). You can accept the default or type in a new file name. Click <OK> to create the table.

Don't be alarmed if you see the message box shown in Figure 9–33. Access 97 is informing you that you have not identified a column as the primary key yet. A primary key is a column or columns that you select as always having a unique value by which the row that contains the key can be quickly selected. You don't need to identify a primary key when you create a table, you can do this later. But, you should use primary keys in the design of your tables as they greatly improve the efficiency of queries.

If you allow Access 97 to create a primary key for you, it will insert a column at the beginning of your table with a name of "ID." Each row in this column is assigned a number, beginning with 1 and incremented by 1 for each row.

Once the table is saved, you can work with the table in either the Table Datasheet view, or you can switch to Table Design view. To do this, with the table opened, click on View|Design View and the perspective will change.

Creating a Table Using the Table Design Method. The advantage of creating a table using the Table Design method is that Access 97 gives you a great deal more control over the composition of the table and the attributes of the columns.

Begin by clicking on the <New> button while in the Database window, with the Table tab clicked (Figure 9–27). You will then see the New Table windows, as shown in Figure 9–28, which is where you select the Design View method to create the table.

When you do this, a blank Table Design form will display, as seen in Figure 9–34.

Then provide a name for the column under the heading Field Name. Be careful that the field names contain no blank characters. Tab to the Data Type column. Click on the down arrow button to see a list box containing all the valid data types available for this column. This list box is shown in Figure 9–35. Click the data type you prefer.

Optionally, you can tab over to the column with the heading "Comments" and provide free form descriptive information.

You can also click in the General tab at the bottom of the window and modify any of the listed attributes for this column (Field Size, New Values, Format, Caption, or Indexed). Most of these attributes display a drop-down list box of the available options when you click inside the text box. For example, Figure 9–36 shows the drop-down list box displayed when the Format text box is clicked. (The attributes that display in the General tab change, depending on the datatype. Therefore, the attributes on your screen may not match what you see in Figure 9–36.)

Figure 9–32 Accept the default table name or type a new one.

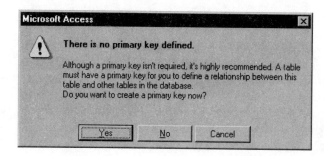

Figure 9–33 Warning box informing you that no primary key has been defined.

One of the data types that you could define for a column is Lookup Wizard. This is a tool that allows you to define how a field retrieves and displays data. Another valid datatype is Hyperlink. This is a new datatype in Access 97 that allows you to specify a hyperlink. To identify a column with a hyperlink datatype, simply click on Hyperlink as a datatype when the data type attribute is selected. This is seen in Figure 9–37.

Or, you could click on the Lookup tab at the bottom of the screen after first selecting one of your columns. You will then see a screen that allows you to specify how the field appears and how its values are retrieved. An example of this screen is seen in Figure 9–38. The attributes that display change, depending on the data type for the column.

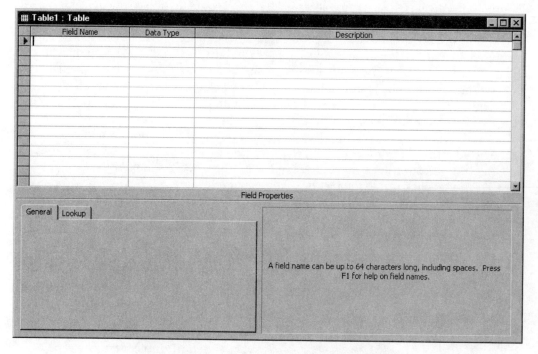

Figure 9–34   A blank Table Design form.

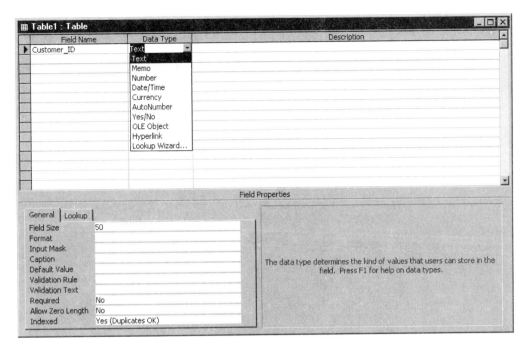

Figure 9-35 A partially completed Table Design form.

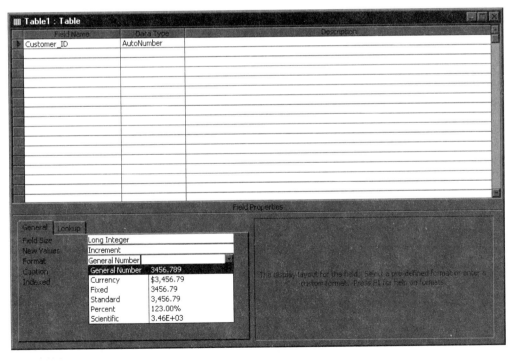

Figure 9-36 The options for the Format attribute.

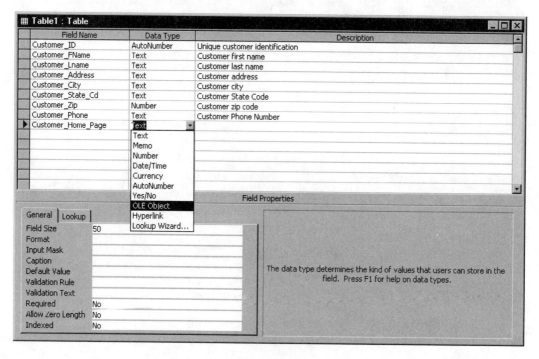

Figure 9–37   The Hyperlink Datatype.

Click on the `Field Name` column in the next row of the table to define the next column in your table. Continue modifying the columns until all required columns have been identified.

As seen in Figure 9–39, you can modify the default properties and attributes for columns. To do this, click on the `Tools|Options` menu item, then on the `Tables/Queries` tab. Modify any of the default items appearing on this screen and click on <OK> to save your changes.

When you have finished adding columns and modifying their attributes and properties, click on `File|Save` to save the newly defined table. You will see a screen like Figure 9–40 that asks you to provide a name for the table. Input a value (or you *could* accept the default) and click <OK>.

If you have not identified at least one of the columns as a primary key, you will see a warning message like Figure 9–33. This is an informational message box, unless you click <Yes>, telling Access 97 that you want it to add a column to the beginning of the table with a name of "ID" that contains a unique index for each row. Unless you want Access 97 to create this new column for you, click <No>, and you will have saved your new table.

Now that you have seen the two primary methods for creating a table manually, the following section shows you how to use the Table Wizard to automate many of the steps of table creation.

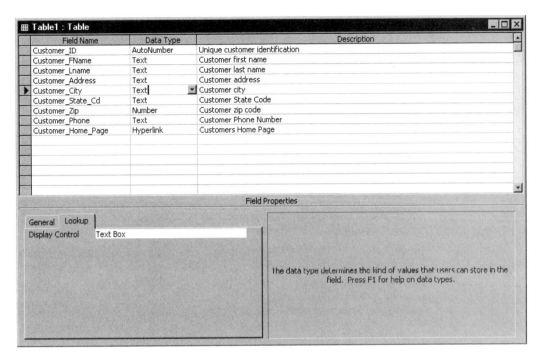

Figure 9–38   Modifying the way the column retrieves its data.

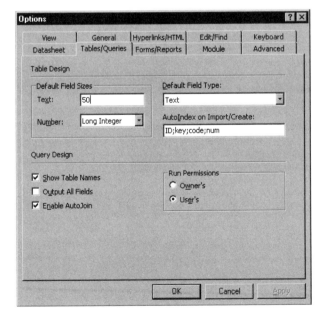

Figure 9–39   Modifying the Tables/Queries options to suit your needs.

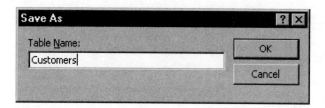

Figure 9–40 Providing a
name for your creation.

Creating a Table with the Table Wizard

Creating a table using the Table Wizard is a much simpler process than what you've read
about so far. The Table Wizard allows you to create a table based on a number of predefined templates. These templates define all the information needed to create and identify
the table, including column names, data types, comments, general properties, and lookup
properties.

The Table Wizard allows you to select which fields from a predefined table template
you want to use, rename the fields according to your liking, provide a new table name,
allow Access 97 to identify a primary key (which you can override and change), and establish relationships with other tables.

Click on the <New> button while in the Database window with the `Tables` tab selected. This is seen in Figure 9–27.

On the New Table window, as seen in Figure 9–41, click on the Table Wizard item in
the list box. This instructs Access 97 that you want to use the Table Wizard to create a
new table. Click on <OK> to continue.

From the Sample Tables and Fields window (shown in Figure 9–42), you progress
through an iterative process of selecting a table, selecting the fields on that table to use in
your new table, selecting another table, selecting the fields from this new table to add to
the table you are creating, etc. The Sample Tables and Fields window allows you to
change the name of a column, or you can change it later. When you are done selecting the
columns, click on <Next>.

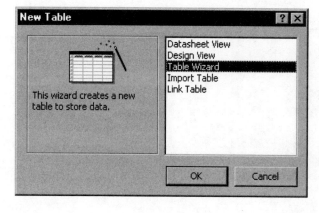

Figure 9–41 Select the Table
Wizard option to use this
valuable tool.

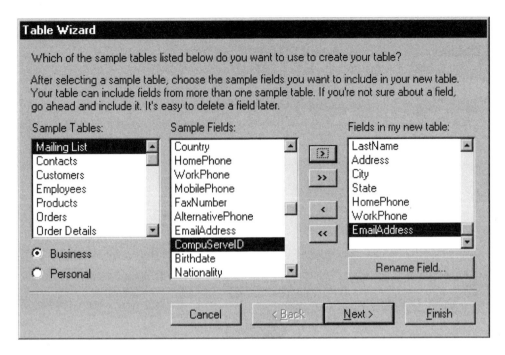

Figure 9–42   The Sample Tables and Fields window.

The next window allows you to accept the default name or change the name for the table you are creating. This is seen in Figure 9–43. Either accept the default name or change it, and select one of the two radio buttons to let Access 97 know if you want it to establish a primary key for you. Click on <Next> to continue.

Figure 9–44 is the screen you'll see next, where you identify the column to use as the primary key, or optionally let Access 97 try to assign it for you. Either accept the best guess that Access 97 can make, or identify a column and click <Next>.

You will then see the window that allows you to identify the relationships that may exist between this table and other tables. All the tables that exist in this database are candidates and therefore display in the table-relationship list box. To identify a relationship, click on the table that you want to link to, and then click on the <Relationships> button. You will see a window that looks like Figure 9–45. Select the type of relationship that exists and then click on the <OK> button.

You're just about done at this point. Figure 9–46 shows the final screen you will see that lets Access 97 know if you want to modify the table design, enter data directly into the table, or enter data directly into the table using a form created for you by the Table Wizard. Make one of these selections and click on <Finish>. Based on the option selected, you will either go back into the table design process or you will be able to begin entering data.

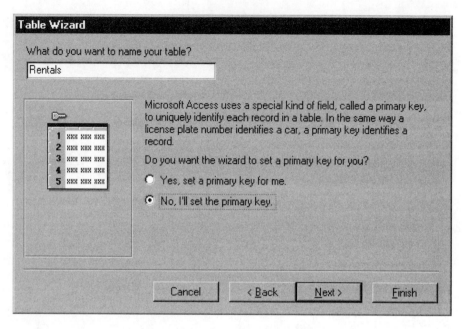

Table Wizard

What do you want to name your table?

Rentals

Microsoft Access uses a special kind of field, called a primary key, to uniquely identify each record in a table. In the same way a license plate number identifies a car, a primary key identifies a record.

Do you want the wizard to set a primary key for you?

○ Yes, set a primary key for me.

◉ No, I'll set the primary key.

Cancel   < Back   Next >   Finish

Figure 9–43 Accept the default or change the name of the table.

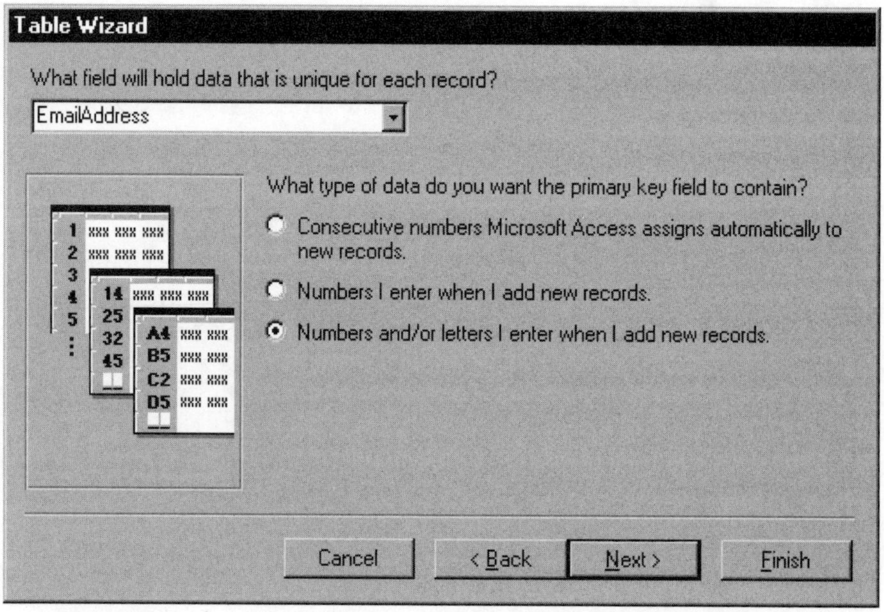

Table Wizard

What field will hold data that is unique for each record?

EmailAddress

What type of data do you want the primary key field to contain?

○ Consecutive numbers Microsoft Access assigns automatically to new records.

○ Numbers I enter when I add new records.

◉ Numbers and/or letters I enter when I add new records.

Cancel   < Back   Next >   Finish

Figure 9–44 Assigning a column to be the primary index.

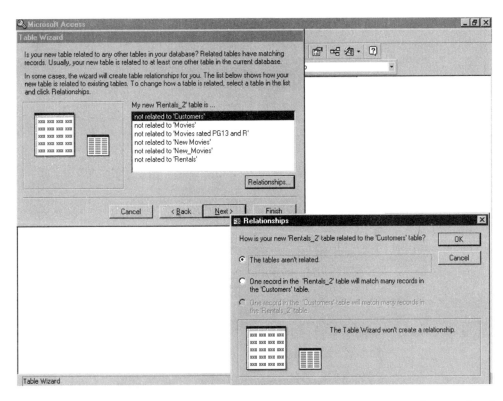

Figure 9–45 Identifying the relationship between the primary key and other tables.

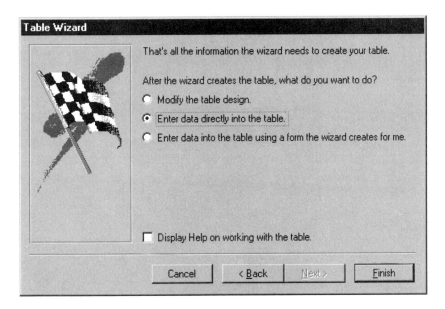

Figure 9–46 The last window in the Table Wizard process.

Now, you're done. That's all there is to using the Table Wizard to automatically create a new table in Access 97.

Moving On

This chapter introduced you to the new features in Access 97 that are tailored for Web database application development. You learned how to use these, as well as received an introduction on how to define databases and database objects, including populating tables with data.

In Chapter 10, "Access 97 Queries," you will learn how to construct simple queries against this data. You will build and execute these queries in Access 97. The concepts behind constructing efficient and effective queries, filtering data, sorting query results, which are accomplished via SQL, are discussed as well.

CHAPTER 10

Access 97 Queries

I n this chapter, you will learn how to construct simple queries against this data. You will see how to build and execute these queries in Access 97. The concepts behind constructing efficient and effective queries, filtering data, and sorting query results, which are accomplished via SQL, are discussed as well.

Introduction to Access 97 Queries

In Chapter 9 you learned how to use the new features in Access 97 that support Web database application development. You also learned how to create and modify databases and tables, as well as define indexes and associated indexes with other tables. In this chapter you will learn how to build and execute simple queries in Access 97. You will also learn how to use an external data source, including Open DataBase Connectivity (ODBC), in your Access 97 tables and queries. This information will assist you if you are using a development tool besides Access 97 to build your front-end Web database application.

Query, like Database, is a word that is often misused when applied to relational database technologies. The correct traditional definition of the word query is an SQL statement that enables the user to view information contained in one or more database tables. This term has been expanded recently to include any type of database access initiated by a user, including update and delete processing. So, for the purposes of this book, I'll define a query as any user-initiated SQL statement that performs a specific action against a database table.

In terms of Web database application development, queries are the components in the application that actually perform the database processing necessary to satisfy the request supplied by a user via a Web page. In this chapter you'll see the facilities in Access 97 to build and execute queries. With this as an introduction, you will learn how queries are formatted and submitted in Web database applications via Common Gateway Interface (CGI) programs in Chapter 13 of this book.

Access 97 includes some very nice query building facilities that you can incorporate in a number of ways in the construction of your Web database application.

- If you are using Access 97 as your front-end application development tool, write and execute the queries as part of your Web database application when you use the Publish to the Web Wizard.

- If you are not using Access 97 as your front-end application development tool, write and perfect the execution of the queries using the Query design tools, and then translate those queries to whatever front-end development tool you are using.

In this book I'll occasionally use the terms front-end and back-end. Front-end refers to the portion of the application that the user sees on his or her computer monitor and the processing that occurs on the user's computer, while back-end refers to the database components and access that are also a part of the application.

If you are not using Access 97 as your front end tool, you will like the Convert to SQL options. With it, the queries that you create using the Query by Example (QBE) interface can be converted to SQL syntax that you can then copy and paste into another Windows application. The QBE grid is a good place to start our discussion of writing and saving queries in Access 97. It is thought by many, including me, to be one of the very best (and easiest) query construction tools available.

Query Boundaries

As is the case with all software tools, Access 97 has limits to the queries that you can write. These are presented in the list below.

- Maximum number of tables in a single query is 32
- Maximum number of fields in a record set is 255
- Maximum number of characters in a parameter query is 255
- Maximum amount of hard disk space used in a record set is 1 gigabyte
- Maximum number of sorted fields in a query is 10
- Maximum number of nested levels in a query is 50
- Maximum number of characters in a QBE cell is 1,024
- Maximum number of AND, WHERE, or HAVING clauses is 40
- Maximum number of characters in an SQL statement is 64kb

As you can see, Microsoft has, in most cases, built large boundaries for you in Access 97. Although other more commercial RDBMS products such as Oracle and Sybase offer more extended boundaries, my belief is that the constraints described above are more than adequate for most commercial applications.

The following section introduces you to the Query by Example (QBE) grid; the graphical interface built by Microsoft to help you construct your queries.

The QBE Grid

As is the case with some of the other components in Access 97, there are a number of ways that you can access the QBE grid and build a query. All of these are accessed by clicking the Query tab on the Database window, as seen in Figure 10–1.

When you begin the process of designing a new query, Microsoft gives you a number of choices. These options are:

Design View	Launches the Query by Example grid process
Simple Query Wizard	Semi-automatically constructs a query based on fundamental pieces of information that you supply
Crosstab Query Wizard	Constructs a specialized cross tabulation query
Find Duplicates Query Wizard	Constructs a specialized query that helps you to find duplicate rows in a table

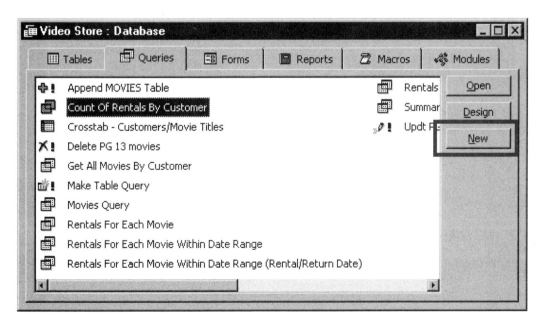

Figure 10–1   The Query tab of the Database window.

Find Unmatched Query	Constructs a specialized query that helps you find records in one table that don't have related records in another table. For example, you can find customers who don't have orders.

The Crosstab Query Wizard, Find Duplicates Query Wizard, and Find Unmatched Query processes are not discussed in this book as they are a type of query you probably won't use in a Web database application. If you want to learn more about how to construct these types of queries, I'd suggest one of the books listed at the beginning of Chapter 9.

Accessing the Design View Query Window

The Design View query process is very useful if you have at least a basic level of understanding of SQL queries. This process gives you the greatest amount of control of the structure of the query and the presentation of the result set. Also, because of the amount of control you have in the form of a graphical interface to how the query is constructed in the Design View mode, you don't have any issues of deleting unwanted columns or adjusting the format and layout of data from the way that the Simple Query Wizard would have constructed it.

Let's look at an example of a situation where the Design View method of creating a query would be used over the Simple Query Wizard. Let's say that you had some basic skills in writing SQL and your boss came to you asking for a report of the balance of all customers owing at least $25,000 to your company where the debt is at least 60 days old. In addition, he wants the results sorted and displayed in alphabetical sequence within geographical regions. Because of your knowledge of the database, you realize that to satisfy this request you have to:

- Join two tables (customer name and address table with the account aging table)
- Perform a complex search (list all customers whose account balances are greater than $25,000 and whose debt is at least 60 days old)
- Sort the result set by company name, within the 5 geographical regions in which the company operates

Because of this criteria, you know that the best way to construct this query is in Design View mode—the Simple Query Wizard just doesn't give you the flexibility and efficiency you need to construct this query as quickly as you could do it using Design View mode.

Let's take a look at how you would use the Design View mode to construct a query. To create a new query using the Design View process, follow these steps.

1. Open the Access 97 database that contains the database objects that you want to use. Do this by clicking on File|Open Database, and then selecting the desired database.

2. Click on the <New> button on the Database window. This brings up the New Query window, as seen in Figure 10–2.

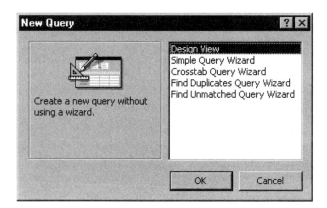

Figure 10–2   The New Query window.

3. If you click on the Design View option, then <OK>, you will be shown a window of all the tables in the currently opened database, as you see in Figure 10–3.

4. Repeatedly click on the table names that you want included in the query and then on the <ADD> button, until all the tables that are going to be part of the query are selected. Once this is accomplished, you will see the Query window in Figure 10–4.

Once you've come this far, you are ready to start building your query. Because of the amount of control and flexibility you have to tailor a query, there is too much information to cover in this chapter. I'll leave this discussion here and refer you to the entire Chapter 11. I do want to show you now how to access and construct a query using the Simple Query Wizard. The next section covers how to access the Query Window using the Simple Query Wizard process. The Simple Query Wizard, much like the Database and Table Wizards, allows you to more conveniently create a query with a much more intuitive, point-and-click interface.

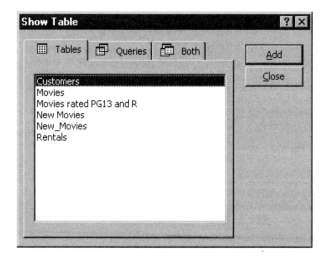

Figure 10–3   Select the tables that are part of the query.

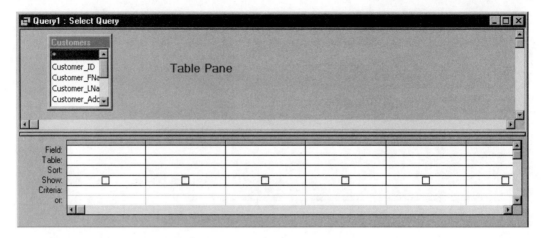

Figure 10–4   The Query window.

Accessing the Simple Query Wizard Query Window

The Simple Query Wizard is a great tool to use if you have very little or no experience using SQL or if you have experience using SQL but just need to create a simple SELECT-type query. Although you have no control over the structure of the query or the layout of the presentation of the result set, it does give you quick and easy access to your data.

Let's say that you have no skills in writing SQL and your boss comes to you asking for a report of all the customers in the Customer table in the database. You know that the best way to construct this query is using the Simple Query Wizard because you only need to access one table in the database and there are no selection criteria or sorting of the result set required. Let's take a look at how you would use the Design View mode to construct a query, using the Simple Query Wizard.

Open the Access 97 database that contains the database objects that you want to use. Do this by clicking on `File|Open Database`, and then selecting the desired database.

Click on the <New> button on the Database window. This brings up the New Query window, as seen in Figure 10–2.

First, click on the `Simple Query Wizard` option.

Then click on the <OK> button, and you will see a screen as in Figure 10–5. Use this window to select the table (or query) objects that are part of the query you are building. You can select the table(s) or queries that contain the objects in the Table/Queries list box, and then repeatedly click on the `Field Name` and right arrow (>) buttons to move the identified fields to the list of selected fields. You should notice that Access 97 uses the two-part dot notation to identify the database objects. The convention for this type of syntax is:

```
database-object-type.database-object-name
```

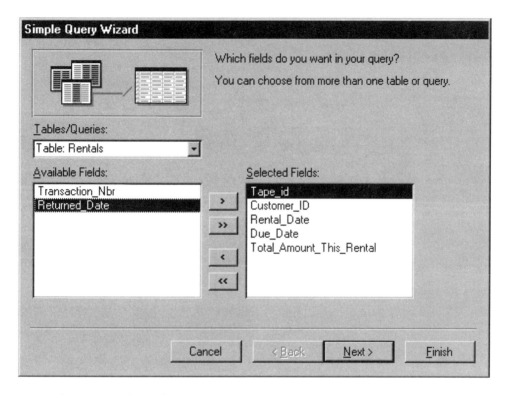

Figure 10–5 Select the table objects that are part of the query.

Warning! If two or more objects are in the table pane of the query, and no relationship exists between the objects, the output of the query will be a Cartesian Product. You want to avoid this! A Cartesian Product is a database table join process where every row of one table is concatenated to every row of another table, yielding a result set that combines the columns of both tables and has as many rows as the product of the number of rows in each. In simpler terminology, you'll get a really big table as a result that's a complete mess.

Using this interface, you can select as many fields as you like from as many database objects as are listed. (See the section titled Query Boundaries at the beginning of this chapter for a list of the limits that exist in Access 97.) Once you have selected all the fields that comprise your new query and pressed the <Next> button, you will be prompted to let Access 97 know if this is a detail or summary query.

Detail queries display every field selected of every record and provide no aggregation capabilities. Summary queries, as seen in Figure 10–6, allow you to specify aggregate functions on the fields selected for the query that are defined as integers.

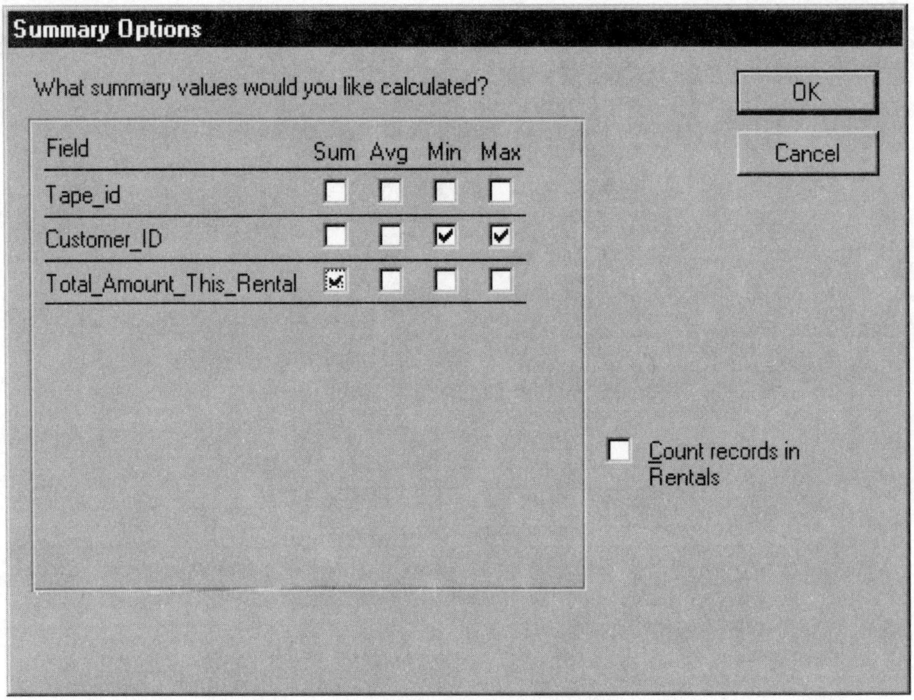

Figure 10–6 The Summary Query window where you define the fields to aggregate.

After you click <Next>, and if there are fields defined as dates in your field selection list, you will see the Date Aggregation screen, as seen in Figure 10–7.

If you don't want to group the result set by date, click the Unique date/time radio button. Otherwise, select the type of data grouping that you want to include in this query and then click the <Next> button.

When you do this, you will see the final window in the Simple Query Wizard process, as seen in Figure 10–8. This window asks if you want to open the query or modify the query design. If you are not happy with the query, click on the Modify query design radio button, otherwise, click on the Open the query to view information radio button.

When you have done one of the above steps, click on the <Finish> button to perform the following two steps automatically:

Save the query with the name specified in Figure 10–8. When you save a query, Access 97 saves it in a table that is only accessible from within Access 97. However, you can save the query in ASCII text format if you so choose using the File|Save As menu function.

Execute the query and show the result set, as seen in Figure 10–9.

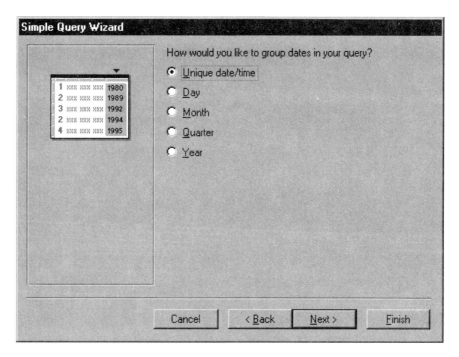

Figure 10–7   The Data Aggregation window.

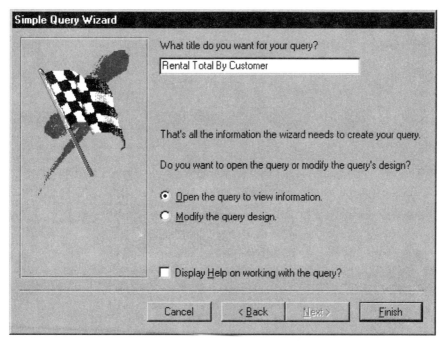

Figure 10–8   Supply a name for the newly created query.

Tape_ID	Rental_Date	Due_Date	Min Of Custom	Max Of Custon	Sum Of Total
1	3/1/97	3/2/97	1	1	$2.00
2	2/12/97	2/15/97	3	3	$6.00
3	3/18/97	3/19/97	2	2	$4.00
4	4/5/97	4/8/97	2	2	$4.00
5	2/12/97	2/15/97	3	3	$6.00
5	2/28/97	3/2/97	3	3	$8.00
5	4/2/97	4/3/97	5	5	$4.00
7	4/1/97	4/3/97	5	5	$4.00
8	3/11/97	3/12/97	5	5	$4.00
9	4/3/97	4/4/97	3	3	$8.00
12	4/11/97	4/12/97	5	5	$4.00

Record: 1 of 11

Figure 10–9   The result set from executing the query.

Queries are no different from other database objects—they all have properties. These properties can be modified to suit the needs of your application. Now that you've seen how to access the primary two methods of creating a query, let's take a look at setting the properties of Access 97 queries.

Setting Query Properties

Every object in an Access 97 database has properties. You access the properties dialog window for an object by right-clicking on that object. When you do that over a query object, you will see a Query Properties window, as seen in Figure 10–10.

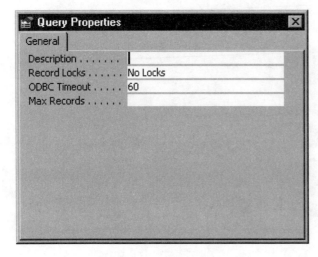

Figure 10–10   The properties dialog window for a query.

You assign properties to each individual query in a database. These properties become part of the query object to which they are defined. To adjust the properties for an individual query, follow the steps listed below:

1. Open the Access 97 database that contains the database objects that you want to use. Do this by clicking on `File|Open Database`, and then selecting the desired database.
2. From the Database window, click on the Query tab.
3. Select the query whose properties you want to modify by clicking once on its name.
4. Click on the `<Design>` button to access the Query Design screen.
5. With your cursor anywhere inside the table pane of the Query window, double-click to bring up the Query Attributes window. A brief description of each of the property attributes is shown in Table 10–1.

Each query has property settings that you can change to alter the way the query behaves and how the query results look. Because Access 97 gives you the ability to adjust the properties for each of your queries, the following list should give you some ideas on how the properties can be adjusted to fit any requirements that you may have.

- The server in which your Access 97 database is located is frequently down and unavailable during the day. You don't know when you run a particular query whether or not the database containing the data that the query reads is available or not, and you don't want your query to "hang" endlessly. So, you set the `ODBC Timeout` property to 15 seconds, thinking that if the query has not attached to the desired database in 15 seconds the conclusion is that the database is probably not available. This way, when the query runs and after 15 seconds still has not established a database connection, the user will receive an error message describing the problem.

- The table that the query reads is huge, with over 1.5 million records. A SELECT ALL query against such a huge dataset would ordinarily take a very long time and would create a huge result set. So, you set the `Max Records` property to 1000 rows, thinking that you can see what you're looking for in those 1000 rows. This way, when the query runs, it will only provide a result set that has a maximum of 1000 rows of data.

- The table that you want to access from within a query does not reside in the current database, but does exist in another database. Since you don't have to provide database/table information for queries that run against tables in the same database within which the query exists, this presents a problem. So, you set the `Source Database` property to point to the database that contains the table which the query needs to read. This way, when the query runs, it will automatically find and access the table it needs to read that exists in another database.

These are just a few of the ways that you can adjust query properties to tune them to your specific environment and needs. The next section introduces you to the process of joining tables in a query.

Table 10–1   Query Properties

Property	Description
Description	Up to 255 characters of descriptive information
Output All Fields	Specifies whether every field on the QBE is visible when the query runs
Top Value	Specifies the top nth percent of the records in the query
Unique Values	Specifies whether unique records only are returned
Unique Record	Similar to the Unique Values attribute, except this specifies whether only the unique records based on all fields in the underlying data source are returned.
Run Permissions	Specifies whether a user who would not otherwise have the necessary permissions is given permission to perform an action within the query
Source Database	This specifies a source database if the default is not to be used. The default database is the one that contains this query. This option allows you to execute queries defined for one database against another.
Source Connect String	This is a corollary attribute to Source Database in that it specifies the name of the application (and any additional database connection parameters) that was used to create or connect to the database.
Record Locks	In a multiuser system, this attribute specifies how the records are locked while the query is executing. Options are: No Locks, All Records, and Edited Records.
Recordset Type	This specifies whether the result set from the query is a dynaset or a snapshot. A dynaset is an editable result set returned from the execution of a query and a snapshot is a non-editable result set returned from the execution of a query.
ODBC Timeout	An important attribute when the database connected to it is networked, this establishes the length of time the executing workstation checks for a network connection response before the user is notified that she or he is no longer connected to the network.
Filter	This specifies a filter to be used when executing the query. This attribute is similar to the Filter by Form button in terms of what it does, but the Filter attribute does not require the user to know the correct syntax to specify a filter as the Filter by Form requires.
Order By	Very much like the Filter attribute, the Order By attribute allows the developer to specify a column by which to order the result set of the query without knowing the precise syntax to accomplish this.
Max Records	Specifies the maximum number of records to include in the result set when connecting to an ODBC data source

Joining Tables in a Query

Table joins is a method whereby you can relate the contents of one database table to the contents of another database table. For example, you may have a table that contains a list of all the employees in a company, and another table of all the departments that exist within a company. It would be advantageous to somehow relate the two tables so you can identify the names of the employees who work in each of the departments in the company. You can do such a thing by joining the employees table to the departments table and then executing your query from the joined result set.

When you view a query in the Design View mode (selected by clicking on `View|Design View` while viewing a query), any relationships that exist between the tables in the query are displayed in a manner similar to that in Figure 10–11. The lines that display in the window are drawn either *manually* or *automatically*.

Joining Manually

You can manually establish a relationship between two tables by following these six steps.

1. Open the Access 97 database that contains the database objects that you wish to use. Do this by clicking on `File|Open Database`, and then selecting the desired database.

2. Click on the `Query` tab to display all the queries defined to this database.

3. Select one of the queries by clicking on it and then click the `<Design>` button.

4. Click and hold down the left mouse button on any column in Table A from which you wish to form a relationship.

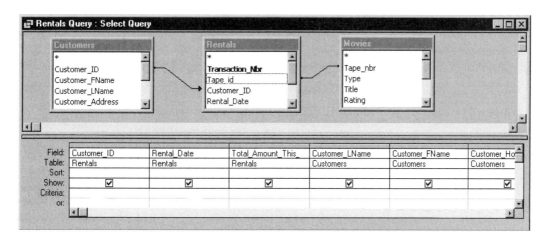

Figure 10–11   The Query Design view showing table relationships.

5. Drag the icon over to any column on Table B with which you wish to form a relationship.

6. Release the left mouse button and you will see that a line is drawn between the two selected columns/tables, indicating the acceptance of the relationship.

Joining Automatically

You can have Access 97 join relationships automatically, but before you do you must turn on the AutoJoin option. If it is not on, Access 97 will not attempt to perform the AutoJoin process. To enable AutoJoin, perform the following six steps.

1. Open the Access 97 database that contains the database objects that you wish to use. Do this by clicking on `File|Open Database`, and then selecting the desired database.

2. From the Database view, click on the `Query` tab.

3. Select a query by single-clicking on it and click on the `<Design>` button to enter the Query Design facility on the selected query.

4. Click on `Tools|Options`, and then on the `Tables|Queries` tab. This brings up the screen as seen in Figure 10–12.

5. To enable the AutoJoin process, make sure the Enable AutoJoin checkbox is checked. To disable it, remove the check from the box.

6. Click on `<OK>` to accept the changes.

Access 97 automatically identifies and describes a join relationship between columns in two tables in one of two ways; first, by determining a pre-existing relationship (a join, established either manually or automatically and saved) between the tables and second, based on the naming conventions used for the columns in the tables, by joining the fields in two or more tables if the fields have the same names and data types. In other words, if columns exist in two tables that have the same name and datatype, this will trigger an automatic join if these two tables are part of the same query.

It is good practice whenever you create a new query to check the join relationship that Access 97 recognizes. This is due to the facility built into the product which attempts to automatically join two tables. On occasion, Access 97 may establish a join relationship different from the one you want.

You can also access the Join Properties dialog box to identify or modify the type of join that exists between two tables. You do this in the manner described here.

1. Open the Access 97 database that contains the database objects that you wish to use. Do this by clicking on `File|Open Database`, and then selecting the desired database.

2. From the database view, click on the `Query` tab.

3. Select a query to work with and then click on the `<Design>` button.

4. Right click the mouse when the cursor is positioned on the join line that you want to look at or change. This brings up a dialog box letting you tell Access 97 whether you

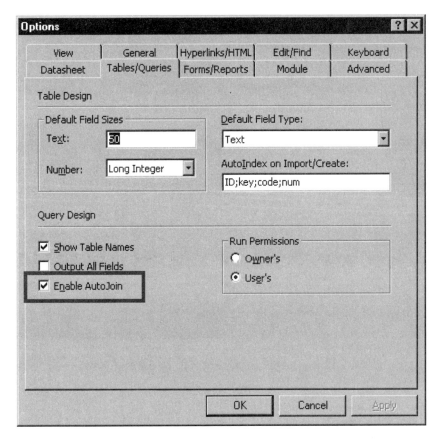

Figure 10–12   The AutoJoin option on the Options dialog box.

want to delete (remove) the join or work with the join properties. An example of this is seen in Figure 10–13.

5. Click on `Join Properties` and the dialog box seen in Figure 10–14 will display. On this screen you can identify one of three (and only three) possible join scenarios for the join operation. Select the type of join that suits your needs and click <OK>.

Types of Join Relationships

Access 97 recognizes three types of join relationships, as seen in Figure 10–14. These are described below.

• *Inner Join*. This is the default type of join. It joins the two tables *only* when the values in the two joined fields are equal.

• *Left Join*. This type of join takes all the records from the left-most table, regardless of whether the right-most table has any matching values in it. The left join frees you from having to concern yourself with whether or not there are any matching records in the right-most table. If there are none, the result set will be the left-most table.

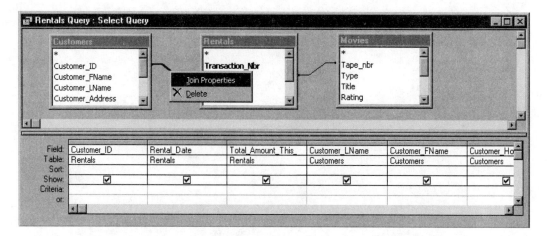

Figure 10–13 Let Access 97 know if you want to delete the Join or modify the properties.

- *Right Join*—This type of join takes all the records in the right-most table, regardless of whether the left-most table has any matching values in it. The right join frees you from having to be concerned with whether there are matching values in the left-most table as the result set will be the entirety of the right-most table only if there are none.

Accessing External Data

Up to this point you've seen how Access 97 queries can access Access 97 databases and tables, but this is not the only type of data that can be accessed from within Access 97. Access 97 gives you three methods you can use to access external (non-Access 97) data from within Access 97. These are:

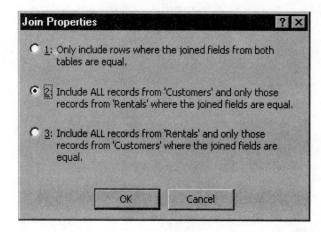

Figure 10–14 Select one of three possible join scenarios.

- Link the external table to the Access 97 application
- Open the external table directly from within the Access 97 application
- Import the data in the external table into the Access 97 application

The method you use in your application depends on many factors. To help you determine the best method for each situation, you should consider the following.

- If the application needs to access data held in the external table frequently, you should link to the external table. This is because Access 97 maintains the connection to linked tables for the duration of a session. The process of establishing and terminating a connection to an external table consumes a lot of resources and consequently takes a lot of time.
- If the data resides on an ODBC data source, you should always link the table rather than attempt to open it directly.
- If the table is installed on an Indexed Sequential Access Method (ISAM) data source, you could either link to the table or open it directly, depending on the unique requirements of your application.

External Data Access Requirements

You need to make sure that a few requirements are in place before you connect to an external data source. These requirements are:

- The external data needs to be accessible by your users, from an architectural perspective. In other words, if the data that the Access 97 application needs to read is on a server that is not recognized on the network, Access 97 surely won't find it either.
- The necessary ODBC drivers must be correctly installed and registered on your system. If you are using an Access 97 query to read a table in a Sybase database, you need to make sure that you have access to the correct Sybase ODBC drivers.
- The query you write that accesses the external data must not be prohibited. For example, OODBMS systems allow a data type of BLOB. Access 97 does not support this data type. If you tried to connect to this data source, your application would fail.

Establishing Access to External Data

Access 97 gives you two methods to use to establish access to external data, linking and importing. Linking allows you to access an external data source dynamically. As the data in the linked-to data source changes, your application views the changed data immediately. The connection to the linked data is established whenever a process is initiated from within Access 97 that needs the data.

Imported data is data that is imported once into an Access 97 table. If this data changes at the source at any time after it is imported into Access 97, your Access 97 application won't know about the changes.

Linking to External Data. To link to an external data source from within the Access 97 shell, perform the following steps:

1. Open the Access 97 database that contains the table that you want to receive the linked data. Do this by clicking on `File|Open Database`, and then selecting the desired database.

2. Click on `File|Get External Data`. Then click on the `Link Tables` option on the dialog popup.

3. As seen in Figure 10–15, you then identify the location and file name to which you want to establish a link. If you are attempting to link to an ODBC data source, one must already exist for the link to become effective. Once you have identified the correct data source, click on the `<OK>` button.

Once you have created a link, the type of link that it is can be modified afterwards. To do this, click on the `Tools|Add-ins` menu item, then click on the `Linked Table Manager` item.

To Import External Data.   To import external data into your Access 97 table(s), perform the following steps.

1. Open the Access 97 database that contains the table that you want to receive the imported external data. Do this by clicking on `File|Open Database`, and then selecting the desired database.

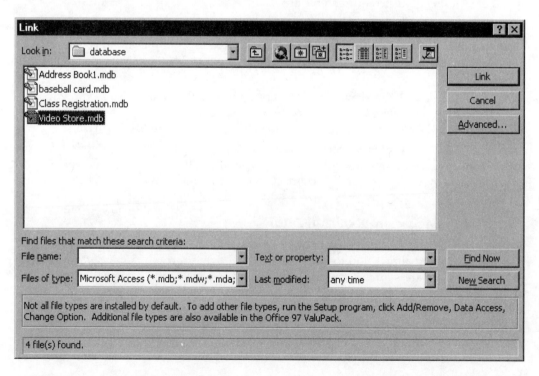

Figure 10–15   Selecting the location and name for the linked source data.

2. Click on `File|Get External Data`. Then click on the `Import` option on the dialog popup.

3. As seen in Figure 10–16, you then identify the location and file name from which you want to import data. If you are attempting to import from an ODBC data source, one must already exist for the import to work properly. Once you have identified the correct data source, click on the `<OK>` button.

Open DataBase Connectivity (ODBC) is Microsoft's standard cross-platform SQL API that allows programmers to create a gateway connection between an application program and a database engine. In the case of Access 97, this means that you can have an Access 97 query read and process information stored in a database from any vendor that supports ODBC, such as Oracle, Sybase, Informix, etc. The next section describes how to work with ODBC from within an Access 97 application.

Working with ODBC Connections

Access 97 works very well with ODBC. You'd expect this, though, as the same company is behind both the language and the standard. In this section you will learn how to manipulate the ODBC connections in Access 97.

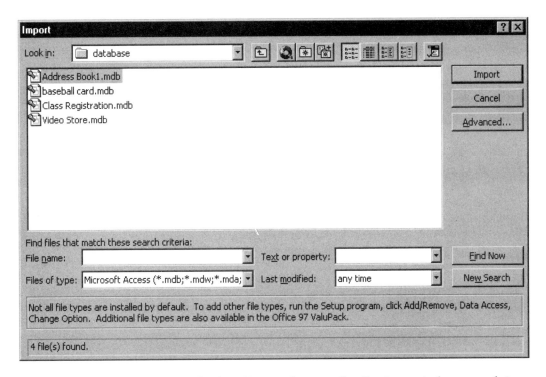

Figure 10–16 Selecting the location and name for the imported source data.

ODBC Connection String

As you've read, Access 97 tables and queries can connect directly to ODBC data sources. In a Web database application, this capability gives you tremendous flexibility in the design of the system. For example, you can have an Access 97 database, located outside the corporate firewall, link to Oracle data that resides behind the firewall in a secure environment. Or, you can populate an entire Access 97 database with replicated Access 97 data that resides in a database in a remote location with complete transparency to the user.

To connect a defined table to an ODBC data source, the required ODBC connection string is stored in the Description property of the table. It is created automatically by Access 97 if you link a table from the Access 97 menu. This was described in detail in Chapter 9, "Introduction to Access 97," but is presented again in these steps for reference purposes.

1. Open the Access 97 database that contains the table to which you wish to provide an ODBC link. Do this by clicking on `File|Open Database`, and then selecting the desired database.
2. Click on the Table tab in the Database window to provide you with a list of tables known to this database.
3. Click on a table to which you want to establish an ODBC link.
4. From the main menu, click on `File|Get External Data`.
5. From the submenu that displays, click on `Link Tables`.
6. Select the drive/path/location name of the table that you want to link to and click `<OK>`.

The connection strings in the following examples are supplied by the ODBC drivers that are provided by various database vendors. Their syntax and the meaning of the parameters does not usually need to be modified. However, if you do need to modify them, consult the documentation provided by the database vendor.

The following is an example of an ODBC connection string to link to another Access 97 table via ODBC as seen in the description property of a table:

```
DSN=Accounting;DBQ=H:\Finance\Database\Accounting.mdb;DriverID=25;FIL=MS
Access;MaxBufferSize=512;PageTimeOut=5;
```

In this example, the table name is `Accounting` and it resides in an Access 97 database located in a database named `Accounting.mdb` on the `h:\finance\database` disk/directory. These are the parameters indicated by you. The rest of the parameters in the connect string are provided by the ODBC driver.

The following is a connection string to attach to an SQL Server table:

```
ODBC;DSN=Pubs;APP=Microsoft Access;WSID=08;DATABASE=pubs;TABLE=dbo.
finance
```

In this example, the table name is `dbo.finance` and it resides in a database named `Pubs` that is in a disk/directory that SQL Server knows about but which is not required in this connect string. The rest of the parameters in the connect string are provided by the ODBC driver.

You should note that in each example, the connect strings are different. This is because of the nature of ODBC. Each RDBMS vendor that provides an ODBC interface into its product requires information to set up and manage the ODBC connection. The connect string supplies that information.

I'll give you an example of how to use connect strings to attach to an ODBC-compliant database (supplied by the fictitious ABC Database Corp.) from a Web database application that primarily accesses an Access 97 database.

Assume that you are a developer on a project for a company that sells widgets. Management wants you to build a Web application that lists all the different types of widgets the company makes and the number of each type available for order. Because of the design of the existing data, the information you need to list the different types of widgets is in an Access 97 table. Also, the inventory information that lists how many widgets are available for order are in a table managed by the ABC database. This, as you've seen above, is ODBC-compliant.

The first thing you do is to create an Access 97 table of inventory data, using an ODBC connection to link to the same information stored in the ABC inventory table. Once this is done, you build an Access 97 query that reads the information in your Access 97 product type table and matches it with the inventory information of number of products on hand in inventory as stored in the new Access 97 inventory table.

Now that the query is built that reads the required information, you build the necessary HTML Web pages and CGI programs to communicate with the Web users to read their requests and provide the results of the query. You are done.

Connect strings are established in a number of different ways. The most convenient way is to use the ODBC Data Source Administrator supplied with Windows NT and Windows 95. A print of this screen is seen in Figure 10–17. The use of this tool is outside the scope of this book because ODBC by definition must be non-Access 97 if you are running an Access 97 database or application. However, its intuitive and friendly graphical interface makes it a snap to identify a data source and establish an ODBC connection, provided the ODBC drivers exist. RDBMS vendors are responsible for providing the ODBC drivers. Microsoft keeps a pretty comprehensive collection of them on their Web site, `http://www.microsoft.com/odbc/`.

I can recommend the following for a more detailed analysis of ODBC:

Title:	Microsoft ODBC 3.0 Software Development Kit and Programmer's Reference
Author:	Microsoft
Publisher:	Microsoft Press
ISBN:	1-57-23151-64

Title:	Teach Yourself ODBC in 21 Days
Author:	Bill Whiting, Bryan Morgan, Jeff Perkins
Publisher:	Sam's Publishing
ISBN:	0-67-230609-3

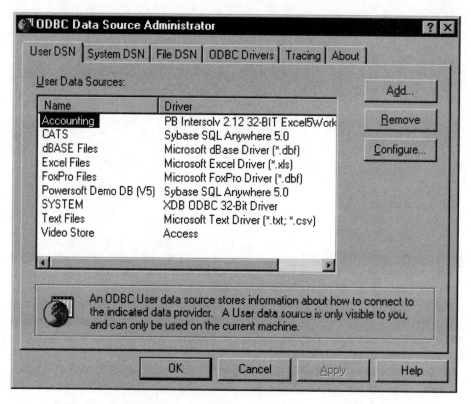

Figure 10–17   The ODBC Data Source Administrator.

Title:	Windows 95 Multimedia & ODBC API Bible
Author:	Richard J. Simon (Editor), Tony Davis, John Eaton, R. Murray Goertz
Publisher:	Waite Group Press
ISBN:	1-57-169011-5

Moving On

This chapter continued our foray into Access 97. You learned how to write a simple query using two methods, the Query Wizard and the QBE grid. With this as an introduction, you learned how to establish and maintain relationships between tables. Finally, you read about the capabilities in Access 97 to link to and read from external data sources, including ODBC data sources. In the next chapter, you will continue to learn more about Access 97 queries, this time focusing on the more advanced features.

CHAPTER 11

Designing
Advanced
MS Access
Queries

In this chapter you will go deeper into the facilities in Access 97 to create advanced queries. This includes using multiple aggregate functions, applying criteria in the query, parameter queries, nested queries, and optimizing performance of queries.

Specifically, we will discuss using the following SELECT statement clauses:

- The FROM clause
- The WHERE clause
- Using the GROUP BY clause
- The HAVING clause

The information discussed in this chapter is valuable to any developer using Access 97 as their back-end RDBMS, regardless of what front-end design and HTML tool is being used.

SELECT Statement Clauses

Before you begin learning the advanced query facilities in Access 97, a brief review of the clauses that comprise the SELECT statement is appropriate. If you are already familiar with these, skip to the *Using Group By* section of this chapter.

The SELECT clause is the primary way in which you, the developer, interact with the tables in a database. It is the basic SQL statement in not only Access 97 but all RDBMS products. The SELECT clause provides tremendous power and flexibility not only in querying data, but also in creating and deleting it.

Let's take a look at what happens when you write and submit the following SQL code from within a CGI program or Access 97:

```
SELECT last_name, first_name FROM name_table;
```

The Access 97 database engine receives the SQL code and translates it into machine-executable form. The Access 97 database engine then performs the SELECT. In this case, the query is designed to return the `last_name` and `first_name` fields for all the rows (records) that exist in the `name_table` table. Finally, the Access 97 database engine extracts the result set of the query from the `name_table` table and sends it back to the initiator (the CGI program or Access 97).

SELECT clauses can be written and executed from a number of sources. For the purposes of this book, the two primary sources are from within CGI programs and from within the Access 97 product. For the purposes of this chapter, it doesn't matter a bit which of these two methods initiate the SELECT statement. The operation of the query and the result sets returned are identical.

The control you exercise over what the SELECT statement does is available to you by using the various clauses in the SELECT statement. Let's take a look at a quite complex SELECT clause. I've picked a complex one as an example to illustrate the clauses that are discussed in this chapter.

The following SELECT statement is one you'd write if you worked for a Video Rental store and your boss came to you with a request to produce a report that showed the following:

- The aggregate total of the tape rental for each customer for all the times he or she had rented movies from the store

- The average amount of tape rental paid by each customer for each time he or she came to the store to rent movies

- The least amount paid at any one time by each customer who had ever been in the store to rent movies

- The most amount paid at any one time by each customer who had ever been in the store to rent movies

Further, the SELECT statement creates a result set of this information and places the result set in Customer_Id sequence.

```
SELECT DISTINCTROW Rentals.Customer_ID, Rentals.Rental_Date,
Rentals.Due_Date, Customers.Customer_LName, Customers.Customer_FName,
Sum(Rentals.Total_Amount_This_Rental) AS [Sum Of Total_Amount_This_
Rental], Avg(Rentals.Total_Amount_This_Rental) AS [Avg Of Total_Amount_
This_Rental], Min(Rentals.Total_Amount_This_Rental) AS [Min Of
Total_Amount_This_Rental], Max(Rentals.Total_Amount_This_Rental) AS [Max
Of Total_Amount_This_Rental], First(Customers.Customer_Home_Page) AS
[First Of Customer_Home_Page], Count(*) AS [Count Of Rentals]
```

```
FROM Customers INNER JOIN Rentals ON Customers.Customer_ID = Rentals.
Customer_ID
GROUP BY Rentals.Customer_ID, Rentals.Rental_Date, Rentals.Due_Date,
Customers.Customer_LName, Customers.Customer_FName
ORDER BY Rentals.Customer_ID DESC;
```

The clauses in the SELECT statement must appear in the following sequence, otherwise, you'll probably receive a syntax error.

```
SELECT tablename(s).column(s)
  FROM        tablename(s)
  WHERE       condition(s)
  GROUP BY tablename(s).column(s)
  ORDER BY tablename(s).column(s)
  HAVING      condition(s);
```

Using the QBE forms though, you won't have to touch the SQL very much, but you still need to be familiar with it and understand it if you're going to use another front-end other than Access 97 to query your Access 97 database.

Table 11–1 lists the various clauses in the SELECT statement. All the clauses are not mandatory. In fact, the only clause that is mandatory in a SELECT statement is: `SELECT column-list FROM table-name`. In the syntax of the following SELECT statement, the boldface components are required words, while the italicized components are to be provided by you:

Table 11–1   The SELECT Clause Parameters

Clause	Description
SELECT	Lists the column(s), data function(s), or aggregate function(s) to include in the result set.
FROM	Identifies the table(s) or query used as the source against which to execute this query. A query identified in the FROM clause of a SELECT statement is an example of a *nested query*.
WHERE	This clause is used a number of different ways: To qualify the result set to specified criteria To link tables listed in the FROM clause To specify a criteria for an UPDATE or DELETE process
GROUP BY	Combines rows with matching values into groups using one or many functions. This clause is almost always used with aggregate functions.
ORDER BY	Sorts the result set of the query into a specified sequence. The default sequence is ascending.
HAVING	This is a corollary clause to the GROUP BY clause and limits the amount of data returned to the result set by the aggregate function.

```
SELECT  tablename(s).column(s)
   FROM          tablename(s)
   WHERE         condition(s)
   GROUP BY tablename(s).column(s)
   ORDER BY tablename(s).column(s)
   HAVING        condition(s);
```

The complex query example listed previously for the video rental store includes a number of aggregate clauses, such as SUM and AVG. Later in the chapter, in the section titled Aggregate Functions, you'll see how to create nested queries. For now though, think of aggregate functions as components of the SELECT statement that give you the ability to perform arithmetic functions on the result set returned from a SELECT statement. Before getting into aggregate functions and nested queries, you should learn a bit more about the Group By clause.

If two or more tables are joined in a SELECT statement, the query must include either a WHERE or a JOIN clause. Failure to do so will create a Cartesian Product result set, and you will not be invited to the annual Christmas party thrown by the company's DBA.

The FROM Clause

The one and only purpose of the FROM clause is to inform the SQL processor what tables in the database against which the query is to be executed. It is not only possible (and frequently required) that you identify more than one table in the FROM clause, but these tables do not need to be in the same database as the other tables. In the video store example earlier in this chapter, the FROM clause indicates that the SELECT statement is to execute against two tables, the RENTALS table and the CUSTOMER table.

For example, consider an application in which you want to compare information that resides in a table in the current database against archived information for the same table in a backup database. As seen here, this is possible:

```
SELECT Accounts.Acct_nbr, Hist_Accts.*
   FROM      Accounts, Hist_Accts IN
   MyCompany.MDB
   WHERE     Accounts.Acct_nbr = Hist_Accts;
```

This code will match a table in the current database named Accounts with a table in a database named Hist_Accts (this is the FROM clause at work), and produce a result set that contains the Acct_nbr column in the Account table and all the fields in the Hist_Accts table whenever there is a match on the Acct_nbr columns in the two tables that are a part of this query.

Another common use for the FROM clause is to assign *aliases* to table names. An alias is a temporary name given to a table that is only active for the execution of the query. This is frequently done to condense the amount of code that is written to create the SQL statement. Using the previous example, it could be rewritten using aliases as follows:

```
SELECT Accounts.Acct_nbr, Hist_Accts.*
   FROM      Accounts AS A, Hist_Accts IN
   MyCompany.MDB AS B;
   WHERE     A.Acct_nbr = B;
```

Now that you've seen how the FROM clause in a SELECT statement works, let's take a look at the WHERE clause, which you know is being used to accomplish one of the following:

- To qualify the result set to specified criteria
- To link tables listed in the FROM clause
- To specify a criteria for an UPDATE or DELETE process

The WHERE Clause

The WHERE clause has a dual purpose in an SQL statement:

- To constrain and reduce the size of the result set of a query and
- To join two or more tables together.

The format of the WHERE clause in an SQL statement is as follows:

```
WHERE tablename.columnname or [expression] [OPERATOR] [comparison value]
```

An example of a simple WHERE clause is:

```
WHERE MOVIES.RATING = "PG13"
```

An example of a WHERE clause using an expression as its operand is:

```
WHERE (format([RENTALS.DATE_RENTED],'yymmdd')) > 970401
```

The [OPERATOR] can be an Access 97 mathematical operator (in the example above the OPERATOR is the greater than sign, ">") or one of the operators described in Table 11–2.

As you know, one of the uses of the WHERE clause is to join two or more tables together for the query. There are five ways that tables can be joined (Inner Join, Self Join, Left Outer Join, Right Outer Join, and Full Outer Join), all of which are discussed in the following sections.

Table 11–2   The Operators Allowed in a WHERE Clause

Operator	Description
AND	Used to join two or more conditions together
OR	Used to identify two or more conditions that will return a result set if any of the specified conditions are found true
IN	Used to compare the values in a column against a series of possible values
BETWEEN	Used to compare the values in a column as being in a range of values identified by a lower and an upper boundary
IS NULL	Used to extract all the rows where the values for a specified column are NULL
LIKE	Used to extract rows where a column that is defined as text contains a specified string pattern

Inner Join.   This is the most common type of join and is the result of linking two tables together on a matching, common column. When the columns for the identified tables (the FROM clause) are matched, the entire row for each table is made available as the result set. The following is an example of an inner join.

```
SELECT ACCOUNTS.ACCOUNT_NBR, HISTORY.*
  WHERE ACCOUNTS.ACCOUNT_NBR = HISTORY;
```

In this example, the ACCOUNTS and HISTORY tables will be joined together on a column named ACCOUNT_NBR. Inner joins only select rows from the listed tables where the joined fields are equal.

Self Join.   A self join is a type of join where one table is joined to itself, producing a result set that is the sum of tables duplicated. This is the least frequently used type of join and is only used in rare circumstances. The following is an example of a self join.

```
SELECT A1.Acct_Desc, A1.Acct_Bal, COUNT(A1.Acct_Owner)
  AS Acct_Rank
  FROM [Account_Stats] AS A1, [Account_Stats] AS A2
  WHERE (((A1.Acct_Bal) < [A2].Acct_Bal]))
  GROUP BY A1.Account_Desc, A1.Acct_Bal
  ORDER BY COUNT(A1.Acct_Owner);
```

This query produces a result set as seen below:

Account_Desc	Acct_Bal	Acct_Rank
Deposits	$1,120.05	1
Withdrawal	$912.00	2
Service Charge	$21.18	3
Reversals	$18.11	4

In this code example, you recognize that this is a self join because of the FROM clause, which assigns different alias names to the same table. The purpose of this SELECT statement is to aggregate and then rank the balances of the different types of accounts in the Account_Stats table, and then to list the ranking order in the result set.

Access 97 does not allow self joins at this time. The description above is provided to give you an understanding of this type of join as many other tools provided by RDBMS vendors allow this type of join.

Left Outer Join.   A left outer join is a join in which all the columns in the left-most table (the first table listed in the FROM clause) are included in the result set, whether or not there is a matching value in the right column (the second table listed in the FROM clause). It is useful in a situation where you want to include in the result set all the rows in the first table listed in the FROM clause, and only those rows in the second table listed in the FROM clause that are a match to the first table.

The type of join you want, Left Outer Join or Right Outer Join, is determined by the order that the tables are listed in the FROM clause.

Table 11–3 shows the tables that will be used to explain the left outer join, right outer join, and full outer join.

Table 11–3   The Rows and Columns in Two Very Small Tables

Table A		Table B	
C1	**C2**	**CA**	**CB**
A	10	10	S
B	20	20	T
C	20	60	U
D	40		
E	50		

A left outer join on the tables in Table 11–3 would produce the following result set.

C1	**C2**	**CA**	**CB**
A	10	10	S
B	20	20	T
C	20	20	T
D	40	Null	Null
E	50	Null	Null

Right Outer Join.   A right outer join is the opposite of a left outer join. In a right outer join, all the columns in the right-most table (the last table listed in the FROM clause) are included in the result set, whether or not there is a matching value in the left columns (the first table listed in the FROM clause).

A right outer join on the tables would produce the following result set:

C1	**C2**	**CA**	**CB**
A	10	10	S
B	20	20	T
C	20	20	T
Null	Null	60	U

Full Outer Join.   A full outer join is a combination of both the left outer join and the right outer join. It also combines all of the columns in the left-most table (the first table listed in the FROM clause) that do not have a match with any of the columns in the right-most table (the last table listed in the FROM clause), and all of the columns in the right-most table that do not have a match in the left-most table.

A full outer join on the tables would produce the following result set:

C1	C2	CA	CB
A	10	10	S
B	20	20	T
C	20	20	T
D	40	Null	Null
E	50	Null	Null
Null	Null	60	U

Access 97 does not have a full outer join clause at this time. The information described above is provided to help you understand what a full outer join is as some of the other RDBMS tools provided by other software vendors provide this.

Now let's take a look at the GROUP BY clause, which is used to describe how matching rows of data are combined and summarized.

Using GROUP BY

GROUP BY is a component of the SELECT statement that is used to combine matching rows of data and to return the summarized result set. GROUP BY functions are normally used in combination with aggregate functions—but this is not a requirement. GROUP BY can also be used to group individual columns. The query in Figure 11–1 is an example of a query using the GROUP BY clause.

In this example, you see that the query will group the output by the column `movies.title`, and it will use the `count` function to count the number of entries (rows) there are in the Rentals table. This is precisely what we'd want to see in a query that was designed to show us the most popular movies. The SQL that executes the query shown in Figure 11–1 is seen in Figure 11–2. When you are in the QBE grid, you can see the SQL automatically generated by clicking on `View|SQL View` on the menu.

Figure 11–3 shows the Datasheet view for this query. You access the Datasheet view by clicking on the `View|Datasheet View` menu item.

To identify a column that you want to include in a Group By clause, do the following:

1. While in the Datasheet view window, at the bottom of the screen in the grid area, click on the row titled Total.

2. Right click in the right hand side of this cell and you will see a drop-down list box of the various Total options Access 97 allows on the identified column. This is seen in Figure 11–4.

3. Scroll the list until you find the Group By item. Make sure it is selected (in reverse video) and left click on it to select it.

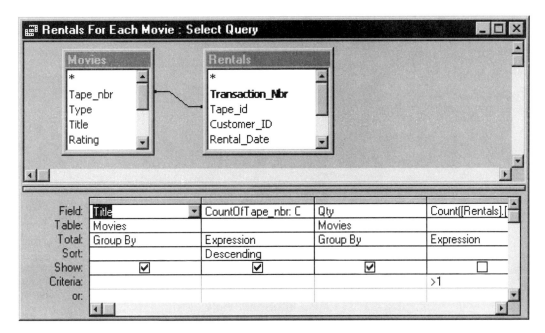

Figure 11–1   A query using GROUP BY.

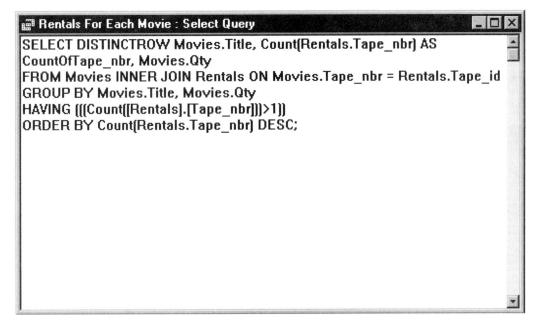

Figure 11–2   The SQL generated showing the GROUP BY clause.

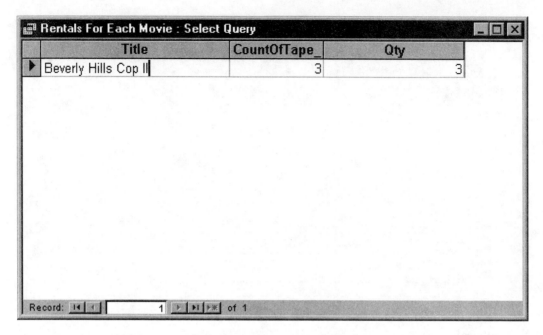

Figure 11–3   The DataSheet view of the query.

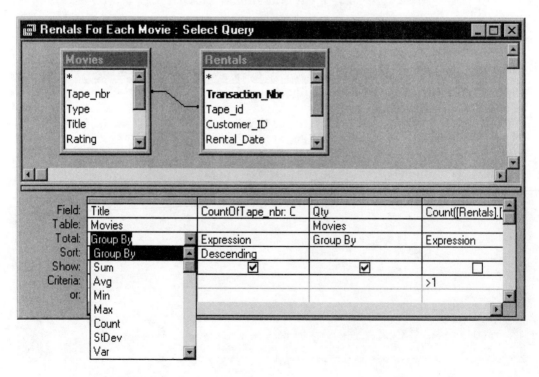

Figure 11–4   Specifying a GROUP BY clause.

An Example of the GROUP BY Clause.   In the examples in this section, you'll see the effects of identifying a specific column in a table to include in a GROUP BY clause, and how the result set changes based on how you specify the GROUP BY clause. As seen in Figure 11–5, the first example specifies that you are wanting to execute the Count function on the `Tape-Nbr` column. You would do this if you wanted to see how many times each movie had been rented, or what are the most popular movies.

Figure 11–6 shows the results of executing the query specified in Figure 11–5.

Now, if you change the type of query by requesting a Group By clause on the `Tape_nbr` column, as seen in Figure 11–7, the result set from the query looks quite different, as seen in Figure 11–8.

Aggregate Functions

Using aggregate functions in a SELECT statement allows you to perform arithmetic functions on a specific group or groups of data. Table 11–4 lists the available aggregate functions and the datatypes against which the function is valid.

Aggregate functions are selected and used the same way that a GROUP BY clause is identified in the QBE grid. As seen in Figure 11–9, the COUNT aggregate function is selected for the `Tape_nbr` column and in this example provides a list of the number of times each movie had been rented. The result of this should be a count of the number of rows that exist in the source table for each movie title.

The result of this query is seen in Figure 11–10. As expected, this shows the number of times each movie title has been rented.

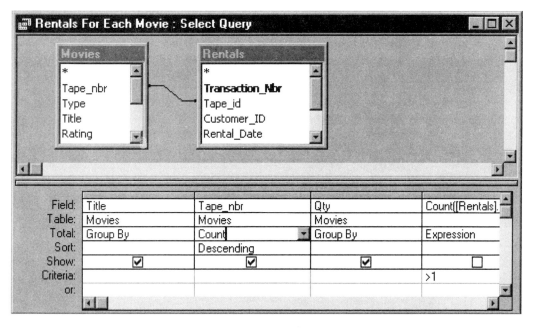

Figure 11–5   Specifying the Count function on the Tape_nbr column.

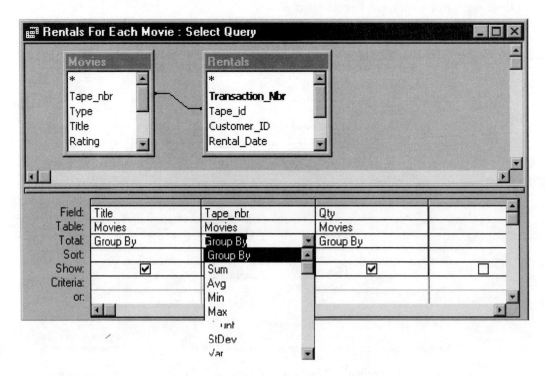

Rentals For Each Movie : Select Query

Title	CountOfTape_	Qty
▶ Beverly Hills Cop II	3	3
Speed	1	8
Somewhere In Time	1	12
Lion King	1	18
Cinderella	1	17
Bridges Of Madison County	1	29
Beverly Hills Cop	1	4
Best Of The WWF	1	10
Apollo 13	1	10

Record: 1 of 9

Figure 11–6 Results of using the Count function on the Tape_nbr column.

Rentals For Each Movie : Select Query

Movies
- *
- Tape_nbr
- Type
- Title
- Rating

Rentals
- *
- **Transaction_Nbr**
- Tape_id
- Customer_ID
- Rental_Date

Field:	Title	Tape_nbr	Qty	
Table:	Movies	Movies	Movies	
Total:	Group By	Group By	Group By	
Sort:		Group By		
Show:	☑	Sum	☑	☐
Criteria:		Avg		
or:		Min		
		Max		
		unt		
		StDev		
		Var		

Figure 11–7 Specifying the GROUP BY clause on the Tape_nbr column.

228

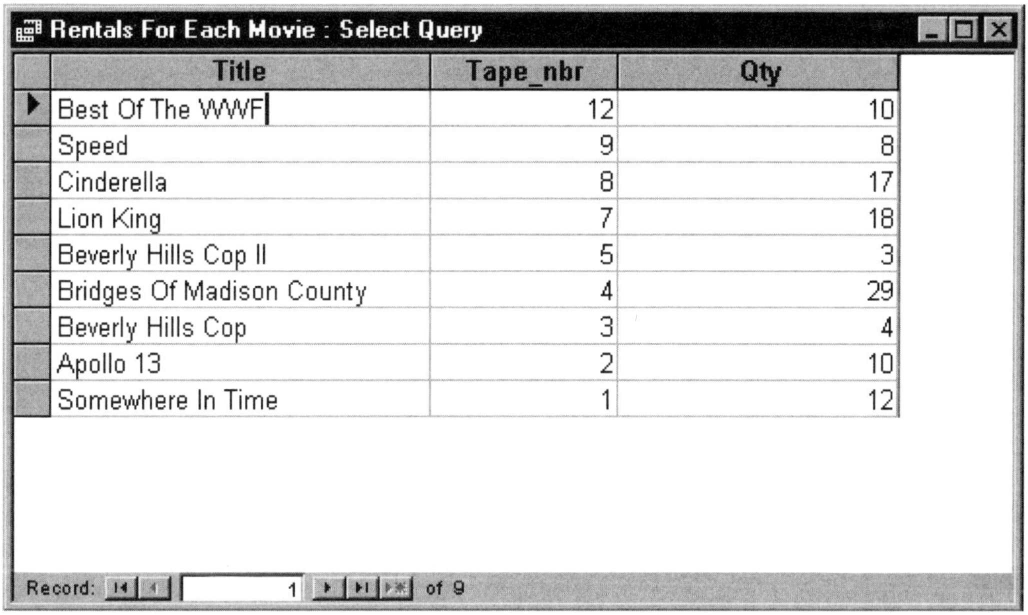

Rentals For Each Movie : Select Query

Title	Tape_nbr	Qty
Best Of The WWF	12	10
Speed	9	8
Cinderella	8	17
Lion King	7	18
Beverly Hills Cop II	5	3
Bridges Of Madison County	4	29
Beverly Hills Cop	3	4
Apollo 13	2	10
Somewhere In Time	1	12

Record: 1 of 9

Figure 11–8 Results of using the Group By clause on the Tape_nbr column.

Table 11–4 Aggregate Functions Allowed in a SELECT Query

Function	Description	Datatypes
SUM	Adds the values in a column	Number, Date/Time, Currency, AutoNumber
AVG	Averages all the values in a column	Number, Date/Time, Currency, AutoNumber
MIN	The lowest value in a column	Text, Number, Date/Time, Currency, AutoNumber
MAX	The largest value in a column	Text, Number, Date/Time, Currency, AutoNumber
COUNT	The number of non-null rows in a column	All
STDEV	Standard deviation for a sample of all the values in a specified column	Number, Date/Time, Currency, AutoNumber
STDEVP	Standard deviation for all the values in a column	Number, Date/Time, Currency, AutoNumber
VAR	Variance for a sample of all the values in a specified column	Number, Date/Time, Currency, AutoNumber
VARP	Variance for all the values in a specified column	Number, Date/Time, Currency, AutoNumber
FIRST	The first row's value for the specified column	All
LAST	The last row's value for the specified column	All

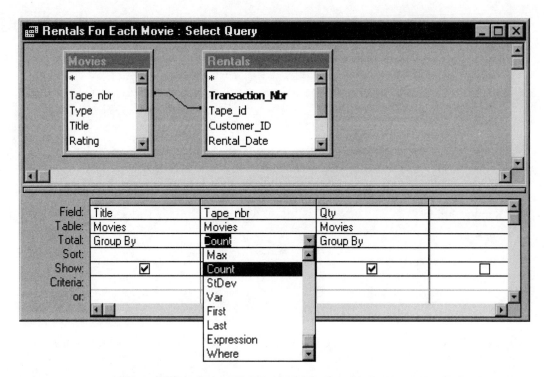

Figure 11–9   Using the Count aggregate function.

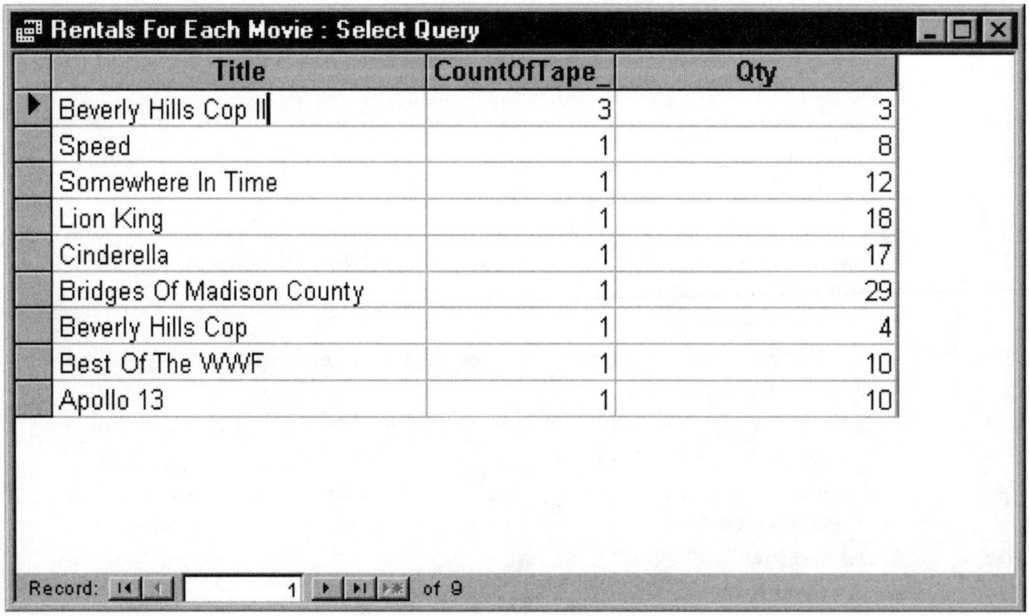

Title	CountOfTape_	Qty
Beverly Hills Cop II	3	3
Speed	1	8
Somewhere In Time	1	12
Lion King	1	18
Cinderella	1	17
Bridges Of Madison County	1	29
Beverly Hills Cop	1	4
Best Of The WWF	1	10
Apollo 13	1	10

Record: ◄◄ ◄   1   ► ►► ►* of 9

Figure 11–10   The results of executing the Count aggregate function.

If the query that includes the aggregate function returns a result that contains less than three rows, the STDEV, STDEVP, VAR, and VARP aggregate functions will return an empty (blank) result set. This is because the result set can not be calculated for these functions.

The HAVING Clause

Like the GROUP BY clause, the HAVING clause is used in conjunction with aggregate functions. It limits the size of the result set returned from the query in a way similar to the WHERE clause. What is dissimilar is that the HAVING clause can limit the data returned in the result set based on an aggregate function. Using a HAVING clause is what is sometimes referred to as post criteria aggregation.

You specify the HAVING criteria on the QBE grid in the row labeled Criteria. Looking back to Figures 11–9 and 11–10, you can see that the result set returned from the query contains nine rows, with a value in the CountOfTape_nbr column ranging from a high of three to a low of one. Consider a query where you'd only want to see the titles of the movies that were rented more than one time. This is a good example of a post criteria aggregation that results in the addition of a HAVING clause included in the SELECT statement.

As seen in Figure 11–11, the HAVING clause specification of only showing the movie titles that have been rented more than one time is done in the Criteria row on the QBE form. In the Criteria row on the QBE grid, under the column heading Tape_Nbr, you see a value in the cell that reads > 1. This is the HAVING clause.

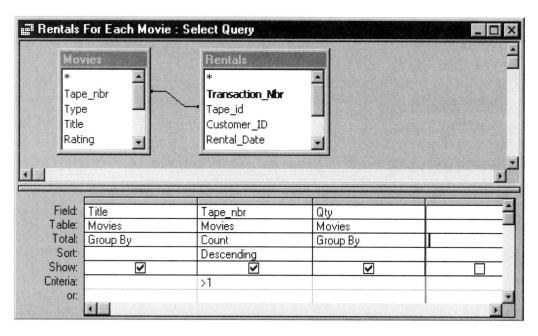

Figure 11–11 Specifying the HAVING clause.

Figure 11–12 shows what the SQL would look like for this query, and Figure 11–13 shows the result set returned when this query is run.

Parameter Queries

Parameter queries are an important part of a Web database application in that they allow the user to specify at run-time a value or range of values as input to the way the query processes. They are invaluable in situations where you want to design a query that allows the person who executes the query to supply critical selection values at the time the query is run. When a parameter query is run, Access 97 displays a small dialog box that prompts the user to supply the missing parameter.

Consider an example where we again turn to our Video Store business. In any family-oriented video rental business, there are videos in the store that are rated from G to NR. You could design and write a number of queries that list the movies in stock for each of the rating categories. Or, you could design and write one query that allows the user to specify the rating of the movies he or she are interested in at the time the query is executed. This is an example of a situation for which a parameter query is ideally suited.

Syntax of Query Parameters

If you want to include a parameter in a query, Access 97 lets you do this by enclosing the parameter in square brackets ([ ]). Square brackets in an Access 97 query signify an alphanumeric prompt. For example, consider the QBE form as seen in Figure 11–14. You

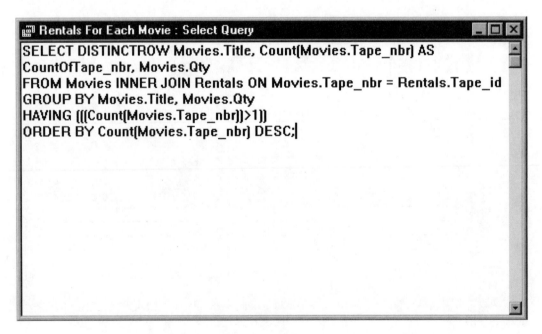

Figure 11–12   The SQL for a SELECT using the HAVING clause.

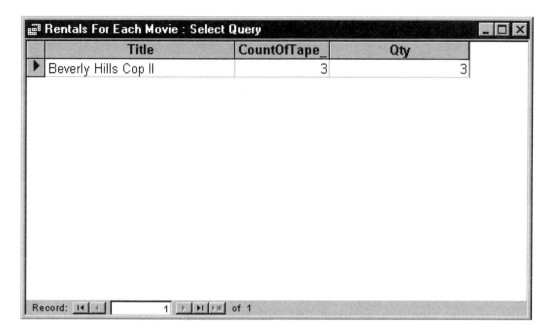

Figure 11–13   The result set from a Having-clause query.

can see that a criteria is specified and enclosed in square brackets. The text enclosed in the brackets is "State of Residence."

In Figure 11–15, the line of code immediately before the SELECT statement instructs Access 97 to prompt the user to supply the information requested. You must supply a data type if one is not supplied for you by Access 97.

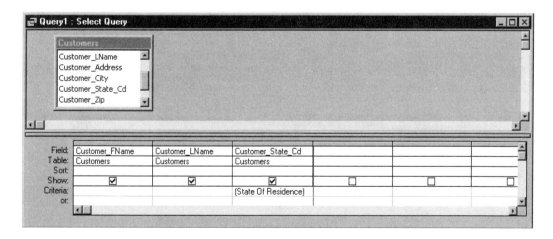

Figure 11–14   The QBE form with a parameter query.

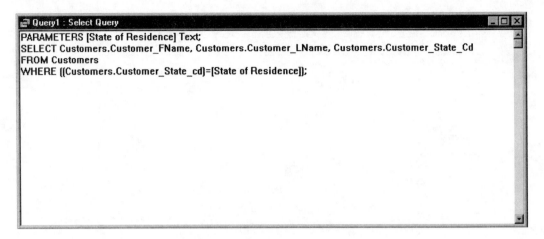

Figure 11-15   The SQL syntax for a parameter query.

When this query executes, Access 97 will format and display a query box, asking the user to supply the required information prior to the execution of the query. This is seen in Figure 11-16.

Finally, when the user supplies the information and the query executes, the result set displayed will be for the query the user requested, as seen in Figure 11-17.

Multiple Parameter Queries

The syntax and processes used to define and use a multiple parameter query are identical to those used to define a single parameter query. Consider the following example.

In the Movie Rental database, you want to define a query to extract the names of all the movies that have a rating and rental date within a range that you won't be able to determine until run time. The first step is to use the Query Wizard to build a basic query, extracting the columns you want to see. Once this is done, you can go into the SQL View of the query, as seen in Figure 11-18, and describe the parameters (movie rating and beginning and ending of date range) that you will provide at runtime.

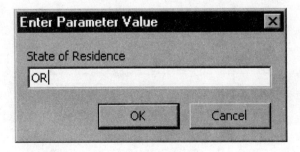

Figure 11-16   The parameter query prompt box.

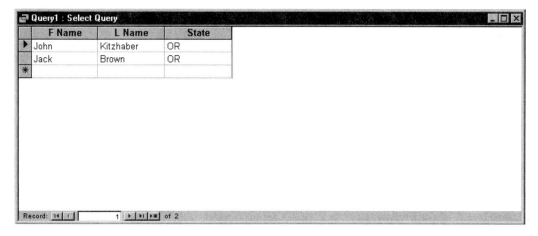

Figure 11–17   The result set from the parameter query.

When you switch to Design View, you will see the parameters on the two columns displayed in the QBE grid (Figure 11–19).

You could also specify the multiple parameters in your query using the QBE grid. I am familiar with SQL syntax and feel more comfortable adding the parameters in the SQL View.

Figures 11–20 through 11–22 are the dialog windows displayed during runtime. Once the required parameter information is supplied, the query can run.

The result from this query is shown in Figure 11–23.

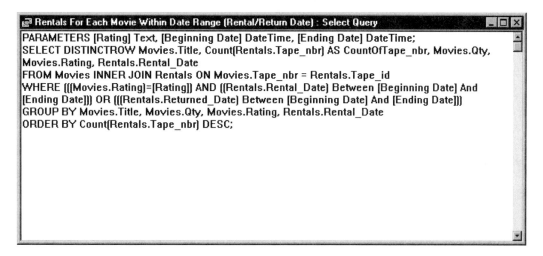

Figure 11–18   Describing the parameters in the multiple parameter query.

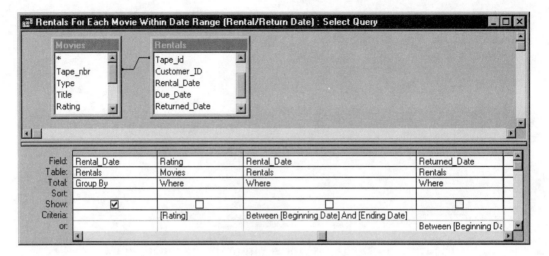

Figure 11–19   The QBE grid and multiple parameters.

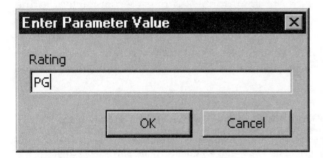

Figure 11–20   Supplying the Rating runtime parameter.

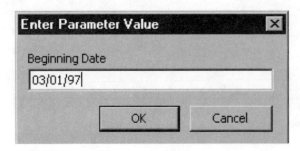

Figure 11–21   Supplying the Beginning Date runtime parameter.

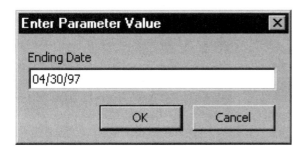

Figure 11–22   Supplying the Ending Date runtime parameter.

Specifying Multiple Occurrences of the Same Query Parameter

The same parameter can be used to select from multiple columns. Access 97 recognizes that this is your intention provided you abide by one single requirement; the parameter name must be the same among the columns that you intend it to be the same on.

Consider an example of a situation in which you want to query the database for all tapes of a certain rating that were either rented or returned within a certain range of dates. When this query executes, since the date range you provide is the same, you do not want to have to enter the date range two times—once to compare with the rental_date column and once again to compare with the return_date column.

Figure 11–24 shows what this query would look like in the QBE grid. Notice that the names for the parameters in the Criteria row for the rental_date and return_date columns are identical. This is what you'd want. In Figure 11–25, you see what this query looks like in the SQL View.

Rentals For Each Movie Within Date Range (Rental/Return Date) : Select Query				
Title	**Tape_nbr**	**Qty**	**Rating**	**Rental_Date**
Best Of The WWF	12	10	PG 13	4/11/97
Speed	9	8	PG 13	4/3/97
Cinderella	8	17	PG 13	3/11/97
Lion King	7	18	PG 13	4/1/97
Beverly Hills Cop II	5	3	PG 13	2/28/97
Beverly Hills Cop II	5	3	PG 13	4/2/97
Bridges Of Madison County	4	29	PG 13	4/5/97
Beverly Hills Cop	3	4	PG 13	3/18/97
Somewhere In Time	1	12	PG 13	3/1/97

Record: |◄|◄| 1 |►|►||►*| of 9

Figure 11–23   The result set from the multiple parameter query.

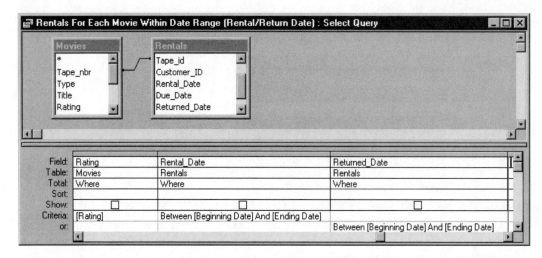

Figure 11–24   Supplying multiple occurrences of the same parameter.

When this query executes, the user will be prompted to enter just three pieces of information before the query actually executes.

- The rating of the movie
- The beginning date in the date range to check against the Rental_Date and Return_Date columns
- The ending date in the date range to check against the Rental_Date and Return_Date columns

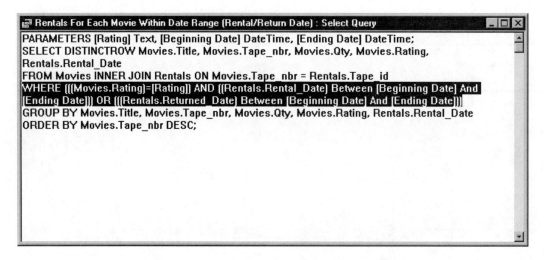

Figure 11–25   SQL View of this query.

When the requested information is input and the query executes, the result set returned will contain the results of the query with all three selection criteria applied.

Specifying Parameter Data Types

Access 97 attempts to determine the correct data type for a parameter you specify as part of a query. Most of the time, it gets it right. When it doesn't guess right, your query will not run. There are two methods you can use to specify the data type for parameters.

- While in the SQL View, add a PARAMETERS line before the SELECT statement, as seen in Figure 11–26. On this line supply the parameter names and a specification of the data type.
- While in the Design View, click on `Query|Parameters`. This will bring up a Query Parameters dialog box where you can explicitly describe the data types for any or all supplied parameters. This is seen in Figure 11–27.

Nested Queries

Nested queries are queries that are based on the result set of another query (or combination of queries and tables). There are a number of reasons why you would want to design a nested query. These are:

- To accelerate query design by query reuse
- Because nested queries are more manageable
- To offload as much of the processor requirements onto the server machine
- To propagate changes made in queries by changing base queries

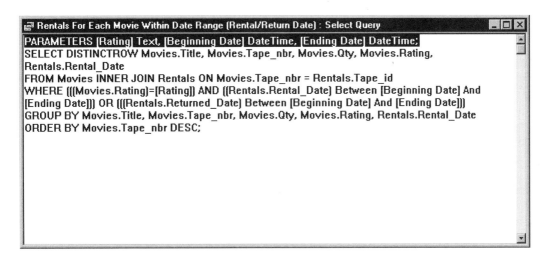

Figure 11–26   The SQL View method of supplying a parameter data type.

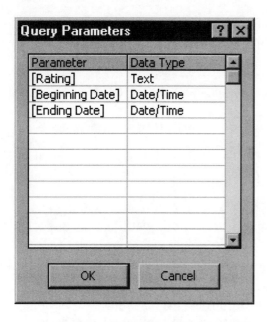

Figure 11–27   The Design View
method of supplying a parameter data
type.

If you are not familiar with nested queries, the best way that I've found to conceptualize them is to think of a query running and producing a result set. That result set is then used automatically (and without you having to do anything special) as the source data for a second query. The result set for the second query is what is returned. Although it is possible to have many levels of nested queries, the truth is that they rarely exceed two levels, and almost never exceed three levels.

Creating a Nested Query

In most cases, the inner most SELECT in a nested query is a join of some sort on two or more tables. The columns in the result set of this inner query are frequently the product of the tables being joined. The outer queries then summarize or manipulate the result set from the inner query.

In Figure 11–28, you see that an inner join query is written that selects some of the columns from the Customer, Movie, and Rental tables. Figure 11–29 shows what this query looks like in Design View mode. Even though we are not including any of the columns on the Rentals table in the result set, we need to include this table in our query to prevent a Cartesian Product result set.

Once this inner-most query is written and perfected, save it. Now you are ready to write the outer query—the one that will act upon the result set of the inner-most query. At this point, it doesn't matter whether it is a left-outer, a right-outer, or a full-outer query.

Start this process by creating a new query. In the Table/Query pane of the QBE window, right click and select the Show Table option, as seen in Figure 11–30. This shows the tables that are a part of the query and allow you to select or deselect tables.

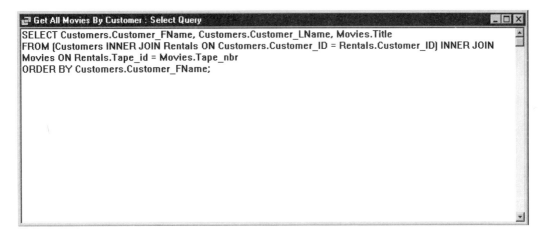

Figure 11–28 The inner-most query of the nested queries.

When you click the Show Table option, click on the Query tab of the Show Table window, as seen in Figure 11–31, where you will see a list of all the saved queries.

Select a query to use as the inner-most query and click <Add>. You will see this query in the Table/Query pane of your QBE window, as seen in Figure 11–32. Once you are here, you select the columns to display in your result set, as well as all the query details you have already learned about. In Figure 11–32, the result set will include the customers last name and a count for how many times that customer has rented a movie [this is done by way of COUNT(title)].

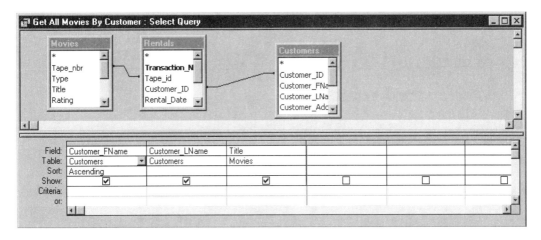

Figure 11–29 The inner-most query in Design View mode.

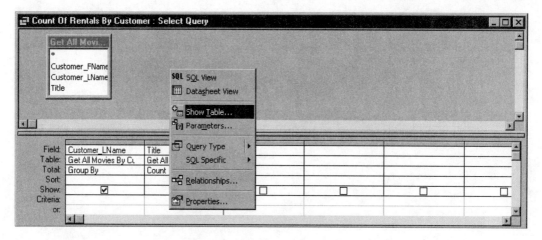

Figure 11–30 The first step in selecting a query to use in a nested query.

Figure 11–33 shows what the nested query looks like in SQL View mode. Note what Table/Query is referenced in the FROM clause of the SELECT statement. It is [Get All Movies By Customer], which is the name of the query saved as the inner-most query.

Action Queries

Action queries alter the content or composition of a table and fall into one of four categories, Make Table, Update Query, Append Query, or Delete Query. Access 97 gives you the ability to write and execute all four of these queries.

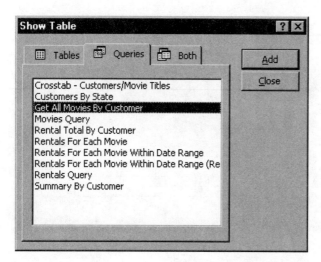

Figure 11–31 Click on the Query tab.

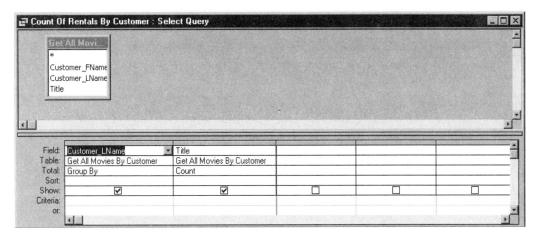

Figure 11–32 The Query Design view of a nested query.

Make Table Query

A Make Table query is a type of query that creates and populates a table with data that is selected from a source table—all in one SELECT statement. The process of creating a Make Table query is fairly straightforward. In a Web database application development project, this is an important capability. For example, you may want to provide a subset of a master table that contains confidential information. In this case you would strip out the confidential information and only make available (presumably outside the firewall) the non-confidential data.

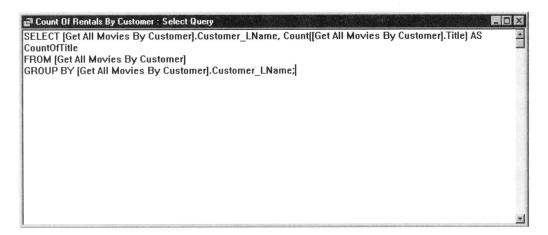

Figure 11–33 The SQL View of a nested query.

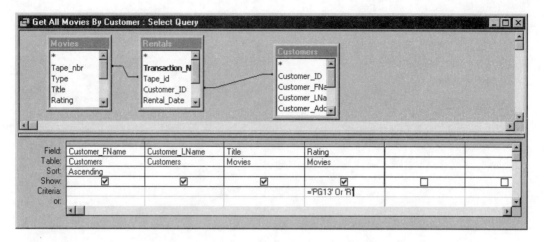

Figure 11–34   Defining the query that is used to populate the new table.

As seen in Figure 11–34, open a new, blank query and select the table(s) that will be used as source for the Make Table query. Select the column(s) in the table(s) that will be used to populate the new table.

In Figure 11–35, you use a Make Table query to create a new table that contains all the rows and columns in the source table that have a Rating equal to "PG13" or "R."

Figure 11–35   Selecting the Make Table option on the Query menu item.

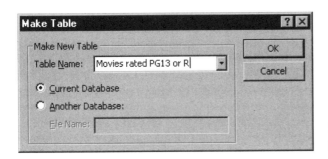

Figure 11–36 Specifying a name for the new table.

When you click on the Query|Make Table option, you will see a dialog box asking for the name of the table that is created from this query. As seen in Figure 11–36, the name assigned to the new table is "Movies rated PG13 and R."

Once you provide a name for the new table and save the query, it is ready to run. Access 97 will display a dialog box informing you that it is about to create a new table (and will automatically delete an existing one if one of the same name currently exists!). It then provides you with a count of the number of rows it is about to add to the new table, as seen in Figure 11–37. If this is acceptable and you want to proceed, click <OK> to create the table and populate it with data, otherwise <Cancel>.

Update Table Query

The Update Table query is a powerful tool used to apply mass updates against a table. For example, you could increase the price of all the products in a table by 12 percent; change the department number that employees work in from 1221 to 2112; or change the address for all purchase records in a database for a particular customer. The update query updates the data residing in a table in place, as opposed to the Make Table query that creates a new table using an existing table as source data.

Let's begin by defining a new query (or select an existing one) that executes a SELECT against a table and returns a result set of the rows that you want to update. When this is done, click on Query|Update Query, as seen in Figure 11–38. This action inserts a row in the QBE grid with the label Update to Figure 11–39.

In Figure 11–39, all rows in the MOVIES table that have a RATING equal to "PG13" will have the rating changed to "PG 13" (with a space). When you have the specifications

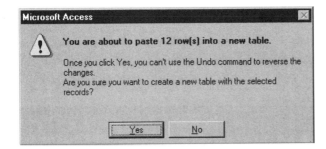

Figure 11–37 Dialog box warning you of the pending table creation.

Figure 11–38   Selecting the Update Query option from the Query menu item.

supplied for the Update Table query, save the query with a distinctive, indicative name, as seen in Figure 11–40. Believe me, you will be glad to have named your queries carefully as you begin to accumulate more and more of them.

Then, when you run the query, Access 97 displays a warning box as seen in Figure 11–41. This warning box tells you that Access 97 is about to update an existing table and asks for confirmation to continue. If this is acceptable and you want to proceed, click <OK> to create the table and populate it with data, otherwise <Cancel>.

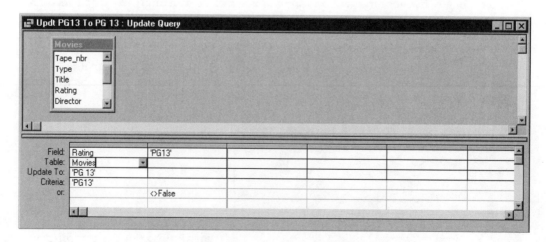

Figure 11–39   Specifying the value(s).

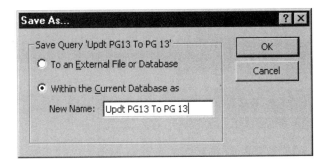

Figure 11–40 Picking a name
to identify the Update query.

Append Query

The Append query is used to add data to a pre-existing table. One or more tables of data
are used for source data to add to the table that is to be appended. The main benefit of
using an Append query is that the user saves time by not having to re-key data.

Prior to building an Append query, you must identify the table(s) to be appended,
as well as the source table, and any selection criteria you want to apply.

Define a new query that will be the Append query. To this, select the table(s) that
you will use as the source table information. In Figure 11–42, a table named New Movies
will be appended to the existing table named Movies.

Apply any selection or sort criteria necessary to place the data in a format compati-
ble with the target table. When this is done, click on the Query|Append Query menu
item, as seen in Figure 11–43. This causes a window to display where you can supply the
name of the target table—the table that is to be appended. In the example in Figure 11–44,
you are selecting the MOVIES table to be the appended table.

Once the table to be appended is identified, it shows up in the QBE grid in the row
labeled Append To. Once the query has been created and written to your satisfaction,
save it with a name descriptive of what it does, as seen in Figure 11–45.

Once the Append Query is written, saved, and then executed, a dialog box similar to
the one seen in Figure 11–46 will display, warning the user that a table is about to be appended. If this is acceptable and you want to proceed, click <OK> to create the table and
populate it with data, otherwise <Cancel>.

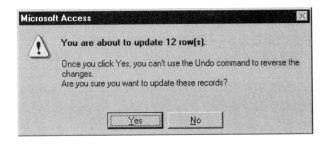

Figure 11–41 Access 97 is
about to update a table.

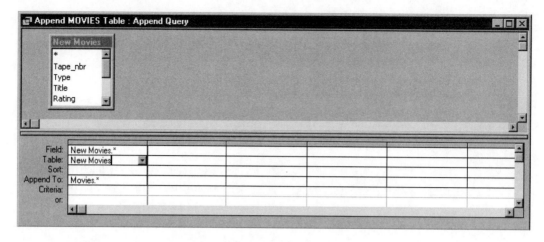

Figure 11–42   Selecting the source table(s) for the Append query.

Figure 11–43   Selecting
Query|Append Query.

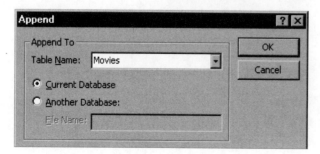

Figure 11–44   Naming the
table that is to be appended.

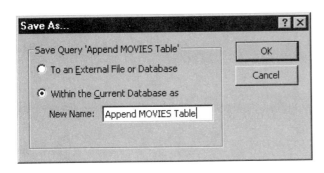

Figure 11–45 Saving the Append Query with a descriptive name.

Delete Query

The Delete Query is used to update one or more rows in a table in a mass-update style. It simplifies the process of deleting a group or collection of rows, especially if those rows are identifiable by applying a selection criteria.

A Delete Query is very simple to create. With the exception of the addition of one step, it is a normal SELECT query. The process of defining a Delete Query is defined here.

Write a normal SELECT query as you did earlier. Apply whatever selection criteria you want to identify the rows that you want to delete. This is shown in Figure 11–47 where a query is being written to extract all rows that have a Rating of "PG 13." It's important to remember to back up the data to be deleted, to run a SELECT against the table that is going to have data deleted from it, and to verify that your DELETE identifies the correct rows.

Run the SELECT query and scrutinize the results closely. If you are satisfied with the results, click on the `Query|Delete Query` menu item, as seen in Figure 11–48. When you do this, you'll notice some changes to the QBE grid, most important, the addition of a Delete row in the grid, as seen in Figure 11–49. When you look at the Query in SQL View, you'll notice the verb DELETE has replaced the verb SELECT, as seen in Figure 11–50. Clicking on `Query|Delete Query` is the one critical step that transforms a SELECT query into a DELETE query.

As seen in Figure 11–51, save the query with a descriptive name—you don't want this one inadvertently executed.

When the query is executed, as is the case with the other Action queries, a warning box will display to inform you of the pending delete action. This is seen in Figure 11–52. If

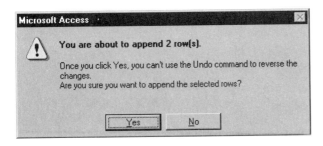

Figure 11–46 Warning supplied by Access 97 before a table is appended.

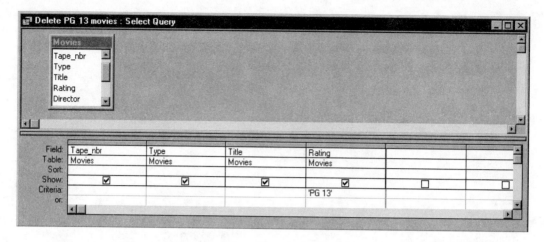

Figure 11–47   A SELECT query that is to become a DELETE query.

Figure 11–48   Converting the SELECT query to a DELETE query.

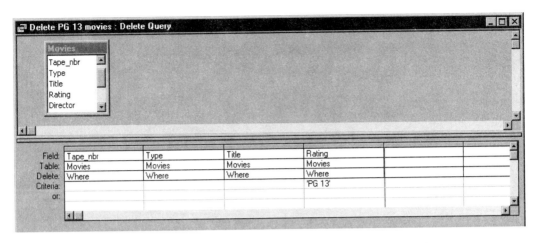

Figure 11–49 The QBE grid after making the query a Delete query.

this is acceptable and you want to proceed, click <OK> to create the table and populate it with data, otherwise <Cancel>.

Optimizing Queries

Simple queries that run against tables with few rows and limited row lengths do not require much thought from the developer to determine the most efficient way to write the query. As the complexity of the query increases, or as the number of rows in the table(s) increases, or as the length of the rows in the tables increases, the developer must become increasingly concerned about optimizing the query for performance.

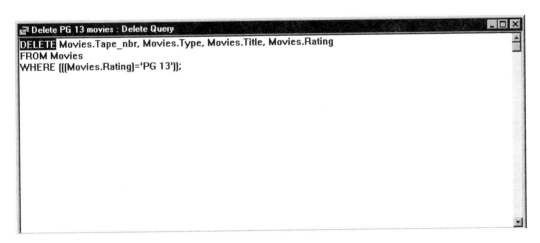

Figure 11–50 The SQL View for the Delete query.

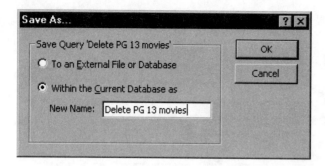

Figure 11–51   Saving the Delete Query with a descriptive name.

Access 97 is good about optimizing the query for you. However, it cannot overcome sloppy database design or query coding techniques. Fortunately, there are a number of things that you can do to optimize the performance of your queries.

- Place indexes on the fields that are joined. This decreases the time required by Access 97 to access the correct rows because it will search the indexes of the table, which avoids having to scan the file directly.

- Pick the smallest data type appropriate for table columns. This will help to reduce the size of the table, thus decreasing the amount of time required to access the table and transmit query result sets to the requestor.

- Limit fields in a query. Obviously the more data Access 97 has to format and include in a result set, the more time it will take to create that result set and transmit it across data lines to your machine or browser.

- Avoid restrictive query criteria. Restrictive query criteria applied on calculated and non-indexed columns increases the amount of time it takes Access 97 to execute the query.

- Avoid calculated fields in nested queries. If calculated fields are a requirement in a nested query, attempt to structure the query so the calculated field is formed by the outer-most query.

- Index sorted columns. When possible, it is best to place an index on a column that is sorted in a query. This will increase the efficiency of the sort algorithm and return the result set to you more quickly.

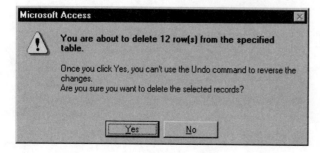

Figure 11–52   The warning box issued when the Delete Query is run.

- Limit the use of Group By columns. Using a Group By on a column that does not require grouping slows the efficiency of Access 97 in supplying you with a result set.
- Use nested queries over total queries with joins. It is generally advantageous to split a total query that has a join into a nested query. The inner-most query performs the joins on the table(s) while the outer-most query calculates the totals.
- Use the Performance Analyzer. The Performance Analyzer is a tool supplied in Access 97 as an aid in determining where and why queries might run into performance problems.

Analyzing Query Performance with Analyzer

The performance analyzer is a tool included in Access 97 to help you identify problems with queries and all the components in your Access 97 database. The analyzer identifies potential areas where performance might be stymied, and recommends alternatives you can use to address the performance problem areas identified.

You do not have to have a query running or a table open to use the Analyzer. In fact, you are prevented from having a query executing or table open when you run the Analyzer. Because queries are one of the slowest components of an RDBMS system and Web database application, it is a wise idea to run the query performance analyzer against your queries before releasing them to production status.

You access the Performance by clicking on `Tools|Analyze|Performance`, as seen in Figure 11–53. This displays the Performance Analyzer, as seen in Figure 11–54.

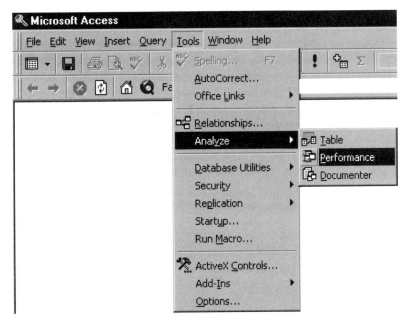

Figure 11–53   Accessing the Performance Analyzer.

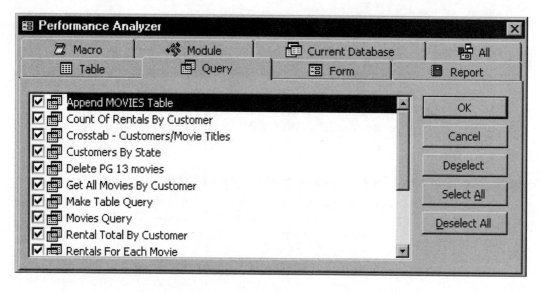

Figure 11–54   The Performance Analyzer.

From the tabs that display on the Performance Analyzer window, you can select specific components in your database, or all components in the database. Select the various components you want the Performance Analyzer to scrutinize and click the <OK> button to start the analysis.

Depending on the size and complexity of the database, and the configuration of your hardware, the analysis process can take anywhere from a few seconds to several minutes. But, once the analysis is done, if there are no errors you will see a window describing Access 97 recommendations, such as the one shown in Figure 11–55.

You'll notice that the performance analysis returns the results broken into four categories, Recommendations, Suggestions, Ideas, and Fixed. If you click on either Recommendations or Suggestions, Access 97 proposes steps to follow to increase performance. When a specific item or items are highlighted, the <Optimize> button is enabled and you can click on it. If you do, Access 97 will make the recommended changes automatically. Idea items require action by you—Access 97 will not do these automatically.

You might think that having Access 97 make changes to your database automatically is great. In most cases, it is. Be careful, though, as Access 97 will may make suggestions that you do not want to implement. Scrutinize the recommendations and suggestions very carefully before clicking the <Optimize> button.

Moving On

This chapter focused on presenting some of the more advanced components and features in Access 97 for building queries. You learned how to use aggregate functions and multiple aggregate functions, to apply criteria to queries, parameter queries, and nested queries, and how to optimize the performance of queries. This is vital information if you

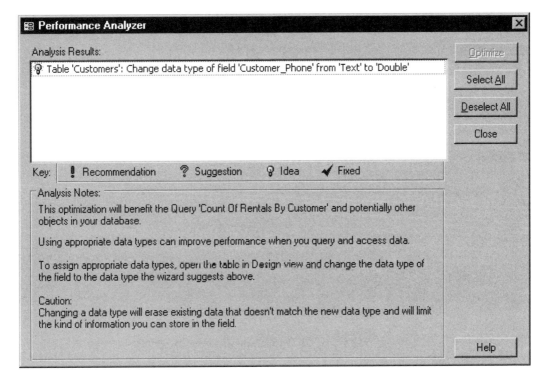

Figure 11–55   The results of a performance analysis.

are building a Web database application because you need to know the facilities that exist in the Access 97 product to read and manipulate the data contained in Access 97 tables. You will use this information not only in the design of HTML forms that access databases (the subject of Chapter 12), but also when designing and writing CGI programs that access Web databases (the subject of Chapter 13). Also, you learned about the Performance Analyzer.

Using the last two chapters as a foundation to the Access 97 RDBMS product, the next few chapters present material specific to front-end Web application design and construction. Specifically, Chapter 12 describes how to use HTML markups and extensions to access corporate databases.

Section III: Interfacing with the Internet User

CHAPTER 12

HTML Forms and Database Access

This chapter continues with the subject that was introduced in Chapter 6, "Overview of HTML." Specifically, Chapter 12 shows you how to build a well-designed HTML form to accept user input and display the results of database queries.

An HTML form can appear anywhere in an HTML document and is designed to accept user input for subsequent processing; for instance, posting of the information to a database, use of the information to query a database, or generation of custom HTML pages based on user-supplied input.

This chapter gives you a thorough introduction into the markups (controls) available to construct and transmit an HTML form. These markups, and the actions and attributes you code to the controls on the form, are the input mechanism into your Web database application.

Objects

There are seven basic objects on an HTML form that you have available to receive input from users. These are shown in Table 12–1. Figure 12–1 is a screen print of what each of these input controls looks like on a finished HTML page.

When the user clicks on the <Submit> or <Press To Send> buttons, it is then that the HTML markup formats a CGI send request as discussed in Chapter 7, "Overview of CGI." Once this request is received by the server, it initiates the processing of a CGI program that interprets and processes the input provided by the user. It is the responsi-

Table 12–1   Objects Appearing on an HTML Form

Object Type	Description
Checkbox	Allows the user to select one or more items from a selection of choices
Command Buttons	Allows the user to cause an action to occur to the form. The most common choices are Submit (in Figure 12–1, this is labeled `<Press To Send>`) and Reset.
List Box	Allows the user to select one of a list of choices that displays when a control, usually a down arrow, is clicked
Password	Allows the user to input a character string while the echo of that string is asterisks (*), thus masking the input data stream
Radio Button	Allows the user to select one, and only one, of a group of choices displayed
Text	Allows the user to input a character string
Text Box	Allows the user to input a series of text lines

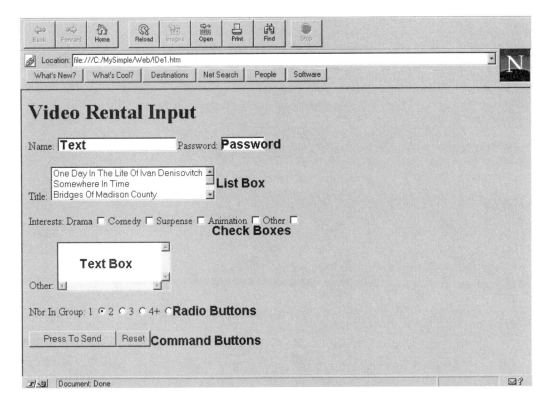

Figure 12–1   The various types of HTML form input objects.

bility of the CGI program to format and transmit a response back to the browser (the user). This response could be a simple confirmation of receipt or it could be a display of a result set from a database query.

> The screen images you see in this chapter are not glitzy or even very aesthetically appealing. They are functional, however, and that is their purpose. Excessive graphics would detract from what I want you to see on these forms. This chapter is meant to introduce you to the various controls and facilities available to you when using HTML forms for database query and updates—it is not meant to be a GUI design chapter. A solid presentation of GUI design principles would take a book of its own.

Syntax of HTML Markups

The following code snippet gives the HTML markup syntax for the form shown in Figure 12–1. The following section describes the syntax and components for these and a few other types of HTML markups.

```
<HTML>
<HEAD>
<TITLE>Demo2</TITLE>
<META NAME="GENERATOR" CONTENT="HAHTsite 2.0"></HEAD>
<BODY>
<FORM NAME=Form1 ACTION="Demo2.htm">
<H1>Video Rental Input</H1>
<P>Name: <INPUT TYPE=TEXT NAME=Renter_name SIZE=25 MAXLENGTH=40>
Password: <INPUT TYPE=PASSWORD NAME=Password SIZE=8 MAXLENGTH=8></P>
<P>Title: <SELECT MULTIPLE NAME=Movie_Titles SIZE=3>
<OPTION VALUE="One Day In The Life Of Ivan Denisovitch">One Day In The
Life Of Ivan Denisovitch</OPTION>
<OPTION VALUE="Somewhere In Time">Somewhere In Time</OPTION>
<OPTION VALUE="Bridges Of Madison County">Bridges Of Madison County</
OPTION>
<OPTION VALUE="Beverly Hills Cop">Beverly Hills Cop</OPTION>
<OPTION VALUE="Beverly Hills Cop II">Beverly Hills Cop II</OPTION>
</SELECT></P>
<P>Interests: Drama <INPUT TYPE=CHECKBOX NAME=I_Drama> Comedy <INPUT
TYPE=CHECKBOX NAME=I_Comedy> Suspense <INPUT TYPE=CHECKBOX NAME=
I_Suspense> Animation <INPUT TYPE=CHECKBOX NAME=I_Animation> Other
<INPUT TYPE=CHECKBOX NAME=I_Other></P>
<P>Other: <TEXTAREA NAME=Other_Interest_Text COLS=20
ROWS=3></TEXTAREA></P>
<P>Nbr In Group: 1 <INPUT TYPE=RADIO NAME=RadioGroup1 HAHTNAME=Group_1
CHECKED> 2 <INPUT TYPE=RADIO NAME=RadioGroup1 HAHTNAME=Group_2> 3 <INPUT
TYPE=RADIO NAME=RadioGroup1 HAHTNAME=Group_3> 4+ <INPUT TYPE=RADIO
NAME=RadioGroup1 HAHTNAME=Group_4></P>
<P><INPUT NAME=Send_Button TYPE=SUBMIT VALUE="Press To Send"><INPUT
NAME=Reset_Button TYPE=RESET VALUE=Reset></P>
```

```
</FORM>
</BODY>
</HTML>
```

Form Specification

The `<FORM>` . . . `</FORM>` HTML tag pair is used to define the entire form. There are three parameters available when using this tag (METHOD, ACTION, and ENCTYPE).

`<FORM METHOD="GET|POST">`. As you learned in Chapter 7, there are two methods of sending information to a CGI script, GET and POST. When using the GET method, character strings and field names supplied by the user on the form which are intended to be sent to the CGI program are placed in environmental variables that the CGI program then retrieves for processing. When using the POST method, as seen here, the character string is sent to the CGI program directly on the URL that is sent back to the server.

Forms designed to transmit a single user input are well suited to use the GET method. Forms accepting several user inputs should be written to use the POST method because the amount of data that can be passed using the GET method is limited.

`<FORM ACTION="specified URL or CGI script")>`. The ACTION method is used to initiate a specific CGI program or trigger an identified URL. Such is the case in the following example:

```
<FORM ACTION="http://teleport.com/cgi-bin/acct_inq.exe">
```

The ACTION attribute is the way to trigger the execution of a CGI program on a server. In this code sample, the program named `acct_inq.exe` that resides in the `cgi-bin` directory on the `teleport.com` server is targeted as the program that is to be executed.

`<FORM ENCTYPE="application/x-www-form-urlencoded">`. The ENCTYPE attribute specifies the encoding used for the content of the HTML form. This is specified to ensure complete and accurate transmittal of all user-supplied data. This attribute is infrequently used as the default encoding (as seen above) and is usually acceptable.

Input Specification

There are a number of markup and specifications available to define user input. The following are discussed in the following sections:

- Checkbox
- Command Button
- List Box
- Password
- Radio Button
- Text
- Text Box

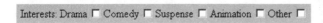

Figure 12–2 A checkbox as seen in a browser.

Checkbox. Checkboxes are used to allow a user to select between 0 and *n* non-exclusive choices, where *n* is the total number of checkboxes in the group. A checkbox is termed a two-state input field—that is, it can be either on (checked) or off (unchecked). The following code shows the actual HTML code used to create the checkboxes seen in Figure 12–2.

```
<P>Interests: Drama <INPUT TYPE=CHECKBOX NAME=I_Drama>
Comedy <INPUT TYPE=CHECKBOX NAME=I_Comedy> Suspense <INPUT TYPE=CHECKBOX
NAME=I_Suspense> Animation <INPUT TYPE=CHECKBOX NAME=I_Animation>
Other <INPUT TYPE=CHECKBOX NAME=I_Other></P>
```

The specific format for the checkbox syntax is:

```
<INPUT TYPE=CHECKBOX NAME=name>
```

In this example, the character string identified by *name* is the name part of the name/value pair that is sent to the CGI program. The `value` part of the name/value pair is determined by whether the control is checked or not. If it is checked, then the value is `yes`. If it is not checked, then neither the name or the value is sent to the CGI program.

In this example, the checkboxes are placed horizontally across the page. You could combine HTML codes and place them vertically down a page in an ordered or unordered list. If a checkbox is checked when the user presses the `<Submit>` button, then a name/value pair will be sent to the server. In the case of this code and Figure 12–2, if the user had checked the Comedy and Suspense checkboxes, then the following name/ value pairs will be sent to the server:

```
I_Comedy=yes&I_Suspense=yes
```

Command Buttons. When the user has completed the form and is ready to send it off to the server, he or she can press the `<Submit>` button. This causes the browser to format the CGI request using one of the 3 methods already discussed, and pass the request to the server which interprets the URL and identifies the need to execute a CGI program.

There are two basic types of command buttons, `<Submit>` and `<Reset>`. Each of these do different things. The `<Submit>` button performs the action just described while the `<Reset>` button causes the form to be cleared of all input values.

The following code sample shows the actual HTML code used to format the `<Submit>` and `<Reset>` buttons.

```
<P><INPUT NAME=Send_Button TYPE=SUBMIT VALUE="Press To Send"><INPUT
NAME=Reset_Button TYPE=RESET VALUE=Reset></P>
```

The code sample here is standard HTML syntax and is the only way to describe a command button, short of using other types of development suites that customize how they handle command buttons from standard HTML syntax. The value attribute allows the de-

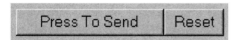

Figure 12–3   Command buttons as seen in a browser.

veloper to specify the label on the button. In this case, I have chosen the label of <Press To Send>.

It is possible to have multiple command buttons on an HTML form, each sending a different name/value pair to the server. In such a case, a value must be supplied for each name attribute so the server can identify which command button initiated the action. In the code above, and reproduced in Figure 12–3, only one command button is shown, and as you can see, this formats a name/value pair for transmission to a server. The <RESET> button simply clears the form—it doesn't transmit anything to the server. The following name/value pair would format the form for transmission to the server if a user clicked on the <Press To Send> button:

```
UserRequest=Press+To+Send
```

List Box.   List boxes allow a user to make an exclusive or non-exclusive selection from a list of choices. This list could be hard, or it could be retrieved from a database. If the values are retrieved from a database, a development tool suite that supplies necessary extensions to standard HTML syntax is required. These extensions actually populate the list box with values retrieved from a database table. The main point here is to recognize that this capability exists and understand where to go to acquire it.

In the following listing, list boxes are accommodated in HTML code using the <SELECT> . . . </SELECT> tag pair. The results of this HTML code are shown in Figure 12–4.

```
<P>Title: <SELECT MULTIPLE NAME=Movie_Titles SIZE=3>
<OPTION VALUE="One Day In The Life Of Ivan Denisovitch">One Day In The
Life Of Ivan Denisovitch</OPTION>
<OPTION VALUE="Somewhere In Time">Somewhere In Time</OPTION>
<OPTION VALUE="Bridges Of Madison County">Bridges Of Madison County
</OPTION>
<OPTION VALUE="Beverly Hills Cop">Beverly Hills Cop</OPTION>
<OPTION VALUE="Beverly Hills Cop II">Beverly Hills Cop II</OPTION>
</SELECT></P>
```

To make a list box accept multiple user selections, include the keyword MULTIPLE in the <SELECT> tag as seen in the code listing. To force the list box to allow only one selection, exclude the MULTIPLE keyword from the <SELECT> tag as shown here:

Figure 12–4   A list box as seen in a browser.

```
<SELECT NAME=Movie_Titles SIZE=3>
```

When a user selects one or more items from the list box, the browser formats a name/value pair for each item selected. For example, if the user had selected *Somewhere in Time* and *Bridges of Madison County* as multiple selections, the browser would format and transmit the following name/value pairs to the server for the CGI program:

```
Movie_Titles=Somewhere+In+Time&Movie_Titles=Bridges+Of+Madison+County
```

Password. Password markups are an extension of text markups; what the user types in the input area is replaced with asterisks (*) in the form. This is most often used to control access to a site or a database.

What the user actually types in a password field is what is transmitted to the server—not the asterisks that are seen in the browser. This should be an area of concern if you are worried about hackers in that a clever hacker would be able to intercept the password that is sent to the server. The exception to this is if the browser and server both explicitly support data encryption. Data encryption is a more secure way to transmit data between browsers and servers and is discussed in Chapter 18 of this book.

There is one basic way to write the HTML code for a password control. The SIZE=8 and MAXLENGTH=8 parameters can be increased to 255 characters each, but most passwords are 8 characters in length. The results of the HTML code below are seen in Figure 12–5.

```
<INPUT TYPE=PASSWORD NAME=Password SIZE=8 MAXLENGTH=8>
```

When a user completes a form that has a password control on it and presses <Submit>, a name/value pair is created and sent to the server. That name/value pair is then interpreted on the server by a CGI program. If it is found to be incorrect, the common procedure is to give the user two more tries before preventing him or her from making any further attempts. In the example just shown (assuming a password of SD12107 was entered) the following name/value pair would be sent to the server:

```
Password=SD12107
```

Radio Button. Radio buttons allow a user to make an exclusive selection from a list of possible alternatives. When one button is selected, the other buttons in the group are deselected, and there is no way to deselect all the radio buttons in a group. If such a need exists, that is, to not select any of the available alternatives, you should consider using checkboxes without the MULTIPLE attribute.

The following code snippet displays the HTML code necessary to format and display the radio buttons seen in Figure 12–6.

```
1 <INPUT TYPE=RADIO NAME=RadioGroup1 HAHTNAME=Group_1 CHECKED>
2 <INPUT TYPE=RADIO NAME=RadioGroup1 HAHTNAME=Group_2>
```

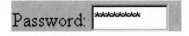

Figure 12–5   A password as seen in a browser.

Figure 12–6   Radio buttons as seen in a browser.

```
3  <INPUT TYPE=RADIO NAME=RadioGroup1 HAHTNAME=Group_3>
4+ <INPUT TYPE=RADIO NAME=RadioGroup1 HAHTNAME=Group_4>
```

The specific syntax for a radio button is:

```
<INPUT TYPE=RADIO NAME=group_name HAHTNAME=haht_group (CHECKED)>
```

Note the following about the HTML code:

- `INPUT TYPE=RADIO` identifies this form control as being a radio button
- `NAME=group_name` is a name given to a group of radio buttons. It is by giving a collection of radio buttons the same group_name that gives the control the ability to have only one radio button selected at a time
- `HAHTNAME=haht_group` is an extension to standard HTML code made by HAHT-site IDE
- `(CHECKED)` indicates that the radio button that carries this optional parameter is seen initially in a browser as being in an ON status

When using radio buttons, it is wise to identify all the buttons that belong together in a group. In the code just shown, the group name for the radio buttons is `Radio-Group1`. This allows the browser to select or deselect the appropriate radio buttons when a selection is made.

After a radio button is selected and the user clicks on the `<Submit>` button, the browser formats a name/value pair for transmission to the server and ultimately to the CGI program.

```
RadioGroup1=Group_2
```

It is by interpreting this name/value pair that the CGI program determines which radio button was selected (clicked) by the user. It is then that it can take whatever action is appropriate based. In the context of the figure and example in this section, the CGI program would determine that the second radio button in the group of four was selected, meaning that the user indicated that there are two people in the group.

Text.   Text areas are used when short text strings are expected from a user. Longer text strings are provided for in text boxes, which are discussed in the next section. Text areas can be defined to a prespecified maximum length (a good thing when you are using the GET method).

The following code sample shows the HTML code used to format a text area on an HTML page. The results of this code are seen in Figure 12–7.

```
<INPUT TYPE=TEXT NAME=Renter_name SIZE=25 MAXLENGTH=40>
```

The specific syntax for the text form control is:

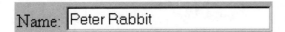

Figure 12–7 Text area as seen in a browser.

```
<INPUT TYPE=TEXT NAME=control_name SIZE=control_size
MAXLENGTH=maximum_length>
```

INPUT TYPE=TEXT indicates that this HTML specifies a text control. NAME=`control_name` is a name given to the form control to uniquely identify the control. SIZE=`control_size` specifies the number of characters, with a maximum of 255, that are viewable in the control on the form as seen in a browser. MAXLENGTH=`maximum_length` specifies the maximum number of characters, up to a limit of 255, that the control length could be.

If the MAXLENGTH value is greater than the SIZE value, the user will be able to scroll left or right inside the control to view all the input characters.

The text area defined in this code allows a user to input a text string of up to forty characters. The first twenty-five characters will display in the window and she or he can scroll horizontally to view up to the fortieth character. Any text input beyond forty characters is truncated.

When a user inputs a text string in the text control and presses the <Submit> button, a name/value pair is formatted and transmitted by the browser to the server. In this example above and in Figure 12–7, this name/value pair is:

```
Renter_name=Peter+Rabbit
```

This name/value pair indicates that the user supplied the character string Peter Rabbit in the text control named Renter_name. The browser translates the space between the words Peter and Rabbit and makes the character string, or the value portion of the name/value pair, be Peter+Rabbit. This name/value pair would be transmitted to the CGI program which would interpret it and take whatever action is provided and described in the program code.

Text Box. A text box is identified in HTML code with the <TEXTAREA> . . . </TEXTAREA> tag pair and is used to accept character input that might be too long to fit inside a text area. The following code snippet shows the HTML code necessary to create a text box and Figure 12–8 shows the result of the HTML code in an HTML browser.

```
<TEXTAREA NAME=Other_Interest_Text COLS=20 ROWS=3></TEXTAREA>
```

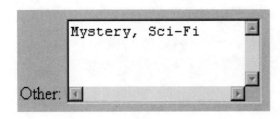

Figure 12–8 Text box as seen in a browser.

Text boxes are defined within the <TEXTAREA> . . . </TEXTAREA> tag pair by a column (COLS) and rows (ROWS) attribute. These define the horizontal and vertical size of the text box. An attribute can be input that defines the word wrapping capabilities of the text box. This attribute is WRAP and its values can be either off, virtual, or physical. Off means that all text entered will appear as a single line until an <Enter> key is pressed. Virtual means that individual lines will word-wrap on the screen and when they are sent to the server. Physical means that individual lines will word-wrap on the screen but not when sent to the server, thus causing each line to be transmitted individually. If these attributes are supplied, they can appear anywhere between the left bracket (<) and the right bracket (>) that define the boundaries of the TEXTAREA control.

When a user inputs values in the text box, the browser formats a name/value pair that is transmitted to the server. In the last code sample, this name/value pair would be:

```
Other_Interest_Text=Mystery,+Sci-Fi
```

Assuming this name/value pair was sent to the CGI program from the user's browser, the CGI program would determine that the user had input the character string Mystery, Sci-Fi, and that the blank character that was input between the words Mystery, and Sci-Fi was translated to a plus sign (+) for transmission. Once this is determined by the CGI program, the program will perform whatever processes are needed and specified by the programmer.

Now that you've seen the syntax for controls that can appear on a form, the following section presents information on some of the limitations that you will encounter when placing objects on HTML forms. Included in this discussion are suggestions you could implement to overcome these limitations.

Overcoming Limitations of Placing Objects on HTML Forms

You have limited control over where you place objects, controls, and text on an HTML form. For example, you have only three choices as to where on an HTML page or form you can place controls; on the left margin, in the center, and on the right margin. Also, there are no tab stops when you format text and objects, and you can not include more than one blank character to place white space between objects on a page.

In this section you'll learn about four ways to control the layout and placement of objects on an HTML page and form. These are:

- Using tables
- Using null graphics
- Using <PRE> . . . </PRE> tag pairs
- Using server-side includes

Using Tables

One of the ways to exercise what limited control you do have is by using tables. You can define a borderless table with deliberately empty cells to accommodate the placement of objects in a way you like. Figure 12–9 is a screen print demonstrating how to place two types of list boxes on an HTML page using tables—in this case, a borderless table.

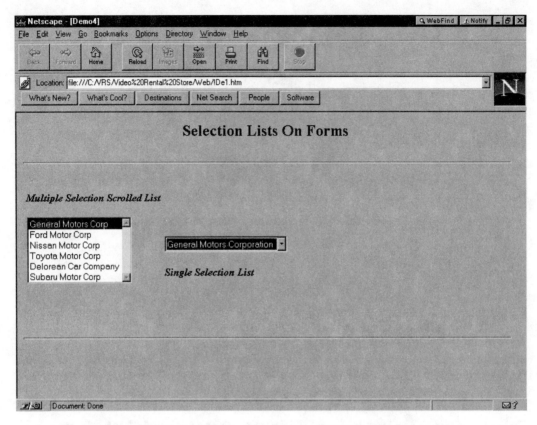

Figure 12–9   Two types of selection lists placed on a page.

The following code snippet is the actual HTML code used to create these two list boxes within a borderless table.

```
<HTML>
<HEAD>
<TITLE>Demo4</TITLE>
<META NAME="GENERATOR" CONTENT="HAHTsite 2.0"></HEAD>
<BODY>
<P ALIGN=CENTER><FONT SIZE="+2">
<STRONG>Selection Lists On Forms</STRONG></FONT></P>
<P><HR></P>
<FORM NAME=Form1 ACTION=SELF>
<TABLE>
<TR>
<TD><P><STRONG><EM>Multiple Selection Scrolled List</EM></STRONG></P>
<SELECT MULTIPLE NAME=List1 SIZE=6>
<OPTION VALUE=Chev>General Motors Corp</OPTION>
<OPTION VALUE=Ford>Ford Motor Corp</OPTION>
```

```
<OPTION VALUE=Nissan>Nissan Motor Corp</OPTION>
<OPTION VALUE=Toyota>Toyota Motor Corp</OPTION>
<OPTION VALUE=Delorean>Delorean Car Company</OPTION>
<OPTION VALUE=Subaru>Subaru Motor Corp</OPTION>
</SELECT></TD>
<TD><P> </P><P> </P><P><SELECT NAME=Combo1 SIZE=1>
<OPTION VALUE=Delorean>Delorean Motor Corp</OPTION>
<OPTION VALUE=Ford>Ford Motor Corporation</OPTION>
<OPTION VALUE=Chevy>General Motors Corporation</OPTION>
<OPTION VALUE=Nissan>Nissan Motor Corp</OPTION>
<OPTION VALUE=Subaru>Subaru Motor Corp</OPTION>
<OPTION VALUE=Toyota>Toyota Motor Corp</OPTION>
</SELECT></P><P><STRONG><EM>Single Selection List</EM></STRONG></P></TD>
</TR>
</TABLE>
</FORM>
<P> </P>
<P><HR></P>
</BODY>
</HTML>
```

One of the things you should notice about the definitions of the items in the table is the use of the `Value=` attribute. This is seen here:

```
<OPTION VALUE=Chev>General Motors Corp</OPTION>
<OPTION VALUE=Ford>Ford Motor Corp</OPTION>
<OPTION VALUE=Nissan>Nissan Motor Corp</OPTION>
```

It is a good idea to use the `VALUE=` attributes in selection lists to provide a better level of control when coding CGI scripts, as well as to limit the number of characters needed to be entered or transmitted.

Using Null Graphics

Another way in which you have control over the placement of controls and objects on an HTML page is by using null graphics as spacers. Null graphics are graphic objects that are transparent, thereby taking up space on an HTML page without rendering an image. Dependent on the size of the null graphic, you have control over the placement of visible objects. For example, if you want a text box to appear on a form ten spaces from the left margin, you already know that you can not include ten spaces in the HTML page. But, if you define a null graphic whose width is the equivalent of ten characters, you can supply the spacing by placing the null graphic on the left margin, and then placing the text box directly to the right of it. Figure 12–10 and the code sample that follows are the actual image and HTML code used to demonstrate this.

```
<HTML>
<HEAD>
<TITLE>Demo4</TITLE>
</HEAD>
<BODY>
```

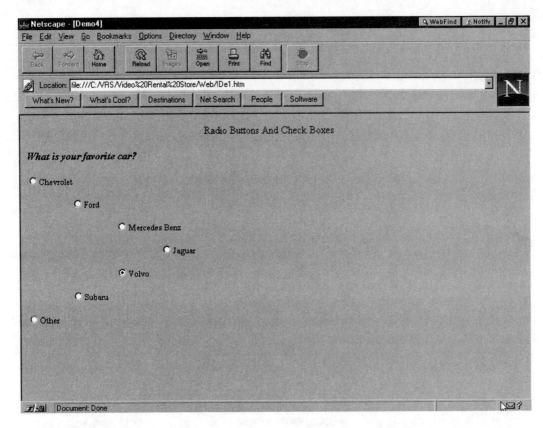

Figure 12–10 Browser view of null graphics and radio buttons.

```
<P ALIGN=CENTER>Radio Buttons And Check Boxes</P>
<FORM NAME=Form1 ACTION=SELF>
<P><STRONG><EM>What is your favorite car?</EM></STRONG></P>
<P><FONT SIZE=-1><INPUT TYPE=RADIO NAME=RadioGroup1
HAHTNAME=Radio1></FONT><FONT SIZE=-1>Chevrolet</FONT></P>
<P><FONT SIZE=-1><IMG SRC="SimpFold/Images/Spacer.GIF" WIDTH=70 HEIGHT=7
NOAUTO-RESIZE VSPACE=1></FONT><FONT SIZE=-1><INPUT TYPE=RADIO NAME=
RadioGroup1 HAHTNAME=Radio2></FONT><FONT SIZE=-1>Ford</FONT></P>
<P><FONT SIZE=-1><IMG SRC="SimpFold/Images/Spacer.GIF" WIDTH=140 HEIGHT=7
NOAUTO-RESIZE VSPACE=1></FONT><FONT SIZE=-1><INPUT TYPE=RADIO NAME=
RadioGroup1 HAHTNAME=Radio7></FONT><FONT SIZE=-1>Mercedes Benz</FONT></P>
<P><FONT SIZE=-1><IMG SRC="SimpFold/Images/Spacer.GIF" WIDTH=210 HEIGHT=7
NOAUTO-RESIZE VSPACE=1></FONT><FONT SIZE=-1><INPUT TYPE=RADIO NAME=
RadioGroup1 HAHTNAME=Radio4></FONT><FONT SIZE=-1>Jaguar</FONT></P>
<P><FONT SIZE=-1><IMG SRC="SimpFold/Images/Spacer.GIF" WIDTH=140 HEIGHT=7
NOAUTO-RESIZE VSPACE=1></FONT><FONT SIZE=-1><INPUT TYPE=RADIO NAME=
RadioGroup1 HAHTNAME=Radio5></FONT><FONT SIZE=-1>Volvo</FONT></P>
```

```
<P><FONT SIZE=-1><IMG SRC="SimpFold/Images/Spacer.GIF" WIDTH=70 HEIGHT=7
NOAUTO-RESIZE VSPACE=1></FONT><FONT SIZE=-1><INPUT TYPE=RADIO NAME=
RadioGroup1 HAHTNAME=Radio8>Subaru</FONT></P>
<P><FONT SIZE=-1><INPUT TYPE=RADIO NAME=RadioGroup1
HAHTNAME=Radio6></FONT><FONT SIZE=-1>Other</FONT></P>
</FORM>
</BODY>
</HTML>
```

The actual code to position the graphic, and to give it a height and width dimension is:

```
<IMG SRC="SimpFold/Images/Spacer.GIF" WIDTH=70 HEIGHT=7 NOAUTO-RESIZE
VSPACE=1>
```

Using `<PRE>` . . . `</PRE>` *Tag Pairs*

The preformatted tag pair is used to generate HTML documents that will appear exactly the same in a browser as they appeared when created. All blank spaces, carriage returns, and blank lines enclosed within the `<PRE>` . . . `</PRE>` tag pair are retained when viewed by a browser.

Figure 12–11 displays what the use of this tag pair looks like when viewed in a browser. The code listing that follows is the HTML code that was written to create the page seen in Figure 12–11.

```
<HTML>
<HEAD>
<TITLE>Demo4</TITLE>
</HEAD>
<BODY>
<FORM NAME=Form1 ACTION=SELF>
<P ALIGN=CENTER><STRONG>Text Input And The PRE Tag</STRONG></P>
<P>A pre-filled, 3 row x 24 column TEXTAREA input control:</P>
<P><TEXTAREA NAME=MLText1 COLS=24 ROWS=3>Peter Piper picked a peck of
pickled peppers. If Peter Piper picked a peck of pickled peppers, how
many pickled peppers did Peter Piper pick?</TEXTAREA></P>
<P>Password: <INPUT TYPE=PASSWORD NAME=Text1 SIZE=8 MAXLENGTH=8
VALUE=Password></P>
<PRE>   Preformatted text with a bunch of spaces.</PRE>
<P>Name: <INPUT TYPE=TEXT NAME=Text2 SIZE=30 MAXLENGTH=40 VALUE="Enter
your name"></P>
<P>A Quotable-Quote From You:
<INPUT TYPE=TEXT NAME=Text3 SIZE=80 MAXLENGTH=256></P>
</FORM>
</BODY>
</HTML>
```

The actual code using the `<PRE>` . . . `</PRE>` tag pair is:

```
<PRE>    Preformatted text with a bunch of spaces.</PRE>
```

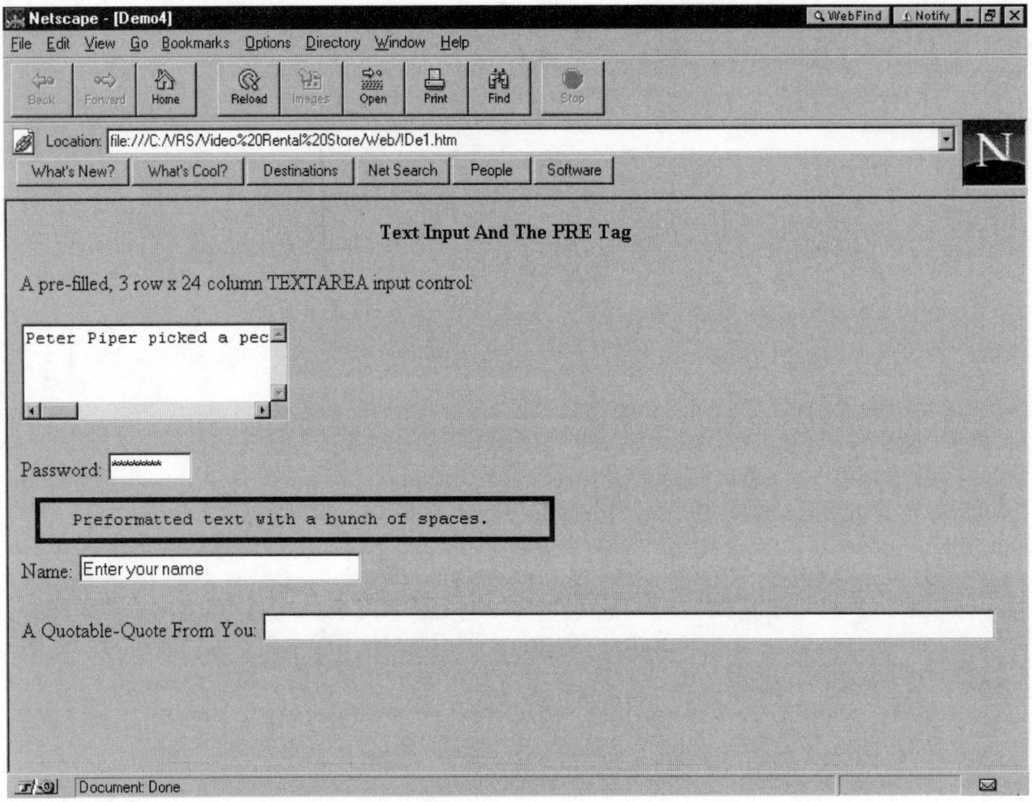

Figure 12–11   Browser view of `<PRE> . . . </PRE>` tag pair

The biggest limitation that the use of this tag pair overcomes is the inclusion of more than one blank character before the control or text. In the last example, there are five blank spaces between the left margin and the first word of text.

Using the `<PRE> . . . </PRE>` tag pair with a string of blank characters to the left of a control or graphic is another way to control the placement of these objects on the HTML page or form. For example, if you want a graphic to appear twenty-five characters from the left margin, you could use the `<PRE> . . . </PRE>` tag pair with twenty-five spaces between the tag pair, followed immediately by the graphic.

Using Server-Side Includes

If your site includes several objects, controls, or text that are consistent among HTML pages, you should consider using virtual includes—or what is sometimes referred to as server-side includes. By using server-side includes, you can embed a reference to a file of pre-written (and hopefully pre-tested) HTML code that resides on the server. By doing this the HTML page is formatted in preparation to being sent to the browser by incorporating the copied code from the server.

Using server-side includes is much the same in concept as including header files in C programs, PBLs in PowerBuilder programs, or copybooks in COBOL programs. They overcome the limitation of having to write code for every action in every HTML page (or program) by giving you the capability of reusing code that is tested and verified.

Consider the following code:

```
<FORM METHOD="POST" ACTION="http://teleport.com/cgi-bin/mergeit"
<!--#include virtual="/common/html/headings.shtml" -->
<!--#include virtual="/common/html/banners.shtml" -->
… HTML code for the body of the page …
<!--#include virtual="/common/html/buttons.shtml" -->
</FORM>
```

In this example, the server would begin to interpret this HTML code and come to the first include statement:

```
<!--#include virtual="/common/html/headings.shtml" -->
```

At this point, it would retrieve the contents of the `headings.shtml` file from its `/common/html/` directory.

The file extension does not *need* to be `*.shtml`. In the example here, this file actually contains HTML code, and could just as well have the file extension of *.SHTML, *.HTM or *.HTML. It is a commonly recognized convention to use a file extension of SHTML to represent server-side includes.

The contents of the `headings.shtml` file could be:

```
<H1>ABC Corporation</H1>
<H2>Our World-Wide Web Internet Site</H2>
```

Once this file is retrieved and placed in the HTML code, the server reads and interprets the next line of HTML code that requests a server-side include:

```
<!--#include virtual="/common/html/banners.shtml" -->
```

As expected, the `banners.shtml` file is retrieved from the `/common/html/` directory and merged into the body of the HTML form. The remainder of the HTML code is read and interpreted by the server until the last include is read:

```
<!--#include virtual="/common/html/buttons.shtml" -->
```

When this line is read, the `buttons.shtml` file is retrieved from the `/common/html/` directory and merged into the body of the HTML form. Once all the server-side include files have been read and merged into the HTML document, it is then transmitted to the browser.

Now that you've seen how to overcome some of the limitations that exist in HTML placing objects on an HTML page where you want them, let's look at how to accommodate database queries in HTML. There are very limited specifications that allow you to connect to and access a database from HTML. You will see in the next section how to handle this situation.

Database Queries and HTML

HTML specifications provide no direct method for querying a database, and you can not directly access a database from within a Web page or HTML form. There are a number of different methods you can use to build database connectivity into your HTML form without relying on the current HTML specification. This is a good thing as the current HTML specification provides no support for directly connecting to a database. The methods are:

- *Code-less interfaces*—These are software tool sets that work in tandem with developer defined template files. The purpose of the templates is to define various views into the database and describe how data is to be displayed once it is retrieved. When these forms are incorporated into an HTML page and sent to the server for processing, they are processed by CGI programs that perform the actual querying and formatting of the data.

- *Custom CGI programs*—These are gateway programs that are specifically written to accept and process SQL queries. These programs receive the user's request for DBMS data, parse the user inputs and create a query to accommodate the user's request, and then dynamically create an HTML document that transmits the result set back to the user.

- *HTML embedded SQL extensions*—These are special HTML extensions supplied by RDBMS and other tool vendors that provide a mechanism to embed SQL statements directly into the body of the HTML file that is passed from the user to the HTTP server. When received at the server, this HTML file is parsed to pull out the SQL statements that are subsequently passed to a CGI program.

You'll note from the above three ways to accomplish database access that they all rely in one form or another on the use of a CGI program. Recalling from Chapter 7 that the execution of a CGI program on a server is triggered from an HTML form, you can rightly conclude that the only way to cause a database access to occur on a server is from a CGI program that is initiated from a form that appears on a Web page and sent by a user.

The examples presented in the remainder of this chapter are created using the HAHTSite IDE, by Haht Software. The purpose here is not to teach you how to use this tool, rather, it is to demonstrate how a set of HTML pages can be written to:

- Connect to an Access 97 database
- Query the database
- Format and display the result set

The ways in which the HAHTSite IDE software accomplishes this are quite similar to other Web database application development tool suites. Understanding this is a necessary element to understanding how Web applications accomplish database access.

Connecting to a Database

The HAHTSite IDE provides a GUI-based mechanism to connect an application to a database as seen in Figure 12–12.

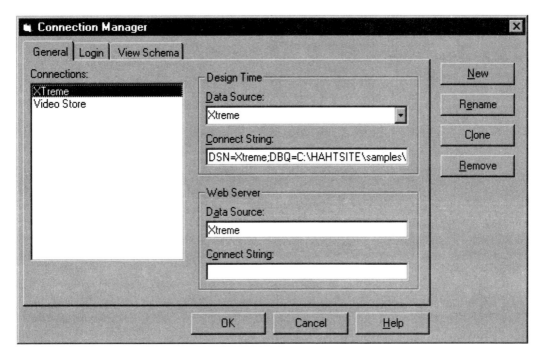

Figure 12–12 The Connection Manager dialog box.

The Connection Manager is a tool that is accessed from the main toolbar within the HAHTSite IDE. Its purpose is to identify the database to which the Web pages in the application are to connect and to initiate the connection to that database. This database could be an Access 97, Oracle, SYBASE, Informix, or any other ODBC compliant database. When configured properly, this connection becomes an attribute of the project—or in our case, the database application. It defines the name of the connection, the data source name, and an optional connect string that is passed automatically to the DBMS when a database connection is made.

Once the Connection Manager is configured correctly to a data source either directly or through ODBC, all the tables in that database are accessible by HTML pages. In HAHTSite IDE, as is the case with other Web database application development suites, the connection to a database is identified in the additional and proprietary HTML code that the tool adds to the HTML form that you create. The users don't see this additional HTML code when viewing the page in their browsers, but the Web server and CGI programs running on the Web server receive, interpret, and act on the additional HTML code to provide the necessary database access.

Querying the Database

The DB Table Widget, in HAHTSite IDE, is an object placed on a HTML page that is not viewable in a user's browser but which accomplishes the actual format of the database query and display of the result set. To use the DB Table, you simply drag the DB Table

Widget icon as seen in Figure 12–13 and drop it on the HTML page where you want the result set of the query to be placed.

Once this object is placed on an HTML page, you can modify the attributes of the query in the Database Table Properties dialog box. As seen in Figure 12–14, you can identify the table in the database to be queried. You can also perform table joins.

There are four tabs on this dialog box that define the type of query and the way the result set will display. The SQL tab is the one you'd use to specify the exact nature of the query and result set. If you know and like to code SQL you can write it directly into the SQL dialog box, as seen in Figure 12–15. If you'd prefer to use a GUI interface, an SQL Assistant feature will guide you through the process in a friendlier environment.

Now, when you click on <OK>, the query will have been defined via SQL, and the query will execute when needed against the Access 97 database table identified in the previous section titled, Connecting to a Database.

Please refer back to Chapter 5, "Application Development Suites," to learn more about some of the other tools in this category.

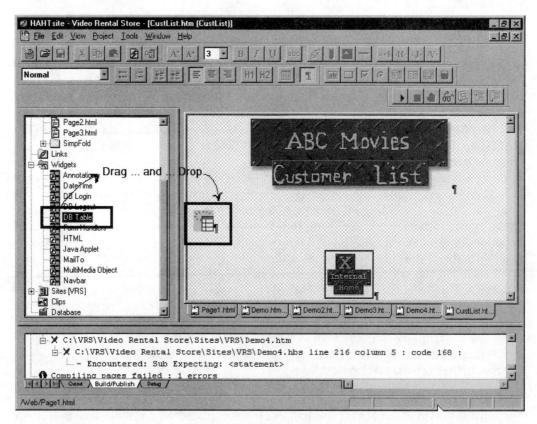

Figure 12–13   The DB Table Widget icon and the HTML page painter.

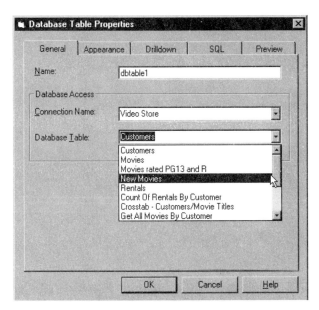

Figure 12–14 Selecting a table to query.

Formatting and Displaying the Result Set

Once you have defined the query, you can click on the Preview tab in the Database Properties dialog box (Figure 12–14) to see what your data will look like in the HTML form. An example of what the Preview tab looks like for a defined query is seen in Figure 12–16.

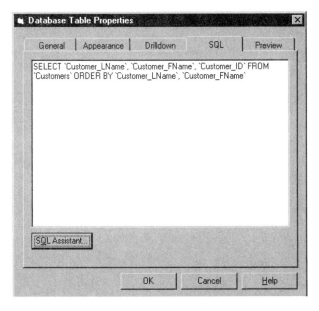

Figure 12–15 Describe the exact nature of the query.

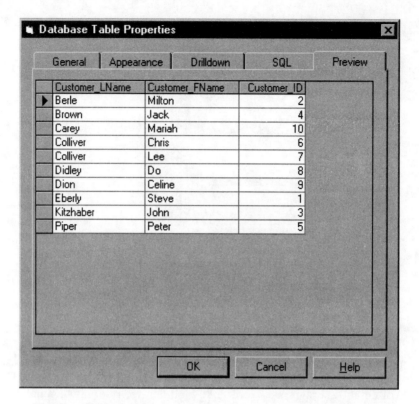

Figure 12–16   The Preview tab look of a defined query.

There are a number of ways in which you can modify the look of the result set. The one I use the most is to adjust the width of each column. Especially in a result set that contains a large number of columns, you want to be careful to include as little white space as possible. There is a nice and easy to use facility in HAHTsite IDE to do this, as is the case with the other tools that fall into the category of Web database application development suites.

Once you have adjusted the way the result set will look, click on <OK> to accept the definition.

At this point in the process, you have identified the database the application is to connect with, identified the table(s) to attach to, created the SQL to perform the query, and formatted the layout of the result set. Running the application is the only thing left to do.

As seen in Figure 12–17 from a Netscape browser, the result set formats and displays beautifully. Because of the definition of the DB Table Widget within HAHTsite, you should notice a few navigation prompts at the top of the table. These are placed automatically by the DB Table Widget.

The screen print in Figure 12–17 is the result set generated from a query against an Access 97 table. However, once the data exists, Access 97 does not need to be running or

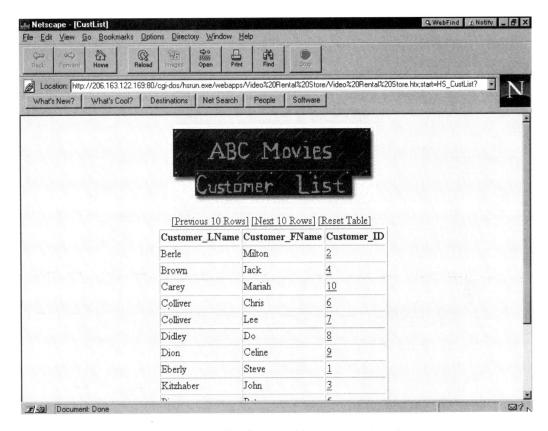

Figure 12–17   A database table as seen in a browser.

active for the data that resides in its database tables to be accessed from the Web database application. That is the purpose of ODBC as discussed in multiple locations in previous chapters.

Drilling Down in a Web Database Application

Most Web database application development suites offer a capability commonly referred to as drilling down in their tools. What this means is that if you, as a user, click on a particular cell in the display of a database query, another query based on the values of the clicked cell will initiate and display in a subsequent HTML page.

You'll notice in Figure 12–17 that each cell in the column headed Customer_Id is underlined. This is the universally accepted format for a hot-link or hypertext link. If a user clicked on one of the values in any row underneath the column heading Customer_Id, she or he would trigger a subsequent query to display a detail record of the customer whose ID had been selected (clicked).

Notice in Figure 12–14 that one of the tabs in the Database Table properties dialog box is labeled Drilldown. This is where you'd go as the first step. The Drilldown window, which appears in Figure 12–18, allows you to specify which column in the result set is the drilldown column.

You'll also notice that an item labeled "Destination Page" in the Drill To section has a HTML page identified in it. This instructs HAHTSite IDE that when a user clicks in a cell that allows a drilldown, the results of the query are to display in an HTML page with an identifier of HS_Page_3. This is the internal identifier for Page_3. The HTML filename is Page_3.html, but HAHTsite (HS) precedes the page name with HS_.

Figure 12–19 shows what HS_Page_3 looks like inside the HAHTsite IDE. You'll notice in the painter window (middle right side of the screen image) there are some fields defined for each of the fields in the row selected. Specifically, for each field there is a text identifier describing the field and a text box that will hold the actual database field.

At this point, you've almost finished defining the drill down function. What is left is a process of identifying the source of the data for each of the display items on the HTML

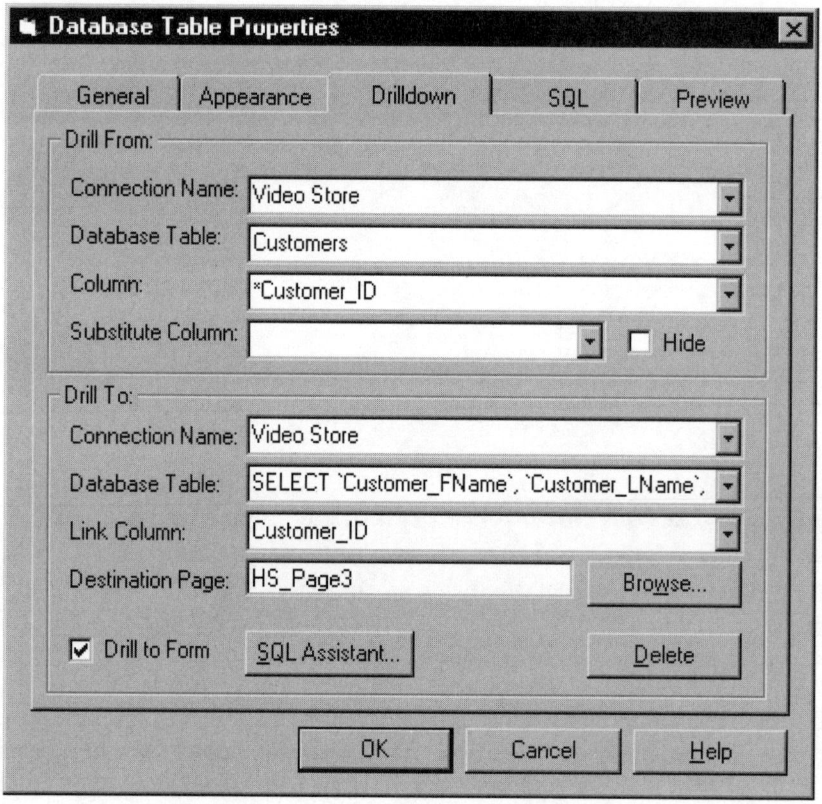

Figure 12–18   The drilldown tab.

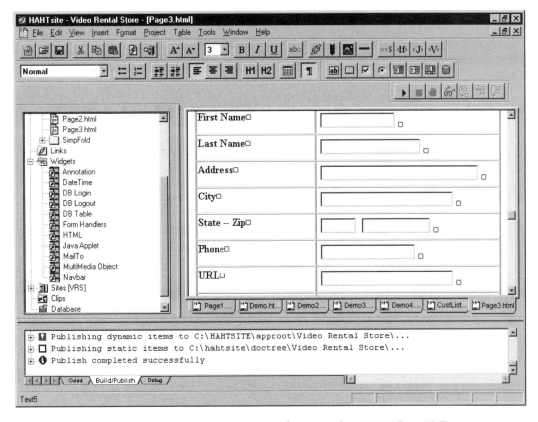

Figure 12–19 The "Drill To" form in the HAHTSite IDE.

page. Since all of the display items originate from the same database row, I'll show you how to do this for the first field, First Name.

Double-click on the text box and you will see a Text Box Properties dialog box, as seen in Figure 12–20. Click on the Database tab, where there are just two fields you need to specify. The first is the Data Set name and the second is the Data Field name.

Provide these two values and click <OK>. That's it! That's all there is to it. Now, do you want to see how it all works?

Let's say you click on the `Customer_ID` for a row in the Customer List window, as seen in Figure 12–17. Assume that you click on `Customer_Id = 9`, which happens to be Celine Dion, (my favorite singing artist). You will go to the Customer Update screen, known as `Page_3.html`, with the contents of the row in the database for Celine Dion displayed on the page! The results of this drill-down are shown in Figure 12–21. Pretty cool, isn't it?

Of course, you know that the magic to all this is the interface between the HTML page and the extensions provided to HTML by HAHTsite and the interpretation of those extensions by a CGI program running on the server. To the user of this application, however, it looks like a very interactive and useful capability to a database application.

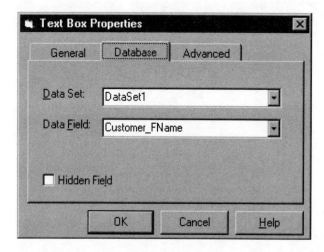

Figure 12–20 The Text Box properties dialog box.

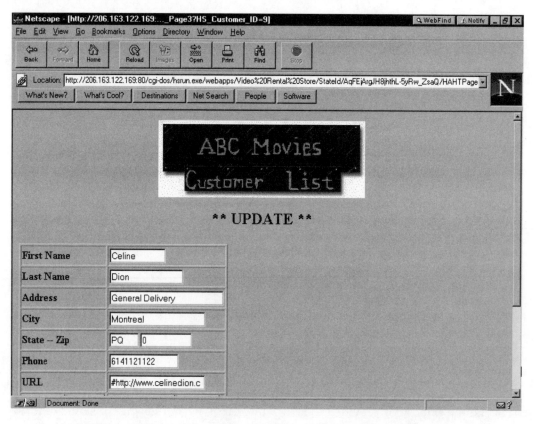

Figure 12–21 The effects of doing a drill-down operation.

OK, by now you should know that Access 97 provides no direct mechanism to access its database tables from within a Web page. Although you can use the Publish To The Web Wizard as discussed in Chapter 9 to create a static Web page of data that exists in an Access 97 table, and then incorporate this Web page in your Web application, any changes that are made to the data in the tables after this page is created are not included until another Publish To The Web process is accomplished.

HAHTsite IDE is one of a growing number of tools that fall into the category of Web database application development suites. These are tools that provide proprietary extensions to HTML that accomplish the steps necessary to connect to a database, format and execute the query, and format and display the results on a Web page.

If at this stage in the chapter you don't think you can use the HAHTsite IDE tool, this is good. The intent has not been to teach you this. If, however, you have a sense of what functions Web database application development tool suites contain and even perhaps the mechanism by which they work, then that is the intent here.

In the following section, I'll take the information presented so far one step further. Here you'll learn the facilities that exist in tools of this type to perform database updates and how these facilities are incorporated in HTML.

Database Updates and HTML

So far, you've seen how easy it is to structure and execute a query against a database from within an HTML form using HAHTSite IDE and the extensions it provides to the HTML specifications. Hopefully, you recognize that other tools of this type perform the same functions in similar ways. Querying databases is fine, but what do you do if you want to insert rows, update existing information, or, delete rows of information? No problem.

Figure 12–21 shows you the form that displays when you do a drilldown operation on a selected customer. At the bottom of the screen are a number of buttons that are of interest; Update, Delete, and Insert. These are seen in Figure 12–22. You should also notice two database movement buttons that are labeled << Previous Next >>.

Because of the point-and-click, graphical interface built into the current generation of Web database application development tool suites, adding these buttons into your forms and causing them to perform the database functions required is very easy. The buttons, and their functions as discussed in this section, need not appear on every Web form. In fact, very few of the Web pages you create will include forms that provide buttons that initiate database update actions. But, as the industry begins to grow more comfortable with the concept of allowing database update access from Web applications, the demand to include this capability in the applications that you design and write will increase.

I'll show you how easy it is.

Step 1: Place Control on the Form

There are three simple activities to this step, as seen in Figure 12–23.

1. Position your cursor in the form where you want to add the control. You do this by right clicking at the correct position.

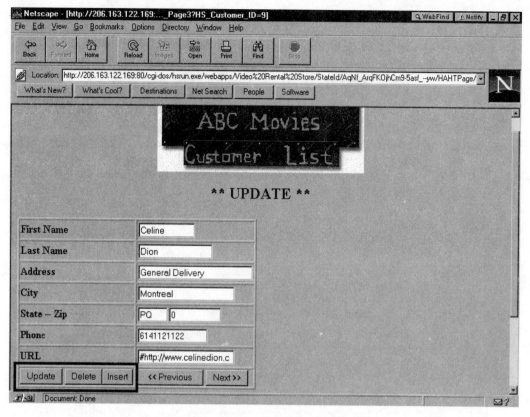

Figure 12-22   The database update and movement buttons.

2. On the toolbar you'll see a command button icon. Right click on time on this control.

3. During step 2, the command button control will be placed into your form at the position indicated. You'll notice that the name of the button is `<Submit>`. This is OK for now—you will change it in the section below labeled Step 2: Assign Caption and Action to the Button.

Step 2: Assign Caption and Action to the Button

If you double-click on the button just placed on the form, you will see the Button Properties dialog box, as seen in Figure 12-24. There are two tabs in this window, the first is labeled General. There are two actions needed on this tab.

1. Supply a caption to the control. The caption is what will appear as a name for the control when it is displayed. Above the caption text box is a text box titled, Name. This is the internal name assigned to this control for use by some extended HAHT-Site IDE functions.

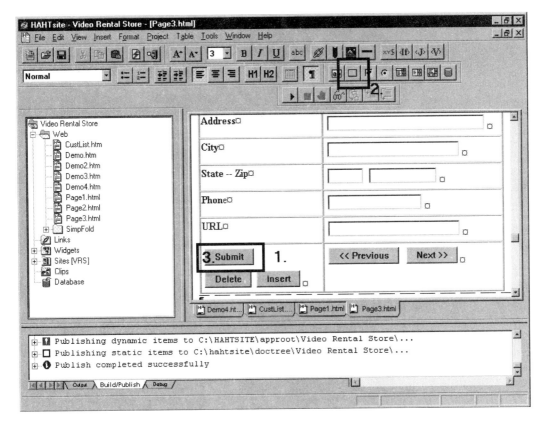

Figure 12–23   Place the control on the form.

2. Click on a radio button to indicate the type of action this button is to have. Since this is an <Update> button, click on the Button radio button.

Step 3: Select the Type of Database Action

When you click on the Database tab in the Button Properties dialog box, you'll see two areas needing information from you, as shown in Figure 12–25. These are specification of a dataset against which the database action is performed and the type of action to be performed.

1. In the Dataset drop down list box, select the dataset against which the intended action is performed.

2. In the Action drop down list box, select the type of action that the button is to perform against the dataset identified above. Notice in Figure 12–25 that there are a number of different actions you can specify, such as Insert, Update, Delete, MovePrevious, and MoveNext.

3. When done specifying the button properties, click the <OK> button.

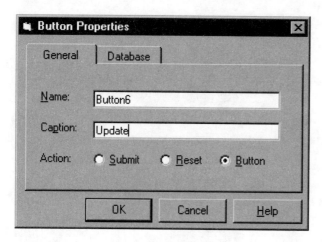

Figure 12–24 Button Properties look at the General tab.

You've seen how to create an <Update> button. In the Action drop down list box in Figure 12–25 you'll see the MovePrevious and MoveNext actions. These are the actions you would select for a <Previous> and a <Next> button on an HTML form.

You've just seen how to place a control on a form that causes an update operation to be applied to the database when it is clicked. The CGI program running on the server is the component that does all the work for you—and you don't even have to write it.

Form Design Tips

The majority of this chapter deals with using HTML objects and HTML extensions to build forms that access Access 97 databases. The following are some form design tips and considerations of which you should be aware.

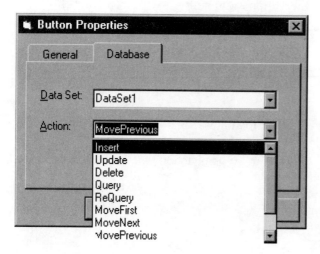

Figure 12–25 Supplying dataset and action information to the button.

- Group input objects together on a form. You can do this by theme, function, data type, etc. This becomes an especially critical action as the length of the form increases.

- Columns that users will want to use to perform a drill-down query have to display on the parent form. This may seem obvious, but columns are sometimes left off when the forms are initially designed.

- Giving a consistent appearance to your forms will help users become comfortable with them more quickly. This means:
  - Use consistent fonts, colors, backgrounds, and graphics.
  - Place labels for objects on a page in a consistent manner. Make a decision and stick with it to either place your text describing the control to the left or to the right of the control.
  - Orient controls in a consistent manner. Your radio buttons and check boxes should all appear vertically or horizontally oriented.
  - Be consistent in where you place button bars. It is customary to place these at the bottom of the form, but if you deviate from this custom, be a consistent deviate.

- Pick meaningful, concise descriptions for controls. A text box labeled "TIN" is much less meaningful than one labeled "Social Security Number."

- Consider the tab order of the text-input objects when placing them. It is awkward for a user to have a tab order on text-input be Name-City-State-Zip-Address. It is much better that the tab order be Name-Address-City-State-Zip.

- Limit the size of the text box and text area controls on the form to the size of the data they will contain. It is wasteful and not very pleasing to look at when a text-input box that allows for 80 characters of input is placed on a form where the text-input box can only hold 8 characters—such as the one you'd have for a password.

- Use the various methods described in this chapter to control the position of the controls on the form. You can really dress up the form if you take some time to lay out the objects well.

- Decide what objects to use based on the type of data to be displayed. It is much better to use Male | Female radio buttons than Male | Female check boxes. A person can be either male or female, but never both or never neither. They have to be one or the other. A group of radio buttons serves this purpose nicely while check boxes would be confusing and could cause erroneous data to be sent.

- When a form requires data input from the user, this should be clearly indicated on the form. It is very aggravating to complete a multi-page form, press the <Submit> button, and then be informed that some needed pieces of information were not supplied.

- If you're writing your own CGI programs for database interactions, be aware of the naming limitations of the language being used to write those CGI programs. You could assign a name to an object on an HTML form that would not be acceptable to certain languages.

- Whenever possible, present defaults in controls such as buttons, check boxes, and lists. Be careful though, you could overdo this.

- Involve users in the design of the HTML forms. With HTML and some of the HTML editors and development tools available, you can very rapidly prototype pages. Take advantage of this capability by involving users to aid in designing an effective user interface. Remember, what looks good to you, the developer, may not look as good to the person using it.

There are a number of books available that will help you design effective Web forms. The following list below is a great start.

Title:	Hybrid Html Design: A Multi-Browser HTML Reference
Author:	Kevin Ready, Janine Warner
Publisher:	New Riders Publishing
ISBN:	1-56-205617-4

Title:	Mastering Web Design
Author:	John McCoy
Publisher:	Sybex Press
ISBN:	0-78-211911-5

Title:	Creative HTML Design
Author:	Lynda Weinman, Bill Weinman
Publisher:	New Riders Publishing
ISBN:	1-56-205704-9

Moving On

This chapter focused on designing HTML forms that access databases. You know that HTML specifications provide no direct capability to access databases—that this capability is provided by one of three ways that were presented in the section titled Database Queries and HTML. This chapter used a hybrid of two of these methods, Code-less interfaces and HTML embedded SQL extensions. Toward this end you saw how the use of a tool like HAHTSite IDE facilitates this.

The next chapter presents material on the third way that you can incorporate database queries in HTML—by using a Custom CGI program.

CHAPTER 13

Accessing Web Databases Using CGI Programs

This chapter begins with a review of the CGI basics you learned in previous chapters in this book. You will learn about CGI input and output processing, and some of the different ways that exist in which a client can make a request to the server when an HTML form is submitted. Then, you will see how CGI programs can be used to generate HTML.

Later in this chapter you will learn how to write a CGI program to perform whatever type of database access is required by your Web database application. Rather than use a specific programming language, I will present examples written in pseudocode. That way you can choose whichever language best suits your needs. These examples will address the following issues:

- Query (select) records from an Access 97 database
- Insert records in an Access 97 database
- Update records in an Access 97 database
- Modify records in an Access 97 database

If you have limited skills in a CGI programming language, refer back to Chapter 3 for a list of books that will help you with many of the most popular languages.

Basics of CGI Programs

Recall what you learned in Chapters 5 and 12—that is, that Web application development suites allow you to create applications with full database access capabilities without having to write CGI programs that accomplish this back-end processing. These development tools usually include a CGI program that is already written and supplied with the product that does this database processing. If you are using one of these tools, then you will still find value in this chapter. The reason is that even though the CGI database access programs are already written and supplied for you, you may still find value in writing your own CGI programs in some situations. Some reasons for writing your own CGI programs are to:

- Create non-database query/update processing, such as:
  - Randomly modify the wallpaper that your application uses
  - Create a registry of people that have visited your site
  - Keep a count of the hits your Web site has had
- Provide financial transaction processing to your applications
- Provide statistic functionality to your application
- Supply documents stored in a document repository to the user

---

Tip: Even though I am not including specific code samples that show you how to perform the above, I would like to point you to a very useful URL for this type of CGI program. The URL is `http:\\www.worldwidemart.com\scripts\`. The name of this site is *Matt's Script Archive*. It is run by a CGI wire head named Matt Wright and is the home of a bevy of well-written free CGI scripts, including the ones listed above.

If you are not using a Web application development suite, then this chapter will be one that you refer to often. You will see specific examples of code that perform a number of different types of database access. Before we proceed into the actual code used to accomplish various types of database processing, let's take a look at the CGI process.

The CGI Process

Figure 13–1 displays the normal CGI process flow. This process is described below.

1. A user, accessing a Web browser, sends a request to a Web server via HTML. This HTML includes a request to execute a CGI program, as well as any parameters the CGI program might need.
2. The Web server receives the request from the browser, processes the HTML, and encounters the request to execute a CGI program. The Web server initiates the CGI program's execution by calling it and passing it any parameters that were received from the browser.
3. The CGI program executes. In its execution, it may:
   - Access no other resources
   - Access databases either locally or remotely
   - Access other applications or initiate the execution of other programs
   - Access other network resources
4. The Web server receives a result set from the CGI program if one is returned, and sends the data and/or response back to the browser via HTML.

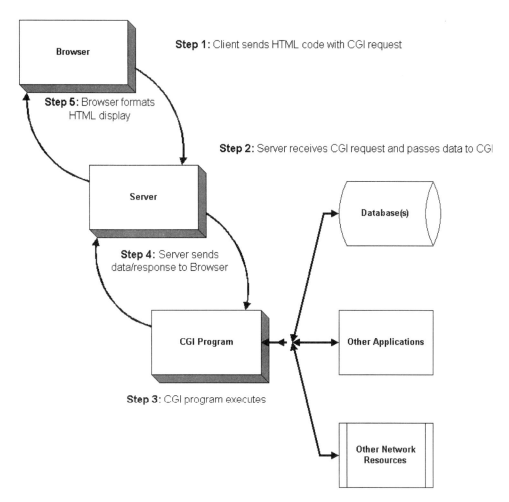

Figure 13–1   The CGI process flow.

5. The browser receives the HTML sent to it from the Web server and formats and displays the data received.

CGI Data Input and Output

CGI input data is data that is passed to the Web server from the user's browser, with the intent that the Web server will pass it to the CGI program. The CGI program uses this data to determine its logical execution path and to (potentially) format a query to a database.

Additionally, the Web server can format and pass information to the CGI program that describes the type of data that was passed. This is what happens when data is passed to a CGI program via standard input. By providing this type of information, the CGI program can determine how to process the data it receives.

The Web server not only initiates the execution of the CGI program by sending it data that is passed from the browser and launching the program, but it is the machine on which the CGI program executes. Then, the CGI program returns program output to the Web server for formatting and sending back to the browser.

There is one, and only one, way that CGI programs return output. That is by standard output. Even in the rare situation when a CGI program returns no data, it still formats and generates a response via standard output that indicates there was no data sent.

CGI standard output data is returned in one of two formats, *parsed header output* and *non-parsed header output*. With parsed header output the data created by the CGI program is received and interpreted by the Web server and then sent to the user's browser. With non-parsed header output, the Web server has the responsibility (and overhead) of generating the header information and sending it, along with the rest of the response, to the user's browser.

CGI Environmental Variables

CGI environmental variables can be thought of as little buckets of information, each one with a unique name, that are used to hold data passed from one program or process (in this case the Web server) to another program or process (in this case the CGI program). CGI scripts use environmental variables for a number of reasons—not the least of which is to pass data between the Web server and the CGI program. There are two types of CGI environmental variables, *request-specific* and *not-request-specific* variables.

Request-specific variables are those environmental variables that are specific to the client request that the CGI program is fulfilling. Not-request-specific variables are those environmental variables that are set during all client requests. Request-specific variables are those that are very specific to the type of request received from the user's browser while not-request-specific variables are those that are generic to any or all types of requests received from the user's browser.

CGI environmental variables, regardless of their type, are used by CGI programs to:

- Specify the type of processing and database request the CGI program must perform
- Indicate the type of browser the client is using
- Maintain and pass state information

For a listing of these environmental variables and the type of information contained in each, refer to Chapter 7 which gives a thorough description and explanation of them.

Passing CGI Data Streams

There are several ways that a Web client can transmit data strings to a CGI program with three being the post popular. These are:

- GET
- ISINDEX
- POST

These are described in this section.

GET Method to Transmit CGI Data Streams.   You use the GET method when passing data provided by users via HTML forms to CGI programs. Because of the limitation on the amount of data (usually 256 characters) that can be passed to a CGI program using the GET method, it is the least desirable way of the three listed to transfer data to the CGI program. Its strength is in its ease of use when passing only a few data fields.

The GET method causes a query string to append to the action URL when the user presses the <Submit> button on a form. A complete string (including the request for a CGI process and the passed parameters, which is the part in italics) passed to the Web server may look like:

```
GET /cgi-bin/processform.pl?action=READ&screen=QUERY HTTP/1.1
```

What this string does is to cause the Perl script named processform.pl, that is located in the cgi-bin directory on the server, to begin executing, while also passing two name/value pairs to it. The two pairs are the name action, with a value of READ, and the name screen, with a value of QUERY. The processform.pl Perl script would accept and interpret these two name/value pairs and perform whatever processing the programmer had designed into the program.

ISINDEX Method to Transmit CGI Data Streams.   You use the ISINDEX method when the need exists to perform database queries. The latest HTML specifications allow for the addition of the <ISINDEX> tag to your HTML code. This tag allows the HREF URL to perform a query based on data input by a user. The syntax for this is:

```
<HEAD>

<ISINDEX HREF="URL-CGI Program">

</HEAD>
```

In this example, URL-CGI Program is the URL for the CGI program to execute. Therefore, assuming an URL for a CGI executable as http://teleport.com/cgi-bin/processit.exe, and passed parameters to this program of ?lastname+taxyear, the HTML code would look as follows:

```
<HEAD>

<ISINDEX HREF="http://teleport.com/cgi-
bin/processit.exe?lastname+taxyear">

</HEAD>
```

Following this example, the Web browser would pass the following string to the Web server:

```
http://teleport.com/cgi-bin/processit.exe?lastname+taxyear
```

The Web server receives this string, and causes the processit.exe CGI program to begin executing with a passed command string of: lastname+taxyear.

POST Method to Transmit CGI Data Streams.   The POST method is conceptually similar to the GET method, with much broader application. Whereas the GET method appends the user supplied data to the ACTION URL, the POST method is formatted and sent to the server in a stream of data of varying length which is passed to the CGI program.

A specific example of using the POST method to receive CGI data streams follows.

```
POST /cgi-bin/processit.exe HTTP/1.1

Accept: text/plain

Accept: text/html

Accept: */*

Content-type: application/x-www-form-urlencoded

Content-length: 42

state=OR&politics=Republican&Minimum=25000
```

When this data stream is received by the Web server, it passes it directly to the CGI program named `processit.exe`. The `processit.exe` program might then do something like format and execute a query against an Access 97 database to extract the names, addresses, and telephone numbers of all the contributors to the Republican party in the state of Oregon who made a contribution of at least $25,000.

Tip: The Content-Length environmental variable is not required, but it is a very good idea to include it—and to be accurate when using it. The reason you should use it is that some servers do not send an end of file marker to CGI programs. Without the Content-Length variable, the CGI program may not receive the correct data. The reason it is important to establish the correct parameter to signify the passed string length is that you may end up truncating the data or sending extraneous data to the CGI program in the passed string.

Reading User Data into CGI Programs

You've seen in the previous section three ways to get user-supplied data streams to a CGI program. In this section you'll see how to read and process that data in a CGI program.

As you know, CGI programs can be written in a number of different languages. You have your favorite one, which may not be mine. Therefore, the basic steps to read user data into a CGI program are described below in *pseudo-code*:

```
Determine the method used to transmit the data by querying the
REQUEST_METHOD and QUERY-STRING environmental variables

IF the GET method was used to transmit data THEN
  Parse the QUERY_STRING environmental variable name-value pairs into
  their respective components

ELSEIF the ISINDEX method was used to transmit data THEN
  Parse the QUERY_STRING environmental variable into its component parts

ELSE
```

Read the value of the passed string from the CONTENT_LENGTH environmental variable and parse this number of characters from the string in the QUERY_STRING environmental variable.

END

Once the passed string is either separated into its component parts or parsed appropriately, it can be processed by the CGI program accordingly.

Now that you've reviewed the basics of what CGI is and how data is received into, processed from, and output by a CGI program, its time to see how a Web server uses the power of a CGI program to access databases by submitting and processing queries on behalf of a Web client.

Common Web Database Access Methods

As you learned in Chapter 12, HTML specifications provide no direct method for querying a database. There are a number of different methods you can use to build database connectivity into your HTML form. These are:

> *Code-less interfaces*—These are software toolsets that work in tandem with developer defined template files. The purpose of the templates is to define various views into the database and describe how data is to be displayed once it is retrieved. When these forms are incorporated into an HTML page and sent to the Web server for processing, they are processed by CGI programs that perform the actual querying and formatting of the data.

> *Custom CGI program*—These are "gateway" programs that are specifically written to accept and process SQL queries. These programs receive the user's request for DBMS data, parse the user inputs and create a query to accommodate the user request, and dynamically create an HTML document that transmits the result set back to the user. This method of database access is the one that is presented in this chapter.

> *HTML embedded SQL extensions*—These are special HTML extensions supplied by RDBMS and other tool vendors that provide a mechanism to embed SQL statements directly into the body of the HTML file that is passed from the user to the Web server. When received at the server, this HTML file is parsed to pull out the SQL statements that are subsequently passed to a CGI program.

Why Use Custom CGI Programs for Database Access?

Custom CGI programs are the most common method of accessing corporate databases, far eclipsing the other two methods described above. Although code-less interfaces and HTML embedded SQL extensions may someday catch up to and surpass the popularity of custom CGI programs, this is not expected to happen for many years. And, when that time does come, the need and use for custom CGI programs will continue—in fact, it may never end. There will always be an inherent limit to the power and flexibility of code-less interfaces and HTML-embedded SQL extensions that custom CGI programs will exceed.

This is why all the major development toolkits provide API interfaces to more powerful languages.

Ways CGI Programs Access Databases

The following are some of the ways that custom CGI programs access databases.

SQL Queries—These are the most common way, as well as the way used to access Access 97 databases.

Non-SQL Queries—These are used to access non-RDBMS databases, including network databases, and hierarchical databases such as IMS.

ODBC/JDBC—These are APIs made available by the RDBMS vendor and CGI programming tool vendor to act as an interface between the front-end development tool and the back-end database.

Stored Procedures—Stored procedures are RDBMS-specific database instructions that are executed either on a predefined schedule or at will by a calling (accessing) program.

Ways CGI Programs Provide Advantages over Other Methods

CGI programs give you, the developer, several advantages over other back-end programs. Some of these are shown in Table 13–1.

Now that you've seen some of the advantages to using a CGI program in your Web database application, the following section describes some of the factors to consider in choosing the right programming language.

Choosing a CGI Programming Language

As you learned in Chapter 3, choosing a CGI programming language is not much different from choosing a programming language for any other type of application. In fact, many of the factors discussed below are the same.

Whereas Chapter 3 discussed many of the actual programming language options you have in deciding which to use for your CGI programs, the information in this section is provided to help you recognize the factors to consider when choosing which language to use.

Code Libraries—Unless you are using a really obscure CGI programming language, have unlimited time, or have a very simple CGI program to write, you will probably need to make use of code libraries. The general rule of thumb is: Don't reinvent the code if you can get it already written!

Cost—The amount of money available in the project budget for support tools, development tools, testing tools, etc. should all be considered when evaluating CGI

Table 13–1 Advantages of CGI Programs

Advantage	Description
Choice	There are a wide number of languages (more than 15) from which you can chose to write your CGI programs. These are broken into the following categories:
	Compiled Languages—These are languages in which the original code syntax must be translated to a platform-specific set of binary executable code before it can be processed on a given platform. Examples of these are; C, C++, Fortran.
	Interpreted Languages—These are languages where the original code syntax is read by, translated, and executed by the target machine at runtime. Examples of these are; Perl, Visual Basic, Java.
Complexity	Because of the power and control the developer has in most CGI programming languages, custom CGI programs can be written to accomplish very complex tasks. This could include validation of user input before posting to a database, integration of the Web database application with other non-Web applications, and generation of dynamic HTML data presentations.
Control	CGI programs give you total control over the data input to your database, how that data is processed, how it is extracted from the database, and how it is presented to the user.
Exploitation	Because of the API interfaces provided by most CGI programming-language tool vendors, you can exploit the power of other tools that interface with the CGI programming language to extend the functionality of the CGI program.
Flexibility	CGI programs give you the ability to access a wide variety of databases. Additionally, you can access more than one type of a database, from more than one database vendor, from within a single CGI program.

programming languages. Some of these tools are free, while others are quite expensive. For example, most testing tools are very expensive. If the scope of your project requires that you use a testing tool of some sort, then you must consider the cost of testing tools in relation to the programming language in the decision making process.

Function—Your CGI program will require that certain functionality be provided from the language in which program is developed.

Integration—If your CGI program will not interface with any other applications, then this is a non-issue. However, if this is not the case, you should consider the integration afforded by candidate languages with other applications and the languages used by those other applications.

Learning Curve—In addition to the current skill set of the present development team being a consideration factor, the amount of time in the project schedule to develop adequate skills in the proposed CGI programming language is a decision factor when choosing the language.

Life-Cycle—The amount of rework that the CGI program is expected to endure during its life cycle is a decision factor in choosing the language it is written in. Very rarely are programs of any sort, including CGI programs, written and placed into production that never require any type of maintenance.

Present Skills—The skillset that exists in the development team should be considered carefully when choosing a CGI programming language. For example, a skilled Visual Basic programmer does not possess the skills needed to master the Perl language nearly as easily as a skilled C++ programmer.

RDBMS Interfaces—Certainly one of the most significant (if not the most significant) consideration in writing a CGI program to access a Web database is the RDBMS interfaces provided by the candidate CGI programming languages. I generally choose Visual Basic to write CGI programs that access MS Access 97 databases due to the direct interface that is supplied and the speed of data access thus afforded.

Schedules—The amount of time available to write the CGI program is critical to choosing a CGI programming language. C programs are generally more efficient than Visual Basic programs, although Visual Basic is generally a more productive programming language.

Speed—Certain types of processing are more intensive than others. Different programming languages handle certain functions with different efficiencies. For example, C++ offers more efficient string handling capabilities than Visual Basic, although Visual Basic provides generally quicker access to Access 97 databases than does C++.

What you've read so far in this chapter is meant to be a review of CGI and the information in Chapter 7. With this as a foundation, the rest of the chapter will show you how to use CGI to read and process against Access 97 databases in Web applications.

Accessing Web Databases Using CGI Programs

Figure 13–2 is a generalized flowchart of the data and logic flows through a CGI program. What is not shown is the supplemental program logic that you would write to support whatever processing is required of the application to support business rules. Being a programmer, you should already have a good handle on this.

As you know, once the CGI program determines the FORM method that was used to place user-supplied data by the server in an accessible location, the program flow is not too dissimilar from the flow you may expect in any other program that processes against a database.

In reality, you will probably know what FORM method is used by your application to place user-supplied data in a place and format in which the CGI program can access it. You will know this because you probably will be the one to write it! The first decision branch is therefore included for documentation purposes to show you the two different ways in which you could retrieve the data into your CGI program—each based on the

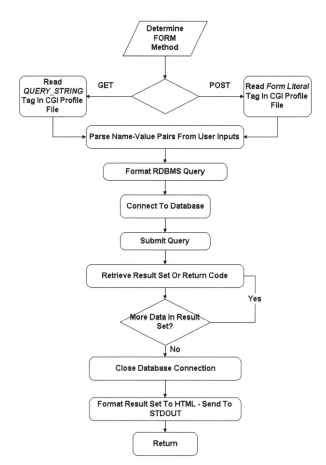

Figure 13–2 CGI database program flow.

FORM method used. For an in-depth description of the different FORM methods, refer to Chapter 7.

Contents of the CGI Profile File

The CGI profile file is used when the POST FORM method is used. It is a mechanism used to pass information sent from the browser through the server, and into the CGI program. The following briefly describes the process used by a Web server to decode data passed to it from the browser (in the URL) and place it into the CGI profile file for use by the CGI program.

For each name/value pair that exists in the URL encoded string, the server decodes the value and places a line in the [Form Literal] section of the CGI profile file for each name/value pair. Each of these lines is in the format:

```
name=value
```

If the decoded value is 255 characters or more in length, the server places the decoded value in a temporary file. It then places a line in the [Form External] section of the CGI profile file in the format:

```
name=pathname length
```

where `pathname` is the path and name of the temporary file and `length` is the size in bytes of the decoded value

If the length of the name/value pair is 65,536 bytes or more, the server does not decode the name/value pair. The server marks the location and size of the value in the CGI content file and lists the name in the [Form Huge] section of the CGI profile file in the format:

```
name=offset length
```

where `offset` is the offset from the beginning of the CGI content file at which the raw data first appears and `length` is the length of the raw data expressed in bytes.

There are seven sections in a CGI profile file, but not all are required. The sections contained in a CGI profile file for your application are dependent on the CGI programming language and your architectural and operating environments. The seven sections are:

- Accept
- CGI
- Extra Headers
- Form External
- Form Huge
- Form Literal
- System

Each of these are shown here as they might appear in a CGI profile file.

```
[Accept]
xxx/yyy=zzz…                  If the MIME types found in the request header
as:
   Accept: xxx/yyy; zzzz...
xxx/yyy=Yes          If only the MIME type appears in the request header

[CGI]
Authentication Method=  Method used for authentication (e.g., "Basic")
Authenticated Password=  If present is the Password in the request
Authentication Realm=  Name of realm for users/groups
Authenticated Username=  If present is the username in the request
CGI Version=                  The version of CGI running and recognized by
the server
Content Length=          Length specified in bytes of information sup-
plied with the request
Content Type=            MIME content type of info supplied with request
```

Executable Path=	Physical pathname of the back-end cgi directory
From=	E-Mail of client user
Logical Path=	Extra path info in logical space
Physical Path=	Extra path info in local physical space
Query String=	String following the "?" in the request URL sent by the browser
Referer=	URL of referring document
Remote Address=	The remote client's network address
Remote Host=	The remote client's network hostname
Request Method=	The method specified in the request (e.g., "GET", "POST")
Request Keep-Alive=	Does the client request connection be re-used? (Yes|No)
Request Protocol=	The server's request protocol (e.g. HTTP/1.0)
Request Range=	Byte-range specified with the request
Server Admin=	E-Mail address of server's administrator
Server Name=	Server's network hostname (or alias from config)
Server Port=	Server's network port assignment
Server Software=	Version of the Web server software
User Agent=	String describing client/browser software/version

[Extra Headers]
```
; These are any "extra" headers that may be
; found in the request that initates the CGI
; program. They are listed in "key=value"
; form.
```

[Form External]
```
; If the decoded value string is more than 254
; characters long, or if the decoded value
; string contains any special control
; characters or quote marks the server puts
; the decoded value into an external tempfile
; and lists the field in this section as:
;     key=<pathname> <length>
;     where <pathname> is the path and name of
;     the tempfile containing the decoded
;     value string
;     <length> is the length in bytes of the
;     decoded value string.
```

[Form File]
```
; If the form data contained any uploaded
; files, they are described in this section
; as:
;     key=[<pathname>] <length> <type>
;          <encoding> [<name>]
;          where <pathname> is the path and name
;          of the tempfile containing the
;          uploaded file,
```

```
;        <length> is the length in bytes of
;        the uploaded file,
;        <type> is the content type of the
;        uploaded file as sent by the browser
;        <encoding> is the content-transfer
;        encoding of the uploaded file,
;        <name> is the original file name of
;        the uploaded file.
```

[Form Huge]
```
; If the raw value string is more than 65,536
; bytes long, the server does no decoding. In
; this case, the server lists the field in
; this section as:
;   key=<offset> <length>
;        where <offset> is the offset from the
;        beginning of the Content File at which
;        the raw value string for this key is
;        located
;        <length> is the length in bytes of the
;        raw value string. You can use the
;        <offset> to perform a "Seek" to the
;        start of the raw value string, and
;        use the length to know when you have
;        read the entire raw string into your
;        decoder.
```

[Form Literal]
```
; If the request was a POST from a Mosaic form ; (with content type of
"application/x-www-
; form-urlencoded"), the server will decode
; the form data. Raw form input is of the form
; "key=value&key=value&...", with the value
; parts "URL-encoded." The server splits the
; key=value pairs at the '&', then splits the
; key and value at the '=', URL-decodes the
; value string and puts the result into
; key=value (decoded) form in the [Form
; Literal] section of the INI.
```

[System]
Content File=   Pathname of file containing raw request content input
to CGI processing
Debug Mode=   Indicates if the server's CGI debug flag is set
(Yes|No)
GMT Offset=   Offset of local timezone from GMT, seconds
Output File=   Pathname of file to receive results of CGI processing

Querying a Database

Let's take a look at an example of a HTML form initiating the query of a database. To be sure, and at the risk of being redundant, the process summarized is:

- The HTML form initiates the query by the FORM METHOD used and written in the HTML code
- The FORM METHOD is interpreted by the Web server
- The Web server begins the execution of the CGI program that actually queries the database.

Each step in this process is described in detail. For the sake of clarity, all extraneous images, text, controls, and other objects that would ordinarily appear on a Web page are removed from this and the other examples in this section.

The Web Database Query Page

The following HTML code is used to generate the Web page as seen in Figure 13–3. The purpose of this Web page is to have the user select a movie rating to use in the WHERE clause of a SELECT statement.

```
<IITML>
<HEAD>
<TITLE>This is a SELECT Query Example</TITLE>
</HEAD>
<BODY>
</BODY>
<FORM METHOD=POST ACTION="http://teleport.com/cgi-bin/query.exe">
<P>Rating: <SELECT MULTIPLE RATING=Movie_Rating SIZE=3>
<OPTION VALUE="PG">PG</OPTION>
<OPTION VALUE="PG 13">PG13</OPTION>
<OPTION VALUE="R">R</OPTION>
<OPTION VALUE="NR">NR</OPTION>
</SELECT></P>
<P><INPUT NAME=Sub_button TYPE=SUBMIT VALUE="SUBMIT"></P>
</FORM>
</HTML>
```

Web Server Action on Receiving the Query Request

In the HTML code, you'll notice a few items and controls that are significant to the execution of this process. First is the <FORM METHOD> tag, that appears as follows:

```
<FORM METHOD=POST ACTION="http://teleport.com/cgi-bin/query.exe">
```

When the request which is initiated from the browser is received at the Web server, the Web server places the data passed to it in various sections of the CGI profile file, and then begins the execution of the query.exe program. This program is located in the cgi-bin directory on the Web server identified by http://teleport.com. Note that this is an example of URL addressing.

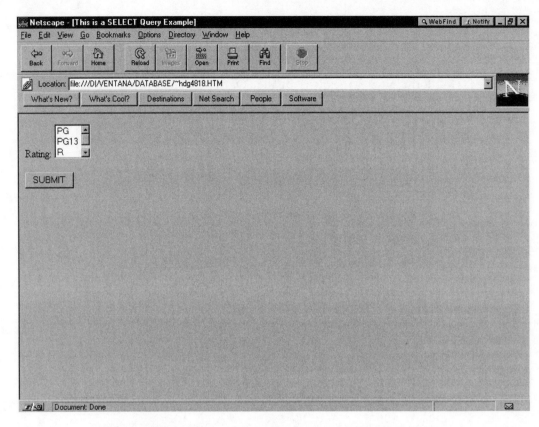

Figure 13–3   The Web page initiating a database query.

Some of the information placed in the CGI profile file by the Web server upon receiving this request is identified here:

```
[CGI]
Authentication Method=  Basic
CGI Version=            2.0
Content Type=           MIME content type of info supplied with request
Executable Path=        d:\webpage\cgi-bin\query.exe
Request Method=         POST
Request Keep-Alive=     NO
Request Protocol=       HTTP/1.1
Server Name=            teleport
Server Port=            126.160.112.50
Server Software=        WebSTAR 2.1

[Extra Headers]

[Form External]

[Form File]
```

[Form Huge]

[Form Literal]
MOVIE_RATING=PG 13

[System]

Take note that because the Web page uses the POST method, the passing of data to the CGI program is achieved by placing the data in the FORM LITERAL section of the CGI profile file. If, on the other hand, the GET method had been used, then the Web server would have placed the passed information it received from the client browser into the QUERY STRING tag in the CGI section of the CGI profile file. It would have then calculated and placed the length of the passed string in the CONTENT LENGTH tag, which is also in the CGI section of the CGI profile file.

Execution of the CGI Program for a Database Query

Referring back to Figure 13–2, you see that the first action performed by the CGI program is to determine the FORM method used. Also note that, in most cases, the person writing the CGI program will know which FORM method was used to pass information to the program. However, to determine the type of FORM method used is a simple process of querying the value of the Request Method tag in the CGI section of the CGI profile file. In this example, the value is POST.

Depending on the programming language used to write your CGI program, the process of querying the value of a tag in a profile file varies. Also, some of the other steps discussed in this section require different techniques. The steps are the same, but the actual coding and processes may be different. Consult the documentation for the programming language you are using to determine how to accomplish the steps described in this section.

Once the FORM method is determined, you have only to parse the name/value pairs before you can get down to the actual database query. Depending on the FORM method, the parsing is different. If the FORM method is POST, then the name-value pairs are stored in the CGI profile file, in the FORM LITERAL section. Since you are using the POST method, the following lines appear in the CGI profile file:

[Form Literal]
MOVIE_RATING=PG 13

If you are using the GET method, then the process is a bit more complicated, but not too difficult for most programming languages. It is a simple process of the following:

- Retrieve the contents of the Query String line in the CGI section of the CGI profile file
- Iteratively extract the name/value pairs, recognizing that each is separated by an ampersand (&).

Therefore, the following value in the Query String would extract to the associated name/value pairs:

CompanyName=ABC Systems Computers&Street=&URL=http:\\teleport.com

Name/value pairs:

```
CompanyName=ABC Systems
Street=
URL=http:\\teleport.com
```

Referring back to Figure 13–2, you see that once the name/value pairs are parsed, the next steps are to:

- Format the Access 97 query
- Connect to the database
- Submit query
- Retrieve result set
- Close database connection

At this point in the process, there is nothing special about this program and the fact that it originated from a Web initiated request—the program logic and process flow are *exactly* the same as if the program was *not* part of a Web database application. Because I want to keep the presentation of the material in this section as language-independent as possible, you'll see no sample code here. You would accomplish all of the steps exactly the same as you would if this were not a Web-initiated program. Once the database connection is closed, however, it is time to format the result set to HTML and send it to the standard output device.

Types of CGI Output Responses

Earlier in this chapter you learned that CGI programs communicate back to a client via CGI standard output. Given this, there are two ways to package a response to a Web client from a CGI program using CGI standard output/*direct* and *indirect*. In the direct method, the Web server is involved only as a transport mechanism. The following is a code example of what a CGI program might produce if it is using the direct method.

```
HTTP/1.1 200 OK
Date: Tuesday, 22-Apr-97 16:02:10 GMT
Server: WebSTAR 1.0
MIME-version: 1.0
Content-type: text/html
Content-length: 1096
Last-modified: Tuesday, 22-Apr-97 16:02:10 GMT

<HTML>

. . .

</HTML>
```

Notice the existence of the HTTP/ character string in the first line of the sample code. To know what type of output processing a CGI program is using, the Web server inspects the first line of the CGI output file. If the first line starts with the character string

`HTTP/`, the Web server knows that this is a direct response. If this text string is missing, the Web server assumes the CGI program is using the indirect response.

In the indirect method, the Web server takes a more proactive role in the communication between the CGI program and the Web client by packaging the CGI response with header information. The following is a code example of what a CGI program might produce if it is using the indirect method.

```
Content-type: text/html

<HTML>

. . .

</HTML>
```

Notice the lack of existence of the `HTTP/` character string in the first line of the sample code. This tells the Web server that the CGI program has generated output using the indirect method.

Output from a CGI Program Doing a SELECT Query

Once you determine what type of CGI output processing you want to use, creating the HTML code to send back to the browser is relatively simple. The key is to realize that the CGI program creates and outputs the HTML code necessary to format an HTML page.

The following listing is a partial example of the HTML code needed to generate the Web page shown in Figure 13–4.

```
Content-type: text/html
<HTML>
<HEAD>
<TITLE>Output From SELECT Query</TITLE>
</HEAD>
<BODY>
<TABLE BORDER=1>
<TR><TD><STRONG><CENTER>Title</CENTER></STRONG></TD>
<TD><STRONG><CENTER>Type</CENTER></STRONG></TD>
<TD><STRONG><CENTER>Rating</CENTER></STRONG></TD>
<TD><STRONG><CENTER>Male_Star</CENTER></STRONG></TD>
<TD><STRONG><CENTER>Female_Star</CENTER></STRONG></TD>
<TD><STRONG><CENTER>Qty</CENTER></STRONG></TD></TR>
<TR><TD>Best Of The WWF</TD>
<TD>Action</TD>
<TD>PG 13</TD>
<TD>Hogan</TD>
<TD></TD>
<TD>10</TD></TR>
<TR><TD>Tornado</TD>
<TD>Action</TD>
<TD>PG 13</TD>
<TD></TD>
<TD>Hunt</TD>
```

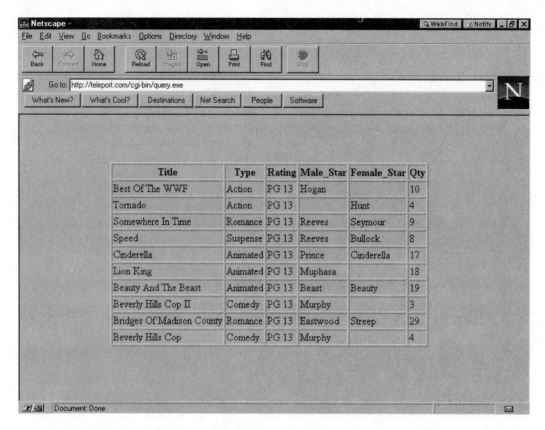

Figure 13–4   The output from the CGI program as seen in a browser.

```
<TD>4</TD></TR>
<TR><TD>Somewhere In Time</TD>
<TD>Romance</TD>
<TD>PG 13</TD>
<TD>Reeves</TD>
<TD>Seymour</TD>
<TD>9</TD></TR>
</TABLE>
</BODY>
</HTML>
```

You should note a couple of things from this code sample. The first line of code reads:

```
Content-type: text/html
```

As you know, this tells the Web server that the developer of the program is using the indirect method. Second, the HTML code is exactly the same as you would write if you wanted to write an HTML page.

The key to this process of having the CGI program generate the HTML code for the result page of the database query is quite simple. Simply format the display of the result set in your CGI program exactly as you would format report lines of the query, with the exception that you have to include embedded HTML tags and tag pairs around the data.

Basically this involves formatting a series of what you can think of as "report lines" within your CGI program. Each of these report lines, when output from your CGI program, is shown in the last example. Because of the MIME header (`Content-type: text/html`), the server recognizes that what follows is HTML code and treats it as such.

If you are confused about what is going on here, think about it this way. A program, in this case a program that we call a CGI program, queries an Access 97 database and receives a result set. The program then formats a report from the result set. In this case, the report is the data retrieved from the database query along with a series of HTML tags placed where needed to achieve the desired result when the report is viewed in a browser. The first report line written from the CGI program, (`Content-type: text/html`), is one that instructs the server that all the report lines that follow from this CGI program are HTML code. The server then knows to interpret the remainder of the report lines that it receives from the CGI program as HTML code, and to send the HTML code back to the client.

Redirecting CGI Output

It is sometimes necessary to redirect the output from your CGI program to another information resource as its response. This is possible by generating a Location or an URL header line as the first line of the CGI output. The syntax of these header lines is:

```
Location: absolute or relative URL
URL: absolute or relative URL
```

If the Location or URL header line generated as the first line from the CGI program points to a resource or resource file on the Internet, and if that reference contains no references in it to other resources on the Internet, then this is termed an *absolute URL*.

In some cases though, the resource file referenced by an URL could be a data file that contains HTML code. In that HTML file, the first line could contain a link to still another resource or resource file located on the Internet. If this is the case, then the Location or URL header line generated as the first line from the CGI program is said to be a *relative URL*.

Therefore, the following one line of code could be generated from your CGI program:

```
Location: /teleport.com/cgi-bin/redir.out
```

The contents of the `redir.out` file would then contain the HTML code that formats and displays the result set of the query in the user's browser.

There are a number of advantages to redirecting output from your CGI program. When the CGI program needs to generate a static HTML page instead of a dynamic page of the query results, it is best to have these types of pages predefined. For example, if the result set of the query contained zero rows, you'd want to send a message to the user indicating this. If you are not sure of the format or layout of a result set, you could have the

CGI program format a redirected output line, referencing a dataset that contains HTML code that indicates this. If another program other than the CGI program creates the result set, you would want to reference this other program's output file from the CGI program so it can be seen in the client's browser.

Returning an Error Code

A Windows CGI program could have a need to send a status code and message to the user to indicate that there was something wrong when trying to process the SELECT query. This is accomplished using a special Status header line that immediately precedes the MIME header line that reads: `Content-type: text/html`. The format for this line is:

```
Status: code description
```

The `code` is a HTTP status code and `description` is an explanation of the status code. Therefore, the following is a sample of some HTML code that could be generated from the CGI program to return an error code to the Web client.

```
Status: 400 Bad Request
Content-type: text/html
<HTML>
<TITLE>400--Bad Request</TITLE>
<BODY><H1>Bad request--error code 400</H1></BODY>
</HTML>
```

When seen in a browser, this CGI output would resemble that seen in Figure 13–5.

A CGI program in a Web database application is really very little more than any other type of program that you'd write in a non-Web database application. The main differences between the two are:

- The CGI program begins execution because a Web server has received a request from a browser to start the program.
- After querying the database, the CGI program wraps a bunch of HTML tags around the data that it formats in the shape of a report before it spits it out.

Inserting Rows in a Database from a Web Application

Let's now see how you'd place functions in your Web database application to add rows of data to your Access 97 database from the Web front-end. As before, each step in this process is described in detail. Also, again for the sake of clarity, all extraneous images, text, controls, and other objects that would ordinarily appear on a Web page are removed from this and the other examples in this section.

The Web Database Insert Row Page

The following HTML code is used to generate the Web page as seen in Figure 13–6. The purpose of this Web page is to have the user provide the information that will be used to create a new row in a table in the Access 97 database.

```
<HTML>
<HEAD>
<TITLE>Add a Record</TITLE>
```

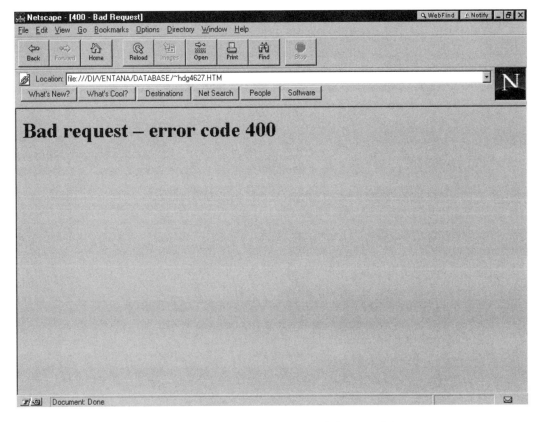

Figure 13–5   An error code generated from a CGI program.

```
</HEAD>
<BODY>
</BODY>
<FORM METHOD=GET ACTION="http://teleport.com/cgi-bin/addrec.exe">
<TABLE BORDER=4>
<TR><TD>TITLE:</TD><TD>
<INPUT NAME="M_Title" TYPE="TEXT" COLS=30 SIZE="30">
</TD></TR>
<TR><TD>TYPE:</TD><TD>
<INPUT NAME="m_type" TYPE="RADIO" VALUE="Action"> Action
<INPUT NAME="m_type" TYPE="RADIO" VALUE="Drama"> Drama
<INPUT NAME="m_type" TYPE="RADIO" VALUE="Mystery"> Mystery
<INPUT NAME="m_type" TYPE="RADIO" VALUE="Romance"> Romance
<INPUT NAME="m_type" TYPE="RADIO" VALUE="Comedy"> Comedy
<INPUT NAME="m_type" TYPE="RADIO" VALUE="Animated"> Animated
<INPUT NAME="m_type" TYPE="RADIO" VALUE="SPORTS"> Sports
<INPUT NAME="m_type" TYPE="RADIO" VALUE="RL"> Real Life
</TD></TR>
<TR><TD>RATING:</TD><TD>
```

```
<INPUT NAME="m_rating" TYPE="RADIO" VALUE="PG"> PG
<INPUT NAME="m_rating" TYPE="RADIO" VALUE="PG 13"> PG 13
<INPUT NAME="m_rating" TYPE="RADIO" VALUE="R"> R
<INPUT NAME="m_rating" TYPE="RADIO" VALUE="NR"> NR
</TD></TR>
<TR><TD>MALE STAR:</TD><TD><INPUT NAME="Male_Star" TYPE="TEXT" COLS=20
SIZE="20">
</TD></TR>
<TR><TD>FEMALE STAR:</TD><TD><INPUT NAME="FEMALE_STAR" TYPE="TEXT"
COLS=30 SIZE="30">
</TD></TR>
<TR><TD>QTY:</TD><TD><INPUT NAME="Qty" TYPE="TEXT" COLS=3 SIZE="3">
</TD></TR>
</TABLE>
<INPUT NAME="Submit" TYPE="SUBMIT" VALUE="ADD RECORD">
<INPUT NAME="Clear" TYPE="RESET" VALUE="CLEAR">
</FORM>
</HTML>
```

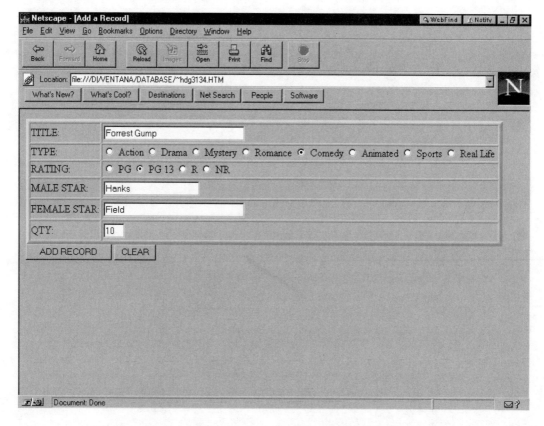

Figure 13–6   The Web page adding a row to a database.

Web Server Action on Receiving the Add Row Request

In the HTML code just shown, you'll notice a few items and controls that are significant to the execution of this process. First is the `<FORM METHOD>` tag, that appears as follows:

```
<FORM METHOD=GET ACTION="http://teleport.com/cgi-bin/addrec.exe">
```

You remember that the database query example in the previous section used the `FORM METHOD=POST`, while this example uses `FORM METHOD=GET`. In the section below you'll see how the Web server treats this type of request.

Some of the information placed in the CGI profile file by the Web server upon receiving this request is identified here.

```
[CGI]
Authentication Method=    Basic
CGI Version=                 2.0
Content Type=             MIME content type of info supplied with request
Executable Path=          d:\webpage\cgi-bin\addrec.exe
Query String=                 m_title=Forrest Gump&m type=comedy&m_
rating=PG 13&male_star=Hanks&female_star=Field&qty=10
Request Method=           GET
Request Keep-Alive=       NO
Request Protocol=         HTTP/1.1
Server Name=              teleport
Server Port=              126.160.112.50
Server Software=          WebSTAR 2.1

[Extra Headers]

[Form External]

[Form File]

[Form Huge]

[Form Literal]

[System]
```

Take note that because the Web page uses the GET method, the passed data is sent to the CGI program in the `Query String` tag of the CGI profile file.

Execution of the CGI Program to Add a Database Record

Once the FORM method is determined, you have only to parse the name/value pairs before you can get down to the actual database query. Depending on the FORM method, the parsing is different. If the FORM method is POST, then the name/value pairs are stored in the CGI profile file, in the `Form Literal` section. Since you are using the GET method, the following lines appear in the CGI profile file:

```
Query String=     m_title=Forrest Gump&m_type=comedy&m_rating=PG
13&male_star=Hanks&female_star=Field&qty=10
```

This process is a bit more complicated than using the POST method, but not too difficult for most programming languages. It is a simple process of the following:

- Retrieve the contents of the `Query String` line in the `CGI` section of the CGI profile file.
- Iteratively extract the name/value pairs, recognizing that each is separated by an ampersand (&).

Therefore, the following value in the Query String would extract to the associated name/value pairs:

```
m_title=Forrest Gump&m_type=comedy&m_rating=PG
13&male_star=Hanks&female_star=Field&qty=10
```

Name/value pairs:

```
m_title=Forrest Gump
m_type=comedy
m_rating=PG 13
male_star=Hanks
female_star=Field
qty=10
```

Referring back to Figure 13–2, you see that once the name/value pairs are parsed, the next steps are to:

1. Format the SQL query
2. Connect to the Access 97 database
3. Submit SQL to add the record
4. Close database connection

Given the contents of the Query String environmental variable described earlier in this section, the specific SQL string to insert the row into the Access 97 table named `movies` will look like:

```
INSERT INTO movies
        (m_title, m_type, m_rating, male_star, female_star, qty)
VALUES        ('Forrest Gump', 'comedy', 'PG 13', 'Hanks', 'Field', '10');
```

With this processing complete, the program logic and process flow are *exactly* the same as if the program was *not* part of a Web database application. You'll see no sample code here. Once the database connection is closed, however, it is time to format the result set to HTML and send it to the standard output device.

Output from a CGI Program Doing an INSERT Row

Typically, there are two types of responses that you want to send from the CGI program when it processes an INSERT row request on an Access 97 database. First, assuming there were errors in the input data provided, you'll want to inform the user of the error and give her or him a chance to correct the error. Second, assuming there were no errors in the input data and the new row was successfully added to the database, you'll want to inform the user of this—that their Access 97 database has been updated. In this section, you'll see how each of these two scenarios are accomplished.

Error on Input.   Figure 13–7 shows what a screen might look like just before the `<Add Record>` button is clicked. You'll notice that this should cause an error—there is nothing input for the movie title.

The Web Server would receive the request from the client's browser and place the following string in the `Query String` tag in the `CGI` section of the CGI profile file.

```
m_title=&m_type=comedy&m_rating=PG 13&male_star=Hanks&female_star=
Field&qty=10
```

Before formatting the RDBMS query (in this case an INSERT) to the Access 97 database, the program should do some edits to make sure the data it received was substantial enough and of the correct format to be usable.

In this example, the CGI program would find that the user had provided no data for the m_title field—an obvious mistake. The most common process at this point is for the CGI program to format an HTML page and form that looks very similar to the one the

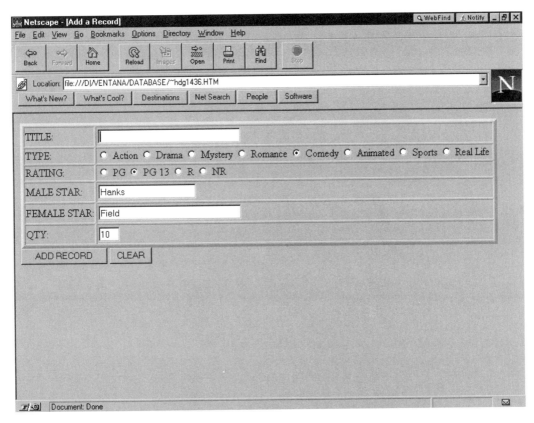

Figure 13–7   Oops, an error on input.

user just saw, with the addition of a notification of the error. The following HTML code is an example of this. Figure 13–8 shows what this HTML code looks like in a browser, including the error message.

```
Content-type: text/html
<HTML>
<HEAD>
<TITLE>Add a Record</TITLE>
</HEAD>
<BODY>
</BODY>
<FORM METHOD=GET ACTION="http://teleport.com/cgi-bin/addrec.exe">
<TABLE BORDER=4>
<TR><TD>TITLE:</TD><TD>
<INPUT NAME="M_Title" TYPE="TEXT" COLS=30 SIZE="30">
</TD></TR>
<TR><TD>TYPE:</TD><TD>
<INPUT NAME="m_type" TYPE="RADIO" VALUE="Action"> Action
<INPUT NAME="m_type" TYPE="RADIO" VALUE="Drama"> Drama
<INPUT NAME="m_type" TYPE="RADIO" VALUE="Mystery"> Mystery
<INPUT NAME="m_type" TYPE="RADIO" VALUE="Romance"> Romance
<INPUT NAME="m_type" TYPE="RADIO" VALUE="Comedy"> Comedy
<INPUT NAME="m_type" TYPE="RADIO" VALUE="Animated"> Animated
<INPUT NAME="m_type" TYPE="RADIO" VALUE="SPORTS"> Sports
<INPUT NAME="m_type" TYPE="RADIO" VALUE="RL"> Real Life
</TD></TR>
<TR><TD>RATING:</TD><TD>
<INPUT NAME="m_rating" TYPE="RADIO" VALUE="PG"> PG
<INPUT NAME="m_rating" TYPE="RADIO" VALUE="PG 13"> PG 13
<INPUT NAME="m_rating" TYPE="RADIO" VALUE="R"> R
<INPUT NAME="m_rating" TYPE="RADIO" VALUE="NR"> NR
</TD></TR>
<TR><TD>MALE STAR:</TD><TD><INPUT NAME="Male_Star" TYPE="TEXT" COLS=20
SIZE="20">
</TD></TR>
<TR><TD>FEMALE STAR:</TD><TD><INPUT NAME="FEMALE_STAR" TYPE="TEXT"
COLS=30 SIZE="30">
</TD></TR>
<TR><TD>QTY:</TD><TD><INPUT NAME="Qty" TYPE="TEXT" COLS=3 SIZE="3">
</TD></TR>
</TABLE>
<INPUT NAME="Submit" TYPE="SUBMIT" VALUE="ADD RECORD">
<INPUT NAME="Clear" TYPE="RESET" VALUE="CLEAR">
<P>
<STRONG><FONT COLOR=#FF0000>Error!</FONT> You must provide a Title for
the movie.</STRONG>
</FORM>
</HTML>
```

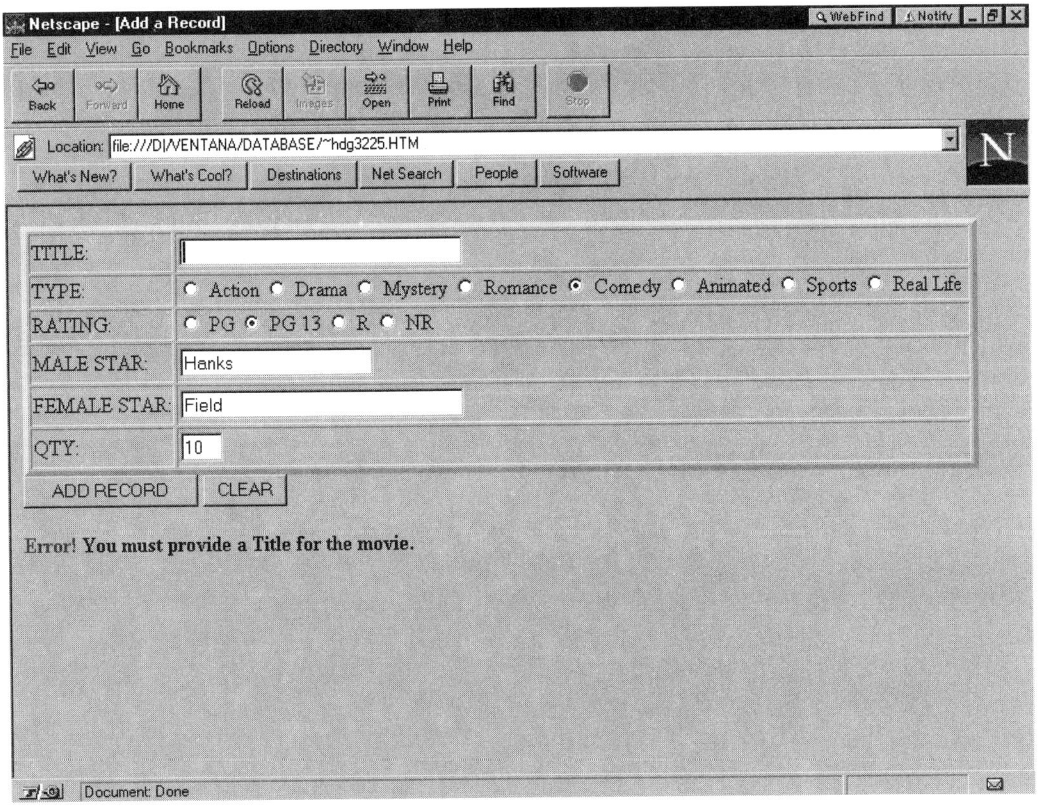

Figure 13-8   An error message displayed on the HTML input form.

The first line of code is using the direct method of response to communicate with a Web server from a CGI program.

```
Content-type: text/html
```

The majority of the HTML code is exactly what the user last saw, with the exception of the error message. The lines of HTML code that accomplish the display of this are:

```
<P><STRONG>Error! You must provide a Title for the movie.</STRONG>
```

Once the user views this Web page, provides a title for the movie, and presses the `<Add Record>` button again, the Web server and CGI program processes this request.

The processing described in this section could easily apply to a variety of errors that might be encountered. For example, if the user provides data to be inserted into a database that would cause an invalid duplicate situation, you can simply modify the error message that displays at the bottom of the browser to inform the user of this situation.

Add Record Was Successful.   Assuming the data provided by the user was successfully added to the Access 97 database, you'll probably want to inform him or her of this fact. Simply format a CGI response from your CGI program as an HTML page and then send that response to the standard output from your CGI program. An example of what this HTML code might look like is seen in the following code sample.

```
Content-type: text/html
<HTML>
<HEAD>
<TITLE>Add Record Was Successful</TITLE>
</HEAD>
<BODY>
You successfully added the movie titled: Forrest Gump to the database.
Press the <IMG SRC="file:///d|/ventana/images/ch13-18/backbutt.gif"> to
continue.
</BODY>
</HTML>
```

This HTML code would appear in a browser as seen in Figure 13–9.

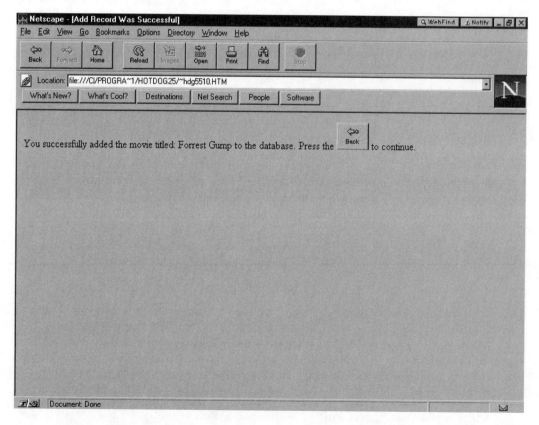

Figure 13–9 Notifying the user their "add record" was successful.

At this point, the user could press the `<Back>` button on the browser and go back to the last viewed Web page.

Deleting a Row from a Database Using a Web Application

Let's now see how you'd place functions in the CGI program of your Web database application to delete rows of data from your Access 97 database. This is shown in the following section.

The Web Database Delete Row Page

The HTML code that follows is used to generate the Web page seen in Figure 13–10. The purpose of this Web page is to have the user provide the information that will be used to delete a row from the Access 97 database.

```
<HTML>
<HEAD>
<TITLE>Delete a Record</TITLE>
</HEAD>
<BODY>
</BODY>
<FORM METHOD=GET ACTION="http://teleport.com/cgi-bin/delrec.exe">
<TABLE BORDER=4>
<TR><TD>TITLE:</TD><TD>
<INPUT NAME="M_Title" TYPE="TEXT" COLS=30 SIZE="30">
</TD></TR>
<TR><TD>TYPE:</TD><TD>
<INPUT NAME="m_type" TYPE="RADIO" VALUE="Action"> Action
<INPUT NAME="m_type" TYPE="RADIO" VALUE="Drama"> Drama
<INPUT NAME="m_type" TYPE="RADIO" VALUE="Mystery"> Mystery
<INPUT NAME="m_type" TYPE="RADIO" VALUE="Romance"> Romance
<INPUT NAME="m_type" TYPE="RADIO" VALUE="Comedy"> Comedy
<INPUT NAME="m_type" TYPE="RADIO" VALUE="Animated"> Animated
<INPUT NAME="m_type" TYPE="RADIO" VALUE="SPORTS"> Sports
<INPUT NAME="m_type" TYPE="RADIO" VALUE="RL"> Real Life
</TD></TR>
<TR><TD>RATING:</TD><TD>
<INPUT NAME="m_rating" TYPE="RADIO" VALUE="PG"> PG
<INPUT NAME="m_rating" TYPE="RADIO" VALUE="PG 13"> PG 13
<INPUT NAME="m_rating" TYPE="RADIO" VALUE="R"> R
<INPUT NAME="m_rating" TYPE="RADIO" VALUE="NR"> NR
</TD></TR>
<TR><TD>MALE STAR:</TD><TD><INPUT NAME="Male_Star" TYPE="TEXT" COLS=20
SIZE="20">
</TD></TR>
<TR><TD>FEMALE STAR:</TD><TD><INPUT NAME="FEMALE_STAR" TYPE="TEXT"
COLS=30 SIZE="30">
</TD></TR>
<TR><TD>QTY:</TD><TD><INPUT NAME="Qty" TYPE="TEXT" COLS=3 SIZE="3">
</TD></TR>
```

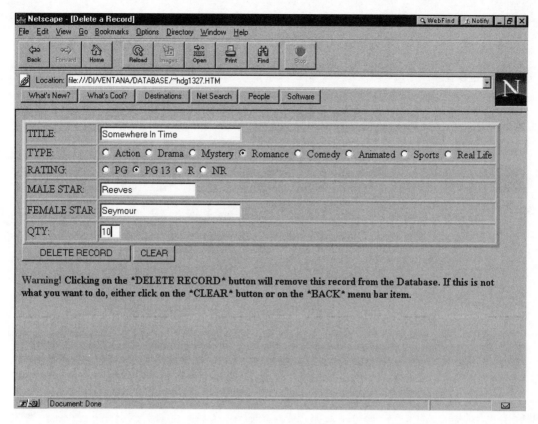

Figure 13–10   The Web page deleting a row from the database.

```
</TABLE>
<INPUT NAME="Submit" TYPE="SUBMIT" VALUE="DELETE RECORD">
<INPUT NAME="Clear" TYPE="RESET" VALUE="CLEAR">
<P>
<STRONG>Warning! Clicking on the *DELETE RECORD* button will remove this
record from the Database. If this is not what you want to do, either
click on the *CLEAR* button or on the *BACK* menu bar item.</STRONG>
</FORM>
</HTML>
```

Web Server Action on Receiving the Delete Row Request

In the HTML code above, you'll notice a few items and controls that are significant to the execution of this process. First is the <FORM METHOD> tag, that appears as follows:

```
<FORM METHOD=GET ACTION="http://teleport.com/cgi-bin/delrec.exe">
```

Some of the information placed in the CGI profile file by the Web server upon receiving this request is identified here:

```
[CGI]
Authentication Method=    Basic
CGI Version=                2.0
Content Type=             MIME content type of info supplied with request
Executable Path=          d:\webpage\cgi-bin\addrec.exe
Query String=               m_title=Somewhere In
Time&m_type=Romance&m_rating=PG 13&male_star=Reeves&female_star=Seymour
&qty=10
Request Method=           GET
Request Keep-Alive=       NO
Request Protocol=         HTTP/1.1
Server Name=              teleport
Server Port=              126.160.112.50
Server Software=          WebSTAR 2.1

[Extra Headers]

[Form External]

[Form File]

[Form Huge]

[Form Literal]

[System]
```

Here, the Web page uses the GET method, the passed data is sent to the CGI program in the Query String tag of the CGI profile file.

Execution of the CGI Program to Delete a Database Record

Once the FORM method is determined, you have only to parse the name/value pairs before you can get down to the actual database query. In previous sections, you've seen how this is done. When the parsing is complete, you would have the following name-value pairs defined.

Name/value pairs:

```
m_title=Somewhere In Time
m_type=Romance
m_rating=PG 13
male_star=Reeves
female_star=Seymour
qty=10
```

Once the name/value pairs are parsed, you then need to format the Access 97 query, connect to the database, submit SQL delete request, and then close database connection.

Given the contents of the Query String environmental variable described earlier in this section, the specific SQL string to delete the row the user specified from the Access 97 table named `movies` will look like:

```
DELETE FROM movies
    WHERE m_title = 'Somewhere In Time';
```

Once the database connection is closed, however, it *is* time to format the result set to HTML and send it to the standard output device.

Output from a CGI Program Doing a DELETE Row

Typically, there are two types of responses that you want to send from the CGI program when it processes a DELETE row request. First, if there were errors in the input data provided, you'll want to inform the user of the errors and give her or him a chance to correct the error. Second, if there were no errors in the input data and the new row was successfully added to the Access 97 database, you'll want to inform the user of this. In the previous section titled "Output From a CGI Program Doing an INSERT Row," you saw examples of how to accomplish both of these types of responses.

Updating a Database Row from a Web Application

By now you might be able to infer what needs to be done to update a row of data in an Access 97 database from a Web application. Just to make sure you understand, this section will show you.

The Web Database Update Row Page

The HTML code that follows is used to generate the Web page seen in Figure 13–11. The purpose of this Web page is to have the user provide the information that will be used to update an existing row in the Access 97 database.

```
<HTML>
<HEAD>
<TITLE>Update a Record</TITLE>
</HEAD>
<BODY>
</BODY>
<FORM METHOD=GET ACTION="http://teleport.com/cgi-bin/updrec.exe">
<TABLE BORDER=4>
<TR><TD>TITLE:</TD><TD>
<INPUT NAME="M_Title" TYPE="TEXT" COLS=30 SIZE="30">
</TD></TR>
<TR><TD>TYPE:</TD><TD>
<INPUT NAME="m_type" TYPE="RADIO" VALUE="Action"> Action
<INPUT NAME="m_type" TYPE="RADIO" VALUE="Drama"> Drama
<INPUT NAME="m_type" TYPE="RADIO" VALUE="Mystery"> Mystery
<INPUT NAME="m_type" TYPE="RADIO" VALUE="Romance"> Romance
<INPUT NAME="m_type" TYPE="RADIO" VALUE="Comedy"> Comedy
<INPUT NAME="m_type" TYPE="RADIO" VALUE="Animated"> Animated
<INPUT NAME="m_type" TYPE="RADIO" VALUE="SPORTS"> Sports
```

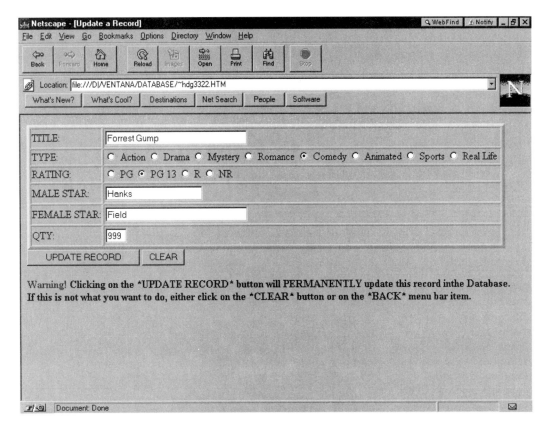

Figure 13–11   The Web page updating a row in a database.

```
<INPUT NAME="m_type" TYPE="RADIO" VALUE="RL"> Real Life
</TD></TR>
<TR><TD>RATING:</TD><TD>
<INPUT NAME="m_rating" TYPE="RADIO" VALUE="PG"> PG
<INPUT NAME="m_rating" TYPE="RADIO" VALUE="PG 13"> PG 13
<INPUT NAME="m_rating" TYPE="RADIO" VALUE="R"> R
<INPUT NAME="m_rating" TYPE="RADIO" VALUE="NR"> NR
</TD></TR>
<TR><TD>MALE STAR:</TD><TD><INPUT NAME="Male_Star" TYPE="TEXT" COLS=20
SIZE="20">
</TD></TR>
<TR><TD>FEMALE STAR:</TD><TD><INPUT NAME="FEMALE_STAR" TYPE="TEXT"
COLS=30 SIZE="30">
</TD></TR>
<TR><TD>QTY:</TD><TD><INPUT NAME="Qty" TYPE="TEXT" COLS=3 SIZE="3">
</TD></TR>
</TABLE>
```

```
<INPUT NAME="Submit" TYPE="SUBMIT" VALUE="UPDATE RECORD">
<INPUT NAME="Clear" TYPE="RESET" VALUE="CLEAR">
<P>
<STRONG>Warning! Clicking on the *UPDATE RECORD* button will PERMANENTLY
update this record inthe Database. If this is not what you want to do,
either click on the *CLEAR* button or on the *BACK* menu bar item.</STRONG>
</FORM>
</HTML>
```

Web Server Action on Receiving the Update Row Request

In the HTML code above, you'll notice a few items and controls that are significant to the execution of this process. First is the <FORM METHOD> tag, that appears as follows:

```
<FORM METHOD=GET ACTION="http://teleport.com/cgi-bin/updrec.exe">
```

Some of the information placed in the CGI profile file by the Web server upon receiving this request is identified below:

```
[CGI]
Authentication Method=    Basic
CGI Version=               2.0
Content Type=             MIME content type of info supplied with request
Executable Path=          d:\webpage\cgi-bin\updrec.exe
Query String=              m_title=Forrest Gump&m_type=Comedy&m_rating=
PG 13&male_star=Hanks&female_star=Field&qty=999
Request Method=           GET
Request Keep-Alive=       NO
Request Protocol=         HTTP/1.1
Server Name=              teleport
Server Port=              126.160.112.50
Server Software=          WebSTAR 2.1

[Extra Headers]

[Form External]

[Form File]

[Form Huge]

[Form Literal]

[System]
```

Take note that because the Web page uses the GET method, the passed data is sent to the CGI program in the Query String tag of the CGI profile file.

Execution of the CGI Program to Update a Database Record

Once the FORM method is determined, you have only to parse the name/value pairs before you can get down to the actual database update operation. In previous sections, you've seen how this is done. When the parsing is complete, the following name/value pairs are defined.

Name/value pairs:

```
m_title=Forrest Gump
m_type=Comedy
m_rating=PG 13
male_star=Hanks
female_star=Field
qty=999
```

Referring back to Figure 13–2, you see that once the name/value pairs are parsed, the next steps are to:

- Format the RDBMS query
- Connect to the database
- Submit SQL to update the row
- Close database connection

Given the contents of the Query String environmental variable described earlier in this section, the specific SQL string to update the row the user specified in the Access 97 table named `movies` will look like:

```
UPDATE movies
   SET m_type = 'Comedy'
       m_rating = 'PG 13'
       male_star = 'Hanks'
       female_star = 'Field'
       qty = '999'
   WHERE m_title = 'Forrest Gump';
```

With the processing complete, there is nothing special about this program and the fact that it originated from a Web initiated request—the program logic and process flow are *exactly* the same as if the program was *not* part of a Web database application. You'll see no sample code here. You would accomplish all of the above steps exactly the same as you would if this were not a Web-initiated program in the CGI programming language of your choice. Once the database connection is closed, however, it is time to format the result set to HTML and send it to the standard output device.

Output from a CGI Program Doing a Update Row

As you've seen, there are typically two types of responses that you would possibly send from the CGI program when it processes an UPDATE row request. The first is used if there were errors in the actual update process. In this case, you'll want to inform the user of the error and give her or him a chance to correct the error. Second, assuming there were no errors in the input data and the row in the Access 97 database was updated successfully, you'll want to inform the user of this. In the section titled "Output from a CGI Program Doing an INSERT Row," you saw examples of how to accomplish both of these types of responses.

In most cases, you do not want to give the user the ability to modify the keys of the data in your Access 97 database. If you do, though, you can provide for this programmatically. If you do not, either place the key data on the form in a hidden field that is not modifiable, or place a warning message on the screen telling the user which field(s) they should not modify. This, and many more topics relating to security, are discussed in detail in Chapter 18.

The information in the previous sections showed you how to select, add, delete, and modify rows in an Access 97 database from a Web database application. Did you notice that these four functions were fulfilled using four different HTML pages, and four different CGI programs? This may be sufficient, but what if you want to provide these four functions in one HTML page, using one CGI program—in what I call *full database access*? The following section shows you how to accomplish this.

Providing Full Database Access from Your Web Application

With the understanding you've acquired so far, the information in this section should come fairly easy to you.

The Web Full-Database AccessPage

The following HTML code is used to generate the Web page seen in Figure 13–12. You'll notice from this figure that a new row is added to the bottom of the table featuring four radio buttons Query, Add, Delete, and Update.

```
<HTML>
<HEAD>
<TITLE>Full function DB access</TITLE>
</HEAD>
<BODY>
</BODY>
<FORM METHOD=GET ACTION="http://teleport.com/cgi-bin/procrec.exe">
<TABLE BORDER=4>
<TR><TD>TITLE:</TD><TD>
<INPUT NAME="M_Title" TYPE="TEXT" COLS=30 SIZE="30">
</TD></TR>
<TR><TD>TYPE:</TD><TD>
<INPUT NAME="m_type" TYPE="RADIO" VALUE="Action"> Action
<INPUT NAME="m_type" TYPE="RADIO" VALUE="Drama"> Drama
<INPUT NAME="m_type" TYPE="RADIO" VALUE="Mystery"> Mystery
<INPUT NAME="m_type" TYPE="RADIO" VALUE="Romance"> Romance
<INPUT NAME="m_type" TYPE="RADIO" VALUE="Comedy"> Comedy
<INPUT NAME="m_type" TYPE="RADIO" VALUE="Animated"> Animated
<INPUT NAME="m_type" TYPE="RADIO" VALUE="SPORTS"> Sports
<INPUT NAME="m_type" TYPE="RADIO" VALUE="RL"> Real Life
</TD></TR>
<TR><TD>RATING:</TD><TD>
<INPUT NAME="m_rating" TYPE="RADIO" VALUE="PG"> PG
<INPUT NAME="m_rating" TYPE="RADIO" VALUE="PG 13"> PG 13
<INPUT NAME="m_rating" TYPE="RADIO" VALUE="R"> R
<INPUT NAME="m_rating" TYPE="RADIO" VALUE="NR"> NR
</TD></TR>
```

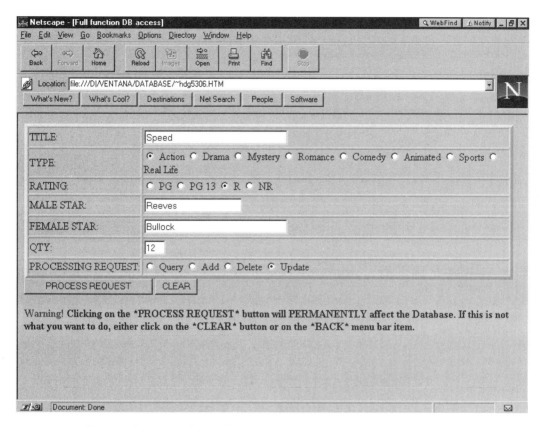

Figure 13–12   The Web page providing full database access.

```
<TR><TD>MALE STAR:</TD><TD><INPUT NAME="Male_Star" TYPE="TEXT" COLS=20
SIZE="20">
</TD></TR>
<TR><TD>FEMALE STAR:</TD><TD><INPUT NAME="FEMALE_STAR" TYPE="TEXT"
COLS=30 SIZE="30">
</TD></TR>
<TR><TD>QTY:</TD><TD><INPUT NAME="Qty" TYPE="TEXT" COLS=3 SIZE="3">
</TD></TR>
<TR><TD>PROCESSING REQUEST:</TD><TD>
<INPUT NAME="p_type" TYPE="RADIO" VALUE="QUERY"> Query
<INPUT NAME="p_type" TYPE="RADIO" VALUE="ADD"> Add
<INPUT NAME="p_type" TYPE="RADIO" VALUE="DELETE"> Delete
<INPUT NAME="p_type" TYPE="RADIO" VALUE="UPDATE"> Update
</TD></TR>
</TABLE>
<INPUT NAME="Submit" TYPE="SUBMIT" VALUE="PROCESS REQUEST">
<INPUT NAME="Clear" TYPE="RESET" VALUE="CLEAR">
<P>
```

```
<STRONG>Warning! Clicking on the *PROCESS REQUEST* button will PERMA-
NENTLY affect the Database. If this is not what you want to do, either
click on the *CLEAR* button or on the *BACK* menu bar item.</STRONG>
</FORM>
</HTML>
```

Web Server Action on Receiving the Database Request

In the HTML code shown, there a few items and controls that are significant to the execution of this process. First is the <FORM METHOD> tag, that appears as follows:

```
<FORM METHOD=GET ACTION="http://teleport.com/cgi-bin/procrec.exe">
```

Some of the information placed in the CGI profile file by the Web server upon receiving this request is identified as follows:

```
[CGI]
Authentication Method=   Basic
CGI Version=              2.0
Content Type=             MIME content type of info supplied with request
Executable Path=          d:\webpage\cgi-bin\procrec.exe
Query String=                 m_title=Speed&m_type=Action&m_rating=R&male_
star=Reeves&female_star=Bullock&qty=12&p_type=Update
Request Method=           GET
Request Keep-Alive=       NO
Request Protocol=         HTTP/1.1
Server Name=              teleport
Server Port=              126.160.112.50
Server Software=          WebSTAR 2.1

[Extra Headers]

[Form External]

[Form File]

[Form Huge]

[Form Literal]

[System]
```

Because the Web page uses the GET method, the passed data is sent to the CGI program in the Query String tag of the CGI profile file. Also, there is one extra parameter in the Query String tag of the CGI section. This extra parameter is &p_type=Update. The other options that the field named p_type could be are Query, Add, or Delete, depending on which radio button the user selected.

Execution of the CGI Program to Take Action on a Database Record

Once the FORM method is determined, you have only to parse the name/value pairs before you can get down to the actual Access 97 database operation requested by the user. When the parsing is complete, you would have the following name/value pairs defined.

Name/value pairs:

```
m_title=Speed
m_type=Action
m_rating=R
male_star=Reeves
female_star=Bullock
qty=12
p_type=Update
```

Referring back to Figure 13–2, you see that once the name/value pairs are parsed, the next steps are to:

- Format the Access 97 query
- Connect to the database
- *Submit SQL to cause desired action to take place*
- Retrieve result set (if the process was a query)
- Close database connection

The critical step in this process is the one labeled "*Submit SQL to cause desired action to take place,*" which is given to you in the Query String that you parsed from within your CGI program. The last name/value pair passed in this example is p_type=Update.

Given the contents of the Query String environmental variable described earlier in this section and the value of the p_type tag in the CGI profile file, the specific SQL string to update the row the user specified in the Access 97 table named movies will look like:

```
UPDATE movies
   SET m_type = 'Action'
      m_rating = 'R'
      male_star = 'Reeves'
      female_star = 'Bullock'
      qty = '12'
   WHERE m_title = 'Speed';
```

When you interrogate the value of p_type and depending on the value of this field, your CGI program would either query a row on the Access 97 database, add a row to the database, delete a record from the database, or update an existing record on the database. You could provide these four functions within the one CGI program, or you could accommodate the required processing by calling subroutines. Either option will work. The program logic and process flow, regardless of the method used, are *exactly* the same as if the program was *not* part of a Web database application. Once the database connection is closed, however, it is time to format the result set to HTML and send it to the standard output device.

Moving On

This chapter should have provided you with the information needed to give you a very clear understanding of the role of all the components in a Web database application, and how they work together. Particularly, you learned how the CGI program is used to accomplish the actual database processing as requested by the user via HTML forms.

The next chapter introduces you to MIME, which is the set of agreed-upon formats that enable you to send binary files via e-mail, as e-mail attachments, or by other methods. As you grow in your comfort level with building Web database applications, you will undoubtedly find this a very valuable addition to the scope of your applications.

CHAPTER 14

MIME
and Advanced
Data
Presentation

This chapter discusses MIME and its uses. You will learn about the various MIME types and subtypes, as well as gain an understanding of MIME from both a developer's and a user's perspective.

What Is MIME?

MIME stands for Multipurpose Internet Mail Extension. It is a set of standards that specifies both the type of file being sent from a Web component (either a Web server or browser) to another Web component as well as the method that should be used to turn that message back into its original form. When MIME was first designed, its purpose was to facilitate e-mail over the Internet. Shortly after its introduction however, people found uses for it beyond e-mail. Companies that developed browsers incorporated the ability to define MIME types and subtypes other than e-mail files into their browsers.

MIME standards are evolving. They define a growing set of data types that give you the ability to create Web applications that incorporate either new data types or objects such as audio, video, three-dimensional virtual reality graphics, etc. For example, HTML is a MIME data type. So too is a JPEG graphics file and an audio (WAV) file. In fact, any type of information or file that can be stored electronically could be, and probably already is, a MIME data type.

MIME is *bi-directional*. This means that it is a way for the Web browser to communicate the content of the page to the server and it is the primary way that a Web server tells a Web client about the document that it's sending.

MIME is also the way that a Web client tells a Web server the types of documents that it can receive and process. Some of the new capabilities provided by MIME standards and data types include:

- Including many different types of files, such as audio, video, text, and graphics within a single page
- Sending messages with multiple fonts
- Sending audio, video, graphics, and multimedia files
- Sending text messages without regard to length
- Tagging messages with information so browsers know how best to handle them
- Transmitting character sets besides ASCII

Before MIME, the process of sending non-text and non-HTML files from one Web to another was a complicated one. This process included the following steps. First, the sender had to translate (uuencode) the source data and save it to disk in a place that could be retrieved by the recipient. Then, the receiver had to initiate the request to transfer the uuencoded file to his or her machine.

The receiver, once the file was transferred, had to decode the file back into its original format. Then, the recipient could use or view the file. An example of one of the screens used to identify some of the different types of file formats available to uudecode is seen in Figure 14–1. Uuencode stands for Unix to Unix encoding and is a predecessor method to MIME for converting files from one format to another to allow transmission over the Web.

Figure 14–1 shows one of the screens that a user would have to navigate if they had downloaded a file that was not uuencoded, prior to MIME. On this screen, the user is asked to provide the type of uuendocing done when the file was coded for transmission over the Internet. This is so that it could be properly decoded prior to its being used. With MIME, and the ability to process MIME types and subtypes being included in browsers, this type of screen is no longer required because the browser accommodates the translation.

Uses for MIME on the Web

You've already seen MIME used in this book, although you may not know it. In the previous chapter, you learned how to create a Web page from within a CGI program to transmit back to the user by using the following code:

```
Content-type: text/html
<HTML>
. . .
</HTML>
```

The first line of code (`Content-type: text/html`) is what is referred to as a MIME header. Although you'll learn about MIME headers later in this chapter, for now you should understand that this line of code instructs the receiving browser that the rest of the page contains HTML text data.

MIME is also used to add multimedia, audio, video, and graphic elements to your application. In addition to making your pages more presentable, it also makes them more useful. Consider the following examples.

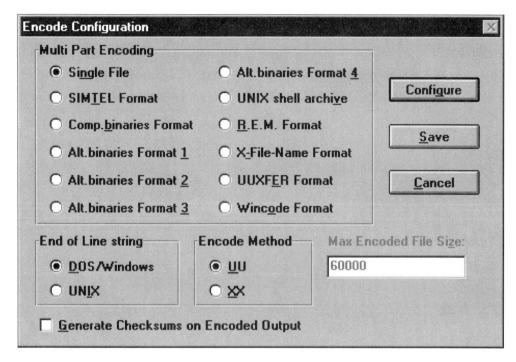

Figure 14–1   An example of an earlier uuencoding method.

Example 1

- *Scenario #1*—You go to a Web site and can read the 1963 inaugural address from President John F. Kennedy

- *Scenario #2*—You go to a Web site and see a picture of President John F. Kennedy standing at the podium in his black tuxedo and hat during his 1963 inaugural address. When you click on his picture, a window pops up and you see a streaming audio/video recording of the actual address.

Which of the above two scenarios do you think carries more punch and has a more significant impact on the user? If you said Scenario #2 to this "no-brainer" question, you'd be right. Let's take a look at another example that is perhaps more aligned with the type of application you might write some day.

Example 2

- *Scenario #1*—You work for a real estate firm and have been asked to place the listings your company manages on a Web page. So, you create a Web page with text descriptions of all the properties.

- *Scenario #2*—You work for a real estate firm and have been asked to place the listings your company manages on a Web page. So, you create a Web page that shows a picture of each property. When a user clicks on a picture of the property he or she is interested in, a multimedia player pops up and displays a walking tour of the house.

I think you'd agree that in both examples, scenario #2 carries more pizzazz, and has a greater impact than scenario #1. Figure 14–2 provides an example of a high-impact page.

You'll notice a couple of things here. Next to the picture of actor Charlie Sheen you'll see two graphics; the first is highlighted with a square box around it and is the image of a microphone while the second is an image of a movie camera. Next, notice at the bottom of the figure I've placed a black rectangle around what appears as an URL:

`http://www.heroes.net/pub/heroes/avis/aviviv.html.`

If you click on this URL, the Web server at the United States Department of State, which is where the page seen in Figure 14–2 originates, will attempt to send an HTML file that contains a streaming video/audio image of Charlie Sheen speaking about the merits of patriotism. The HTML code to accomplish this is seen here:

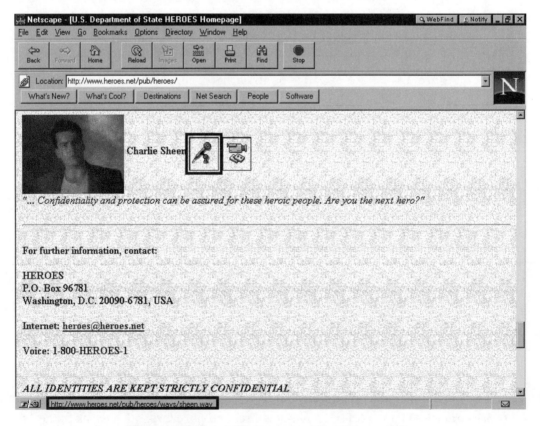

Figure 14–2 A Web page with extra punch.

```
<IMG SRC="http://www.heroes.net/pub/heroes/gifs/sheen.gif"
ALIGN="MIDDLE"></>Charlie Sheen </B>
<A HREF="http://www.heroes.net/pub/heroes/wavs/sheen.wav">
<IMG SRC="http://www.heroes.net/pub/heroes/gifs/audio.gif"
ALIGN="MIDDLE"></A>
<A HREF="http://www.heroes.net/pub/heroes/wavs/sheen.avi">
<IMG SRC="http://www.heroes.net/pub/heroes/gifs/video.gif"
ALIGN="MIDDLE"></A>
```

Assuming you clicked on the graphic of the movie camera, the file named

```
http://www.heroes.net/pub/heroes/wavs/sheen.avi
```

would begin playing in your browser. Your browser would know that it was receiving an audio/video file that it needed to play inside the browser by the MIME header. In this case, the MIME header for this file is:

```
Content-type: video/x-msvideo
```

MIME Headers

The code example used for the Charlie Sheen audio/video file is one of several types of MIME headers—with these MIME headers appearing at the very beginning of the file being transferred. Although there are several more MIME header types required and available for e-mail transmission and receipt, the number of headers used for Web non-e-mail transfers is limited. In fact, you might be surprised to learn that *no* MIME headers are required to transfer a file, and in most cases only one will do.

The following is a snippet of HTML code in which a MIME header appears in italics.

```
Content-type: text/html
<HTML>
<TITLE>An HTML MIME Header</TITLE>
<HEAD></HEAD>
<BODY><H1>This is a test.</H1></BODY>
</HTML>
```

Figure 14–3 shows what this code looks like in a browser. Notice that this appears as you'd expect.

Now, consider the following snippet of HTML code and notice the absence of a MIME header.

```
<HTML>
<TITLE>No MIME Header</TITLE>
<HEAD></HEAD>
<BODY><H1>This is a test.</H1></BODY>
</HTML>
```

When a browser receives this file without a MIME header present, it treats the HTML code as regular non-HTML text. It will not apply any formatting to the character strings and display the HTML code as text—completely unformatted. This is seen in Figure 14–4.

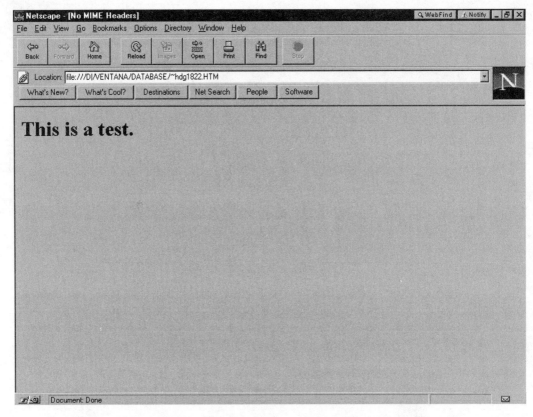

Figure 14–3   A little bit of HTML code with a MIME header.

The lack of HTML formatting and use of a MIME header could be advantageous to you. For example, if you had some ASCII text files that you wanted to make available for viewing without special HTML formatting tags, simply place them on a Web server as ASCII text files, without a MIME header. When a user's browser points to these files, he or she can view them as straight text files. Although they won't appear elegant in a browser, the purpose is still served.

Now that you have a good introduction to the capabilities of MIME, the following sections show you how these capabilities are provided through MIME types and sub-types.

MIME Types and Subtypes

MIME specifications are evolving. They are submitted to and approved by the Internet Assigned Numbers Authority (IANA). Presently, there are seven recognized MIME types, with hundreds of subtypes recognized by the IANA. Table 14–1 describes the approved MIME types, as well as a *partial* sublist of the approved subtypes.

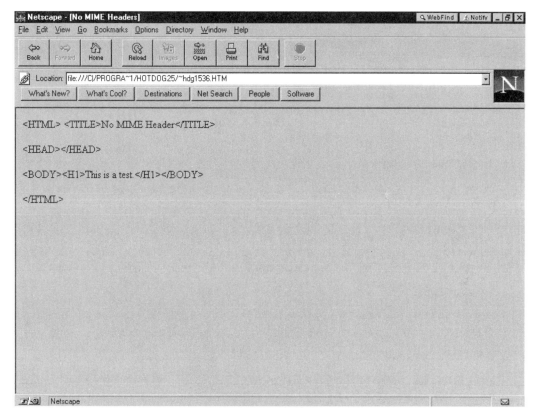

Figure 14–4 A little bit of HTML code without a MIME header as seen in a browser.

Table 14–1 MIME Types and Subtypes

Type	Description	Subtypes
Application	Message is data that does not fit into any of the other MIME types	cybercash, msword, postscript, rtf
Audio	Message is an audio file	32kadpcm, basic, wav
Image	Message is an image	cgm, gif, jpeg, tiff
Message	Message is an encapsulated e-mail message	external-body, news, partial, rfc822
Multipart	Message consists of multiple body parts	alternative, formdata, mixed, report
Text	Message is primarily ASCII text	html, plain, richtext, sgml, tab-separated-values
Video	Message is a video file	avi, quicktime, vnd.vivo

MIME Type/Subtype Examples

The following examples demonstrate the use of a combination of each of these types, along with a selected subtype.

Application Type: `Content-type: application/msword`

Definition: The body of the enclosed message is an MS Word document. The browser automatically launches MS Word and loads the included document when the page is viewed in a browser.

Audio Type: `Content-type: audio/wav`

Definition: The body of the enclosed message is an audio file saved in the WAV format and the WAV file plays automatically when the user clicks on it.

Image Type: `Content-type: image/gif`

Definition: The body of the enclosed message is a graphics file saved in the GIF format and the GIF file displays in the browser with the rest of the page.

Message Type: `Content-type: message/RFC822`

Definition: The body of the enclosed message is encapsulated as an RFC822 message and is processed as an RFC822 file when viewed in a browser.

Text Type: `Content-type: text/html`

Definition: The body of the enclosed message is HTML code and the browser formats it accordingly.

Video Type: `Content-type: video/mpeg`

Definition: The body of the enclosed message is an audio/video file saved in the MPG format which plays automatically when viewed in a browser.

Multipart Type: `Content-type: multipart/mixed; boundary="@@@@@@@@"`

Definition: The body of the enclosed message consists of file elements of different types and/or subtypes which are handled appropriately based on their type and/or subtype.

I can recommend the following book as a resource if you want to learn more about MIME:

Mime, uuencode & Zip
Author: Judi Fernandez
Publisher: MIS Press
ISBN: 1-55-828528-8

Multipart Type Example.   With the exception of the multipart type, the use of the other six MIME types is self-evident. Specifically, the type/subtype MIME header appears before the body of the message. With the multipart type, MIME headers can appear throughout the message body. The following code snippet, with the MIME headers italicized, is an example of this.

```
Content-type: multipart/mixed; boundary="@@@@@@@@"
--@@@@@@@@
Content-type: text/html
<HTML>
<HEAD>Multipart MIME Example</HEAD>
<BODY>
--@@@@@@@@
Content-type: text/plain
Now is the time for all good men to come to the aid of their country.
To be or not to be, that is the question.
Four score and seven years ago.
--@@@@@@@@
Content-type: image/jpeg
... JPEG IMAGE DATA ...
--@@@@@@@@--
```

The beginning of an encapsulated boundary consists of two hyphens (- -) followed by the boundary string. The end of an encapsulated boundary consists of two hyphens (- -) followed by the boundary string followed by two more hyphens (- -).

Custom MIME Types

You can create and use a MIME type and/or subtype combination that does not exist; for example, in an intranet application. This could be to allow an Adobe Acrobat file to be transmitted and viewed by a browser in a usable format. To define and use a customized type/subtype, you'd have to perform the following steps:

1. Identify the type/subtype combination, and making sure it does not exist in the approved list of the IANA. This list can be seen at URL `http://www.isi.edu/ div7/infra/iana.html`. If you want more detail on MIME types and subtypes, then this URL will be of interest to you: `http://www.w3.org/pub/WWW/Proto- cols/ rfc1341/4_Content-Type.html`.

2. Configure the Web server to recognize the new type/subtype.

3. Make sure the browsers accessing the Adobe Acrobat file are configured to use a plug-in that formats and displays the file correctly.

4. Find or build a plug-in to display the file in the correct format A plug-in is a reusable program that dynamically extends the base function of a Web page by adding features such as audio and video playback.

As you can imagine, this is not an easy process. You are much better off contacting the IANA to see if they have an approved type/subtype combination that you can use. Also, hopefully, you can find a plug-in that you could use as well as these are usually quite difficult to write from scratch.

MIME Perspectives

Depending on your perspective, MIME means different things. As a developer, you need to understand MIME from both your perspective and that of the users. You need the users' understanding to design and build an application that is not only easy to use and functional, but fun.

MIME from a Developer's Perspective

Although it sometimes makes good sense to display text or straight HTML pages to your users, you will probably want to frequently include audio/video/graphics capabilities in your Web applications. To do this, you must maintain a keen awareness of available MIME types and subtypes. CGI applications are increasingly incorporating newer media types, such as graphics, server-push animation, 2D and 3D charts, Virtual Reality Modeling Language (VRML), and plots and graphs. The following URLs will help you to keep up with evolving MIME types and subtypes.

- `ftp://ds.internic.net/rfc/`
- `http://www.cis.ohio.state.edu/hypertext/faq/usenet/mail/mime-faq/top.html`
- `http://www.cs.indiana.edu/docproject/mail/mime.html`
- `http://www.netscape.com/assist/helper_apps/media-types.html`
- `http://www.netscape.com/assist/helper_apps/what-is-mime.html`

As you design and develop your Web database applications, be aware of the available MIME types and subtypes. Employ all available resources to make your Web pages as functional *and* attractive as possible.

A common sense design tip when using a MIME type that requires a plug-in is to provide a convenient way for users to acquire the plug-in if it doesn't exist on their machines. You can easily do this with a text or icon hyperlink to a site that contains the needed plug-in.

MIME from a User's Perspective

Your users are becoming increasingly aware of and comfortable with multimedia Web applications. The applications you build for them should not only address the business' needs, but be as enjoyable to use as other Web applications they might use. Therefore, your Web database application will probably need to support, at the very least, some sort of audio output and graphics/video display.

If you limit the design of your application to use only standard types and subtypes, the need for plug-ins should be minimal. In most cases, you will probably be able to design and deliver a very useful and enjoyable Web database application by using nothing other than the standard types and subtypes. If you find the need to build an application that requires the use of a non-standard type or subtype, make it easy for the user to acquire and use the necessary plug-in.

As discussed in the previous section, you can do this by providing a hyperlink to a site that contains the plug-in from the Web page that requires its use. Be aware though that downloading and installing a plug-in does not always ensure that it is configured to be used automatically by the user's browser. Not all plug-ins automatically configure the browser. For example, the plug-ins seen back in Figure 14–2 automatically configure themselves, but they require the user to completely close out of the browser they are using and restart it.

Figure 14–5 shows the screen the user would use to manually configure a plug-in to work with various MIME types and subtypes. Under the column heading File Type is listed the MIME type/subtype combination. The column heading Action lists the application that executes or the action that takes place when the MIME type/subtype is encountered. Finally, the column heading Extension lists the various file extensions that would trigger the action specified.

In Figure 14–5, a MIME type/subtype combination of `audio/x-pn-realaudio` will cause a plug-in program named `raplayer.exe` that is in the `c:\windows\system` directory to execute whenever a file with the extension of `ra` or `ram` is encountered in a Web message. With this definition, this machine is fully configured to automatically

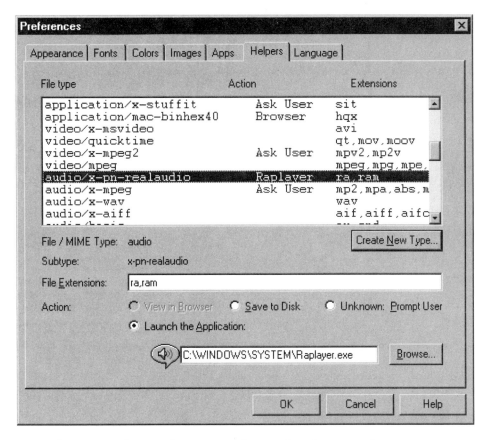

Figure 14–5 Configuring a plug-in for Netscape Navigator.

recognize and play the necessary plug-in whenever a real audio file is received in a Web message.

To get to the Preferences screen (Figure 14–5) using Netscape Navigator, simply click on the Options menu item in the main menu. Then click on the General Preferences menu item and the Helpers tab.

If you'd like to read more about plug-ins, I recommend a book titled *Official Netscape Plug-in Book* written by Shannon Turlington and published by Ventana Media Group (ISBN: 1-56-604468-5).

Moving On

This chapter presented foundation information that you can use to incorporate MIME in your Web database applications to add powerful and attractive multimedia components. You saw how easy MIME is to use, provided that you adhere to a few requirements—specifically use the `Content-type:` line and approved types and subtypes.

Chapter 15 shows you how to manage Web database access and the application state. You will learn how managing the application state gives you the ability to build pseudoconversational applications.

CHAPTER 15

Managing
Web Database
Access
and the
Application
State

Oftentimes, when an application loses track of where it's been, it doesn't know where it needs to go. This chapter describes three different techniques (Hidden Fields on Forms, Database Tables, and Cookies) that keep track of where an application is during the application state.

You should notice that none of these techniques is HTML. This is because the current specifications for HTML do not specifically address support for managing state data. However, as you will see, you can use some of the features of HTML to incorporate the managing of application state.

There has been much discussion lately about expanding HTML specifications to include managing of application state. Netscape Communications seems to be leading this initiative. You should expect to see this added to HTML specifications by the end of 1998.

What Is Application State?

Application state is ability to keep track of which step an application is in, including providing access to all relevant data that step needs, at any point in a process. Application state information, therefore, is the information that is maintained and transferred from one Web page or form or program to another for subsequent processing.

Consider the following example. I've used a VCR rental application in previous chapters to illustrate certain points. Assume that a clerk wants to query all the movies that are rated PG 13, and from that list wants to perform a drilldown query to produce a list of all the movies that are cartoons.

One way to accomplish this would be to build an HTML form similar to the one seen in Figure 15–1, where the clerk is able to specify both the movie rating and the category on a single form. Here, I have stripped out the unnecessary objects, graphics, and controls from the HTML forms used in this chapter for readability.

The following HTML code is used to create the form shown in Figure 15–1. Note the existence of two drop-down list boxes that the user would use to make his or her selection.

```
<HTML>
<HEAD>
<TITLE>Complex Query</TITLE>
</HEAD>
<BODY>
<FORM METHOD=POST ACTION="http://teleport.com/cgi-bin/query.exe">
<P>Rating: <SELECT RATING=Movie_Rating SIZE=2>
<OPTION VALUE="PG">PG</OPTION>
<OPTION VALUE="PG 13">PG13</OPTION>
```

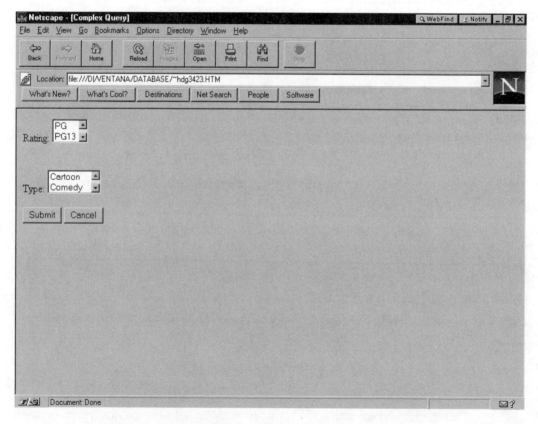

Figure 15–1   Making a form for a complex query.

```
<OPTION VALUE="R">R</OPTION>
<OPTION VALUE="NR">NR</OPTION>
</SELECT></P>
<BR>
<P>Type: <SELECT TYPE=Movie_Type SIZE=2>
<OPTION VALUE="Cartoon">Cartoon</OPTION>
<OPTION VALUE="Comedy">Comedy</OPTION>
<OPTION VALUE="Drama">Drama</OPTION>
<OPTION VALUE="Mystery">Mystery</OPTION>
<OPTION VALUE="Romance">Romance</OPTION>
<OPTION VALUE="Suspense">Suspense</OPTION>
</SELECT>
<P>
<INPUT NAME="Submit" TYPE="SUBMIT" VALUE="Submit">
<INPUT NAME="Cancel" TYPE="RESET" VALUE="Cancel">
</FORM>
</BODY>
</HTML>
```

In this scenario, there is no need to maintain the application state as the user is given the option of supplying enough information to the CGI program running on the Web server so that it can format and execute a complex query. In other words, all the activity required to accomplish a given task is provided for on one Web page, running one CGI program.

But, this approach is limiting because it does not allow for the dynamic *building* of the type list box. For example, the types provided in the drop down list box are Cartoon, Comedy, Drama, Mystery, Romance, Suspense. But, what if there were no movies rated PG *and* of the type Romance? Although this option is selectable in the two drop-down list boxes, it is an invalid combination.

Another exception occurs when the value in the two drop-down list boxes is hard coded and requires changes to the HTML code to modify. Therefore, if a new movie of type Action were to become available, someone would need to make changes to the HTML code to accommodate this new movie type.

If an application could be built so that the results of the first query (the movie rating) are used to construct the second query (the movie type) in a second Web page running a second CGI program, then both of these considerations would be addressed. This means that the application is more flexible to change and requires less maintenance over time. Being able to keep track of the application state will allow us to build such an application.

Now, consider an example where you want to give the users accurate information to make their selections. You want to build an application that walks them through the following steps:

1. The user completes and submits a form specifying the rating of movies the customer wants to see. These ratings are supplied dynamically by performing a query against the database, extracting all the unique movie ratings.

2. From the result set above, the user selects and submits a second form where he or she indicates the type of movie the customer wants to see.

3. The result set from the second step will be a list of all movies that have the rating as specified in Step 1 and are in the category as specified in Step 2.

Given this architecture for the application, a movie rating could be added to or deleted from the database without any coding changes needing to be made in the drop-down list boxes. Such an architecture, requiring multiple steps, could never be accommodated without being able to keep track of where the application is in the series of steps.

A Web database application designed as just described is dynamic, accurate, and does not require modification as new ratings or movie types appear. This reduction in application maintenance increases the life of the application and allows you to spend more time writing new applications and less time maintaining existing applications. All of this is possible because you have designed and constructed the application to maintain and recognize *state* information.

Little attention has been paid to date in the media about the time and cost involved in maintaining Web database applications. This is because the technology is so new that very few (if any) companies have applications that are old enough to require maintenance. However, within two years you will see this become an area in Web application development that garners a tremendous amount of attention.

Authentication and Application State

Authentication means making sure that the person who is accessing all of the Web pages in your Web database application has permission to do so. If your application involves just one Web page, then this is not a problem—you simply provide for the entry and processing of a user ID and password on the one Web page.

But, what if your application involves twenty Web pages? As you know, each Web page has a unique URL. Just because someone entered a user ID and password on the first Web page of the application, which was subsequently authenticated, doesn't mean that he or she has the authority to see or process any of the other pages in the application. Unless you somehow record in the application that the person accessing the Web pages has previously passed a security process you won't be able to protect your pages from unauthorized access.

As a Web database application designer, you must consider the question, "Do you want to make your Web database application accessible to anyone with a browser?" If the answer to the question is, "No," then you must build a program into the application that allows for user authentication and restricted access. This requires the use of application state.

Assume you build a login screen that looks similar to Figure 15–2, with the HTML code necessary to create such a screen.

```
<HTML>
<HEAD>
<TITLE>User ID And Password</TITLE>
</HEAD>
<BODY>
```

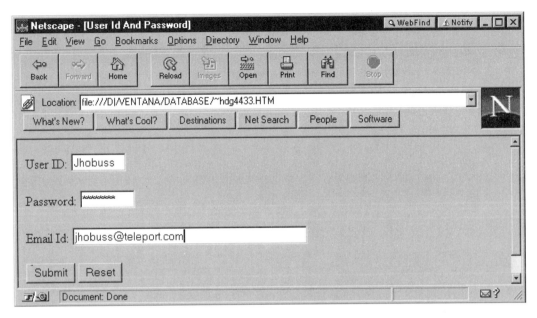

Figure 15-2   An example of a user authentication screen.

```
<FORM METHOD=POST ACTION="www.teleport.com\cgi-bin\pass_ver.exe">
User ID:
<INPUT NAME="User_ID" TYPE="" COLS=8 SIZE="8"><P>
Password:
<INPUT NAME="passwrd" TYPE="PASSWORD" COLS=8 SIZE="8"><P>
Email ID: <INPUT NAME="email_ID" TYPE="" COLS=40 SIZE="40"><P>
<INPUT NAME="Submit" TYPE="SUBMIT" VALUE="Submit">
<INPUT NAME="Reset" TYPE="RESET" VALUE="Reset">
</FORM>
</BODY>
</HTML>
```

In this HTML code you'll notice a special "TYPE" for the INPUT tag PASSWORD. This type causes asterisks (*) to display to the user as they enter data in this field. Also notice that the name of the CGI program that executes on the Web server is pass_ver.exe. Presumably this CGI program would perform some sort of verification of the user_ID/password combination that was entered by the user before access is provided to other system components.

If the user does not pass your security routine then you'd display a message back that tells them so. If the user passes the security routine, then the pass_ver.exe CGI program would format and send a Web page back to the user that gives the user access to sensitive information in your database. Is this the right thing to do? The answer is yes and no.

The answer is "yes" if you want to give authorized users access to the information they want and have authority to access, but you still want to keep the unauthorized user out. But what if the URL that you display to the user, the one that gives them access to sensitive information after they passed your security routines, somehow falls into the hands of someone who shouldn't have access to your system. That person could circumvent your security front-end by merely using the URL of the Web page that follows the security routines. Remember, every Web page has a unique URL. Any URL can be typed into a browser at any time on any machine that is connected to the Internet, thus potentially giving that user the ability to view the Web page associated with the URL. Not a good situation, agreed?

Consider the Web page seen in Figure 15–3. This is an example of a Web page that could be generated from your `pass_ver.exe` CGI program when the user passes the security check. The HTML code used to generate this screen follows. You should notice nothing particularly intriguing about this code.

```
<HTML>
<HEAD>
<TITLE>Access To Sensitive Information</TITLE>
</HEAD>
<BODY>
<FORM METHOD=POST ACTION="www.teleport.com\cgi-bin\empl_adj.exe">
ID Of Employee Whose Salary You Are Adjusting:
<INPUT NAME="empl_ID" TYPE="" COLS=8 SIZE="8"><P>
Percentage Change In Monthly Pay:
<INPUT NAME="change_rate" TYPE="TEXT" COLS=6 SIZE="6"><P>
Increase <INPUT NAME="up_down" TYPE="RADIO">
```

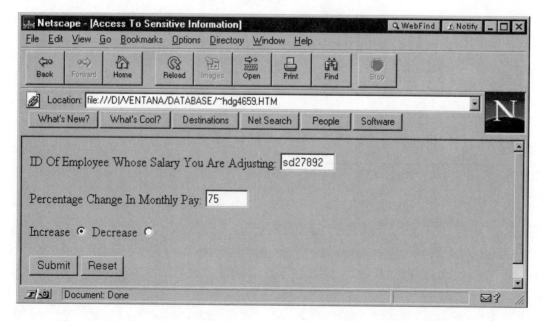

Figure 15–3 A Web page that contains very privileged information.

```
Decrease <INPUT NAME="up_down" TYPE="RADIO"><P>
<INPUT NAME="Submit" TYPE="SUBMIT" VALUE="Submit">
<INPUT NAME="Reset" TYPE="RESET" VALUE="Reset">
</FORM>
</BODY>
</HTML>
```

The VCR scenario in Figure 15–1 and the Employee Salary Adjustment Web page in Figure 15–3 are both excellent examples of situations where you would benefit from maintaining application state. Without the ability to transfer the information from the sign-on page to the data manipulation pages that a user has or has not passed security, anyone who knows the URL of the data manipulation pages could access them and manipulate the data that those pages affect. In the following sections you'll see a number of different ways to accommodate this.

Using Forms to Maintain State

Recall in Figure 15–2 that there were three pieces of information required to be input on this screen, User ID, Password, and Email ID.

Once the user pressed the `<Submit>` button and sent this transaction to the Web server which in turn initiated the `pass_ver.exe` CGI program, it is the responsibility of the `pass_ver.exe` program to perform whatever security validation routines are required. However, it is also the responsibility of the `pass_ver.exe` program to format and send the HTML code as seen in Figure 15–3 back to the user.

What if instead of sending the form that looks like Figure 15–3, the `pass_ver.exe` program formats and sends the form that looks like Figure 15–4? Take a close look at these two figures. Go ahead, look at them again and think about what you see that's different about them.

You should see that there's nothing visibly different about these two Web pages. This is what you'd want both the authorized and the unauthorized user to see as well—nothing visible. However, there is a lot going on in this Web page that is unseen—the critical data passing mechanism to maintain application state. The catalyst to this is the use of hidden fields on forms.

In other words, information gathered on Web page 1, which is sent to and processed by the CGI program pass_ver.exe, is placed in hidden fields that the CGI program pass_ver.exe places on Web page 2. That is then sent back to the user. When the user provides information on Web page 2 and presses the `<Submit>` button, the information that is contained in the hidden fields is returned to the pass_ver.exe CGI program and the CGI program recognizes the existence and verifies the contents of the hidden fields before continuing on with the required processing.

Contrast this scenario with one where a hacker attempts to gain access to your system by typing in the URL of Web page 2 from his or her browser. The hacker would click on the `<Submit>` button to send the Web page to the pass_ver.exe CGI program. But, the pass_ver.exe CGI program would interrogate the contents of the hidden fields contained on this form and determine that there was nothing in them. It would then be able to right-

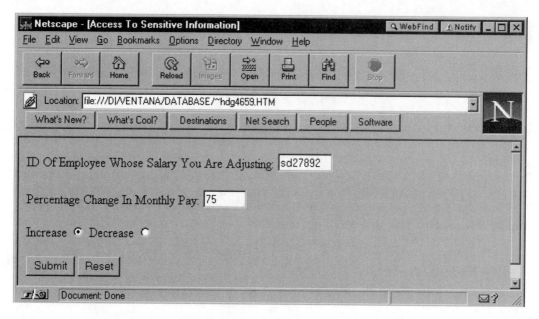

Figure 15–4 A Web page that contains very privileged information—with a hidden field.

fully conclude that the page was submitted by someone who had not initially logged on to the system via Web page 1.

Take a look at the following sample HTML code that was used to create the Web page seen in Figure 15–4.

```
<HTML>
<HEAD>
<TITLE>Access To Sensitive Information</TITLE>
</HEAD>
<BODY>
<FORM METHOD=POST ACTION="www.teleport.com\cgi-bin\empl_adj.exe">
ID Of Employee Whose Salary You Are Adjusting:
<INPUT NAME="empl_ID" TYPE="" COLS=8 SIZE="8"><P>
Percentage Change In Monthly Pay:
<INPUT NAME="change_rate" TYPE="TEXT" COLS=6 SIZE="6"><P>
Increase <INPUT NAME="up_down" TYPE="RADIO">
Decrease <INPUT NAME="up_down" TYPE="RADIO"><P>
<INPUT NAME="Submit" TYPE="SUBMIT" VALUE="Submit">
<INPUT NAME="Reset" TYPE="RESET" VALUE="Reset">
<INPUT NAME="user_ID" TYPE="HIDDEN">
<INPUT NAME="password" TYPE="HIDDEN">
</FORM>
</BODY>
</HTML>
```

You'll notice that what makes this snippet of HTML code different from the code used to generate Figure 15–2 is the following two lines:

```
<INPUT NAME="user_ID" TYPE="HIDDEN">
<INPUT NAME="password" TYPE="HIDDEN">
```

These are the hidden fields which, as the name implies, contain the user_ID and password that are subsequently used to verify and determine the application state. Because these are protected fields, they can not be overtyped or modified by the user. The idea here is that the pass_ver.exe CGI program would transfer the values the user supplied in Figure 15–2 into the two hidden fields that are transmitted back to the user as in Figure 15–4. When the user completes this Web page and presses the <Submit> button which in turn causes the empl_adj.exe CGI program to begin execution on the Web server, this program retrieves, interrogates, and validates the values it receives in the user_ID and password hidden fields, thus determining the application state. In this example, the application state is that the user had successfully entered the required information as seen in Figure 15–2 so they are authorized to view and submit the screen seen in Figure 15–4.

This is all well and good, but what if an unauthorized person input the URL for the Web page that adjusts an employees salary? The answer here is that they would see the Web page exactly as you see it in Figure 15–4, and they may even try to input some values and press the <Submit> button. The problem for them will be when the empl_adj.exe CGI program executes this data and determines that there is nothing in the user_ID and password hidden fields. The program should be written to reject the transaction and log the user ID of the offending intruder.

As you know, the contents of HTML pages, including hidden fields, can be seen in most commercial browsers. This could lead to a compromise of your carefully crafted application. To circumvent would-be intruders you could build or acquire an encryption/decryption interface to your CGI programs that keeps the data in the hidden fields safe.

Using Database Tables to Maintain State

Using Access 97 database tables to maintain state information has its advantages and disadvantages. One of the advantages is that a user's session activity information is maintained from one session to the next. By using hidden fields and not database tables, when users disconnect from the Internet they lose their tracking capabilities. However, by using fields stored in an Access 97 database the information can be saved for later reuse.

An easily understood application of this is in an online shopping application where the user might be called away from his or her computer midway through the shopping activities. When the user logs on later it would be nice (and easy if you are using database tables to maintain state information) if you could display a partially completed order form on a Web page and ask if he or she wants to continue shopping or start over. Such a screen is seen in Figure 15–5.

Another advantage to using tables in an Access 97 database to maintain state information is in the manner of preprocessing user selections. For example, consider our on-

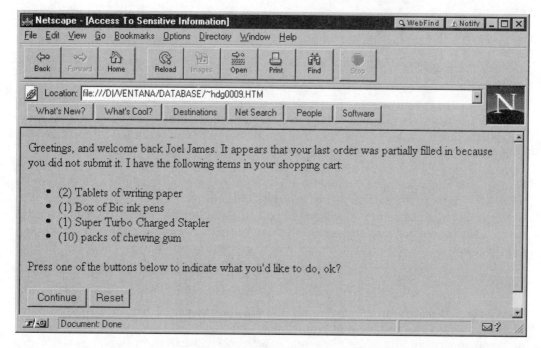

Figure 15–5   The benefit of using database tables to maintain state.

line shopping catalog example. Wouldn't it be beneficial to users to maintain a running tally of their purchases, as they select items and put them in their virtual shopping carts? You can do this easily using database tables to maintain state information—it is quite a bit more complex to do this using hidden fields.

Such advantages are not without disadvantages. One of the most significant disadvantages is the question of what to do with partial information that is left in your database tables. You could find your Access 97 tables quickly filling up with partial data that will never be completed.

Consider again the online shopping catalog example. What if the user browses through your catalog, selects a number of different items (which causes rows to be inserted in an Access 97 database table that keeps track of such things), and then exits your catalog without ever placing and finalizing the order? How do you know when the user did this whether he or she did not intend to finalize the order for the items or whether the Internet connection was inadvertently terminated by the service provider? How long do you keep this information in your tables before a stored procedure deletes it? All of these questions need to be answered when you use database tables in this type of an application to maintain state information.

To maintain state information in an Access 97 database table is a relatively simple process. It involves determining what information needs to be retained to give adequate security while at the same time providing suitable functionality in your application. The process to accomplish this is:

1. Design your Web pages to gather the information necessary to determine your application's state.

2. Build your CGI program to receive this information from the Web page and store it in an Access 97 database table in a format and manner that satisfies the business need.

3. Build a mechanism in your Web pages and CGI program to delete information stored in the Access 97 database when it is no longer needed to maintain state information.

4. Repeat this process until the application is complete.

Using Persistent Cookies to Maintain State

Using cookie is yet another way to maintain an application's state. A cookie is a small packet of data that a Web server stores on a Web client machine to keep track of certain application-specific information. There is a tremendous amount of hard disk space currently being taken up on Web servers with discussion groups dealing with the issue of cookies. You can decide for yourself whether the use of cookies makes sense for your application.

What Is a Cookie?

A cookie is a small piece of data (no more than 4,000 characters in length) that is sent to your browser from a Web server. This data is accepted by your browser, checked for proper length, expiration date, path and domain, and then saved. A popular misconception is that cookies can contain viruses or executable computer code. This is untrue. A cookie can contain whatever data you want, but it cannot contain programs or viruses (which are actually programs). For example, in an application you could create a unique user ID for a visitor, save it as a cookie to that person's hard drive, and then that user would never have to enter his or her user ID again. Instead, the user's browser would read it from the cookie file and ship it to the Web server along with the requested URL.

Additionally, in a virtual mall environment, virtual shopping carts can be created that will allow the browser to quit and twelve months later come back and still have the same products in the cart. You've seen how this is done with database tables, but it could also be done (albeit less glamorously and with less sophistication) with cookies.

How Do Cookies Work?

Using cookies is mostly accomplished by routines built into the user's browser by the developer of the browser. You must add some components to your application that complete the cookie environment, but for the most part the necessary features are already present. Netscape Communications Corporation is the leading proponent for the use of cookies and has built superior functionality into their Navigator browser to handle cookies.

When you click a link to a page, your browser checks the URL of the link against information that is in its cookie database. On a non-Macintosh machine, the name of this file is COOKIES.TXT. On a Macintosh machine, the name of this file is MagicCookie. An example of what the contents of this file looks like is seen in Figure 15–6.

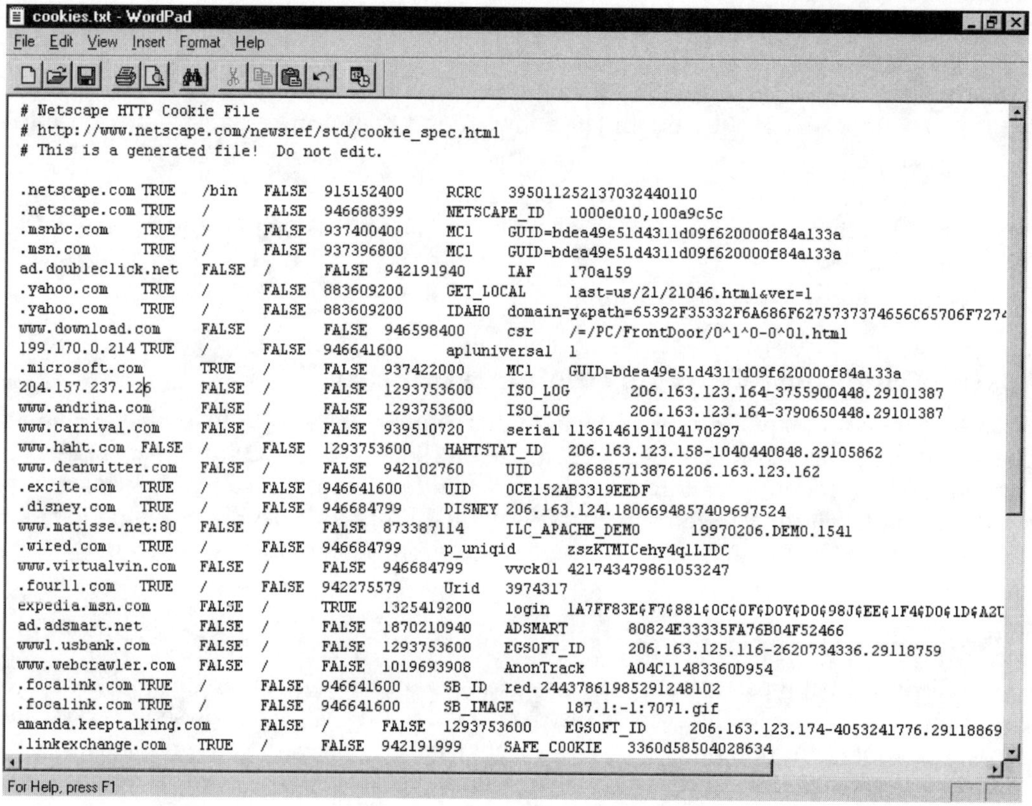


```
# Netscape HTTP Cookie File
# http://www.netscape.com/newsref/std/cookie_spec.html
# This is a generated file!  Do not edit.

.netscape.com TRUE   /bin   FALSE  915152400    RCRC   395011252137032440110
.netscape.com TRUE   /      FALSE  946688399    NETSCAPE_ID   1000e010,100a9c5c
.msnbc.com    TRUE   /      FALSE  937400400    MC1    GUID=bdea49e51d4311d09f620000f84a133a
.msn.com      TRUE   /      FALSE  937396800    MC1    GUID=bdea49e51d4311d09f620000f84a133a
ad.doubleclick.net   FALSE  /      FALSE  942191940    IAF    170a159
.yahoo.com    TRUE   /      FALSE  883609200    GET_LOCAL     last=us/21/21046.html&ver=1
.yahoo.com    TRUE   /      FALSE  883609200    IDAHO  domain=y&path=65392F35332F6A686F6275737374656C65706F727
www.download.com     FALSE  /      FALSE  946598400    csr    /=/PC/FrontDoor/0^1^0-0^01.html
199.170.0.214 TRUE   /      FALSE  946641600    apluniversal  1
.microsoft.com       TRUE   /      FALSE  937422000    MC1    GUID=bdea49e51d4311d09f620000f84a133a
204.157.237.126      FALSE  /      FALSE  1293753600   ISO_LOG       206.163.123.164-3755900448.29101387
www.andrina.com      FALSE  /      FALSE  1293753600   ISO_LOG       206.163.123.164-3790650448.29101387
www.carnival.com     FALSE  /      FALSE  939510720    serial 113614619110417029 7
www.haht.com  FALSE  /      FALSE  1293753600   HAHTSTAT_ID   206.163.123.158-1040440848.29105862
www.deanwitter.com   FALSE  /      FALSE  942102760    UID    2868857138761206.163.123.162
.excite.com   TRUE   /      FALSE  946641600    UID    0CE152AB3319EEDF
.disney.com   TRUE   /      FALSE  946684799    DISNEY 206.163.124.1806694857409697524
www.matisse.net:80   FALSE  /      FALSE  873387114    ILC_APACHE_DEMO      19970206.DEMO.1541
.wired.com    TRUE   /      FALSE  946684799    p_uniqid      zszKTMICehy4qlLIDC
www.virtualvin.com   FALSE  /      FALSE  946684799    vvck01 421743479861053247
.fourll.com   TRUE   /      FALSE  942275579    Urid   3974317
expedia.msn.com      FALSE  /      TRUE   1325419200   login  1A7FF83E¢F7¢881¢0C¢0F¢D0Y¢D0¢98J¢EE¢1F4¢D0¢1D¢A2U
ad.adsmart.net       FALSE  /      FALSE  1870210940   ADSMART       80824E33335FA76B04F52466
www1.usbank.com      FALSE  /      FALSE  1293753600   EGSOFT_ID     206.163.125.116-2620734336.29118759
www.webcrawler.com   FALSE  /      FALSE  1019693908   AnonTrack     A04C11483360D954
.focalink.com TRUE   /      FALSE  946641600    SB_ID  red.2443786198529124810 2
.focalink.com TRUE   /      FALSE  946641600    SB_IMAGE      187.1:-1:7071.gif
amanda.keeptalking.com      FALSE  /      FALSE  1293753600   EGSOFT_ID     206.163.123.174-4053241776.29118869
.linkexchange.com    TRUE   /      FALSE  942191999    SAFE_COOKIE   3360d58504028634
```

Figure 15–6 The contents of a COOKIES.TXT file.

If the file has a cookie that matches the domain and path of the link that was requested, it will send the cookie to the server along with the request for the page. If it has no cookie for the requested URL, then processing continues by the server receiving the URL request. If no cookie exists for the requested URL, but the Web page referenced by the URL needs to insert one in your cookie file, an entry in your cookie file will be created automatically for you.

For instance, let's say that I request the URL `www.matisse.net:80`. My browser would search the COOKIES.TXT or MagicCookie file (if I had a Macintosh machine) to find an entry that matches this URL. So along with the request for the page it would send the rest of the information that is in the COOKIES.TXT or MagicCookie file for this URL.

You should know that when a Web server sends a cookie to a browser, the cookie can only be read by the browser of the person who placed it.

How Can You Use Cookies?

Cookies can be used for a number of things. The three uses listed here are not meant to be conclusive, but rather to give you some ideas on how you can use them in your applications.

Maintain Application State.   When a user logs in to your Web database application, and that application needs to verify the user's login identification and password in a CGI program, upon verification you could send a cookie to the user's machine. This cookie indicates the user's acceptance into your application.

Then, and every time thereafter, when that user accesses your site and requests a secured URL, the cookie data for your site will be sent to your Web server at the same time the URL request is sent. The CGI program executing on the Web server will verify the data passed to it from the cookie file for validity, accuracy, and currency.

Virtual Shopping Mall.   A virtual shopping mall system can be developed using cookies. These cookies would "remember" what people want to buy by recording what they have placed in their virtual shopping carts. By doing this, if a person spends three hours ordering books at your site and suddenly has to get off the net, he or she could quit the browser and return later (weeks, months, or even years if you're so bold!) and still have those items in his or her shopping basket—because those items have been in the COOKIES.TXT or MagicCookie file all along.

Site Personalization.   This is fast becoming one of the most frequently used ways that people are finding to employ cookies. By using cookies to personalize a site, the information users see is tailored to their interests. Perhaps the best use of this that I've seen is what the folks at Yahoo have done. They have published a site where a user can request a slew of different types of information of interest. Every time that user accesses that site again a tailored virtual newspaper is displayed. As seen in Figure 15–7, the information is laid out nicely and the best part is that it is tailored to what each person wants to read.

I can click on the bookmark to my personalized site any time and get up-to-date weather on the cities of my choosing, I can find out what the current price is on investments, and I can find out what the latest news is in the world of Medicine, Technology, or any of a number of other fields.

Additional Information on Cookies

The actual syntax of the COOKIES.TXT or MagicCookie file, and their related commands are rather advanced for this chapter. There are, however, a number of books available that provide good coverage of this topic. These are:

Title:	CGI Developers Guide
Author:	Eugene Kim
Publisher:	Macmillan Computer Publishing
ISBN:	1-57-521087-8

Title:	CGI Programming Unleashed, 2nd Edition
Author:	Berlin
Publisher:	Macmillan Computer Publishing
ISBN:	1-57-521151-3

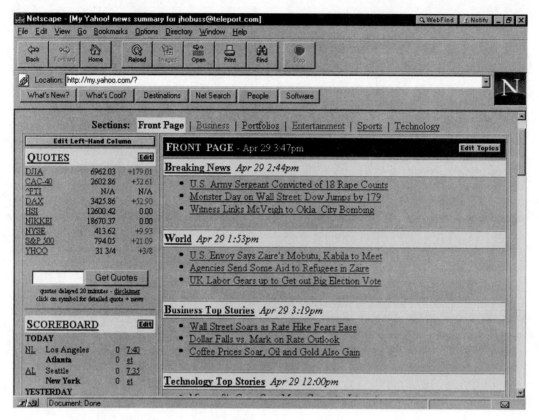

Figure 15-7   A personalized Web site that uses cookies.

Title: CGI Programming in C & Perl
Author: Thomas Boutell
Publisher: Addison Wesley Publishing Company
ISBN: 0-20-142219-0

Moving On

In this chapter you learned how to manage Web database access and the application state by reading about and seeing the three most popular methods available for this, namely hidden fields on forms, database tables, and cookies.

In the next chapter you will read about some of the tips and tricks available to improve the performance of Web applications that use HTML to access databases. Additionally you will read about some key topics in building maintainable Web database applications and actually doing maintenance on those applications.

CHAPTER 16

Improving the Performance of Web Database Applications

I t is no longer enough to merely build a Web application that has access to an Access 97 database and which satisfies a business need. With ODBC and the tools available to integrate Web and database technologies, the "art" in Web Access 97 database application development is no longer in marrying the two toolsets. Rather, the "art" lies in crafting an application that not only meets the business needs *but* is efficient as well. Although Microsoft Corporation has done a wonderful job in building efficiency into their Access 97 product, there are still a number of things you can do to make sure the application you build and the Access 97 database against which it processes are as efficient as possible.

This chapter describes some techniques you can use to build efficiency in your Web database applications. It is segmented into two major parts, Application Optimization and Access 97 Database Optimization.

Application Optimization

Optimizing a Web database application encompasses more than just optimizing queries or indexing tables. There are a number of application-specific issues that directly affect the overall performance of your delivered application. In this section you'll learn about most of these.

Access Speeds

The speed in which users connect to your Web database application has a tremendous impact on the performance of that application. Your goal should be to design and construct an application that gives the user as quick a response as possible. For example, suppose a page in your Web database application displays the results of a query to an Access 97 database in which 72,000 bytes of information are transmitted. Recognizing that it doesn't matter the percentage that this 72k bytes is data versus HTML code, you should know that 72k bytes is not a large amount of data for some queries.

Now, assume a user accessing this Web page is using a 14.4 kbps (kilo bits per second) modem. It will take approximately forty seconds to transfer this data from your Web server to the user's browser. Assume another user accessing this page is using an ISDN line that is comprised of dual 64 kbps channels. It will take approximately nine seconds to transfer the same amount of data from your Web server to this user's browser.

In the current environment of ISDN and T1 data lines, you should not assume that every person accessing your Web pages has access to high speed data lines and modems. If you build your application assuming the worst, then the people accessing your application at higher speeds than the slowest modems will be pleased with its performance.

CGI Programs

CGI programs cause a performance degradation in your application—there is no doubt about this. However, in many cases this is a degradation that you will just have to accept because of the functions you want to build into your application that can not be accomplished in HTML code. The amount of that degradation is very much dependent on the following items specific to CGI programs:

- The language in which the CGI program is written
- The number of functions performed by the CGI program
- The types of database access performed in the CGI program
- The number of CGI programs

Your goal as a designer and builder of a Web database application should be to reduce the performance impacts of CGI programs attributable to these four items.

Recognizing that CGI programs have the potential of seriously degrading the overall performance of your application, you should design these with *at least as much* forethought and consideration as you would to the Access 97 database access modules in a non-Web database application. I have emphasized the phrase *at least as much* because of the number of other issues that contribute to the performance (or lack thereof) of your application other than CGI programs. Fortunately, this is one of the things that you do have some control over.

Change

A Web site that changes is usually a Web site that enjoys repeat visitors. A number of tools are available now that automatically notify users when a Web site in which they are interested changes so they can make more informed decisions about whether or not to revisit the site. It behooves you to consider this aspect when designing your Web site.

Occasionally a Web site designer will lose sight of performance issues when designing the program to integrate change into the Web site. In addition, broken links to other Web resources could develop when a site changes frequently. This causes a degradation in the performance of the completed application as well as impacting the productivity of the developer of the Web pages. Therefore, when designing a Web site and the pages on that site, consider the degree and frequency of change to the site after it goes online.

Most of the tools that scour the Web and report on changes to Web sites do little more than read the contents of the <TITLE> . . . </TITLE> tag pair on the site's home page. Therefore, if you want to build what appears to be a frequently changing site, you may get away with doing little more than changing the contents of the <TITLE> . . . </TITLE> tag pair.

Development Suites

Development suites are highly productive. I believe there is about as much productivity improvement in using a development suite to build a Web Access 97 database application as there is in using a development suite to build a non-Web Access 97 database application.

Consider the time it takes to build a non-Web database application with a development suite tool like PowerBuilder versus building the same application with a programming tool like C. In other than the rarest of circumstances, a developer can build an application with PowerBuilder much more quickly than it takes to build the same application with C. So too, can a Web Access 97 database application developer create an application more quickly using a development suite than by using a straight programming language.

You should also know that an application written using a development suite may have performance problems when it executes because of the nature of the development suite. For example, in the previous paragraph I compared writing an application in PowerBuilder versus writing one in C, noting that in most cases an application can be written more quickly using PowerBuilder than using C. However, in most cases the application written in C will execute more quickly and be more responsive than the Power-Builder application. Although there are many reasons for this that are outside of the scope of this book, (e.g., executing compiled code versus interpreted code, size of object modules, included or called libraries, etc.) you should understand that your use of a development suite to develop a Web database application may negatively affect the performance of that application when it is in production.

Functions in Web Pages

The number and types of functions you place in your Web pages directly affect their performance. For example an HTML page that displays static text information performs much more quickly than a dynamic HTML page that requires several complex operations to format and display a page.

In Chapter 12, "HTML Forms and Database Access," you saw how you can retrieve the values that display in a drop-down list box on an HTML page from a database query. Although this type of function will result in an accurate and current representation of the data in the drop-down list box, your application will perform much better if the values in the drop-down list box are static HTML values. This is certainly true if the values come from an Access 97 database table due to the fact that the values are retrieved from a query to the database. This is a query that does not occur if the values in the drop-down list box are static.

The decision to be made in this example is how important is it to always retrieve the values that display in a drop-down list box from a database query and thus suffer the negative performance impact? If the information is very dynamic in nature and contains a small result set, then go ahead and populate the drop-down list box with a database query. However, if the information is a parts list that never changes (or is a large row re-sult set—who wants to scroll through a 100 item list in a drop-down list box?), then save the CPU cycles and format the drop-down list box using static values.

Java Applets

There is no doubt about it, Java applets are wonderful additions to a Web Access 97 data-base application that needs the functions supplied by them. However, you also know that it takes time to transfer the applet to the user's machine—and the larger the applet, the longer it takes to transfer. Therefore, use this feature sparingly if you are not sure the users already have the applet on their machines.

Web Component Size

All of the following components of your Web Access 97 database application must be downloaded to the user's machine *before* they can be viewed:

- Web pages
- Audio/visual/graphic components
- Some components in an intranet application
- Result sets of database queries

Since very few people have access to dedicated T1 or ISDN lines, the amount of time it takes to download the various application components should be evaluated carefully when designing the application to minimize the download time as much as possible. This is not to say that you should not use graphical elements in your application. To the con-trary, as you've read in previous chapters, the effective use of multimedia components in your Web Access 97 database application is very important to the acceptance of the appli-cation. However, you need to carefully balance the size of the modules that you create against their value when viewed in a user's browser.

Take the Web page viewed in Figure 16–1 as an example. This one page is 192,000 bytes. The majority of this space is taken by a Java applet and graphic *.GIF file that are both downloaded so that the flag seen in the middle of the page appears to be waving in the wind. With no intended lack of respect to the author of this page, this is an example of a module size that is unnecessarily large due to a graphic and applet that are not needed.

I would have preferred to have this page display in my browser in 15 percent of the time that it did take and not seen a flag waving than to have to wait 53 seconds for the graphic and applet to download. Seeing the flag waving was not worth the wait! This is especially true in that the page on which this graphic appears is a junction page—that is, it contains very little useful information and only acts as a router to other, more meaning-ful pages.

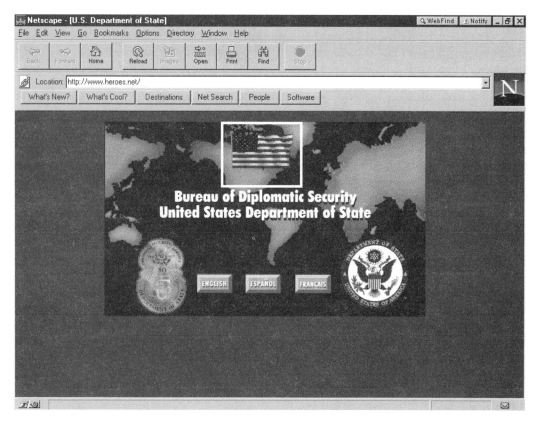

Figure 16–1   A very large module with very little added benefit.

Multimedia Components

As you know, multimedia application components such as *.AVI (movies), *.WAV (sounds), and *.JPG (graphic images) files take a very long time to transfer to a user's machine. For example, an *.AVI file that plays a 60-second interview with the company's CEO takes about 6,340,000 bytes of hard disk space to store. Over a 28.8 kbps modem this file would take about 29 minutes to download! That means the user would be waiting almost half an hour for a file to download so it could be viewed in the browser. This is the bad news.

The good news is that via MIME header types and companion applications, you have the ability to embed multimedia components in your Web database applications. However, use this capability sparingly as the performance impact is significant.

Number and Types of Graphics

For the same reason that you should limit the use of multimedia components in your Web database application, you should also limit the number of graphics. The more graphics that appear on a Web page, the longer it will take to view the page in a browser. It is a conundrum that one of the things that transformed the Internet to the Web is also one of the things that is contributing to the increasingly negative performance on the Web.

Use graphics in your Web Access 97 database applications often enough as is necessary to communicate the message you want to send and to make the pages appealing. But, use them frugally. At the same time you are weighing the value of placing graphics on your Web pages, consider the file type of the graphics you use.

For example, an image saved in *.GIF format occupies about half as much disk space, and therefore transfers to a user's browser about twice as fast as the same image saved in *.PCX format. Although it is true that a file saved in *.PCX format will be more crisp in a browser than the same file saved in *.GIF format, in most cases the difference is negligible. Consequently, consider the performance impact associated with the time it takes to transfer a graphic image when deciding the type of graphics to use in your Web Access 97 database application.

Searchability

Providing an appropriate search facility in your Web Access 97 database application is almost a necessity—this is especially true as the number of pages in your Web site increases. You owe it to the people browsing your site to make as much information about your site available to them in as convenient a manner as possible. Searchability provides this.

In a Web database application, searchability takes on different proportions than in a non-Web database application. In addition to providing the ability to flexibly and efficiently find information contained in the Web pages on your site, you may also want to provide a custom search mechanism in your database. In either case, providing search engines in your Web application could negatively impact the performance of that application and therefore, they need to be designed carefully.

Figure 16–2 is an example of how one company, Powell's Bookstore in Portland, Oregon, has built an efficient and effective search capability into their site. This company has tens of thousands of titles cross indexed and categorized in a number of different ways, yet a search of all of their titles is very efficient. As you can see, you can easily provide search criteria and get a well-defined search result. Take a look at their site and try out their search engine.

If you don't have a book or author to look for, use this book as a search target. But, don't be surprised if Powell's lists none available on their shelves as this book no doubt is a best seller.

Security

If your application requires the use of some sort of security mechanism (these are discussed in detail in Chapter 18, "Using Firewalls and Security Components to Protect Your Data"), this ultimately adds an additional component to the application and, therefore, probably has a negative impact on the performance of the application. However, this does not *have* to be the case.

Even in applications where sensitive information such as social security numbers, phone numbers, e-mail addresses, or credit card numbers, are transferred through Web pages, a well-designed application that uses a commercial product for handling this information will have a negligible overall performance impact. Figure 16–3 shows how a

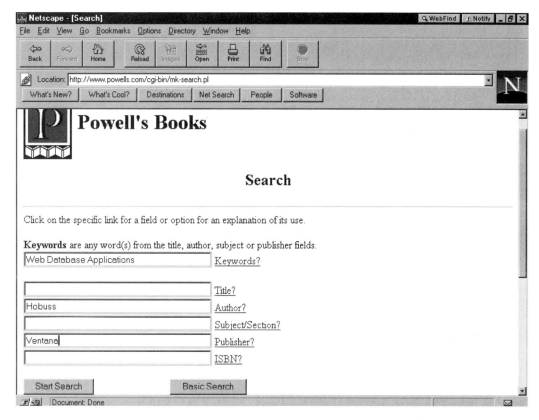

Figure 16–2 An example of a very efficient search capability.

Netscape browser informs users that it is handling a secure transaction—with a key in the lower left corner of the browser. If a transaction was not secure, the key would appear broken.

You will probably also want to protect all the information contained in your databases from prying eyes. Consult with your corporate auditors about this. However, the integrity of your database information is an important issue that may require varying levels of security to be built into the application and this may impact the overall performance of that application.

User-Input Validation

If your applications call for users to input data on forms, you ought to provide at least the same level of on-the-fly input validation in your Web database applications as you would in a non-Web database application. Doing this will improve the overall efficiency of the application.

HTML specifications provide for limited editing capabilities on user input. Therefore, you have a couple of choices to make when it comes to user-input validation:

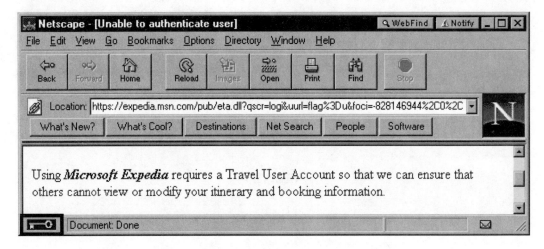

Figure 16–3 Security in an application does not have to impact performance.

- You can create your HTML pages using a scripting language that allows for user-input validation when the data is entered. Examples of these are JavaScript, Visual Basic, etc.

- Or you can provide this capability via a CGI program running on the Web server and transmit any errors back to the user to correct. This is my personal preference due to the fact that the CGI program is running on your server, where you have greater control over it.

The first choice provides for more direct user-input validation as it is done on the user's machine. However, it usually requires more of the developer's time to write the code to create the Web pages. The second choice allows you to create your Web pages more quickly, but requires a CGI program for user-input validation with this validation being done on the Web server. This means that in cases of error, the Web page must be transmitted from the user's machine to the Web server and back again for the user to correct any errors.

If you decide to use a CGI program for user-input validation, make sure that every field that can accept user input is edited in one operation of the CGI program. Nothing is more irritating to a user than completing a lengthy form, pressing the <Submit> button, and then going through a series of corrections while the CGI program notifies them of one error at a time. If there are multiple errors on a form, show the user all the errors at one time.

Access 97 Database Optimization

In the previous section you read about many of the things you can do at an application level to improve the performance of your Web application. In this section you'll read about ways that you can improve the performance of your Web database application that pertain specifically to the data and databases.

Ask Only for What You Need

When querying an Access 97 database, only fetch the rows and columns that you need to satisfy the intent of the query. Extracting unnecessary information negatively affects the performance of your application because of:

- The time it takes your RDBMS to extract the unnecessary data
- The time it takes your CGI program to format the unnecessary data
- The time it takes to transmit the unnecessary data from the Web server to the user's browser
- The time it takes your user to search through the unnecessary data to view the relevant data

Any RDBMS product, including Access 97, will waste precious time retrieving result sets that are larger than those needed. For example, let's call upon our VCR Rental Store application. Assume that the design of a Web page calls for displaying all the movies with a "PG 13" rating. It wouldn't make a whole lot of sense to suffer the overhead of extracting all the rows from the movie database, regardless of their rating, and formatting them on a Web page only to have the user visually select the movie titles in which they are interested.

Create Temporary Tables for Users

If the design of your Web Access 97 database application supports it, you could create a temporary database accessed only by the Web database application. Certainly Access 97 provides the ability to create temporary files. In fact, you saw how to do this in Chapter 11, "Designing Advanced Access 97 Queries." This insures that no other non-Web access will be made to the database that Web users are accessing and therefore maximizes its throughput.

Create Views on the Server and Links to Them

Views of a database are a powerful feature for controlling access to specified rows and columns and joining tables on the server. Using views in your Web application improves the overall performance of the application by restricting the number of rows and columns that are searched in each query to only those necessary to provide an accurate result set.

The Access 97 RDBMS product supports views. By using views in the design of your application, you can control exactly what and how much information a Web database application can access.

Criteria Should Match Server Data Structure

The criteria you specify in a query should match the data structure on the server. This improves the efficiency of the query as Access 97 does not need to translate the requested data structure into the actual data structure.

Consider the following query:

```
SELECT * FROM Movies WHERE [What Is The Rating?] IIF (Movie_Rating = 1,
"PG" , IIF (Movie_Rating = 2, "PG 13", IIF (Movie_Rating = 3, "R", IIF
(Movie_Rating = 4, "NR" ))))
```

This query is poorly written. It takes excessive time to execute because of the way in which Access 97 parses the query and handles the user interaction in the supplying of parameter information, "What Is the Rating?" The following is an example of a correctly written query that extracts the same result set.

```
SELECT * FROM Movies WHERE [Movie_Rating] = IIF (What Is The Rating? =
"PG", 1, IIF ([What Is The Rating?] = "PG 13", 2, IIF ([What Is The Rat-
ing?] = "R", 3, 4)))
```

This example is much improved and will execute more efficiently against an Access 97 database because of the structure of the query. More specifically, the way that Access 97 handles the interaction with the user is to have the user supply the passed parameter for the query, "What Is the Rating?"

Use Distributed Databases

An environment where the Access 97 databases that a Web database application uses are distributed provides the application developer with the opportunity to take advantage of a secure and accessible pool of data. Access 97 supports distributed databases and, in fact, includes features that help to keep the distributed database synchronized. These were discussed in detail in Chapter 9, "Introduction to Access 97."

It is easy for a DBA to replicate a database from production databases and then use the replicated database for Web database application access. The replicated data can then be held in a secure location away from the production data that was used to create it. Distributed databases also give the developer the ability to create an environment where the location of the data is completely transparent to the user.

Do as Much Work on the Server as Possible

You should consider having separate machines for an Access 97 database server and for a Web server. This will improve the overall efficiency of your application due to the improved performance while interacting with your Access 97 database.

The probability is that your Web server is much more powerful than the machines being used by the people accessing your application. Therefore, you will achieve increased performance in your application if you have the server do as much work as possible. This means, among other things, that you should consider formatting and laying out the result set of a query to an Access 97 database in a CGI program running on the server as opposed to a Java program running on the client machine.

Taking this thought one step further, consider locating your Web server on a different machine than your database. This will also increase the performance of your application as you can tune the Web server to handle Web requests and CGI processing while tuning your database to handle data requests.

Do Not Use Drop-Down List Boxes Based on a Large Number of Records

Drop-down list boxes are wonderful additions to HTML forms and can really help your users access pertinent information. A drop-down list box that includes four different movie ratings from which to choose (such as PG, PG 13, R, NR) is much more useful than a drop-down list box with the names of 10,000 movies that you might own as retrieved from a query to an Access 97 database.

In a situation where you really think it would aid the usefulness of your application to have a large result set display in a drop down list box, it is better to add a dialog box. In the dialog box the user could enter selection criteria (e.g., All movies that begin with the word "Beverly") and then click on a `<Submit>` button. This would then return a greatly reduced result set in the drop down list box (i.e., Beverly Hills Cop, Beverly Hills Cop II, Beverly: The Maiden of Green Acres, etc.).

Handle Errors Efficiently

Should handling database errors in a Web database application be any different than handling database errors in a non-Web database application? The answer to this question is, probably not!

For example, attempting to insert a duplicate row in your Access 97 database should result in the same type of error message for both Web and non-Web applications. The difference is that in the Web application, the CGI program that receives the error message should format and send a Web page to the user indicating that an error has occurred. This is exactly one of the scenarios discussed in Chapter 13, in the section titled "Inserting Rows in a Database from a Web Application."

It is important to recognize that it takes a lot longer to communicate an error situation to a user in a Web database application than in a non-Web database application. This is because of the overhead involved in formatting and transmitting this information over the Internet. Therefore, you should attempt to program a Web Access 97 database application to avoid error situations when at all possible. It is frequently not good enough to trap the error and report it to the user in a Web database application—the objective should be to avoid the error in the first place.

Open Web Pages before Retrieving Data

When you first display a Web page, in other than the rarest of circumstances, you should have the user provide some sort of selection criteria prior to clicking on the `<Submit>` button and retrieving data from the Access 97 database. Do not open a Web page with a display of data before the user indicates which type of data they are interested in viewing.

In other words, do not assume what data the user would like to see and provide it for them before they have the opportunity to let you know specifically what they are interested in seeing. If you make this assumption and format and send a page of data extracted from an Access 97 database, you may have wasted the time to do this if the data the user views on the page is of no interest.

Having the user supply search criteria before displaying any data on a Web page accomplishes two objectives in improving the performance of your application. First, it quickly displays the original selection page as this is frequently a static HTML page. Second, it allows the user to specify selection criteria that improves the performance of the selection query and the display of the result set from that query.

Store State Data in a Database

As you read in Chapter 15, it is possible (and sometimes desirable) to store state information about an application in a database. Although in most cases you can either use cookies or simply pass application information from Web page to Web page, it is sometimes necessary to use the database method to maintain information over multiple application sessions.

Because this state information is maintained in database, many more calls to a database are generated to retrieve and store this information. This causes incrementally increased application execution times. Therefore, use this technique sparingly and only when necessary.

Use Stored Procedures

Stored procedures are precompiled SQL programs that execute much more quickly than native SQL and can be executed at any time. They are much the same in concept as subroutines. Although Access 97 does not directly support stored procedures, if your Access 97 Web database application accesses databases from other vendors such as Sybase, Microsoft SQL Server, and Oracle then you should look into using stored procedures as a way to improve the efficiency of your application while performing routine tasks.

Stored procedures also allow you to pass argument data to them. This means that you could have a stored procedure that is a query to which you pass the selection criteria to use during the query. This technique not only performs the database query much more quickly than a native SQL call, but also keeps you from having to write the actual query— you are executing it in the form of a stored procedure.

Moving On

In this chapter you learned some techniques that can be used to build efficiency into your Web database applications. These were categorized by Application Optimization and Database Optimization issues.

In Chapter 17 you will learn about some of the techniques which are useful in migrating data from enterprise data stores to server-based databases. Specifically you'll learn about the features in Access 97 that facilitate this process, such as replication and synchronization. These are two components that are very important in a Web database application that uses Access 97 databases.

Section IV: Advanced Topics in Internet Database Publishing

CHAPTER 17

Migrating Data from Enterprise Data Stores to Server-Based Databases

I n this chapter you will learn about some of the techniques used to migrate data from enterprise data stores to server-based Web databases. By migrate, I mean the process of moving data from one machine or Access 97 database to another machine or Access 97 database. Specifically you'll learn about the features in Access 97 that facilitate this process, such as replication and synchronization.

You'll first read about how to determine what to migrate from your corporate databases to Web servers. This is *not* simply a process of copying a database from one location to another. Next, you'll learn about some of the features in Access 97 that you can incorporate in your overall data strategy that facilitate deployment of corporate databases to be accessed by Web applications. Finally, you will read about backup and recovery principles that you can apply to your Web databases.

What to Migrate

Before you decide what database objects to migrate, you must decide whether or not you *should* migrate data. In other words, just because data that could be used by your Web database application currently exists doesn't mean that you *must* use it.

There are some factors you should consider when deciding whether or not to use existing data within your Web database application, for example, access, location, response time, and security.

Access

In this context the word access refers to the ways in which the data contained in the database is used. For example, if your Web database is to have read-only access, and if the data used by the Web database application currently exists in another Access 97 database that provides full read/write access, then it may be a wise decision to replicate the existing full-access database and create the read-only Web database. This approach yields the following advantages:

- *Separation of Data.* Your Web Access 97 database is a separate file from the production database.

- *Safety.* Your production Access 97 database is isolated and unknown (to Web browsers) and, therefore, is in a safer environment.

- *Response Time.* Your production Access 97 database response time is not impacted by the hits required to support the Web application.

Additionally, if your Web database application only requires a small subset of a production database, then it may make better sense to extract and create the Web database on a predetermined basis from the production database. If you decide to do this, there are a number of ways you can accomplish it, such as replication, stored procedures, and scheduled programs. Each of these techniques is accomplished in a different way, and you can learn how to do each of these actions in one of the book references I listed in Chapter 9, "Introduction to Access 97."

Location

Because the Internet is global, the word *location* in this context means the location of the Access 97 database that is used by the Web application in relation to the Web server. The location of the Web server in relation to the database server is a much more important factor than the relation of the user to the Web server. This is because of the time it takes to transmit data and communicate with the server, as well as because of the necessary security components.

Therefore, in most cases a Web database is better located if it is geographically close to the Web server. This is because the time it takes to transmit data from the Web database server to the Web server is sometimes a function of the distance between the two devices. Certainly high speed digital and satellite communications mitigate the effects of long-distance communications between a Web server and database. However, you should consider the physical location of the database accessed by a Web server when deciding whether or not to migrate data from a production database. If your production database is geographically distant from your Web server, this would favor the decision to migrate the production database to a Web database.

Response Time

The quality of the response time currently existing with your production database, coupled with the degradation added to this due to the hits it will take if it becomes a Web database, may result in a response time for all users that is not acceptable. If this is the case, you should consider migrating data off the production database to the Web server.

You should also consider the impact that the Web server software would have on your production database server if you choose to have both the Web server and database server on the same machine. Most commercial Web servers require at least 16 MB of dedicated memory, while 32 MB is preferred and 64 MB is ideal. If your production database server does not have these resources to spare and you don't want to or can't upgrade the machine, then you have little choice but to make another machine the Web server. Of course, this Web server could access a production database on a different physical machine, and this is an option you should consider.

Security

Security is a significant consideration in the design of your Web database application. In fact, this is such a significant concern that Chapter 18, "Using Firewalls and Security Components to Protect Your Data," is dedicated to this topic. To summarize Chapter 18 and place it in the context of this section, the location of the database accessed by your Web application in relation to your production database is a serious matter. Although the current batch of security and firewall products offer adequate security for your data, you may nonetheless be uncomfortable deploying an application that offers access to corporate data from anyone with a Web browser.

If this describes your comfort level, then migrating the data used by the Web database application from a production database should make good sense to you. However, if you are comfortable with the protection offered by security routines and firewalls, then you should not let this consideration alone stop you from deciding to access your production databases from your Web applications.

Determine What to Migrate

Let's assume you've decided to migrate data from production databases to create your Web databases. How do you decide what to migrate? That's the subject of this section.

ONLY MIGRATE THOSE DATABASE COMPONENTS NEEDED BY YOUR WEB APPLICATION. I've capitalized this point to highlight its significance. If you apply (and you should!) standard data modeling techniques to your Web application, and remove all redundant data in the tables, and design the database with efficiency in mind, you should be assured of accomplishing this objective.

The application of Data Modeling processes is outside the scope of this book. However, there are many books currently available that will help you develop your skills in this area.

Title:	Conceptual Modeling Databases & Case
Author:	P. Loucopoulos
Publisher:	John Wiley & Sons
ISBN:	6-00-084490-5

Title:	Database Modeling & Design, 2nd Edition
Author:	T. Teorey
Publisher:	Morgan Kaufmann Publishers, Inc.
ISBN:	1-55-860294-1

Title:	DB2/SQL
Author:	T. Martyn & T. Hartley
Publisher:	McGraw-Hill
ISBN:	0-07-040666-9

Replication

Centrally stored databases are a thing of the past in corporate IS departments. No longer can companies depend on one database or database site to keep up with the high volume of database requests. With the advent of RDBMS products that support replication, and continuing with the need for databases to support Web applications, more and more computer systems are becoming decentralized. The method most often used to accomplish this decentralization is replication. Database replication is defined as the method of creating synchronized copies of databases for use by different groups of users or over the Internet.

Replication allows you to centrally control access to your database while allowing free exchange of data between the components in the replicated datasets. It also improves the accessibility of the data by bringing it closer to the user. By placing replicated databases on or near a Web server, you can create a distributed environment with much less associated network traffic than if your Web database were located on a network server.

The Access 97 product includes some very nice features for replicating databases. The biggest potential problem that I see with the replication facilities in Access 97 are that synchronization of the replicated databases is a manual process—it does not occur automatically. Someone must initiate a procedure to do this or it must be scheduled into a job scheduler for Access 97 databases that are replicated to become synchronized.

Unfortunately, the decision to replicate or not to replicate a database is rarely a clear and decisive issue. In most cases you will need to weigh the factors which are most important to you to make the correct decision. The following sections describe some of the situations that exist that would lead you to one decision over another.

When to Use Replication

Replication of corporate databases should be used in the following circumstances:

- When users are located in geographically different offices and they have need to access similar information. Such is certainly the case when a production database is considered to be made available to Web database application users.

- When a business need exists to provide 24-hour-per-day, seven-day-per-week access to database data. Such is certainly the case with a Web database application because of the perpetual nature of the Internet.

When Not to Use Replication

There are a number of situations when replication should not be used.

- When the replicated database processes a large number of update transactions. Certainly a replicated database that processes more update transactions than the source database does not show a practical use of replication. This is because, as the transaction volume on a replicated database increases, so too do the data conflicts between the source and replicated databases.

- When it is absolutely crucial that the data in the replicated database is current and up-to-date. Replicated databases are current only when they are created. As time progresses and update transactions are applied to the source database, the replicated database becomes increasingly out of date.

As I wrote earlier, the decision to use or not to use replication is rarely an easy one. My general inclination is to use replicated databases except when the data being accessed in the replicated database is required to be current.

Replication in Access 97

Making a database replicable in Access 97 is a very simple process, as described the following five steps.

1. Start the Access 97 product.
2. Make sure the database you want to be able to replicate is not Open. You can do this by going to the File menu, and then selecting the Close Database option
3. From the Tools menu, select the Replication item, then select the Create Replica submenu item. This is seen in Figure 17–1.
4. As seen in Figure 17–2, you may get a dialog box warning you that the database you are about to replicate is not flagged as replicatable (meaning it is currently open), and that the current database must be closed before you can create a replicated database. Access 97 only allows you to initiate the replication of a database if it is not open.
5. You are then prompted to specify the name and location of the replicated database. Once you do this and confirm your selection, the replicated database is created.

Objects That Can Be Replicatable

All the following objects in an Access 97 database are replicatable:

- Tables
- Queries
- Forms
- Reports
- Macros
- Modules

System objects are not replicatable. But, this should not be a consideration of yours in the design of a Web database application as you would probably never have the need to replicate system objects.

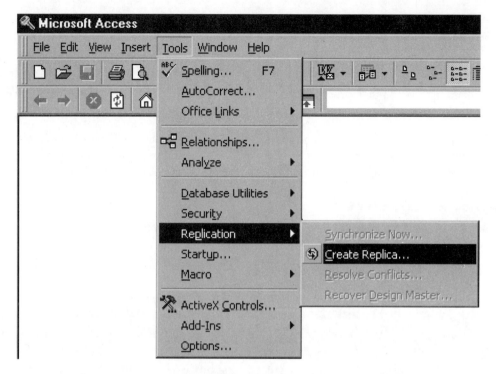

Figure 17–1   Selecting to make a replicated database.

Specifying What Objects to Replicate

When you replicate a database, by default all the objects in that database are replicated. This is something you may not want in your Web database application. You do have the ability to selectively specify which objects are not to be replicated in the following manner:

1. Open the database by clicking on the File menu, then Open Database, then selecting the database with which you want to work.
2. In the database view window, select the object(s) whose replication properties you wish to change by clicking once on it.
3. Right-click on the object to bring up its properties dialog box.
4. Select the last option, which is Properties, and you will see a dialog box similar to the one seen in Figure 17–3. Click on the Replicatable check box to select or deselect it.
5. Click on the <Apply> button to save your changes.

Of course, replication would be of no value if you didn't provide an ability to synchronize the data, which is discussed in the next section. However, synchronization is still an issue even if you are not replicating your database. For example, if you are making a

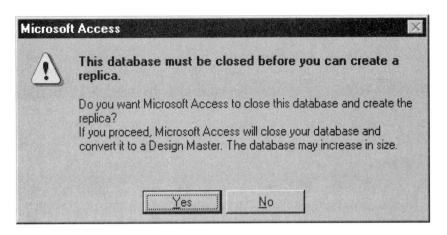

Figure 17-2   A prompt to warn you to close the database before it is replicated.

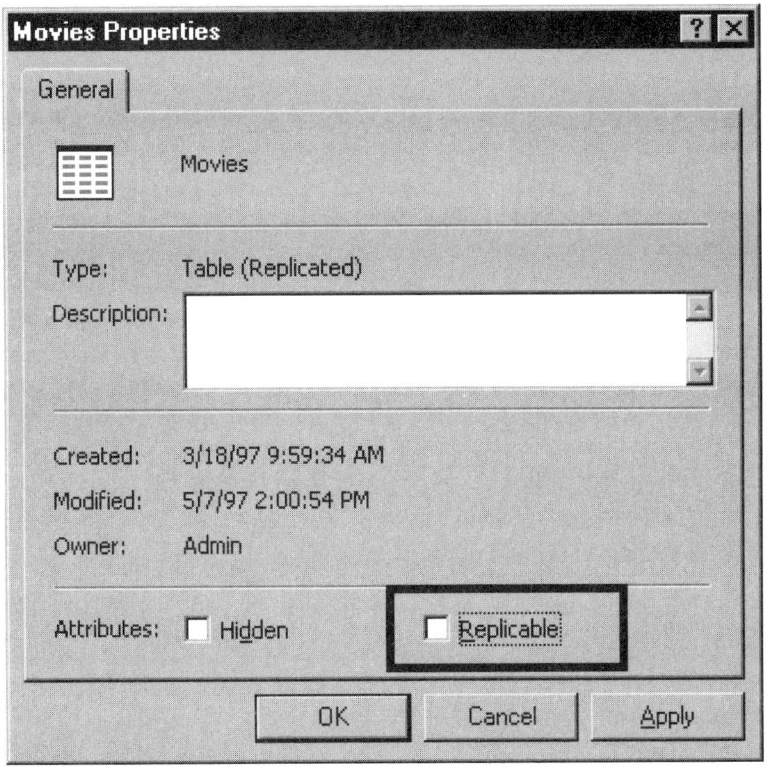

Movies Properties		? X

General

Movies

Type: Table (Replicated)

Description:

Created: 3/18/97 9:59:34 AM

Modified: 5/7/97 2:00:54 PM

Owner: Admin

Attributes: ☐ Hi_d_den   ☐ _R_eplicable

OK	Cancel	_A_pply

Figure 7-3   The Movies Properties dialog box.

read-only copy of an internal use read/write database for access in your Web database application, then you will sporadically need to synchronize the read-only database with the changes made to the read/write database. The following section describes synchronization and how it benefits you in the design and development of an Access 97 Web database application.

Synchronization

Once you've created a replicated database and are comfortable that it is working as desired, you need to be concerned with synchronizing the data in the replicated database with the source database. Access 97 provides a very nice interface to accomplish this process automatically (well, virtually automatically).

Synchronizing Replicated Databases

To synchronize a replicated database with a source, follow the steps listed here:

1. Open the database by clicking on the File menu, then Open Database, then selecting the database with which you want to work.
2. From the Tools menu, select the Replication item, then select the Synchronize Now submenu item. This is seen in Figure 17–4.
3. As seen in Figure 17–5, you will see a dialog box where you can specify the name of the database with which to synchronize. Access 97 will default with the name of the last database that was the target of a synchronization process.
4. Once you specify the name of the database with which to synchronize, click on the <OK> button to start the synchronization.

Synchronizing databases can be done in a manual manner as described here, or in an automated process by writing a Visual Basic script. To automate, compile the Visual Basic script and schedule its execution to occur at a specified time—automatically and regularly. Unlike replication, synchronization can occur when the databases are open. Any of the books listed as references in Chapter 9, "Introduction to Access 97," will show you how to do this.

How often you synchronize data can be a difficult decision. Synchronization should occur as often as necessary to give the users of the replicated database access to current data. How often that is depends on how willing you are to have them view stale data. In other words, a product database that lists the names and prices of various products in your inventory is probably fairly static and therefore a replicated database of this information would not need to be synchronized very often.

However, consider an example where you create a replicated database of an order-entry database. The source order-entry database is constantly being updated throughout the day. In this case, you would want to synchronize the replicated database with the source database at least once per day, possibly more frequently.

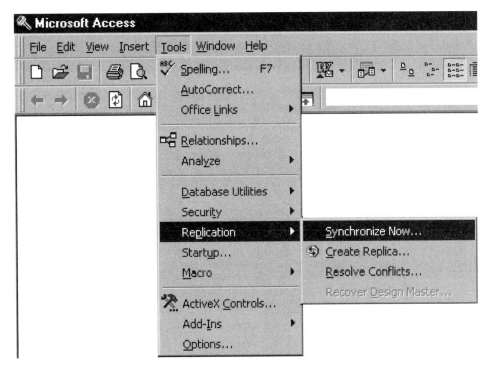

Figure 17–4   Synchronizing a replicated database.

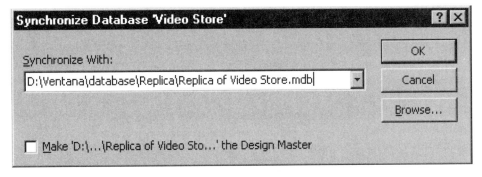

Figure 17–5   The Synchronize Database dialog box.

Backing Up a Web Database

The one factor that most uniquely identifies a backup procedure for a Web Access 97 database is the need to keep that database available 24 hours per day, seven days per week.

If you are backing up a read-only Web Access 97 database, then the possibility of losing changes made to the database after the backup begins and before it finishes is inconsequential. However, if your Web application allows updates to a database, then the availability of the database while it is being backed up is an issue to be addressed. Fortunately, most of the backup and archival tools available, including the backup facility that ships with the Access 97 product, handle concurrent access of the database while it is being backed up.

Microsoft has provided a very nice facility for backing up Access 97 databases. All the components in an Access 97 database are housed in one file, a *.MDB file. Consequently, it is very easy to identify and back up this component at whatever frequency you desire. Backing up a Web Access 97 database is done using the same processes you'd use to back up a non-Web database.

Restoring a Web Database

Unlike Oracle, Sybase, and a few other RDBMS products, Access 97 does not allow you to restore a database while the database is available to Web applications. This means that there's just no way around it—whenever you restore a Web database from a backup that database is unavailable to your Web application until the restoration is complete.

If your Web application is accessing a database that is replicated, you are already familiar with the issue of availability while the databases are being synchronized. Whatever your synchronization frequency is, you are familiar with the issue of availability.

It's a hushed little secret on the Web, but Web Masters very rarely publish or disclose when their sites are scheduled to be unavailable. As a result, you may receive a message similar to the one in Figure 17-6. Consequently, there is no way of knowing for sure if the reason the server can't be located is because you've entered an invalid URL or because the Web site is currently unavailable.

So, when you design your site's backup and restore procedures, recognize that it is acceptable to have your site unavailable for short periods, so long as the frequency or duration of these outages does not become excessive. Mind you, I am not advocating that you pull your Web databases off-line with no notification to your users. I am merely suggesting that current Net etiquette allows your site to be off-line a certain small percentage of time.

Here are some considerations to think about when deciding whether to restore a Web Access 97 database.

- Is the data corrupt, and if so, how corrupt is it? In other words, could the problem that makes you think about restoring the database be solved by deleting some records or perhaps reindexing tables?

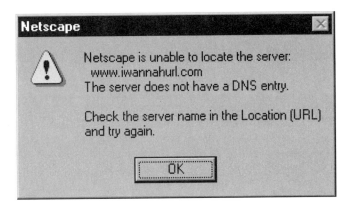

Figure 17-6   A Web site that is unknown, or unavailable?

- What is the impact to the user of restoring a database? Unlike a backup which can be done while the database is being used, a restore makes the database unavailable while it is being restored.

- How much recovery work needs to be done once the database is restored? This has a lot to do with when the database was last backed up and how volatile the data in the database really is. Generally, the more volatile the data that resides in a database, the more frequent the backups should be.

If a database that needs to be restored is replicated, you may be better off by simply deleting the old database and synchronizing it with the replicated database. This technique has the potential of supplying you with a current database without having to restore from a backup.

Moving On

This chapter presented some ideas and techniques you can use to migrate data from enterprise data stores to server-based Access 97 Web databases. You also learned about replication, synchronization, and backup/restore processes.

In the next chapter you will learn about the ways you can implement security modules and procedures in your Web database application to safeguard your data. Hopefully this material will give you the information you need to gain a level of comfort in the design and implementation of your Web database application.

CHAPTER 18

Using Firewalls and Security Components to Protect Your Data

W hat if your Web application involved no interface whatsoever with your corporate databases? Do you think that security of your Web site should still be an issue? You bet it should. It should be of high significance to you. Now, add to this the capability that you build into your application to access (and possibly update) your databases, and you have an issue that should get the hairs on the back of your neck bristling.

This chapter introduces you to the issues of Web-based security and describes some of the things that you can do to secure your Web applications and Access 97 databases.

Access 97 Security

A good place to start this chapter is with a quick review of the security available within Microsoft Access 97. Then you can see how these security features can be applied in a Web database application.

There are two methods of security available in Access, database security that requires a password to access a database and user-level security that can be applied to database objects. By default, security to an Access database is always on. When you first access an Access database, you normally do so with identification as *default user*. The *default user* is a special category of user that has Admin authority and full permissions.

In the following sections I'll show you how to add a new group via the Security routines in Access 97, add a new user to a group, and adjust the permissions for a user or group to Access 97 database objects.

Adding a New Group to an Access 97 Access List

If you are using security to control the access to your Access 97 database objects, and you want to identify a group to which one or more users can share the same access rights to objects in your database, then you will need to add new definitions to the lists of recognized groups to your database objects. You do this by the following:

1. Open the database whose objects you want to modify an access list.
2. Click on Tools | Security | User and Group Accounts, as seen in Figure 18–1.
3. Click on the <New> button on the bottom of the screen and you will see the New User/Group dialog box, as seen in Figure 18–2.
4. Add the new group to the New User/Group dialog box. As seen in Figure 18–3, a new group with the ID of InetGroup is being added with the personal group ID of InetGroup.
5. If you click on <OK>, you will be asked to provide a Personal ID for the previously entered user. As seen in Figure 18–3, the personal ID for the InetGroup user is INet-Group.
6. Click on <OK> when done.

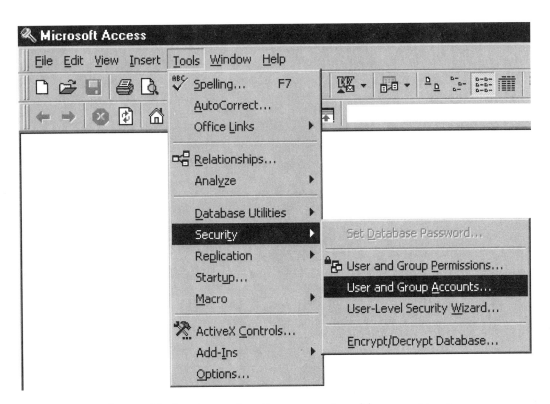

Figure 18–1   Accessing the screen to add a new group.

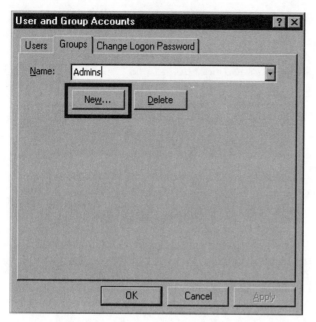

Figure 18-2 Adding a new group.

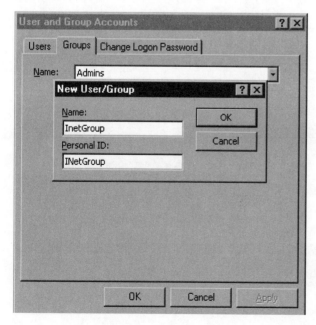

Figure 18-3 Assigning a personal ID to a recently added new group.

Okay, you've added a group definition. A group without users assigned to it is of no value. The next section shows you how to add users to an Access 97 user list. Once this is done, the next section shows you how to add the user list to a group.

Adding a New User to an Access 97 User List

If you are using security to control who gains access to your Access 97 database objects, you will need to add users to the existing lists of recognized users of your database objects. Once you add a user, then you can easily add that user to a group of users who share common access characteristics. You do this by the following:

1. Open the database whose objects you want to modify an access list.

2. Click on Tools | Security | User and Group Accounts, as seen in Figure 18–4.

3. Add the new user to the User And Group Accounts screen, as seen in Figure 18–5. In this case, a new user with the ID of Inet_User is being added with access to the Users and INetGroup groups.

4. If you click on <OK>, you will be asked to provide a Personal ID for the previously entered user. The Personal ID could be a person's name, his or her employee number, social security number, or any other character string that uniquely identifies

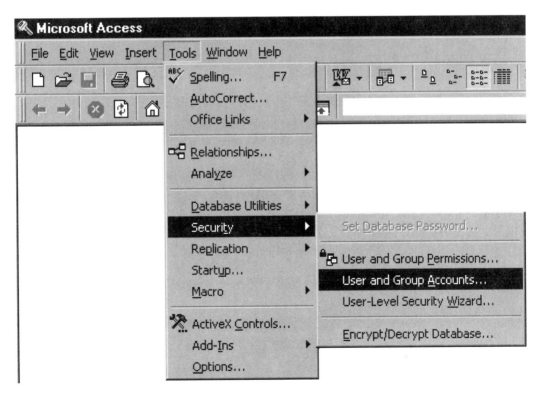

Figure 18–4   Accessing the screen to add a new user.

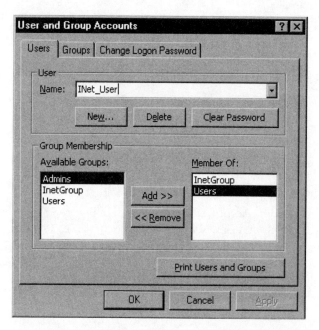

Figure 18–5   Adding a new user.

that user. As seen in Figure 18–6, the personal ID for the Inet_User user is Inet_User. Please note that as long as each user is assigned a unique Personal ID, it doesn't matter what it is.

5. Click on <OK> when done.

Modifying an Access 97 Database Object Access List

Access lists allow you to specify what rights are granted to specific users or groups for specific database objects. Users can be identified individually or collectively as part of a Group.

You can modify the access list to a database or database objects by doing the following:

1. Open the database whose objects you want to modify an access list.
2. Click on Tools | Security | User and Group Permissions, as seen in Figure 18–7.

New User/Group   [?] [X]

Name:
[INet_User]

Personal ID:
[INet_User]

OK

Cancel

Figure 18–6   Assigning a user ID to a recently added new user.

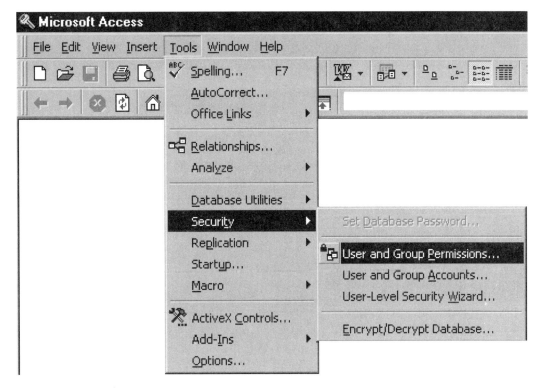

Figure 18–7 Accessing the screen to change a user's permissions to objects.

3. Select the User (or Group) from the list of recognized users (or groups), and adjust the permissions to the various database objects that appear in the User and Group Permissions screen as seen in Figure 18–8. As you can see in this figure, the person with the user ID of JimHobuss is being assigned read-only rights to data in the Movies Table.

4. Click on <OK> when done.

The following describes the types of permissions that you can define for the various objects in an Access 97 database.

Database Objects

- Open/Run—The user or member of the group can open and run the database
- Open Exclusive—The user or member of the group can open and run the database exclusively
- Administer—All other permissions are selected automatically

Table Objects

- Read Data—The user or member of the group can read the data in the table

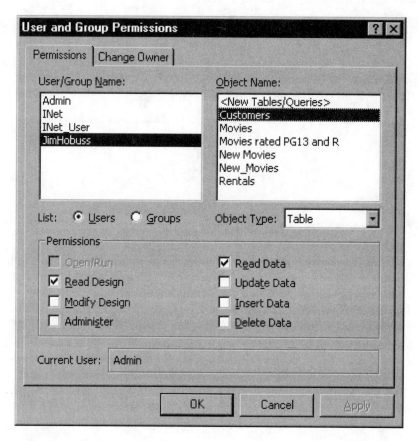

Figure 18-8 Assigning specific access rights to a specific object for a specific user.

- Update Data—The user or member of the group can read and update data in the table
- Insert Data—The user or member of the group can read, update, and insert data in the table
- Delete Data—The user or member of the group can read, update, insert data in the table and delete data from the table
- Administer—All design and data options are selected by default

Query Objects

- Read Data—The user or member of the group can read the data in the table the query accesses
- Update Data—The user or member of the group can read and update data in the table the query accesses

- Insert Data—The user or member of the group can read, update, and insert data in the table the query accesses
- Delete Data—The user or member of the group can read, update, insert data in the table and delete data from the table the query accesses
- Administer—All design and data options are selected by default

Form Objects

- Open/Run—The user or member of the group can open and run the form
- Read Design—The user or member of the group can Open/Run, and read the form
- Modify Design—The user or member of the group can Open/Run, read, and modify the design of the form
- Administer —All design and data options are selected by default

Report Objects

- Open/Run—The user or member of the group can open and run the report
- Read Design—The user or member of the group can Open/Run and read the design of the report
- Modify Design—The user or member of the group can Open/Run, read, and modify the design of the report
- Administer—All design and data options are selected by default

Permissions should be added to a Group level—not a User level. By doing so, it is much more convenient to add a new user to an existing group than to define access rights to all database objects every time you add the new user.

Access 97 Security and Web Database Applications

You may be thinking to yourself that the discussion in the previous sections is pretty cool (hopefully), but are left wondering how this applies to you—a person needing to use Access 97 databases in Web applications. I'll explain that now, and you'll be surprised how transparent the folks at Microsoft have made this.

Whenever you access a security-enabled database either directly or via ODBC, then you must log-in. Access 97 is no different.

As you know, the only way to access an Access 97 database from a Web application is via a CGI program. Depending on the programming language you use to build the CGI program, the syntax for the connection parameters will vary. However, you must provide at least the following parameters when connecting to this type of database:

- Database Name
- Database Type
- Database Location
- User Name
- Password

With the first three items, the operating system can locate and find the correct database that the CGI program needs to access. With the last two items, User Name and Password, the program gains whatever types of security access has been granted to the user that is attempting to log in.

Given this background, you could use the following steps to provide secure access to your Access 97 databases from Web applications:

1. The database objects are created for the database that is accessed from the Web database application.

2. Groups are defined to the Access 97 database that are specific to the types of access rights you wish to give to different levels of user.

3. Users are defined and added to Groups in the Access 97 database based on the types of access they need.

4. A translation database table is then written. This table is used to correlate a user name/password combination that someone enters on a Web page with a User ID/password combination as recorded in the Access 97 database. The reason you do this and don't give Web users their User ID's and passwords as recorded in Access 97 is the potential for a serious breach of security. It is always a good idea to implement a translation process as described here. The Access 97 translation database table often is comprised of just four columns. Those are: *Web User Name,* which is the name that was entered on a Web sign-in page, the *Web Password,* which is the password that was entered on a Web sign-in page, the *Access 97 User Name,* which is the Access 97 user name assigned to the Web User Name, and the *Access 97 Password,* which is the Access 97 password assigned to the Web User Name

5. Write your HTML pages for your application, including the one on which a user supplies his or her user ID and password.

6. Write your CGI program that is called from the HTML page identified earlier. The design and purpose of this program is discussed in detail in Chapters 7 and 13. This CGI program will perform a user ID/password translation as identified in step 4, and then attempt to log in to the Access 97 database needed for the application, based on the Access 97 user ID and password.

7. If the log in to the Access 97 database is successful, the application continues and the application state (the fact that this user has successfully logged in to the Access 97 database) is maintained using one of the methods described in Chapter 15. If the log in was unsuccessful, a message is formatted and sent back to the user from the CGI program notifying the user of this.

Web Site Security—The Problem

Robert T. Morris. Do you remember his name? He's the Ivy league student who is best known as being the creator of the infamous Internet Worm that brought down about half of all the Internet servers in 1988. He was able to do this by making a small change in a C-based `sendmail` program that overflowed an internal buffer and altered a pointer stack to gain unauthorized access to the servers.

Hackers, crackers, thieves, scoundrels. Whatever you choose to call them, they are out there, right now, thousands of them. Their objective ranges from harmless access of unauthorized sites to blatant and catastrophic destruction of data files and potentially hardware. *Hackers* usually don't do any real damage. Most of the time they simply break into a computer installation or site just to see if they can. However, *crackers* will steal data or money or do real damage.

So, what can you do to prevent unauthorized access to your Web site? First, you should understand how all the components in a Web application fit together. Second, you should know what facilities are available to help to prevent unauthorized access to your site. Third, you should build a site that is as difficult to circumvent as possible. Fourth, trust no one.

How you build your site to be as difficult to circumvent as possible is largely dependent on what components you choose to buy and develop.

Security of Your Web Server

Most modern Web server software systems provide facilities for automatic directory listings, which describe the contents of the entire Web site in a convenient and easy to use format. There are many benefits to this capability, such as making all the information that is contained on the sire easily accessible and available to search engines. But, one of the potential problems with it is that users have free access to view all the documents in the Web document domain.

In most situations, this is not a problem as most of the time you place documents in the domain directories so that they *can* be accessed. But, what about files that are placed in these directories which don't have a specific URL that references them? Or, how about files that used to be accessed by Web pages but have had the links to them broken? You may think they are safe, but they are not. Anyone with access to the directories these files are in has the potential to access the files directly.

As a Web Master, you should monitor access to the various directories in your domain as well as to where documents are located. Many companies go so far as to restrict the ability to place files in domain directories to *only* the Web Master.

The following sections describe two ways to provide some level of security for your Web server, *server-side includes* and *child execution privileges.*

Server-Side Includes

As you learned in Chapter 6, "Overview of HTML," Server-Side Includes (SSIs) are HTML commands that reside on the Web server that are included in Web pages when they are constructed. They are typically used to hold HTML tag pairs that are common among a group of Web pages. Think of them as the HTML equivalent of subroutines. The upside of SSIs is that they save a lot of time coding HTML and offer you the ability to standardize the look and feel of certain components of Web pages. The downside risk of SSI's is the ability they give to hackers to cause an unwanted program to execute.

Consider the following SSI entry:

```
<STRONG><!-#exec cgi-"/../cgi-bin/getURL"-></STRONG>
```

This code causes a server-based CGI program named getURL to execute. But what if a hacker or cracker was able to gain access to the domain directory that contained this SSI and change it? The hacker or cracker could change an entry in the SSI that could trigger the execution of a program different from the one you had intended when you created the SSI. Consider the following:

```
<STRONG><!-#exec cmd="rm -rf /"-></STRONG>
```

The result of this changed command executing would be that almost everything on your server's hard disk would be deleted. And, the damage would be done (potentially) long after the hacker made the change and left your site.

The way to prevent this type of unauthorized access is to turn off the Web server's ability to process an "exec" form in an SSI. But, if you do this you also lose the potentially beneficial aspects of being able to process "exec" forms in an SSI. Unfortunately, this is not the only example of a difficult decision you'll have to make when you design the security components in your Web site.

Child Execution Privileges

Child processes are programs that execute from a directory that is subordinate to a parent directory. For example, assume a program named addrec.exe were located in the cgi-bin directory on a Web server. The addrec.exe program might initiate the execution of a program named ver_rec.exe that is located in a subdirectory to the cgi-bin directory named cgi-sub. In this case, the ver-rec.exe program is a child process. The type of privileges assigned to the child process are termed child execution privileges.

It's possible to configure your Web server so that child processes are started as the user root. This, in most cases, is a good thing as it makes program component location simplified. However, it also presents a security problem. The problem is that a CGI program that executes with root privileges could effectively change a user ID from one to another, thus giving the changed-to user ID (i.e., a system administrator) access to your entire Web site. The way to prevent this access is to ensure that your server configuration file is not configured to execute child processes as root.

Secure Sockets Layer (SSL)

SSL is a security protocol that provides Web applications with the ability to communicate with a user in a secure session. The SSL protocol resides between the HTTP and TCP/IP layers, thus providing a shield between the user and TCP/IP. SSL is a protocol that is currently in transition as different groups attempt to define how it should be implemented. It is not a standardized protocol as of this writing, although it should be soon. Then you will see products introduced that give you the ability to handle the secure transmission of server authentication, data encryption, and message safeguarding.

If you want to learn more about SSL, I recommend the following books:

Secure Commerce on the Internet

Author:	Vijay Ahuja
Publisher:	AP Professional
ISBN:	0-12-045597-8

WWW Security: How to Build a Secure World Wide Web

Author: Robert S. MacGregor, Alberto Aresi, Andreas Siegert
Publisher: Prentice Hall
ISBN: 0-13-612409-7

CGI Security

CGI scripts are especially dangerous Web application components in terms of security. Regardless of the quality of the code written in the CGI program, there exists the potential of hacker and cracker subversion of the CGI program. For example, consider the CGI program that sends an HTML form that includes an area for the user to enter text information. If the user enters text information as she or he should, then all is well. But, what if the user enters the following in this text box instead of text data?

```
<IMG SRC="/hidden/badimage.gif">
```

The result would create havoc on your Web server because it could very easily cause the image named `badimage.gif` to be sent to the CGI program, instead of the expected text. Then, depending on how the CGI program was coded, it may cause the CGI program to abend.

Another problem with CGI scripts is that sometimes they (or the libraries that are referenced from within the CGI scripts) contain code that is unwanted at least, and devastating in the extreme. There are many libraries and routines available off the Internet. A large number of developers download and use these routines in the construction of their CGI programs or Web sites. In most cases, there's no problem with this. However, consider the following one line of code that could be embedded in a CGI script that is hundreds or even thousands of lines long:

```
rm -rf
```

This line of code (which incidentally would delete the files from your server's hard disk if it executes) sticks out here, because there is no code surrounding it. But, would you be able to spot it so easily if it were in the middle of a 5,000 line CGI script? This is an issue you need to consider when you download code and libraries from the Internet. It is also an issue to be considered when you are deciding to whom within your company you give access to the cgi-bin directory.

The best advise is to never download and execute object code from any source unless you are 100 percent sure that the code is stable and contains nothing it shouldn't. To be sure that the program will perform as expected is to download only from reputable sources, never download object code (only source code that you can read and scan for improprieties), and seek references from other users of the downloaded code before using it yourself.

Firewalls

Take a look at Figure 18–9. It shows a typical Web site architecture that uses a component called a *firewall* to provide another layer of security for your Web database applications. A firewall is a combination of hardware and/or software that only allows messages to pass through it that are recognized.

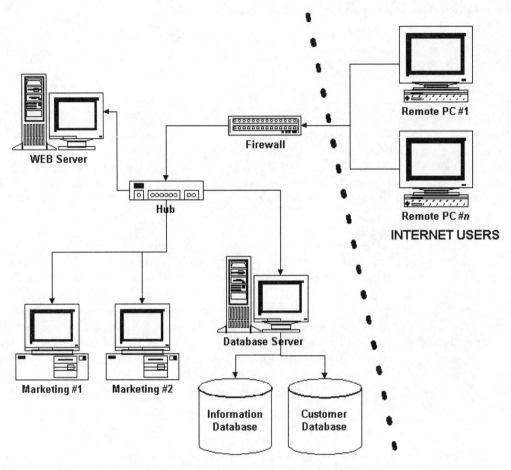

Figure 18–9   Web site architecture with firewall.

Firewalls are user-configurable components that separate a corporation's data from users accessing its Web pages in a Web application. For example, the firewall could be configured so that a set of pre-authorized user IDs are allowed access to data within the firewall while all others are screened out.

If you'd like to learn more about firewalls and how to implement them, refer to the two books listed in the section on Secure Sockets Layer or the following references.

Other Resources

The following sections contain additional resources available to you if you want to learn more about Internet security.

Books on Security

Intranet Firewalls: Planning & Implementing Your Network Security System

Author: Scott Fuller, Kevin Pagan
Publisher: Ventana
ISBN: 1-56-604506-1

Net Security: Your Digital Doberman

Author: Michael Alexander
Publisher: Ventana
ISBN: 1-56-604518-5

Internet Commerce

Author: Andrew Dahl and Leslie Lesnick
Publisher: Simon & Schuster
ISBN: 1-56-205496-1

Special Edition Using Microsoft Commercial Internet System

Author: Peter Butler, Roy Cales, and Judy Petersen
Publisher: Que Books
ISBN: 0-78-971016-1

Web Site Administrator's Survival Guide

Author: Jerry Ablan
Publisher: Sams Net Publishing
ISBN: 1-57-521018-5

Title: Special Edition Using CGI
Author: Jeffry Dwight, Michael Erwin
Publisher: Que Books
ISBN: 0-78-970740-3

Useful URLs

- A FAQ presented by Oxford University on firewalls and their use in Internet security `http://www.lib.ox.ac.uk/internet/news/faq/archive/fire-walls-faq.html`
- A WWW security FAQ presented by Compuserv `http://ourworld.compuserve.com/homepages/perthes/wwwsecur.htm`
- Final Quarterly Report of the UKERNA Secure Email Project `http://www.tech.ukerna.ac.uk/pgp/secemail/q4.html`
- Internet Firewalls Frequently Asked Questions from the V-One Company. `http://www.v-one.com/pubs/fw-faq/faq.html`
- One of the places where hackers meet that contains a huge collection of hacking and related links. `http://incyberspace.com/woodstok/hack/`

Moving On

This chapter introduced you to the features built in Access 97 that allow you to add security to your database objects. You then learned how to use these features in conjunction with a Web deployment of your Access 97 database application. This was followed with a description of some of the things you should be careful of with CGI programs. Finally, you read about the components of a secure Web database application.

In Chapter 19, "Designing an Internet Course Delivery System," you will see how to build a simple class registration Web database application from start to finish.

CHAPTER 19

Designing an Internet Course Delivery System

This is the first of two "summation" chapters. It is a chapter that deals specifically with the issues relating to the analysis and design of a Web database application. In this chapter, you will take what was learned in the previous chapters and see how it is applied to the analysis and design of a Web database application.

There is very little information in this chapter that is specific to the actual construction of an Access 97 database application. That is saved for Chapter 20. I want to include a complete chapter on analysis and design issues for a couple of reasons:

- Without a solid effort in the analysis and design of an application, even a Web database application, the construction efforts and completed application will be, at best, minimally effective and at worst, a disaster.

- Too often Web application developers forego effective analysis and design steps in favor of delivering the application quickly. This is a grave mistake. I want to show you how much critical and valuable information is acquired by performing analysis and design processes.

Recall that in Chapter 8 you learned how to design a Web database application. You will see how the information contained in that chapter, plus various other pieces of information from the other chapters in this book, are applied to the actual design of a Web database application. Then, in Chapter 20, this will be taken to the next logical step, which is the actual construction of a Web database application.

The material for this chapter first appeared as a series of articles published by The Cobb Group and produced by Client Server Associates. As a contributing editor for these magazines, I wrote these articles which are condensed and reprinted here with permission of The Cobb Group.

Background

XYZ Systems, Inc. (a fictitious name for a real company and not to be confused with ABC Company, the fictitious organization profiled in Chapter 20) is a software vendor with 10 products in its inventory. Its education and training curriculum consists of more than 40 instructor-led courses. These courses cover XYZ's products, as well as other companies' products that complement its own. XYZ decided to adapt some of its existing instructor-led courses for delivery in a multimedia format over the Internet.

Management at XYZ had two principal objectives in mind when they funded this project. First, they wanted to give their customers Web access to high-quality training on some of XYZ's core technologies. Second, XYZ must be able to easily and cost-effectively administer the system by having the course administration system interface to existing customer and accounting information. This objective included the desire to build a system that was easy and inexpensive to maintain from a programming standpoint. Management didn't want to spend large amounts of money whenever its Web page changed.

The major architectural components and tools were:

- *Access 97*—This is the DBMS for the existing customer and accounting systems.
- *PowerBuilder v5.0*—This tool is used to build the customer and accounting system. XYZ had the highest staff proficiency using this tool.
- *Macromedia Authorware*—The training coordinator saw this product demonstrated at a conference he attended and felt it held the potential to fill XYZ's need for a tool to develop training materials for delivery over the Net.
- *Existing Web Site*—XYZ had an existing Web site that was built and supported by a Web master. He believed that this would make an excellent platform from which to deliver the training courses.

The members of the project team felt that although it was not chic to do so, what they were building was a client/server system. Most of the characteristics of a client/server system were in place for the course-delivery system, namely:

- *Shared Resources*—The application would take advantage of shared resources.
- *Platform Independence*—Because of the Net delivery of the courses, it certainly was platform independent.
- *Message-Based Interface*—The system had to include a message-based interface.
- *Server Transparency*—Certainly the takers of the courses would have no need to know the location of the server; they only needed to know the URL (Universal Resource Locator) for XYZ.
- *Scalability*—Certainly the delivery of the courses would be scalable.

XYZ's Existing Environment

XYZ's architectural computing environment, including its Web site, looked similar to the diagram in Figure 19–1 at the beginning of the project. XYZ had just implemented an Ethernet 100 mbps network with NetBios communications. The database servers were on Pentium 200MHz processor machines with 128MB of EDO memory running Windows NT version 4.0. The prime DB server was located in the company headquarters in California and was replicated at six sites—three in the United States and three in other countries.

Here's the basic architecture of the client workstation side as well as XYZ's server side. The Web server was also a Pentium 200MHz processor with 64MB of EDO memory running Windows NT version 4.0. The server was also located in the company's headquarters. Each client machine attached to the network was configured with a Pentium 75MHz processor with 16MB of EDO memory running Windows 95.

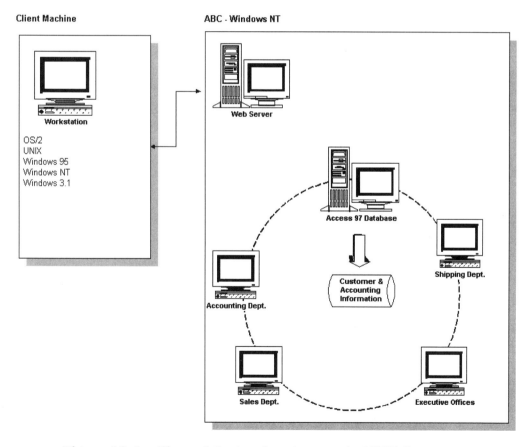

Figure 19–1 The architectural environment at XYZ Company.

Project Analysis

XYZ decided to initiate the project with a four-person project assessment team. The initial four-person team was comprised of:

- Project leader
- Database administrator
- Training coordinator
- Web master

This group was responsible for developing a Joint Requirements Planning (JRP) document. The JRP's purpose would be to:

- Identify the team members and their responsibilities
- Establish the business objectives of the project
- Establish the Rapid Application Development (RAD) approach to be used

JRP Documents

The JRP team published the JRP-Phase I document, which was used to build the project team and to document the developers' perspective of management's expectations for the project. In the JRP-Phase II document, the deliverable would be the primary source document used for the design of the system.

JRP-Phase I.   For the sake of brevity, I've paraphrased the JRP-Phase I document here. The following are the major sections in this document.

Defining Roles and Responsibilities.   Project team members' roles and responsibilities were identified as follows:

Project leader—Leads the project through completion and resolves any issues arising that may impede the team's progress. The PL had first-line responsibility for the success of the project.

Database administrator—Identifies and resolves any database-dependent issues.

Training coordinator—Determines which courses will be delivered over the Net and represents the Training Department's interests.

Web master—Designs and builds the Web pages that facilitate the course delivery.

Curricula developer—Designs and builds the actual courses to be delivered over the Net.

Network engineer—Identifies and resolves any network-dependent issues.

Establishing Business Objectives.   JRP identified the business objectives of the system to be:

- Achieve profitability within nine months after going online.
- Identify four products initially on which to develop courses, followed by four more products within six months.

- Use as much of XYZ's existing architecture and toolset as possible to build this system.

- Design and build the system to require little effort and expense to maintain.

Establishing the RAD Approach. The RAD approach means the definition of the specific method used to conduct a Rapid Application Development activity in connection with the analysis and design phases of a project. JRP established the RAD approach as follows:

- Use the existing Data Dictionary for the tables in the customer and accounting database.

- The project probably wouldn't require data modeling as the data could be used as is. However, XYZ wouldn't know this for sure until later in the project.

- Use PowerBuilder as the GUI painter, application development tool, and prototyping tool.

- Wouldn't use an automated testing tool. XYZ didn't have one and didn't feel one was justified for this project.

Trouble with the JRP Phase I. Upon submission of the JRP Phase I document, management agreed to all of the items in the three major sections, with one exception. They wanted to develop and deliver Internet courses on all 10 of the company's products when the system went online; they didn't want to take the phased approach. In addition, they didn't want to extend the delivery date of the system.

When the Project Leader met with management to resolve this matter, she learned that management had a false expectation for the system. Management believed that if they made the system available only in the western region HQ, and not the rest of the United States or the world, that the time saved could be spent writing the additional course materials. Although the Project Leader didn't correlate the two activities (replication of data with the writing of course materials), she did get management to agree to reconsider this position until after the JRP Phase II document was produced. Her thinking was that the various matrices produced in Phase II would disclose the data dependencies and could be used to either support or refute management's expectations.

JRP-Phase II. The second phase of the JRP activity took three weeks to accomplish and was much more complex than Phase I. Whereas Phase I was accomplished in a couple of meetings, Phase II required a more thorough analysis of the existing network and data structures, as well as the proposed network and data structures.

Experienced in the analysis, design, and construction of client/server applications, the Project Leader determined that the deliverables from the JRP Phase II would be:

- CRUD diagram—CRUD stands for Create, Read, Update, Delete
- Entity/Location matrix
- Entity/Volume matrix
- Action/Frequency matrix

For the sake of brevity, I won't include in this chapter the pre-existing matrices (from the original customer and accounting database creation project) the project team referenced. However, I will discuss the similarities and discrepancies between the existing and new matrices in the following sections.

CRUD diagram.   The CRUD (Create, Read, Update, Delete) diagram needed considerable modification from the one that had been created when the customer and accounting database was first built. Although the CRUD created (and referenced during this project) when the database was first built was specific to accounting and customer information only, the PL believed that a CRUD specific to the new functions would be more beneficial and less disruptive to their short project time frames.

The CRUD diagram that was created is shown in Table 19–1. It included functions that people accessing the system would use, regardless of whether the action touched on the existing database. The CRUD diagram includes functions that all people accessing the system would use.

Entity/Location Matrix.   The purpose of the Entity/Location matrix is to determine, at a very early stage, the consequences and impacts of the application distribution. Because this project entailed adding functions to an existing database, the project team created their Entity/Location matrix ignoring the fact that current data is accessed in the customer and accounting database. They wanted to make sure that what was already de-

Table 19–1   The CRUD Diagram Used at XYZ Company

Entity --> Function V	Web Master	Student	Training Manager	Training Devlpr	Sales	Shipping	Execs
Register/ Take Course		C					
Sell/Record Learning Credits					CRUD	CRUD	
Ship Learning Credit Coupons					CRUD	CRUD	
Adjust Course List	CRUD		CRUD	CRU			
Produce/ View Status		C	R	R	CR	CRU	R
Adjust Learning Credits			CRUD		CRUD	CRU	
Build/Update Web Pages	CRUD						

C = Create, R=Read, U=Update, D=Delete

veloped wouldn't prejudice their thoughts on what needed to be developed. The Entity/Location matrix used by XYZ Company is seen in Table 19–2 below. This Entity/Location matrix developed by the XYZ project team proved that the type of access needed in each location was identical.

What the project team discovered when comparing this matrix against the in-place matrix for the existing customer and accounting database was that, although some of the entities accessing the data were different, the type of access needed in each location was identical. This was a crucial finding in terms of project deadlines and management's expectations for the scope of the project. It meant that XYZ wouldn't need to add any data elements.

Entity/Volume Matrix. The purpose of the Entity/Volume matrix is to determine the data distribution and server sizing issues. The project team discovered several key items when they plotted their data on the Entity/Volume matrix, which is shown in Table 19–3.

First, servers in the western, northern, and southern regions would experience the greatest volume and growth impacts. Second, sales and shipping would be the two entities in the company that had the greatest volume. Third, student access and need for data would be somewhat consistent across all sites. The project team would use this information in the next phase of the project to make some recommendations regarding architectural modifications.

Action/Frequency Matrix. The Action/Frequency matrix is used to determine the network loading considerations. XYZ used the matrix seen in Table 19–4 to help determine the type of processing demand the new system will make on the network.

Table 19–2 The Entity/Location Matrix Used by XYZ Company

Location--> Entity V	Western Region HQ	Northern Region	Southern Region	Eastern Region	Europe	Asia	South America
Web Master	AU	AU	AU	AU	AU	AU	AU
Student	SU	SU	SU	SU	SU	SU	SU
Training Manager	SU	SR	SR	SR	SR	SR	SR
Training Developer	SU	AU	AU	AU	AU	AU	AU
Sales	AU	AU	AU	AU	AU	AU	AU
Shipping	AU	AU	AU	AU	AU	AU	AU
Executives	AR	AR	AR	AR	AR	AR	AR

A = Access ALL occurrences of data, R = Read, S = Access SAME occurrences of data, U = Update, D = Access DIFFERENT subset of data

Table 19–3 The Entity/Volume Matrix Used at XYZ Company

Location--> Entity V	Western Region HQ		Northern Region		Southern Region		Eastern Region		Europe		Asia		South America	
	V	G	V	G	V	G	V	G	V	G	V	G	V	G
Volume/ Growth	V	G	V	G	V	G	V	G	V	G	V	G	V	G
Web Master	5	80	5	80	10	40	5	10	5	10	5	10	5	10
Student	30	75	45	90	50	30	40	20	40	10	40	5	45	5
Training Manager	10	10	15	20	25	10	35	5	35	0	35	0	20	5
Training Developer	10	5	10	5	10	5	10	5	10	5	10	5	10	5
Sales	80	40	90	40	20	5	20	3	5	10	25	30	10	15
Shipping	90	30	30	30	25	30	10	25	5	5	25	20	20	5
Executives	1	0	0	0	0	0	0	0	0	0	0	0	0	0

V = Volume in 1,000s, G = Growth in %/Qtr

The data in the Action/Frequency matrix correlated with the data in the Entity/Volume matrix. Additionally, the project team was pleased to see that the data in the Action/Frequency matrix correlated with the data in the Entity/Volume matrix. Whereas the Entity/Volume matrix showed that the western, northern, and southern regions had the greatest projected volume of data for each entity, these same regions also had the greatest projected frequency for certain actions.

Management on Track

Recall the wrench that management threw in the works at the end of Phase I, when they wanted to implement the delivered system with all the courses at once? Their thinking was that the time saved in not promoting the data to all database server locations could be used to write course materials. With the Entity/Location and Entity/Volume matrices, management saw that data replication and synchronization was already occurring in the regional offices and that very little (if any) time could be shaved from the project by implementing in the HQ offices initially. Having reconciled this difficulty, the project leader secured approval from management to proceed into the next phase of the project, the design of the new system.

The Design Process Described

The Project Team quickly determined that the normal System Development Life Cycle that some members of the team were quite comfortable with would not work for this project. The reason was that they believed that although there would be a clearly recognize-

Table 19–4   Action/Frequency Matrix Used at XYZ Company

Location--> Action V	Western Region HQ		Northern Region		Southern Region		Eastern Region		Europe		Asia		South America	
Volume/ Growth	F	G	F	G	F	G	F	G	F	G	F	G	F	G
Register/ Take Course	80	80	40	80	50	40	25	20	15	10	15	10	15	10
Sell/Record Learning Credits	80	75	50	75	50	60	45	50	5	10	5	10	5	10
Ship Learning Credit Coupons	80	10	0	0	0	0	0	0	0	0	0	0	0	0
Adjust Course List	20	50	0	0	0	0	0	0	0	0	0	0	0	0
Product/ View Status	30	30	30	20	30	20	15	10	10	5	10	5	10	5
Adjust Learning Credits	5	30	30	30	10	40	5	20	10	30	15	10	25	10
Build/ Update Web Pages	80	80	10	10	0	0	0	0	0	0	0	0	0	0

F = Frequency in 1,000s, G = Growth in %/Qtr

able date at which the system would be made available to users (aka "put into production"), that this would be little more than a phase that immediately preceded another development phase. This "iterative" aspect to the application led them to believe that a more refined development methodology was required. What they decided on was a hybrid development process.

With this release cycle as a model, the Project Team determined the following about the Design steps in their project:

• Between the data models developed when the Customer and Accounting database was initially built and the various matrices developed during the analysis phase of the project, they had all the data models they needed to continue with the design and construction of the application.

• They would forego the User Interface Prototype step due to the simple fact that the interface requirements were known at the time.

Release Cycle

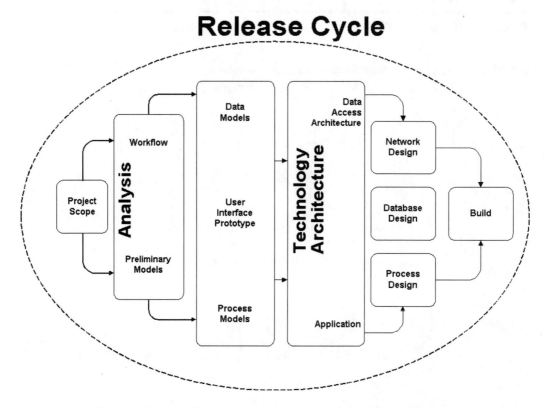

Figure 19-2   The design process used by XYZ Software.

- The Data Access Architecture and Application Architecture were both already known due to the existing Web presence that XYZ had and the Customer and Accounting database.

- The Network Engineer, who was a member of the Project Team, determined that there was no need to perform a rigorous Network Design due to the results of the Entity/Location and Entity/Volume matrices that were produced during the analysis phase.

- The Database Administrator concluded what had been suspected from the beginning of this project—there was no need to perform a Database Design process in the Design phase of the project because the existing Customer and Accounting database met the needs of the training application.

What remained to be done in the Design phase of the project was to do a Process Design. The results of the Project Teams efforts in this regard are described in the following section.

Process Design

The project team used, as a starting point, the functions listed in the CRUD diagram to develop their process design. The CRUD diagram produced during the analysis phase of the project is shown in Table 19–5 below.

What the Project Team decided in terms of the design of their application is described below in a manner specific to each function.

> *Register For Course*—A User accesses the company's Uniform Resource Locator (URL) for the on-line course registration system. This was called the *Account Sign-On Screen*. The user inputs his or her own company name, name, and the company's confidential support number into the *Account Sign-On* Web page—and press `<Enter>` to transmit the request. The request is received by the server at company headquarters and a query is made to the database to perform the following:
> • Verify that the company name and support number entered are valid
> • Extract and display in a Web page sent back to the student the number of credits available (these are the number of credits purchased by the company, less any credits that may have already been used)

Table 19–5 CRUD Diagram Used at XYZ Company

Entity --> Function V	Web Master	Student	Training Manager	Training Devlpr	Sales	Shipping	Execs
Register/ Take Course		C					
Sell/Record Learning Credits					CRUD	CRUD	
Ship Learning Credit Coupons					CRUD	CRUD	
Adjust Course List	CRUD		CRUD	CRU			
Produce/ View Status		C	R	R	CR	CRU	R
Adjust Learning Credits			CRUD		CRUD	CRU	
Build/ Update Web Pages	CRUD						

C = Create, R=Read, U=Update, D–Delete

- Assuming the user input a valid company name/support number combination and the company has support credits available, the Web page displayed to the user lists the number of credits available for use and the courses available to take. This is called the *Support Credit Confirmation Screen*. The course list also lists the number of credits that will be charged to the company's account if the user follows through and begins a course. If the user input an invalid company name/support number combination, or if there were no support credits available to the company, the server will format and transmit an *Invalid Company/Support Number screen*.

- The user selects a course from the list and presses <Enter>. The server receives this Web page and sends back to the user a *Course Request Confirmation Screen* (Web page), which informs the user that if he or she presses <Proceed> the number of support credits the requested course costs will be deducted from the company's account. The user can either press <Proceed> at this point or <Cancel>. If he or she presses <Cancel>, the server will display the *Support Credit Confirmation Screen*. If <Proceed> is pressed, the course credit costs will be deducted from the company's support credits and the course registration process is considered complete.

Take Course—When a student begins taking a course, the server will copy two entities to the student's machine:

- A "cookie" to help keep track of the progress the student makes through the course and
- A Java applet that will actually play the multimedia files that constitute the training course.

As you know, a "cookie" is a mechanism for maintaining application information across multiple sessions. The Web is a "stateless" environment, which means from the transmission of one Web page to the next, each is considered a discrete and totally independent action. This non-conversational nature of the Web means that programmers must manually build a mechanism to keep track of which actions were performed in a series of user-initiated activities to be able to determine which action is yet to be performed. "Cookies," or small files that record the stage of execution of an application, are that mechanism.

Once these two files are copied to the student's machine, the server sends a Web page named *Course Delivery Screen* to the student's machine. The purpose of this HTML page is to do the following:

- Receive the multimedia file that contains the actual course the student requested to take
- Initiate the execution of the Java applet that plays the multimedia course

The architecture of the courses is not described here, but it is exactly the same as a multimedia course that would be taken from a CD-ROM with one exception—the courses developed by XYZ were very small in comparison to most to allow quick transmission to the student's machine. Once the course is completed, the Java applet transmits a HTML page to the server indicating that the course is complete. The server recognizes this HTML page and formats and transmits a *Course Completion Screen* to the user. At the bottom of this screen the student is given a choice to either sign-off or register to take another course. If the student clicks on the `<Sign-Off>` button, the server will format and send a *Have A Good Day* screen. If he or she presses the `<Re-register>` button, the server will format and retransmit the *Support Credit Confirmation Screen*. This completes the process of taking a course.

Sell/Record Learning Support Credits—Learning Support Credits (LSC) are prepaid educational credits which, when redeemed, allow someone to take a specified number of hours of training. Product Support Credits (PSC) are prepaid technical support which, when redeemed, allow the callers to receive technical support on the products they have purchased from XYZ. When a salesperson sells LSCs, he or she inputs this information in exactly the same manner as that used to input PSCs. This is an existing process that requires no modification in terms of application or architecture components.

XYZ sells PSCs at a predetermined rate. These PSCs are redeemed at a given ratio each time an employee from a customer calls the Product Support department for help with a problem. XYZ had a task of determining the ratio of PSCs to LSCs. Once this was done, the project team was able to fully utilize the application components already in existence.

Ship LSCs—Again, because of XYZ's already existing PSC processes, the shipping of LSCs was a very simple process to design. At XYZ, a Visual Basic program scheduled to run nightly produced a report that was routed to the printer in the shipping department. The Visual Basic program queried the database and extracted the number of credits added during the day, and placed this information on the report in the form of a confirmation certificate. This report was formatted in such a way that it could be folded, inserted into an envelope, and mailed to the addressee, who was the purchaser of the PSCs.

The only change required in this process was in the way the Visual Basic program formatted the report. A code on the database would provide a legend that could be interpreted to indicate whether the credits purchased during the day were for LSCs or PSCs. The Visual Basic program would place the correct verbiage on the report.

Adjust Course List—XYZ had been offering instructor led training courses for a long time before they decided to begin offering Web-delivered courses. To support the administration of their instructor-led courses, XYZ had built a couple of tables in their customer and accounting database. These are seen in Figure 19–3 as the ORDER_DETAIL and COURSE tables.

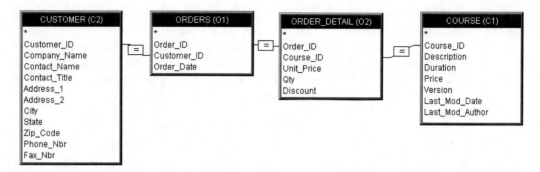

Figure 19–3   The customer and accounting information database.

As you can see from this structure, all the information necessary to accommodate Web initiated account verification and delivery of training exists in the four tables. The "Course_ID" column in the COURSE table is coded to reflect whether or not the course is an instructor-led or Web-delivered course.

With this existing database structure, there was no modification required to handle the adjustment of course lists that would occur from time to time specific to Web delivered courses.

Produce/View Status—This is yet another process that required very little modification to accommodate Web-delivered training courses. The Project Team identified two areas that required slight modification:

- A Customer Account status report, which was executed on a nightly basis via a scheduled procedure, required an additional detail line to show the number of LSCs purchased, used, and available, in addition to the detail line that showed the number of PSCs purchased, used, and available.
- A Customer Account status window needed modification to show the number of LSCs purchased, used, and available, in addition to the detail line that showed the number of PSCs purchased, used, and available.

Other than these two modifications, there was nothing else identified by the Project Team that needed to be addressed to handle this function.

Adjust Learning Credits—This was a function that the Project Team identified would require a lot of "procedural" change and a little bit of coding.

There was very little need to ever adjust PSCs once they were entered into the database, so there was not an identified process that the Project Team could utilize. But, they did recognize that because of the unstable nature of the Web, a student might find that the connection to XYZ's server would break after he or she started taking a course and before the course was finished. This would create a situation where the student's employer would have already had the LSCs deducted but the student would not have finished taking the course.

The procedural change involved receiving notification from the student or his or her employer that an adjustment was necessary and verifying the validity of the assertion. Once the claim was substantiated, the salesperson fielding the call would use a new window that would be developed to adjust LSCs. This would be a Power-Builder window that would allow the salesperson to manually adjust the number of LSCs available to a client company.

By designing such a process, the Project Team felt that this action should initiate two processes:
- An audit record of the transaction so that accountability for adjusting a customer's LSCs could be maintained.
- A confirmation certificate would be automatically generated from a Visual Basic program and mailed to the customer verifying this adjustment. The Project Team identified that this would entail a minor adjustment to the Visual Basic program that was already written to produce PSC and LSC confirmation certificates.

Although management at XYZ recognized the validity of these actions, they rejected including both of them in the initial construction of the Web application. Their thought was that this could be a "Phase II" activity.

Build/Update Web Pages—This was a process that required no changes to the existing architecture, but would constitute the majority of the development work to build this application. To highlight the development activities, the following work was identified by the Project Team:
- Create the Web pages used to support the delivery of training
- Account Sign-On Screen
- Support Credit Confirmation Screen
- Invalid Company/Support Number Screen
- Course Request Confirmation Screen
- Support Credit Confirmation Screen
- Course Delivery Screen
- Course Completion Screen
- Have a Good Day Screen
- Other development efforts
- Use of "cookie" to keep track of course registration and delivery process
- Java applet to play the multimedia course on the client machine
- Modify Visual Basic program to recognize the sale of LSCs and format a confirmation report accordingly
- Modify the Customer Account Status report and Customer Account Status window to add a line showing the number of LSCs purchased, used, and available in addition to the detail line that showed the number of PSCs purchased, used, and available
- Create PowerBuilder window to allow a salesperson to manually adjust the number of LSCs available to a client company

A Slight Change in Toolset

During the Design Phase of the project, the Web Master received an evaluation copy of a Web development tool called HAHTsite IDE. This is a new breed of tool that includes most of the utilities needed to completely build a Web application, including:

- HTML Editor
- GUI Web page construction
- ODBC interface to RDBMS products
- HTML extensions to allow database updates from the HTML
- Sophisticated testing and Web page publication interface

After playing with this tool and getting familiar with it, it was decided that the Web pages should be developed using HAHTSite IDE—not PowerBuilder. It was determined that PowerBuilder would remain XYZ's tool-of-choice to build Windows-based applications. It was also decided that HAHTsite IDE would be used in this development effort and, if proven to work as expected, would become XYZ's tool-of-choice to build and maintain its Web site and Web-delivered applications.

The Development Process

The PowerBuilder developer had 80 hours worth of work on this project. The developer had modified an existing Customer Account Status report and window. He had also written a new window to manually adjust a client company's purchased learning credits should a system fail while a student was in the middle of a course.

The DBA's modifications of the stored procedures to accommodate the selling and shipping of learning credits were quite rudimentary. They involved the following:

- Modified the Visual Basic program that runs nightly to produce a confirmation certificate showing the number of credits purchased during the previous business day, which is subsequently mailed to the customer.
- Modified the Visual Basic program that ran nightly and produced the Customer Account Status report to show the number of learning credits purchased during the day.
- Tested the entire process. This activity took most of the time allocated to the DBA for this phase of the project.

With 152 hours of development work ahead, spanning five calendar weeks, the Web master's development tasks were the most significant development activity in the development phase of the project. Her work is described in detail in the following sections.

Mirrored Sites

Because XYZ's Web site would be used in new ways (i.e., the number of hits would increase substantially, and the length of time people would be connected to the site would increase dramatically while they were taking a course), the project team decided that XYZ needed a mirrored Web site.

A mirrored Web site works in many ways like a replicated database. That is, the Web site objects accessible over the Internet are duplicated in two different locations and are kept in sync. A mirrored Web site is different from a replicated database in that it's rarely accessed from an external user's browser. Rather, a mirrored Web site exists so that the objects that comprise a Web site can be built and tested without affecting the production Web site. Then, when the objects have been satisfactorily tested, they're moved from the mirrored site to the production site.

So, the Web master's first action was to create a mirrored Web site, placing all existing database and Web objects inside it. In this way, when a set of components was successfully tested, it could easily be published into the production site.

Development Approach

The Web master looked at the development activities that were part of this project, as summarized below, and saw marginal value in placing a priority of one task over another.

- Find and employ a Java applet to play the courses.
- Build the "cookie" mechanism to keep track of a lesson's progress.
- Develop seven new Web pages.

Because of the reliance on an externally developed tool to play the courses to the students (the Java applet), the Web master decided that this activity should commence immediately and could occur in tandem with the development of Web pages. Other than this, the project team identified no contingencies between the tasks in the project plan.

The Hunt for a Java Applet.   After an exhaustive search of the tools available on the Net, the project team decided that XYZ would use the *Shockwave Flash* applet, from Macromedia Incorporated. Since the actual courses would be written using Macromedia products, the team believed that that the greatest degree of reliability could be achieved by using its Java applet to play files created using Macromedia products. In addition, XYZ's Web page development tool would incorporate the transfer and playing of Java applets to a user's machine quite nicely.

If you'd like to see this applet in action, visit the Macromedia Incorporated Web site at `http://www.macromedia.com`.

Cookies.   As you've already seen, a *cookie* is a mechanism for maintaining application information across multiple sessions.

Once the Web master spent a little more time with the Web page development tool of choice, the HAHTSite IDE, the team pleasantly discovered that writing a cookie into the application was unnecessary. This is because some of the HTML extensions built into the tool automatically maintain state information, eliminating much of the need for cookies to handle state information.

However, in designing the system, the architects also recognized that a connection might break before the user was finished with a course. Cookies were originally planned to address this situation. But, since the team had decided that cookies were unnecessary, the Web Master decided to change the system's design slightly, thus eliminating the need for a cookie.

The change involved the point in time at which the system would debit the client company's account balance of learning credits. Under the original design, the system charged the company's balance of learning credits before the student began the course. However, if the course credits weren't charged against a client company's balance until after the course was completed, no adjustment was necessary in the event of a broken connection. The user would simply reinitiate the connection and continue the course. When the course was completed and the student saw the Course Completion page, the actual adjustment to the purchased and unused learning credits would occur.

However, this plan contained a security risk—Someone could take a course for free by starting and taking a course but terminating the connection right before finishing the course and being presented with the Course Completion page. To shore up this potential breach, the company decided on the following approach:

- Notify the students early in the course registration process that as soon as the course began, their employer's account balance would be decreased by the number of credits the course costs.

- In a follow-up development activity, build a mechanism to create course completion certificates, which are automatically triggered after the student completes the course and progresses through the Course Completion page. This is where, among other things, the employer's account balance of learning credits would be decreased.

Develop the Web Pages

Figure 19–4 shows the first screen developed by the Web master, which is the first screen in the process a user would follow to sign-up and take a Web course.

What isn't shown on this graphic or included in this chapter is the actual coding and development of each of these Web pages. The intent of this chapter isn't to teach HTML or how to use the HAHTSite IDE, but rather to discuss how to design an application that uses an Access 97 database as the back-end RDBMS to a Web-delivered application.

The process of accomplishing a database connection to an Access 97 database and execution of a query against a table is a graphical process involving just a few steps that have been discussed previously in this book and are presented again in detail in Chapter 20. Since Access 97 tables are ODBC-compliant and the development tool used by XYZ was ODBC-enabled, the actual database connection and query construction were greatly simplified.

Figure 19–5 shows the Support Credit Confirmation screen, which is the next screen displayed to the user once the information supplied on the account sign-up screen is validated against the Customer and Accounting information database. Note that this screen dynamically displays the results of a query extracting the names of the courses that can be taken given the number of learning credits available.

Once this page is displayed, and the user has selected the course to take, the user clicks the <Take Course> button to display the Course Request Confirmation screen. This is the last chance to bail out of the process before the course actually begins. This is also the screen where, when the user clicks the <Proceed> button, the Shockwave Flash Java applet is downloaded to the student's machine.

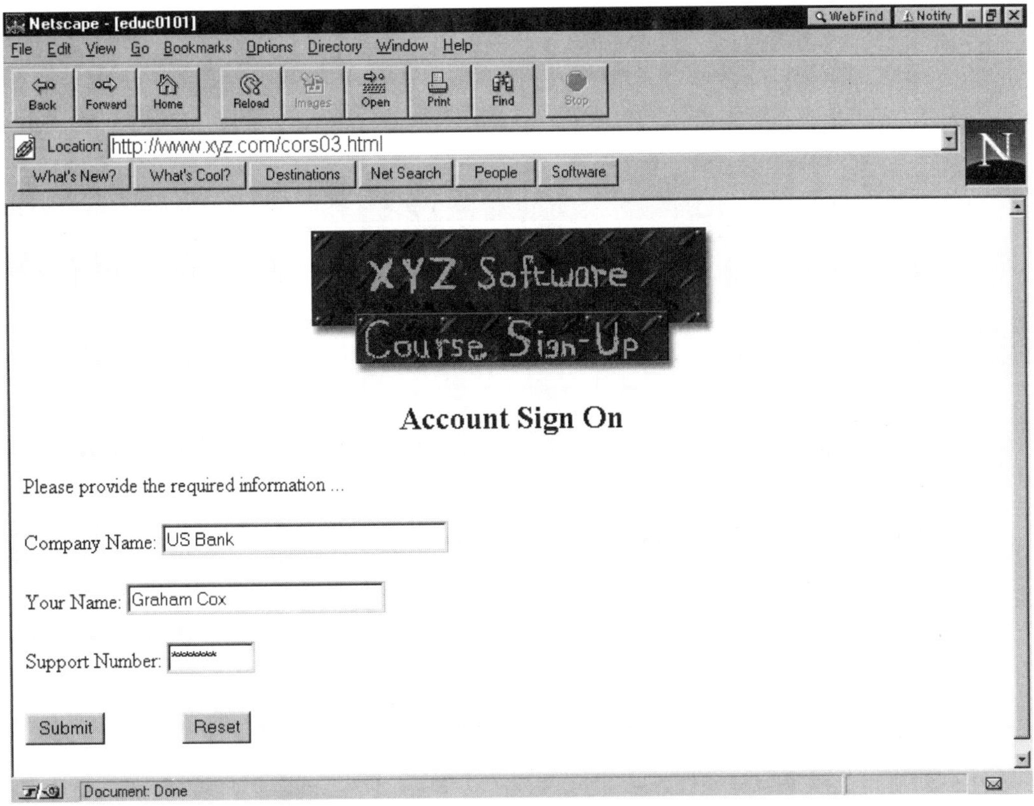

Figure 19–4 The account sign-on screen.

The Web master quickly developed the remaining screens, completing them within the project time frames. XYZ's home page required one last change, adding a button for the user to click on to initiate the whole Internet-delivered course process. The Web master added the highlighted graphical bar element in Figure 19–6 to accomplish this task. Adding this graphical bar (which in HTML terminology is called a hypergraphics link) involved the Web master writing four lines of HTML code.

I'm not including in this section the other three screens (Invalid Company/Support Number screen, Course Completion screen, and Have a Good Day screen) the Web master developed as these are static HTML pages that have no database access.

Implementation

The one problem XYZ encountered during the construction process wasn't in the database or Web page development but in the creation of the actual courses. The curricula developers had a difficult time keeping the course length down to the original mandate of 256,000 bytes. After a couple of meetings between all project team members, management relented and compromised by allowing a maximum course length of 750,000 bytes. Be-

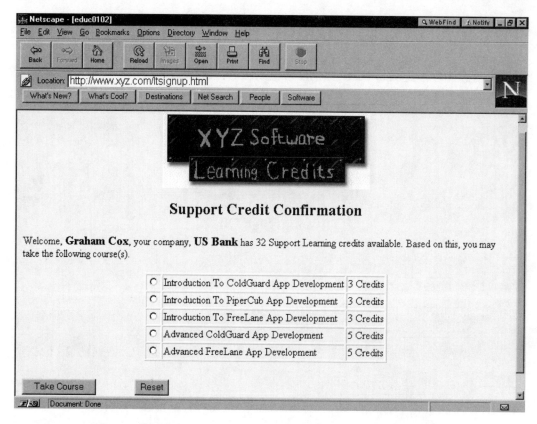

Figure 19–5 The Support Credit Confirmation screen.

tween this and breaking up the courses into more finite and discrete (smaller) components, the curricula developers were able to stay within the appointed guidelines.

XYZ implemented its new system on schedule and within budget following a short beta-testing period. Amazingly (to the management of XYZ) and pleasingly (to the project team), no major modifications were found necessary during beta testing. Therefore, XYZ implemented its new Internet course-delivery system with the following:

- A direct mail campaign to existing customers notifying them of the new service
- A training session in which XYZ's sales force learned how to sell the new service
- A splash page on XYZ's Web site describing the new service. A *splash page* is a temporary Web page that displays prior to the display of a company's home page and is usually reserved for late-breaking or highly interesting information.

Post-Implementation Analysis

XYZ implemented its system at the end of 1996. In the months since implementation, the company has seen better-than-expected response to the system, with revenues from this service 32 percent greater than anticipated. Because of this high demand, XYZ had to in-

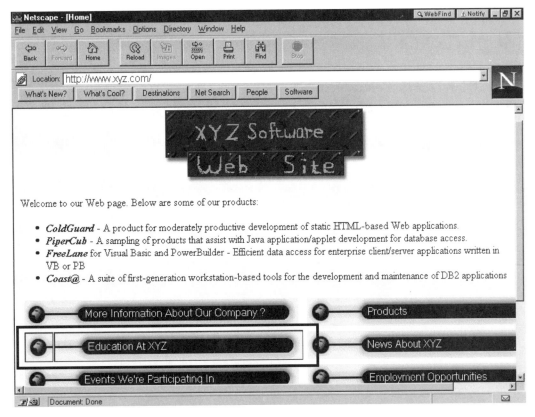

Figure 19–6   XYZ's home page with a link added to the education department's pages and the Web-delivered courses.

stall three additional modems at its server, but XYZ considered it a small price to pay for the extra success.

XYZ recognizes that much of its ability to build and implement this system so successfully came from the exceptional design and configuration of its customer and accounting information database. Without the ability to easily build a Web-based front-end interface to a substantially existing database, XYZ knows that developing this application would have required much more time. Once again, the success of an application, in this case a state-of-the-art Web database application, is highly affected by the design and construction of the database.

Moving On

This chapter presented a case study of the actual analysis, design and construction phases of the Web database application. Emphasis was placed throughout the chapter on the analysis and design component of this application.

In Chapter 20, you'll focus on the actual construction and implementation activities revolving around the development of a Web database Internet and intranet application.

Building
a Simple Class
Registration
System

T his chapter focuses on how to use HTML and a Web database application development suite to construct a Web database application that includes both Internet and intranet access. The company profiled in this chapter is A Better Computer (ABC) Company, a fictitious corporation that provides, among other things, computer training. The Web application profiled in this chapter contains, among other things, a query facility so that Web visitors can see what training classes are held in cities near them. This is the Internet component to the database that is profiled in this chapter. The intranet component presented in this chapter is the facility used by ABC employees to update the Access 97 database that maintains the data that describes ABC Company's course offerings and their availability.

In this chapter I will show you the various components of this application, and describe how it was constructed. You will understand the various components and how they interrelate and interoperate. You will see how the application and application components are constructed. Although the source code and database for this application are included on the CD-ROM, the approach taken here will not be to lead you through the process of installing and executing the application on your hard drive from the CD-ROM. To me, those types of examples, the ones where you install a semi-working application on your hard drive, are never nearly as meaningful as a clear description of how something was constructed so that you can take that description and apply it to your unique circumstances.

Application Configuration

The configuration of this application is based upon several key factors—First, to provide Web access to the inventory of courses that ABC Company has, as well as their availability and second, to provide in-house access to this data for administrative purposes. Although this application provides no capability to actually register for a course on-line, this capability could be easily added.

The basic configuration of this application is as follows:

- Access 97 database with four tables
- HahtSITE IDE used as the application development tool
- Global front-end to the application that provides both Internet and intranet access
- Security log-in screen to protect the application from unauthorized access to the intranet components on the site

Structure of the Database

As seen in Figure 20–1, there are four tables in this database. These are:

Available Courses—This table is accessed over the intranet only by ABC employees who need to maintain the information contained in it by either Inserting, Updating, or Deleting rows. The table contains the following columns:

- *Course_Id*—Datatype: Number. This contains a unique identifier for each course. This column is joined automatically to the column of the same name in the `Class_Registration` table whenever both tables are open at the same time.
- *Course_Name*—Datatype: Text. Contains the name of the course
- *Course_Duration*—Datatype: Number. Contains the number of days in duration for the course

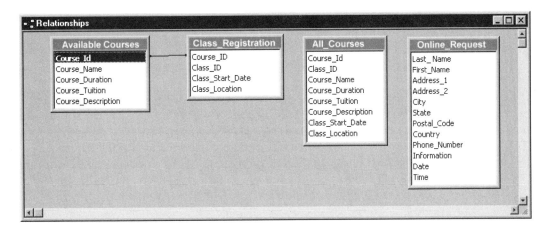

Figure 20–1   The database structure.

- *Course_Tuition*—*Datatype: Currency*. Contains the cost to attend the course
- *Course_Description*—*Datatype: Text*. Contains up to 255 characters of description text for the course

Class_Registration—This table is accessed over the intranet only by ABC employees who need to maintain the information contained in it by either Inserting, Updating, or Deleting rows. The table contains the following columns:
- *Course_Id*—*Datatype: Number*. Contains a unique identifier for each course. This column is joined automatically to the column of the same name in the `Available_ Courses` table whenever both tables are open at the same time.
- *Class_Id*—*Datatype: Text*. Contains a unique identifier for each time the course is offered. In other words, a given course may be offered five times. In such a case, there would be five rows in this table, and the `Course_Id` column would be identical for each row because the course being offered is the same. The `Class_Id` column would have a unique value for each row to identify that row.
- *Class_Start_Date*—*Datatype: Date/Time*. Contains the date that the class starts.
- *Class_Location*—*Datatype: Text*. Contains the city/state in which the class identified by the row is to be held.

All_Courses—This table is accessed by users over the Internet who want to gather information on when and where specific courses are to be offered. The table is created from a Join Query that takes the contents of the `Available_Courses` table and joins it to the `Class_Registration` table on the `Course_Id` column. The table contains the following columns:
- *Course_Id*—*Datatype: Number*. Contains a unique identifier for each course. This column is joined automatically to the column of the same name in the `Available_Courses` table whenever both tables are open at the same time.
- *Class_Id*—*Datatype: Text*. Contains a unique identifier for each time the course is offered. In other words, a given course may be offered five times. In such a case, there would be five rows in this table, and the `Course_Id` column would be identical for each row because the course being offered is the same. The `Class_Id` column would have a unique value for each row to identify that row.
- *Course_Name*—*Datatype: Text*. Contains the name of the course
- *Course_Duration*—*Datatype: Number*. Contains the number of days in duration for the course
- *Course_Tuition*—*Datatype: Currency*. Contains the cost to attend the course
- *Course_Description*—*Datatype: Text*. Contains up to 255 characters of description text for the course
- *Class_Start_Date*—*Datatype: Date/Time*. Contains the date that the class that this record represents starts.
- *Class_Location*—*Datatype: Text*. Contains the city/state that the class identified by the row is to be held.

HahtSITE IDE, the tool used to build this application, does not provide a convenient mechanism to join and access two or more tables from a Web page. Therefore, the `All_Courses` table was created to satisfy Web requests where information from both tables is needed. The `All_Courses` table is either created manually from within Access 97 by someone executing the Join Query or automatically in a prescheduled Visual Basic program that automatically executes the Join Query.

OnLine_Request—This table is accessed over the Internet by users who want to provide input of any type to ABC Company. This input could be a comment on the Web site, a request for product information, or a request to have someone call. The table contains the following columns:

- *Last_Name*—*Datatype: text*. Contains the last name of the person completing the Feedback form.
- *First_Name*—*Datatype: text*. Contains the first name of the person completing the Feedback form.
- *Address_1*—*Datatype: text*. Contains the first address line of the person completing the Feedback form.
- *Address_2*—*Datatype: text*. Contains the second address line of the person completing the Feedback form.
- *City*—*Datatype: text*. Contains the city of the person completing the Feedback form.
- *State*—*Datatype: text*. Contains the state of the person completing the Feedback form.
- *Postal_Code*—*Datatype: text*. Contains the postal code of the person completing the Feedback form.
- *Country*—*Datatype: text*. Contains the country of the person completing the Feedback form.
- *Phone_Number*—*Datatype: text*. Contains the phone number of the person completing the Feedback form.
- *Information*—*Datatype: text*. Contains up to 255 characters of free form text data supplied by the person completing the Feedback form.
- *Date*—*Datatype: date/time*. Contains the date when the person completing this form pressed `<Submit>`.
- *Time*—*Datatype: date/time*. Contains the time when the person completing this form pressed `<Submit>`.

HAHTsite IDE Development Tool

The HAHTsite Integrated Internet Development System merges content creation, client- and server-side logic development, data access (ODBC or native API), automated distributed deployment to multiple sites, team development, and application life cycle management into one seamlessly integrated software system.

HAHTsite IDE uses a proprietary CGI program interface, coupled with proprietary HTML extensions, to free the developer from having to write CGI programs. Here is an example of how helpful a development tool can be to place the Update button (which causes the Access 97 database to be updated with whatever values appear on the screen) as seen in Figure 20–2 and then to make it functional against an Access 97 database is a simple process of:

1. Identifying the connection to the Access 97 database
2. Pasting the controls (including the <Update> button) and objects on the Web page where you want them to appear
3. Double-click on the <Update> button to change its properties
4. Select (Update) as being the database action that occurs when the user clicks the <Update> button

That's it—there's nothing more to it. When a user accesses this Web page, makes changes to the data appearing on it, and then clicks the <Update> button, the interaction

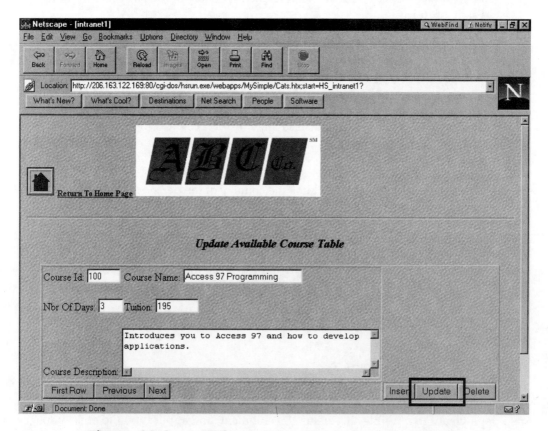

Figure 20–2 A Web page in our application with an <Update> database button.

between the extensions to HTML that are included on the Web page and the CGI pro-gram (supplied by HAHT with the HAHTSite IDE toolkit) running on the Web server cause the Access 97 database to be updated. As you're probably curious as to what these extensions are, I want to show you what the HTML code looks like that the HAHTsite IDE creates *just for* the <Update> button on the Web page as seen in Figure 20–2. This is shown below.

```
NAME=Button5
 TYPE=Button
 VERSION="2.0"
 HAHTVERSION="2.0"
 SAVECONTENTS=True
 IGNORECONTENTS=False
 DISPLAYONLOAD=True
 KEEPCONTENTSONPUBLISH=0
 DYNAMICCONTENT=1
 SetTrace=False
 UseMethod=False
 UserMethod=""
 DataSource=DataSet1
 Action=2
   --><INPUT  NAME=Button5  TYPE=SUBMIT  VALUE=Update><!--HAHT-Extension
/HAHTCHARWIDGET --><!--HAHT-Extension HAHTCHARWIDGET
```

Global Front-End

This Web database application incorporates a front-end that is accessible by both Internet and intranet users. This is seen in Figures 20–3 and 20–4.

Between Figure 20–3 and Figure 20–4, there are four areas on the screen of particular interest in understanding how the front-end to this application works. These are:

1. Toolbar for quick navigation to other Web pages
2. Company logo on every page
3. Hot-links to other Web sites of interest
4. Easy navigation to other Web pages

The following sections describe each of these.

Toolbar for Quick Navigation to Other Web Pages. A toolbar at the top of the home page is a fairly consistent element on most Web sites. Although one of the purposes of the home page is to inform the user which site is being accessed, the primary purpose is to provide a central navigation point to other key sections on the Web site as well as to other areas of interest to the person looking at your Web page.

On ABC's Web site home page, the following hypergraphic links are supplied on the toolbar:

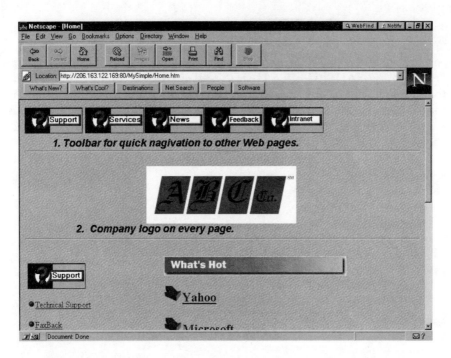

Figure 20-3 The ABC Company's global front-end to its Internet and intranet site.

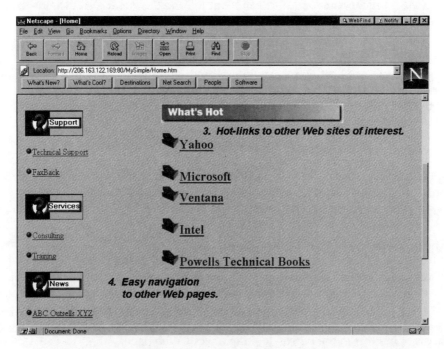

Figure 20-4 Bottom half of the ABC Company's global front-end to its Internet and intranet site.

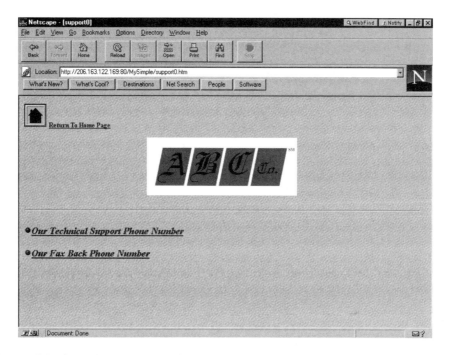

Figure 20–5   What is seen when the user clicks on the `<Support>` icon.

- *Support*—Provides access to the various pages that describe the support phone numbers that are offered by ABC Company. Figure 20–5 shows what the user would see if he or she clicked on the `<Support>` icon. This is a Web page that includes two hypertext links to other Web pages that provide contact information.

- *Services*—Provides access to the various pages that describe the types of services offered by ABC Company, namely Consulting and Training. Figure 20–6 shows what the user would see if he or she clicked on the `<Services>` icon, which is a Web page that includes two hypertext links to other Web pages that provide information on Consulting and Training services. The hypertext link to the Training services page is discussed in detail in a later section as this page performs database access and format of the result set on a Web page.

- *News* —Provides access to the various pages that list the Press Releases issued by ABC Company (Figure 20–7). This is also another fairly typical item on a corporate Web site.

- *Feedback*—Provides access to a customer feedback form (Figure 20–8). Although this is described in detail later in this chapter, feedback forms are quite common items on corporate Web sites. What makes this feedback form unique is that not only is it able to accept new input and then post that input to an Access 97 database, but that the Feedback form is also used to browse and/or update and/or delete existing comments supplied by previous users.

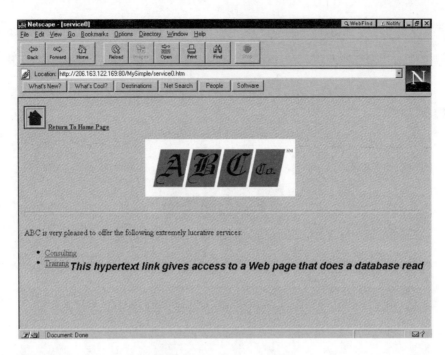

Figure 20–6 What is seen when the user clicks on the `<Services>` icon.

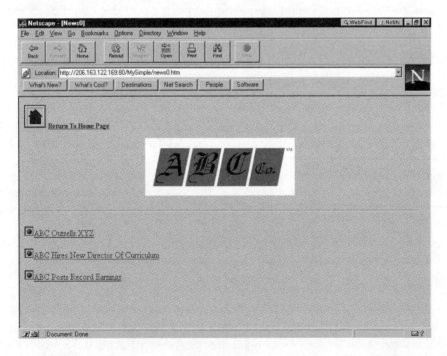

Figure 20–7 What is seen when the user clicks on the `<News>` icon.

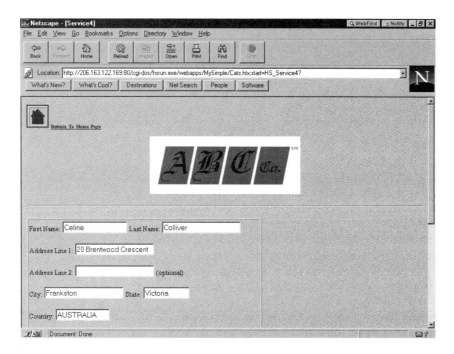

Figure 20–8   What is seen when the user clicks on the `<Feedback>` icon.

- *Intranet*—Provides access to the company's intranet site (Figure 20–9). This is described in detail later in this chapter. For now, you should know that the Web pages accessed from here allow ABC Company employees to update the Access 97 tables on their machines. Employees use these to keep track of the names of courses offered by ABC Company as well as the dates of and locations where those courses are offered. The results of this data entry and update are then viewed externally by users accessing the `Services | Training Services` Web pages.

Company Logo on Every Page.   You'll notice that every page in the ABC Company Web site has a consistent look to it. This look is achieved by the following:

- The background for each page is identical.
- Each page has a Return To Home icon and hypertext link at the top.
- Each page has a company logo on it.

In other than rare circumstances, you should strive for a consistent look to the Web pages in your application. You want to affirm in a very passive way that the page the user is viewing in his or her browser belongs to your site, and that the user has not linked out of your site to another company's site.

Hot-links to Other Web Sites of Interest.   Another common item appearing on corporate Web site home pages are hypertext or hypergraphic links to the Web sites of affiliated companies. This is an aid to people who are browsing your site and wish to go to an-

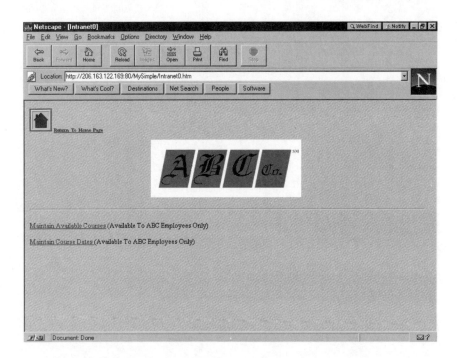

Figure 20–9   What is seen when the user clicks on the
`<Intranet>` icon and after logging in to the database.

other site of a related company. Some companies are finding it lucrative to place references to other organizations' Web sites on their own Web site by charging those other
companies a preset fee to do so. This makes sense and helps all parties concerned because:

- The person browsing the Internet is given a convenient way to move from site to related site.

- Your company receives revenue from the organizations that are listed on your Web
site.

- The organizations that are listed on your Web site have increased hits on their own
Web sites as more people link to them from your site.

Easy Navigation to Other Web Pages.   Along the left border of the home page
you'll see a series of icons that also appear in the toolbar, followed by the hypertext links
to the pages that are contained in those sections. This gives the user the ability to easily
and quickly navigate to the page of his or her choice while avoiding using the toolbar. Let
me give you an example.

Refer back to Figure 20–3, where you'll see the toolbar at the top of the ABC Company's home page. Let's say that someone wanted to find the telephone number for the
FaxBack service. He or she would have to do the following:

- Click on the icon on the toolbar that says `<Support>`.
- Wait for the page, as seen in Figure 20–5 to display in the browser.
- Click on the hypertext link that references the FaxBack telephone number.
- Wait for the page to display in the browser.

This four step process can be expedited by using the hypertext and hypergraphic links that appear on the left side of the ABC Company's home page. To get the FaxBack telephone number using the links on the left side of the home page, the user would simply do the following:

- Look down the left column of the ABC Company's home page, as seen in Figure 20–4 until the hypertext link to the company's FaxBack telephone number was found and click on the link
- Wait for the page requested to display in the browser

That's all there is to it, and the user is pleased at all the time that was saved by this direct link.

Security Login Screen

On the ABC Company's home page, as seen in Figure 20–3, access to the company intranet site is indicated. Although many companies that have Internet and intranet sites have them separated, a growing trend as organizations become more comfortable with security over the Internet is to allow access to an intranet site from the Internet site's Web pages.

Obviously you don't want to allow access to the intranet pages by an unauthorized person. So, you need to build security into your Web database application to keep the unauthorized people out of the pages you don't want them in. You can accomplish this, as seen in the Web database application profiled in this chapter, by providing access to all restricted Web pages from one Web page. In that one Web page you'd require the user to complete a security log-in process. If the user fails security, he or she are not allowed to view any of the pages that follow. If the user passes security, he or she would have whatever access you wish to give by the way you develop the application.

HAHTsite has a very nice way to implement the security log-in process. Basically, it allows you to place what they call a Database Login Widget on any Web page that is contained in an application. When a user accesses a Web page that contains this invisible Database Login Widget (the Web page seen in Figure 20–9 contains one of these) he or she is first presented with a Database Login screen, as seen in Figure 20–10.

Once the needed information is supplied, it is automatically verified against an Access 97 table of authorized users. If the information supplied by the user does not match what is stored in the Access 97 table, a message displays and the user is not allowed to view the Web page. If the information supplied is validated, then the user would see the desired page, in this case, the page seen in Figure 20–9.

The following sections describe the components in this Web application that provide database access to an Access 97 database. These include both Internet application components and Intranet application components.

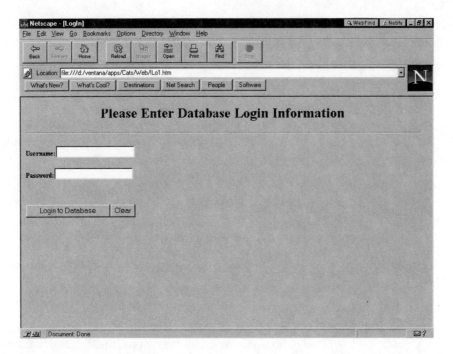

Figure 20–10   The database log-in screen as part of the security process.

Web Database Internet Components in the Application

There are three Web pages that comprise the Internet accessible components in this application. These are:

- Training Course Listing Page
- Course Date/Location Page
- Feedback Page

Each of these are discussed in detail in the following sections.

Training Course Listing Page

From the ABC Company's home page, the Training Course Listing page is accessed by one of the following:

- Clicking on the Services icon in the toolbar and then on the Training hypertext link, or,
- Clicking on the Training hypertext link that is directly below the Services icon that appears along the left side of the home page.

When one of the above is done, the page seen in Figure 20–11 displays.

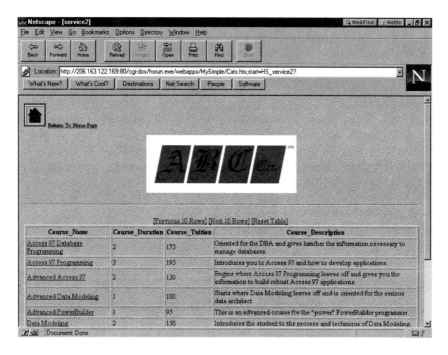

Figure 20–11   The course list page.

What is wonderful about the HAHTsite IDE as a tool to develop Web database applications is the ease with which the page seen in Figure 20–11 was created. Again, I don't want to teach you how to use this tool, but I do want to give you an idea of how easy it is to use development tool suites in the construction of a Web database application. So, the process of creating the page seen in Figure 20–11 is:

- From within the HAHTsite IDE, open the application object.
- Click on `File`, then `New`, then `Page` to create a new page.
- Place the graphics on the page where you want them. For Figure 20–11, these are the house that appears in the upper left corner, the hypertext link to return to the home page, and the corporate logo.
- Click on the Widgets icon, then on the Database Table icon, and drag the icon over and drop it on the new page where you want it to appear.
- Double-click on the Database Table icon just placed on the page, and then on the Database connections tab.
- Click on the Database Connection drop-down list box and select the database connection that you want to access in this Web page.
- Click on the Tables drop-down list box and then select the table that you want to access in this Web page.
- Click on <OK>.

That's it. When this page is viewed in a browser, the HAHTsite extensions to HTML and their interactions with the CGI program supplied by the product take care of establishing a connection to the database, accessing the desired records in the database, formatting the result set onto a Web page, and then transmitting the Web page back to the user.

Do you see the hypertext links at the top of the table in Figure 20–11? These are navigation aids that are automatically supplied by HAHTsite IDE because of the use of the Database Table widget. I did nothing to create these navigation aids that wasn't already provided for in the tool.

The purpose of this page is to list a few pieces of information available for each of the course titles offered by ABC Company, specifically,

- Course Name
- Course Duration
- Course Tuition
- Course Description

You'll notice that each of the items listed under the column heading Course Name is a hypertext link. In HAHTsite IDE, this is termed a *database drilldown*. What this means is that if a user clicked on any of the items listed in the Course Name column, a follow-up query would be generated to retrieve additional information I specified that is based on the course the user selected.

In other words, it doesn't make a whole lot of sense to show all of the course dates and locations for every course on the page seen in Figure 20–11, does it? It's best to give as little information as necessary to allow users to select the course information they need. Then, when they have selected a specific course, give them more detailed information.

Assuming a user clicks on one of the courses listed under the Course Name column, thus triggering a database drilldown, the Course Date/Location page as discussed in the next section will display.

Course Date/Location Page

The Course Date/Location page is only displayed if the user selected a specific course about which to view additional information from the Training Course Listing Page. The Course Date/Location page, as seen in Figure 20–12, contains the following button controls that appear at the bottom of the page:

- *Clear*—Causes all the fields on the form to appear empty
- *MoveFirst*—Causes the records that display one at a time on the page to cycle back to the first retrieved row for the course
- *MoveNext*—Causes the next record retrieved for the requested course to display on the page
- *MovePrevious*—Causes the previous record displayed and retrieved for the requested course to display on the page

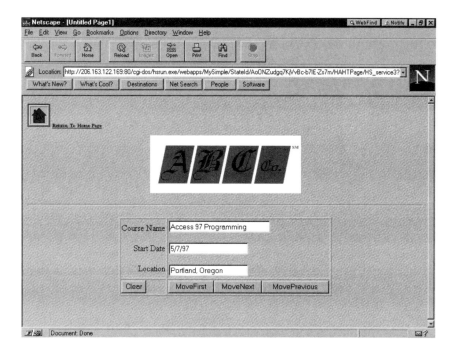

Figure 20–12 The Course Date/Location page.

A user would automatically access this Web page after he or she had indicated a particular and singular course preference by clicking on a specific item that appears under the Course Name column on the Training Course Listing page. Once on this page, the user could view the dates and locations for all the times that this course was taught in order to pick a date and location which fulfilled his or her needs.

Because of the interaction between the extensions to HTML provided by HAHTsite IDE and the CGI program supplied with the HAHTSite product, a person developing this Web page would find it a very easy process to place the buttons on the page that control the movement through the result set. Once placed on the page, causing them to take the action described above is a very simple four-step process. Again for the sake of understanding the power of Web development suites without trying to teach you how to use the HAHTsite product, the process of creating database functionality in a button is described as:

- Double-click on the button to which you want to establish database access while in the HAHTsite IDE.
- On the Button Properties window, click on the Database tab.
- On the Action drop-down list box, select one of the listed database actions (i.e., Clear, MoveFirst, MoveNext, MovePrevious, Insert, Update, Delete, etc.).
- Click <OK>.

Once the above is done by a user, whenever that user clicks on one of the database-update buttons, the action specified for that button will automatically occur—with no additional programming required on your part.

Feedback Page

From the ABC Company's home page, the Feedback page is accessed by one of the following:

- Clicking on the Feedback icon in the toolbar, or,
- Clicking on the Feedback icon that appears along the left side of the home page.

When one of the above is done, the pages seen in Figure 20–13 and Figure 20–14 display.

The Feedback page is quite similar to the other pages you have seen in this application that accept user input and display the results of database queries. The page consists of a form that has various controls on it that accept user input and display the results of queries. What is different about this page is the types of buttons at the bottom of the form. These, and the descriptions of their actions are:

Submit—Once the Feedback form is completed by the user, clicking on the <Submit> button would cause the information supplied by the user to be transmitted to

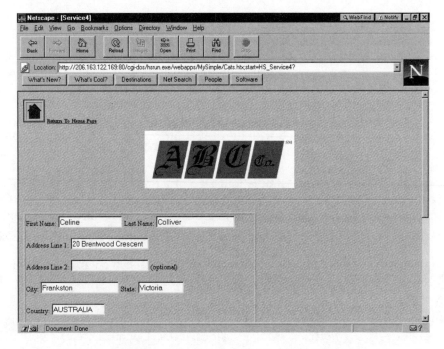

Figure 20–13 The top half of the Feedback page.

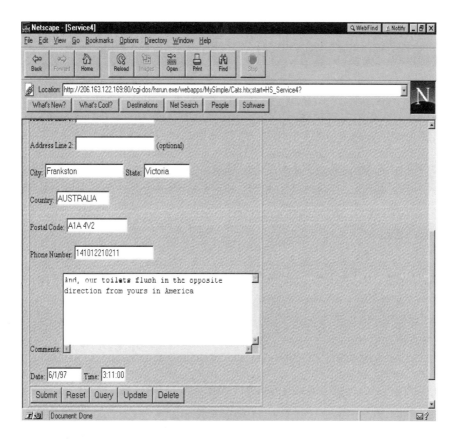

Figure 20–14   The bottom half of the Feedback page.

the CGI program running on the server. The CGI program would format and insert the data into the Access 97 table named: `OnLine_Request`.

Reset—The `<Reset>` button, when clicked, causes all the data that is currently displayed on the form to be cleared from the form. It does not cause the data to be deleted from the database.

Query—A user could enter his or her first and last name in the appropriate form fields, press the `<Query>` button, and the CGI program running on the server would retrieve the record that exists in the `OnLine_Request` table that is a match to the first and last name entered and display the results on this form. The user could then either modify some of the data and press the `<Update>` button or simply press the `<Delete>` button to remove these records from the database.

Update—As described above, the `<Update>` button causes the record that exists in the `OnLine_Request` table that is a match to the first and last name entered on this form to be updated with the values as they exist on the form in the various fields.

Delete—As described above, the <Delete> button causes the record from the On-Line_Request table that matches the first and last name entered on this form to be deleted from the table.

As you learned in the previous section named Course Date/Location Page, the actual process to add the database access functionality described here is a very simple one. The code that actually accomplishes the desired database action is contained in the CGI program running on the server as supplied with the HAHTsite IDE tool.

Web Database Intranet Components in the Application

There are two Web pages that comprise the intranet accessible components in this application. These are:

- Maintain Available Courses
- Maintain Course Dates

Each of these are discussed in detail in the following sections.

Maintain Available Courses Page

From the ABC Company's home page, the Maintain Available Courses page is accessed by one of the following:

- Clicking on the <Intranet> icon that is in the toolbar, or,
- Clicking on the <Intranet> icon that appears along the left side of the home page.

From here, you will see the Database Login screen as seen in Figure 20–10. Complete this screen with your User Name and Password, and click <Submit>. If the information supplied is incorrect, you'll receive an error message. If it is correct, you are allowed access to the intranet site whose first page is the one that appears in Figure 20–9. Click on the hypertext link that says Maintain Available Courses and the Web page as seen in Figure 20–15 will display.

The purpose of this page is to allow authorized ABC Company employees access to update the contents of the Access 97 database table named Available_Courses. This Web page is quite similar to the other Web pages that allow database access, with the difference being that this page provides update access to Access 97 tables that ABC Company wants to restrict to authorized users.

The buttons that appear at the bottom of this page perform the following functions:

- *First Row*—Requery the Available_Courses table and display the first record retrieved on this Web page
- *Previous*—Requery the Available_Courses table but position the record displayed on the row immediately prior to the currently displayed record.
- *Next*—Requery the Available_Courses table but position the record displayed on the row immediately following the currently displayed record.
- *Insert*—Insert the data that appears on the form into the Available_Courses table.

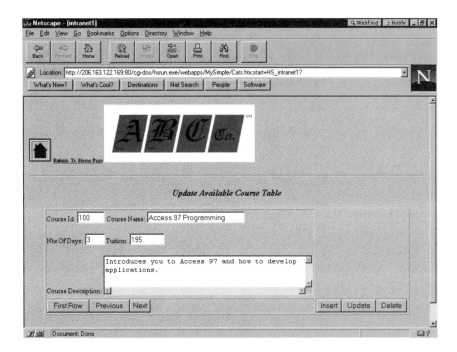

Figure 20–15   The Maintain Available Courses intranet page.

- *Update*—Update the data that is in the `Available_Courses` table with the data that currently appears on the form.
- *Delete*—Delete the row in the `Available_Courses` table that currently appears in the form.

As you learned in previous sections, to cause the actions described above to be assigned to the various buttons is a very simple process. The code that actually accomplishes the desired database action is contained in the CGI program running on the server as supplied with the HAHTsite IDE tool.

Maintain Course Dates Page

From the ABC Company's home page, the Maintain Course Dates page is accessed by one of the following:

- Clicking on the `<Intranet>` icon that is in the toolbar, or,
- Clicking on the `<Intranet>` icon that appears along the left side of the home page.

From here, you will see the Database Login screen as seen in Figure 20–10. Complete this screen with your User Name and Password, and click `<Submit>`. If the information supplied is incorrect, you'll receive an error message. If it is correct, you are allowed access to the intranet site whose first page is the one that appears in Figure 20–9.

Click on the hypertext link that says `Maintain Course Dates` and the Web page as seen in Figure 20–16 will display.

The purpose of this page is to allow authorized ABC Company employees access to update the contents of the Access 97 database table named `Class_Registration`. This Web page is quite similar to the other Web pages that allow database access, with the difference being that this page provides update access to Access 97 tables that ABC Company wants to restrict to authorized users.

The buttons that appear at the bottom of this page perform the following functions:

- *First Row*—Requery the `Class_Registration` table and display the first record retrieved on this Web page.

- *Previous*—Requery the `Class_Registration` table but position the record displayed on the row that is immediately prior to the currently displayed record.

- *Next*—Requery the `Class_Registration` table but position the record displayed on the row that is immediately after the currently displayed record.

- *Insert*—Insert the data that appears on the form into the `Class_Registration` table.

- *Update*—Update the data that is in the `Class_Registration` table with the data that currently appears on the form.

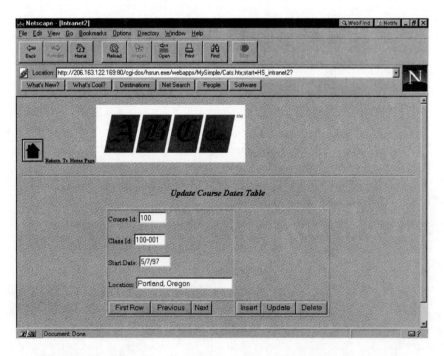

Figure 20–16   The Maintain Course Dates intranet page.

- *Delete*—Delete the row in the `Class_Registration` table that currently appears in the form.

As you learned in previous sections, to cause the actions described above to be assigned to the various buttons is a very simple process. The code that actually accomplishes the desired database action is contained in the CGI program running on the server as supplied with the HAHTsite IDE tool.

Moving On

This chapter examined the Web database application that a fictitious company named ABC Company developed for both Internet and intranet access. Each of the Web pages that provided access to Access 97 database tables was described in detail and how the actual database table access is accomplished was discussed.

In Chapters 6 and 12 you learned how to write HTML code to construct attractive Web pages that could display database data. In Chapters 7 and 13 you learned how CGI programs accomplish the actual database access and function as an interface between the user's request for data and the actual access of the data. In Chapters 8 and 19 you learned how to design a Web database application to take into account the unique considerations of a Web-based database application. In Chapters 9, 10, and 11 you learned how to use the facilities in Access 97 to construct the database objects that would be accessed by a Web database application. And in the other chapters in this book you learned about the other issues to consider when you are tasked with designing and building a Web database application.

APPENDIX A

CD-ROM
Contents

T he CD-ROM included with your copy of this book contains valuable software for the design and development of Web database applications that use an Access 97 database.

The folders on the CD contain demo and evaluation copies of a wide variety of products you could use to help build an Access 97 Web database application.

CD-ROM Contents

Software Folder

HAHTsite.   The product name is: HAHTsite IDE. HAHTsite IDE is a Web database application development suite with a full compliment of tools to help you build Web applications with or without database access. This is the tool that was used in the development of the applications profiled in Chapters 19 and 20 of this book. For more product information, visit HAHT Software's Web site at: http://www.haht.com/.

Web_Wiz.   The product name is: WEB Wizard. Web Wizard: The Duke of URL is a Windows program designed to help you create home pages for the World Wide WEB. With WEB Wizard you can create your own customized home page in just a matter of minutes—guaranteed.

The file on the disc is a self-extracting ZIP filed. If you execute it and the result is WEBWIZ32.EXE, the software should load successfully.

WEB Wizard: The Duke of URL offers these features:

- Quick and easy home page creation
- Ability to specify home page title and subtitle
- Links and bullet lists
- Specify background colors and bitmaps
- Automatically creates a mailto: reference for your e-mail address
- Easily add text to your home page

For more product information, visit ARTA Media Groups Web site at: `http://www.halcyon.com/artamedia/webwizard`.

GIFCLIB. The product name is: gd GIF C Library. gd GIF C Library is a graphics library. It allows your code to quickly draw images complete with lines, arcs, text, multiple colors, cut and paste from other images, and flood fills, and write out the result as a .GIF file. This is particularly useful in World-Wide Web applications, where .GIF is the format used for inline images. For more product information, visit Boutell.Com's Web site at: `http://www.boutell.com/`.

MapEdit. The product name is: MapEdit. Mapedit is a WYSIWYG editor for imagemaps, available for Microsoft Windows and the X Window System. Version 2.24 for Windows 3.1, 95 and NT, as well as 10 variations of Unix, is now available. All these versions support client-side imagemaps, targeting of individual frames, and more. For more product information, visit Boutell.Com's Web site at: `http://www.boutell.com/`.

WebLater. The product name is WebLater. WebLater remembers every URL you copy to your Windows clipboard. Do people mention URLs to you constantly in e-mail and newsgroups and IRC? Would you rather look at them later instead of interrupting your work? That's what WebLater is there for. For Windows 3.1, 95, and NT. For more product information, visit Boutell.Com's Web site at: `http://www.boutell.com/`.

Wusage. The product name is: Wusage. Wusage is a statistics program that helps you determine the true impact of your Web server. It provides valuable marketing information with solid numbers about your Web site's popularity. For more product information, visit Boutell.Com's Web site at: `http://www.boutell.com/`.

PerlMUD. The product name is: PerlMUD. For real-time, interactive teleconferencing, this suite is a complete Internet Multi-User Dimension system written in Perl. The shareware file on the disc is a tar file for UNIX platforms running Perl 5. Establish your own electronic speakeasy, online chat, software support area, or corporate conference call environment. Cross-platform, and now with both "vanilla web" and Java clients. For more product information, visit Boutell.Com's Web site at: `http://www.boutell.com/`.

cgicLibr.   The product name is: cgic CGI Library. cgic CGI Library and it is an ANSI C-language library for the creation of CGI-based World Wide Web applications. cgic CGI Library should be compatible with any CGI-compliant server environment. For more product information, visit Boutell.Com's Web site at: `http://www.boutell.com/`.

Baklava.   The product name is: Baklava. Baklava is Boutell.Com's sprite graphics library for Java programmers. Baklava, a free software product, makes it easy to create animated objects in your Java programs. Give a sprite an image to display and a direction to move in; it'll let you know when it collides with another sprite, right down to the pixel. Many other conveniences for sprite programming are provided. High-level, powerful, fast. For more product information, visit Boutell.Com's Web site at: `http://www.boutell.com/`.

HTMLPro3.   The product name is: HTML Assistant Pro 3. It is a "point and click" editor for making World Wide Web pages. It runs under MS Windows (Version 3.x or Windows 95 but not Windows NT). Making a Web page is easy with HTML Assistant Pro 3. You begin with a blank screen and an idea and start typing. Mark up your page using push button tools so you don't have to remember complicated codes. Including hypertext links (highlighted words that link your page to other Web pages), is simply a matter of copying and pasting the URL (Uniform Resource Locator) for the page you want to point to. Whatever you want to do—share interests or research, advertise your product or service, or publish your ideas, HTML Assistant Pro 3 gets you on the Web easily and quickly. For more product information, visit Brooklyn North Software's Web site at: `http://www. brooknorth.com/`.

HTML_97.   The product name is: HTML Assistant Pro 97. HTML Assistant Pro 97 is the "point and click" editor for making World Wide Web pages. It runs under Microsoft's Windows 95/NT 4.0. You begin with a blank screen and an idea and then start typing. Or convert your existing word processor document to HTML in seconds using our powerful RTF-HTML Instant Converter. Mark up your page using push button tools so you don't have to remember complicated codes. Add Java, Image Maps, Frames, Multimedia, Active X, Tables, Forms, Fonts, the latest and greatest web page enhancements. The customizable Multiple User Tool Bars mean that the program will never be out of date! Whatever you want to do—share interests or research, advertise your product or service, or publish your ideas, HTML Assistant Pro 97 will get you on the Web easier and faster than you ever thought possible! For more product information, visit Brooklyn North Software's Web site at: `http://www.brooknorth.com/`.

URL_Grab.   The product name is: URL Grabber 95. URL Grabber 95 is a small floating tool bar that resides on your MS Windows 95 desktop. With URL Grabber 95 it's easy to "grab" and file URLs from news groups, email messages and other sources, as you are reading them. With a "click" of a mouse, URL Grabber 95 will automatically convert a collection of URLs to active WWW links on an HTML page. For more product information, visit Brooklyn North Software's Web site at: `http://www.brooknorth.com/`.

JDPro.   The product name is: JDesignerPro. Use JDesignerPro to create intranet and Internet Java database applications. Run a live demo, view screen shots, learn about its exciting features and more. JDesignerPro is the Java system which combines both the development environment and deployment system in a single, integrated package. For more product information, visit Bulletproof Software's Web site at: `http://www.bulletproof.com/`.

Alibaba.   The product name is: Alibaba. Alibaba is a Web server product for Windows 95 or Windows NT sold and supported by Computer Software Manufaktur. This is only a short list of Alibaba features available, please look through their manual (also on this CD-ROM) for a complete description of all available features.

Multithreaded High Performance WWW Server; Implemented as NT system service; HTTP 1.0 protocol; SSL Security; Directory listings; CGI (DOS-CGI, WINCGI 1.3, 32bit CGI, DLL interface and ISAPI); GET, POST and HEAD commands; Configurable network port; Multiple Server adresses (Multihoming) (only under NT); Directory ignores; Aliases; Icon extensions for directory listings; Definable Mimetypes; Access logging (Common Logformat 1.2); Error logging with selectable levels; Extended logfiles; Configurable error messages; ImageMaps (NCSA including points and CERN format); Integrated or external image mapper; HTTP access control (by Users, Groups and Sites); Disallow clients; AliAdmin for easy server administration; Remote administration (via NT and via TCP); AliAuth for access and general document administration; File redirection; ISINDEX support; Automatic start of a command script at server startup; Footer and Header (appends automatically a footer to every HTML page); Online statistic, used together with footers; Built-in Server Side Includes with many extensions (like page counters); Server PUSH; Connection Keep-Alive support; Internal and external redirections; Netscape Cookie support; Uninstaller.

For more product information, visit Computer Software Manufaktur's Web site at: `http://www.csm-usa.com/`.

EMWAC.   The product name is EMWAC. EMWAC is a Web server product for Windows NT developed and supported by the Edinburg University, in Edinburg, England. For more product information, visit Edinburg University's Web site at: `http://www.ed.ac.uk/`.

DBArtisan.   The product name is: DBArtisan. DBArtisan is a database administration tool for managing multiple Sybase and Microsoft SQL Servers from a single desktop. The 30-day version on our disc runs under Windows 95. Its unmatched functionality and ease-of-use will help you raise the reliability and availability of your distributed databases. For more product information, visit Embarcadero Technologies Web site at: `http://www.embarcadero.com/`.

ERstudio.   The product name is: ER/Studio. ER/Studio is an Entity Relationship (E-R) Diagramming tool that allows you to design logical and physical data models for client/server and web applications as well as create star-schema models for data marts and enterprise-wide data warehouses.

ER/Studio can generate physical schemas for all major databases as well as reverse engineer existing database schemas into E-R diagrams. ER/Studio data models are database independent. They can be converted automatically from one database platform to another using ER/Studio's powerful data type mapping facilities. The result is faster application development, better data integrity and high performance database designs. For more product information, visit Embarcadero Technologies Web site at: `http://www.embarcadero.com/`.

INET_Creatr.   The product name is: Internet Creator. Internet Creator was developed with the small to medium sized business in mind. The trial version on the CD is a Windows 95 version. It is capable of producing any type of Web site, but has special tools that allow businesses to setup an online catalog or store quickly and easily. The program includes powerful site setup wizards that can collect information about your business, then setup business tools like e-mail based ordering, a shopping basket ordering module, payment and shipping choices, and a sophisticated searching capability. For more product information, visit Forman Interactive's Web site at: `http://www.formaninteractive.com/`.

FolkWeb.   The product name is: FolkWeb Server. FolkWeb Server is shareware that you can try for 30 days before registering. It is a Web server that has the following features:

> Supports Windows NT 3.5 or Windows 95; WIN 32 Multithreading where each connection has a dedicated thread; HTTP 1.0 protocol compliant; Supports GET, HEAD and POST request methods; Supports Content negotiation; Uses built-in NCSA compatible clickable Image-Maps; Uses built-in Database connectivity so that you can publish your Databases without writing a single line of CGI code; Supports Windows CGI/1.2 protocol; Supports ISAPI protocol; Uses GUI based control application for server settings with online help; Supports URL to Path mapping(aliasing); Supports Extension to MIME type mapping; Supports Document to URL redirection; Access Logging; Error Logging; Access Authentication by users or groups; Can change access realms without restarting server; Supports IP filtering; Built-in and configured URLs; Uses built-in Directory listing with image and header extensions; Automatic backing of log files; Database connectivity extensions: adding new records; Change all settings without reloading the server; Capability to run FolkWeb Control Panel from the server; Customized DB reports (background, headnote, footnote, logo); Customized directory listing (background, headnote, footnote, logo); CGI 1.1 support (not to be confused with Windows CGI/1.1 and 1.2 which already supported); Perl CGI 1.1 support; Fully NCSA compliant log files; Improved documentation.

For more product information, visit ILAR Concepts Web site at: `http://www.ilar.com/`.

WebMania.   The product name is: WebMania!. WebMania! is a full-featured shareware HTML editor which includes unparalleled support for Frames, Forms, and Client-Side Image Maps! It also includes 60 user-programmable toolbar buttons, which allow you to add new HTML tags as you learn them, and/or as HTML standards evolve. For this reason alone, WebMania! will NEVER become obsolete! ***New for version 2.0—

SpellChecker, generate CGI forms and Perl scripts, as well as mailto forms, open and edit multiple documents!! Much, much more! You must have VBRun 300.DLL to run this program. If not, look in the transcender program on the CD for the file. For more product information, visit Q&D Software Developments Web site at: `http://www.q-d.com/`.

WebForms. The product name is: WebForms. The WebForms shareware lets you create your own forms which you can link to your home page, allowing you to conduct surveys, collect orders for your products, anything you can think of! Responses are automatically sent to your mailbox, then read by WebFormsTM and collected in a Response Database! It's all controlled by YOU, and all you need is an e-mail address! No CGI?? No problem!! WebForms can handle your forms with or without CGI!! This new version of WebFormsTM contains some fantastic new features, including CGI form and Perl script generation! You must have VBRun 300.DLL to run this program. If not, look in the transcender program on the CD for the file. For more product information, visit Q&D Software Developments Web site at: `http://www. q-d.com/`.

ShowBase. The product name is: ShowBase. Showbase lets you put your database on the Web without programming, you can use ShowBase to index your data and create an interface that provides keyword searching as well as hypertext browsing. The search interface is simple, easy to use, and customizable. As well, you can customize the output to suit your needs. ShowBase supports ODBC compliant databases as well as multimedia files, and is compatible with most Web servers and platforms. When you install the software, you will be prompted for a serial number. The serial number to use for this trial version of the product is: 153256235044582. For more product information, visit Show-Base Inc.'s Web site at: `http://www.showbase.com/`.

Transcender. The product name is: Access Cert 7.0. You will see two folders on the CD: AccessCert and transcender. This Transcender software product is a timed, predictive simulation of the Microsoft Access 97 certification exam. Using it, you will be certain that you are prepared to pass Microsoft's certification exam for MS Access 97. This product offers multiple, full-length exams, complete with explanations of the answers. Most importantly, the sample exams are up-to-date and representative of the real thing. So if you can pass one of our full exams on your first try, you should be ready to tackle Microsoft's exam. For more product information, visit Transcender Corporations Web site at: `http://www.transcender.com/`.

WebMedia. The product name is: Web Media Publisher Pro. It is a Web site development product that boasts the following features:

> 32 Bit; HTML 3.2, Netscape, and MSIE features; Spell Checker; FTP File Upload; Preview Images while adding to Document; Internal Web Browser; Easy Tables Creation; Easy Forms Creation with Preview; Easy Frames Creation; Full JAVA and Shockwave support; User Definable Toolbars; Multi-file Search and Replace; WYSIWYG Background text and background color selection; Target Windows; Default HTML Template; DDE control of Netscape and MS Explorer; Import and Convert NCSA Image Maps in HTML; Convert files between Macintosh, UNIX and DOS format; Unlimited file size; Extended Character List; Choose Font Colors, Size and Face Quickly and Easily; Drag and Drop text editing; Colored HTML tags; Find

and Replace; Relative Path Names; Web Timer; Auto Convert typed foreign characters into HTML Character Entities.

For more product information, visit Web Media Incorporated's Web site at: `http://www.wbmedia.com/`.

CGILIB.   The product is a Perl language library whose name is: cgi-lib.pl. The cgi-lib.pl library has become the de facto standard library for creating Common Gateway Interface (CGI) scripts in the Perl language. Welcome to the official Web site for cgi-lib.pl, with the most up-to-date releases of the library.

The cgi-lib.pl library makes CGI scripting in Perl easy enough for anyone to process forms and create dynamic Web content. The library has the following features:

Extremely simple to learn and easy to use; Designed for operation under Perl5 and Perl4; Very efficient; Compatibility with all CGI interactions, including File Upload; Convenient utility functions; Compatible with Perl5 security features such as taint, warnings (command line options -Tw) and use strict; Debugging facilities; Good starting point for migration to more sophisticated libraries.

For more product information, visit Steven Brenner's Web site at: `http://www.bio.cam.ac.uk/cgi-lib/`.

CGIHTML.   The product name is CGIHTML. Cgihtml is a set of CGI and HTML routines written for C written by Eugene Eric Kim, eekim@eekim.com. It was named one of the top 2 CGI tools in the August, 1996 issue of PC Computing. For more product information, visit E.E. Kims Web site at: `http://www.eekim/`.

SQL_NAV.   The product name is: SQL Navigator. SQL Navigator is the revolutionary GUI tool for server-side database development and management. It provides an integrated environment for schema management and full life cycle support of stored procedure coding, testing and tuning. It was conceived, designed and developed by database developers and DBAs. This is a 30-day trial version. The installation script will prompt you for a password. You should use the password: **gallaxy**. Make sure you enter this password in lower-case characters. For more product information, visit Technosolutions Incorporated Web site at: `http://www.technosolutions.com/`.

Limits of Liability and Disclaimer of Warranty

The authors and publisher of this book have used their best efforts in preparing the CD-ROM and the programs contained in it. These efforts include the development, research, and testing of the theories and programs to determine their effectiveness. The authors and publisher make no warranty of any kind expressed or implied, with regard to these programs or the documentation contained in this book.

The authors and publisher shall not be liable in the event of incidental or consequential damages in connection with, or arising out of, the furnishing, performance, or use of the programs, associated instructions, and/or claims of productivity gains.

The programs on this CD and are presented "as-is." If you have problems running a program, you should contact the software manufacturer for help. Some of the software on this CD-ROM may be shareware; there may be additional charges (owed to the software authors/makers) incurred for the registration and continued use of the shareware. See individual program's README or VREADME.TXT files for more information.

Technical Support

Prentice Hall does not offer technical support for this software. However, if there is a problem with the media, you may obtain a replacement copy by e-mailing us with your problem at: `discexchange@phptr.com`.

APPENDIX B

Frequently Asked Questions

This appendix contains answers to some of the most frequently asked questions about the process of Web database application development. Although these questions and answers will not address *all* of the issues that you may have, you'll find that they provide answers to most of the basic questions you'll encounter. Here are the questions that are answered in this appendix:

- What is the Internet?
- What is the Web?
- What are intranets?
- What is a Web database and why have one?
- What types of databases are accessible in a Web database application?
- What are the advantages of web database applications for the user?
- What are the advantages to a company of building a Web database application?
- What is the role of databases in web applications?
- What are the components in a Web database application?
- What should I consider when choosing a programming language?
- What are some of the languages available to help me build a Web database application?

- What are Web database application development suites?
- What are some of the benefits and limitations to HTML?
- What is a CGI program?
- How does a CGI program fit in the architecture of a Web database application?
- How does data get passed from an HTML page to a CGI program?
- Are there any programming principles that I should be aware of when writing CGI programs?
- Where should security exist in a Web database application?
- What are some of the new features in Access 97 that are specific to Web database applications?
- What types of join relationships are recognized in Access 97?
- What types of objects are allowed on HTML forms?
- How can I format and submit a database query from within an HTML page?
- Why should you use custom CGI programs for database access?
- What is MIME?

What Is the Internet?

The Internet is a global network. It is the communications infrastructure by which our computers communicate with other computers attached to it. This network of computers, when applied on a global level, comprises a community that counts as its members people in nearly every country in the world.

What Is the Web?

Web applications share some common characteristics:

- Understand and use HTML as their display vehicle
- Use the bi-directional Client/Server model of data communications and information collection
- Provide facilities to access a variety of protocols, including HTTP, FTP, Telnet, and Gopher
- Use Uniform Resource Locators (URLs) for document and resource addressing

What Are Intranets?

Recently a new word has become popular when describing a segment of the Internet—*intranet*. An intranet is a private network inside a company or organization that uses the same kinds of software that you'd find on the public Internet, that it is targeted for internal use only. Because of their secure nature (they can usually only be accessed by employees of the company that has the intranet), intranets were the first vehicles for development and deployment of Web database applications.

Intranets, like Internets, are not defined by physical or geographical boundaries. Anyone with a Web browser can access a corporate intranet site from anywhere in the world—although only those people who have security permissions are allowed to enter. A intranet site is usually identified in the same way that an Internet site is identified—by an URL.

What Is a Web Database and Why Have One?

A Web database is not too different from a non-Web database—the distinguishing characteristics are that Web databases are accessed from a Web Browser and Web databases can have no data components that reside on the user's machine. A Web database is part of an application that is deployed over either the Internet (for external user's access) or a corporate intranet (for internal use only). Web databases come in many different varieties such as Microsoft Access 97, Oracle, Sybase, Informix, DB2, and many others.

What Types of Databases Are Accessible in a Web Database Application?

There are four types of databases that are accessible from within a Web database application. These are:

Flat-file database—This is the oldest type of database, and is often referred to as a spreadsheet database. A distinguishing characteristic of a flat-file database is that columns and rows are used to collect and store small and discrete pieces of information into a table.

Relational database—This is a database that contains one or more database tables in which one or more columns of information are related to one or more columns of information in another table. Relational databases hold great promise for Web database application development. They are fast, extremely efficient, and flexible. They are also able to be migrated easily from one physical location to another and most of today's RDBMS vendors provide synchronization facilities in their products to ensure that data which resides in multiple locations is kept in sync automatically (well, pretty much automatically!).

Object-oriented database—An OO database consists of columns and rows, very similar to flat-file and relational databases. Each object in the database has one of three classes; number, text, and date. There are processes (attributes) the database stores for each class of data. For example, it allows manipulation of data stored as dates (i.e., adding a month or subtracting 72 hours), but not data stored as text.

Hybrid database—A hybrid database is considered by many to be the aggregation of the best components and features of RDBMS and OODBMS products. Hybrid databases handle data that RDBMS products can use, as well as non-text items such as pictures, audio/video clips, etc. Hybrid databases allow you to process complex queries.

What Are the Advantages of Web Database Applications for the User?

There are two groups of users of Web database applications. These are people who access your Web database application over the Internet, and the employees of a corporation that has a Web database application accessed over its intranet.

The advantages of a Web database application deployed over the internet are:

- A broader reach than conventional advertising or marketing
- Automated sales force
- Access to company information from the comforts of home (or the workplace)
- Ability to interface with the company data without having to purchase expensive equipment or software

The advantages of Web database applications to intranet users are summarized as:

- Graphical user interfaces to corporate data
- Access to up-to-date company information
- Greater opportunity to interact with other people, departments, and technologies within the company
- Ability to customize their browsers to meet their specific needs
- Integration of the Web database application with other applications running on their machines

What Are the Advantages to a Company of Building a Web Database Application?

The number one reason why a company should do business on the Web by building and deploying a Web database application is that if they don't, with all other competitive issues being equal, their competition will out-perform them. The following list describes some of the reasons why this is the case.

Expanded Reach—On the Web, you can make a sales presentation or put promotional material in the hands of interested people while all your salespeople are sound asleep in their beds. Orders can be taken and product queued for shipment before your first cup of coffee in the morning. You no longer have to pony up the $3–$4k it costs to send a salesperson around the world to meet with customers.

Corporate Image Enhancement—In addition to the marketing and sales opportunities doing business on the Web present, there is a lot of opportunity to conduct Public Relations activities on the Web—thereby performing image enhancement. This includes: corporate mission statement, goals, philosophies, charities to which it donates, and testimonials of what a great company it is to do business with and work for.

Improved Customer Service—Customers are demanding more from the companies they do business with. This includes:

- More product choices
- Less expensive product and services
- Increased customer service

Regarding the last item, the Web provides a tremendous opportunity to provide customer service that is not only very responsive but one of the least expensive to implement.

Lead Generation—When a person browses your Web site, you can track and extract their log-in ID. You know that person is at least a candidate customer—and with the log-in ID you can send follow-up sales and marketing material. If a person downloads something from your Web site that can be accessed and retrieved for free, then you know you have a qualified lead. You can followup on that lead with whatever you decide. The point is that it has incrementally cost you very little to generate this lead.

Product/Service Delivery Channel—The Web represents a new delivery channel for products and services. It is not the only channel for most companies, but it is one that deserves attention. In the coming years, as companies become more astute at doing business on the Web, we will see the recognition that the Web is a viable and significant delivery channel for products and services.

Reduce Operating Expenses—Companies are operating with profit margins that are thinner today than ever before. Doing business on the Web allows companies to reduce their operating expenses by maintaining current sales volumes while decreasing staff counts and expenses, reducing the number of people who work in support, reducing the cost of marketing, reducing public relations costs, and by culling unprofitable products and services due to the improved data on which products and services are profitable and which are not.

Test Marketing—The Web is a great place for a company to "test market" a number of things. These include new products, new services, and new marketing campaigns.

What Is the Role of Databases in Web Applications?

Although you can think of one or more ways that *your* company could make use of a database in its Web applications, the following list is a good introduction.

- Inter-business agreement and document processing, such as ordering, purchasing, invoicing, and automated payment processing.
- Demographics, such as customer, supplier, and business partner profiles that are accumulated and used to improve and customize customer services.
- Customer status and account management used to manage past purchase history, and predict future purchase patterns.

- Establishment and maintenance of customer profiles for use in finely tailored advertising and sales campaigns.

- Inventory management and status to reduce cash reserves held in inventory, to product online and interactive catalogs, to interface with inventory control systems, and to provide virtual shopping malls.

- Sales tracking and call management to monitor, track, and increase the effectiveness of the sales force and various marketing campaigns.

- Technical product specifications that are available to customers and field staff to search for product specifications, parts lists, troubleshooting information, and pricing.

What Are the Components in a Web Database Application?

There are five major components in a Web database application environment. These five components are:

Web Server—The Web server is the software component that reacts to and interfaces with Web browser/client. It has no ability to create or update Web pages or documents. Rather, it reads a request for information coming to it from a Web browser, usually in the form of an URL, locates the requested page, and sends the requested page back to the Web browser.

Application Server—The role of the Application Server is to sit between the Web server and RDBMS and is responsible for maintaining an open connection between the Web server and the RDBMS at all times.

Web Browser/Client—The Web browser/client is the software that runs on a client machine and performs necessary communication functions. The main functions performed by Web browsers/clients are to establish and maintain communications with a Web server, pass user requests and data to the Web server, display information received from a Web server, and to view files not originating from a Web server.

CGI Program—The CGI program, an optional component, is intended mainly to interact with the Web server by using one of a number of different standards. Its primary method of Web server interaction is to connect the Web server to external programs.

Relational DataBase Management System (RDBMS)—The purpose of the RDBMS package is to manage, safeguard, and control the data that is accessed by the Web database application.

What Should I Consider When Choosing a Programming Language?

The decision as to which programming language to use to develop your Web application is not much different from the decision as to which programming language to use to develop any other application. It helps to view a Web database application as just another application development project. It has its own unique set of factors that must be evaluated, but the same statement can be made about any development project.

There are a number of items to consider to determine which is the best programming language to use. These items are:

Skillset of Developers—A knowledge of the skills required for the project and what skills exist in current staff

Scope of the Project—An awareness of the scope of the project and the range of functions and capabilities of the various programming languages

Application Interfaces—Web database applications will interface to either existing or newly created databases as well as potentially to other applications used by the company.

Availability of Support Tools—Regardless of the skills of your developers against the requirements of the task, it is a very valuable investment of time to address the issue of support tool requirements and availability.

Database Interfaces—The type and number of databases your Web database application will access and interface with is an important factor in determining what language you select.

Platforms Application Will Run On—If you are writing an application where components of that application are distributed to a client's machine, then you must be aware of the platforms that run on those machines.

What Are Some of the Languages Available to Help Me Build a Web Database Application?

Although this is not a comprehensive list (new tools and languages are being brought to market at a feverish pace) it is comprehensive in terms of the languages that comprise at least 98% of all the code written in programming languages to create Web database applications. The most popular languages are: C, C++, COBOL, Java, JavaScript, Perl, Power-Builder, Shell Script, Visual Basic, and Visual Basic Script.

What Are Web Database Application Development Suites?

Application development suites are some of the quickest growing segments in the Web market. Companies, both customers and suppliers alike, learned in the early 1990s that a development tool used in isolation and detached from other tools often becomes a little used tool. Application suites remedy this problem by offering a selection of tools used to develop Web applications. For example, most application development suites include the following integrated components: WYSIWYG development interface, an Image Map editor, the ability to write Visual Basic or JavaScript scripts, a basic compiler, a debugger, a Web publishing tool, an application server, and a freeware or evaluation copy of a Web server.

What Are Some of the Benefits and Limitations to HTML?

Although you really don't have much of a choice when deciding to build a Web database application (you *really should* use HTML), some of the benefits available by using HTML are: a rapid development environment, extensive cross-platform support, and support for multiple types of media included on the Web pages.

Like everything else in the world of computing, HTML is not free from limitations. Although the standard is rapidly evolving to remove many of these limitations, the day will probably never come when this tool is free from limitations. The limitations of HTML as a Web page development tool are: limited user-input capabilities, limited page layout capabilities, and limited programmatic capabilities.

What Is a CGI Program?

CGI programs, or scripts (the terms are used interchangeably) are executable files—programs written, compiled, and linked in one of a number of different languages. The most common language for a CGI program is Perl, but other languages include C, C++, Java, JavaScript, Visual Basic, PowerBuilder, etc. Perl's dominance as a CGI development language has recently been challenged not only by many of these other languages but also by Web development tools.

As you know, HTML has no facilities to directly query a database. Through CGI, this capability exists. By utilizing CGI scripts, a request can be sent from within HTML, and processed by the HTTP server, to query the database for specific information, and then display the result set in dynamically built HTML code. With this capability, there is no need to have to change a Web page manually whenever data on that page changes.

How Does a CGI Program Fit in the Architecture of a Web Database Application?

A CGI program is a major component in a Web database application. To understand how it fits in the architecture of the application you need to understand how all the pieces of a Web database application work together. This process is described below.

Step 1: A user, accessing a browser, sends a request to a server via HTML. This HTML includes a request to execute a CGI program, as well as any parameters the CGI program might need.

Step 2: The server receives the request from the browser, processes the HTML, and encounters the request to execute a CGI program. The server initiates the CGI program's execution by calling it and passing it any parameters that were received from the browser.

Step 3: The CGI program executes. In its execution, it may:
- Access no other resources
- Access databases either locally or remotely
- Access other applications or initiate the execution of other programs
- Access other network resources

Step 4: The server receives a result set from the CGI program if one is returned, and sends the data and/or response back to the browser via HTML.

Step 5: The browser receives the HTML sent to it from the server and formats and displays the data received.

How Does Data Get Passed from an HTML Page to a CGI Program?

There are a number of ways that a browser can transmit data strings to a CGI program, with the following three being the most popular. These are GET, ISINDEX, and POST. Each of these are discussed in detail in Chapters 7 and 13 of this book.

Are There Any Programming Principles That I Should Be Aware of When Writing CGI Programs?

The short answer is, "Yes." Assuming you are already a programmer, well schooled in sound programming techniques, there are a few issues unique to CGI programming of which you need to be aware. These are described as application performance, the use of comments, the HTTP protocol and specifications you are supporting in the application, the choice of language and its particular syntax conventions, naming conventions that are standards for the language, the use of a separate development site from the production site, the standards that exist within your company for the development of applications, and the user of libraries as a productivity and system-quality aid.

Where Should Security Exist in a Web Database Application?

The perils of Web commerce have been discussed at length in the media. As a result of all the attention paid to the subject historically, the development and deployment of commercial Web sites is much less dangerous. There are four primary areas where you must ensure that proper security safeguards are in place to protect your data and resources. These four areas are:

Physical—This is perhaps the easiest component area to ensure safety in that the physical security of computers and computing devices has been an issue of concern to MIS managers for a number of years.

Software—Your software is much more vulnerable on a Web site than in almost any other type of delivery method. The Web is a very "open" environment. If you see a graphic on a Web page, or an applet that you'd like, it's easy (albeit illegal) to snag it. Because of this, you must be keenly aware of the security issues which exist as you design your application.

System hacker!—The meaning of these words are clearly understood by even the most neophyte computer user. The consequences of a hacker breaching your system and causing damage of some sort could range in severity from annoyance to catastrophe. Even the variety of breach that is more annoying than anything else will cause you great embarrassment when your boss asks you how someone was able to break through the security layers and gain access to your system. Be warned, making your system too secure from hacker attack is something that would be very hard to do without you making it cumbersome or difficult for the good people to access.

Data—As much as "Protect Yourself" was a byword for the 1980s and 1990s, "Protect Your Data" will become an identifying phrase for the 1990s and beyond. An easy argument could be made for paying more attention to protecting the integrity and confidentiality of the data accessed by your Web database application than to the security of the system as a whole.

What Are Some of the New Features in Access 97 That Are Specific to Web Database Applications?

In Access 97, Microsoft added the following Internet and Web database application development support:

Hyperlink Datatype—Stores hyperlinks in database tables as a valid datatype.

Publish To The Web Wizard—An added `File|Save As HTML` submenu item allows you to save an Access 97 object as an HTML file, or as an optional IDC/HTX file. IDC and HTX are extensions used by the Microsoft Internet Information Server to identify files that include data source information and mapped returned data in field merge codes, respectively.

HTML Import Wizard—Allows you to efficiently import HTML files.

Internet Replication—Features in Access 95 have been enhanced to allow replication of databases over the Web via FTP.

What Types of Join Relationships Are Recognized in Access 97?

Access 97 recognizes three types of join relationships. These are:

Inner Join—This is the default type of join. It joins the two tables *only* when the values in the two joined fields are equal.

Left Join—This type of join takes all the records from the left-most table, regardless of the right-most table having any matching values in it.

Right Join—This type of join takes all the records in the right-most table, regardless of the left-most table having any matching values in it.

What Types of Objects Are Allowed on HTML Forms?

There are seven basic objects on an HTML form that you have available to receive input from users. These are: Checkbox, command buttons, list box, password, radio button, text, and text box.

How Can I Format and Submit a Database Query from within an HTML Page?

HTML specifications provide no direct method for querying a database. There are three main methods you can use to build database connectivity into your HTML form. These are:

Code-less interfaces—These are software toolsets that work in tandem with developer defined template files. The purpose of the templates is to define various views into the database and describe how data is to be displayed once it is retrieved. When these forms are incorporated into an HTML page and sent to the HTTP server for processing, they are processed by CGI programs that perform the actual querying and formatting of the data.

Custom CGI program—These are "gateway" programs that are specifically written to accept and process SQL queries. These programs receive the user's request for DBMS data, parse the user inputs and create a query to accommodate the user request, and dynamically create an HTML document that transmits the result set back to the user.

HTML embedded SQL extensions—These are special HTML extensions supplied by RDBMS and other tool vendors that provide a mechanism to embed SQL statements directly into the body of the HTML file that is passed from the user to the HTTP server. When received at the server, this HTML file is parsed to pull out the SQL statements that are subsequently passed to a CGI program.

Why Should You Use Custom CGI Programs for Database Access?

Custom CGI programs are the most common methods of accessing corporate databases, far eclipsing the other two methods described above. Although code-less interfaces and HTML embedded SQL extensions may someday catch up and surpass the popularity of custom CGI programs, this is not expected to happen for many years. When that time does come, the need and use for custom CGI programs will continue—in fact, it may never end. There will always be an inherent limit to the power and flexibility of code-less interfaces and HTML-embedded SQL extensions that custom CGI programs will exceed those limits. This is why all the major development toolkits provide API interfaces to more powerful languages.

What Is MIME?

MIME stands for Multipurpose Internet Mail Extension. It is a set of standards that specify both the type of file being sent from a Web component (either a Web server or browser) to another Web component as well as the method that should be used to turn that message back into its original form. To you, the person designing or building a Web database application, MIME allows you to incorporate the inclusion of audio, video, and multimedia elements in your application.

APPENDIX C

WWW Database Development Resources

T his appendix contains a list of the available resources accessible over the Internet that provide wonderful examples, documentation, freeware, demoware, or shareware, that will help you in the design and development of Web database applications. This is not an all-inclusive list, but it is certainly substantial enough so that you will get more than enough of what you need to get you moving nicely down the road.

The references are broken down into the following categories:

- Databases
- Programming Languages
- Other
- Reference Material
- Security
- Web Servers

Databases

A site developed and maintained by David Muir Sharnoff that is devoted to being a repository of free Web databases and tools:

```
http://cuiww.unige.ch/~scg/freedb/freedb.list.html
```

A site developed and offered by Bristol Database Resources, Inc. that provides access to a large number of demo applications written for a variety of RDBMS products:

```
http://bristol.onramp.net/
```

A site where you can download a copy of the Postgres95 Web database software:

```
http://s2.ftp.cs.berkeley.edu:8000/postgres95
```

A site where you can download a free copy of the Experimental Multimedia Database—MMDB:

```
http://www.univ.triests.it/cgi-bin/wwwwais
```

A site devoted to disseminating information and links to other commercial sites specific to Web Database Gateway products:

```
http://cscsun1.larc.nasa.gov/~beowulf/db/existing_products.html
```

A site devoted to providing sample scripts and examples of using Oraperl as a CGI/RDBMS interface:

```
http://www.nofc.forestry.ca/features/script.html
```

The Microrim Corporation site that is specific to their R:WEB product:

```
http://www.microrim.com/
```

Oracle Corporation's Web site where you can find copious amounts of information on not only the Oracle RDBMS family of products but related products as well:

```
http://www.oracle.com/
```

The Sybase Corporation's Web site where you can find abundant information on Sybase SQL Server:

```
http://www.sybase.com/products/internet/websql
```

The IBM Corporation site that offers a Web interface for its DB2 database:

```
http://as400.rochester.ibm.com/qdls/400home/ncc/webconn/db2www.htm
```

The Informix Corporation's Web site that is specific to their flagship Informix RDBMS product:

```
http://www.informix.com/informix/dbweb/grail/freeware.htm
```

The Microsoft Corporation Web site that is specific to their Visual FoxPro product:

```
http://www.microsoft.com/vfoxpro/
```

The Borland International site that is specific to dBASE version 5.0 for Windows:

```
http://www.borland.com/product/db/dbase/windbase.html
```

Another site devoted to disseminating information and links to other sites of interest specific to DbPerl, which is a database access applications programming language:

```
http://www.hermetica.com/technologia/dbi/
```

Newsgroup devoted to problem resolution with IBM DB2 databases:

```
news:comp.databases.ibm-db2
```

Newsgroup devoted to Informix database issues:

```
news:comp.databases.informix
```

Newsgroup designed to address issues specific to Microsoft Access:

```
news:comp.databases.ms-access
```

Newsgroup designed to deal with issues specific to the Microsoft SQL Server product:

```
news:comp.databases.ms-sqlserver
```

Newsgroup dealing with topics relating to Oracle SQL database products:

```
news:comp.databases.oracle
```

Newsgroup that offers discussion on Sybase SQL Server:

```
news:comp.databases.sybase
```

Newsgroup that deals with issues specific to the database aspects of Visual Basic:

```
news:comp.lang.basic.visual.database
```

Other

To learn more about SQL and the history of SQL, try these two URLs:

```
http://www.bf.rmit.edu.au/oracle/docs.html#tinalondon
http://waltz.ncsl.nist.gov/~len/sql_info.html
```

A great location to review what some view as standards for developing and using image maps:

```
http://hway.com/ihip/cside.html
```

You can grab a free copy of WinZip, the worlds leading file compression software from this site:

```
http://www.winzip.com/winzip/download.html
```

Macromedia Corporations site that includes Director and Shockwave, two tools useful in developing multimedia applications that might be deployed over the Internet:

```
http://www.macromedia.com
```

The site listed here lists graphics software that is available for downloading:

`http://sun1.bham.ac.uk/s.m.williams.bcm/images/viewers.html`

The following URL contains lists of other links for tips on HTML and graphics:

`http://maui.net/~mcculc/resource.htm`

The newsgroup listed below can help to provide answers to questions about HTML:

`news:com.infosystems.www.authoring.html`

Browsers treat certain HTML tags and tag pairs differently. To see a list of the differences among the various browsers, look at:

`http://www.colosys.net/~rscott/barb.htm`

EDP Markets is a company that makes extensive use of a Web database application to provide its services, which are to find people to fill technical positions for companies willing to pay a fee for this service:

`http://www.edpmarkets.com`

A good example of the use of an image map in a Web application:

`http://www.z100portland.com`

A site sponsored by GNN, a subsidiary of America Online, that provides a set of tools for browsing, authoring, and Web publishing:

`http://www.tools.gnn.com/download.html`

A site put together by Spider Technologies where you can try out a copy of Art Gallery, a Web site development tool:

`http://www.netdynamics.com/action`

The home page for the Edify Electronic Workforce product that is sold and supported by Edify Corporation:

`http://www.edify.com/`

The home page for the IQ Live Web product that is sold and supported by IQ Software, Inc.

`http://www.iqsc.com/`

The home page for Krakatoa, a Web search tool developed and sold by CADIS, Incorporated:

`http://www.cadis.com/`

The web page for LivePAGE, an open, non-proprietary text and information management software developed and sold by Netscape Communications:

```
http://www.netscape.com/comprod/products/tools/
```

The web page for Live Wire and Live Wire Pro, two products developed and sold by Netscape Communications to enable novice users to create and manage Web content, Web sites, and live online Web applications for intranets and the Internet:

```
http://www.netscape.com/comprod/products/tools/
```

The web page for FrontPage, Microsoft Corporation's offering for a Web application development suite:

```
http://www.microsoft.com/frontpage/
```

The web pages for Oracle Designer 2000 and Oracle Developer 2000 Oracle Corporation's Web application development tool suite offerings:

```
http://www.oracle.com/products/tools/des2k/
http://www.oracle.com/products/tools/dev2k/
```

The Web page for Tango, the Web database application development suite from Everywhere Development Corporation:

```
http://www.everyware.com/products/tango/
```

The home page for Webdbc, from Stormcloud Development Corporation, which is a Web database application development suite:

```
http://www.ndev.com/
```

The home page for WebHub from HREF Tools Corporation, which is technology that provides a complete object oriented framework for industrial strength web application development.

```
http://www.href.com/
```

The home page for Webinator, the product from Thunderstone Corporation that is billed as being a Web walking and indexing package that will allow a Web site administrator to create and provide a high quality retrieval interface to collections of HTML documents.

```
http://www.thunderstone.com/
```

The home page for Web Objects, the development tool suite from NeXT Software that is described as being an environment for developing and deploying World Wide Web applications:

```
http://www.next.com/webobjects/
```

Microsoft Corporation keeps a pretty comprehensive collection of ODBC drivers on its Web site at the following URL:

```
http://www.microsoft.com/odbc/
```

Programming Languages

A relatively new scripting language that is beginning to gain a loyal following is named Eva. You can find out all about this language and get a demo copy of the product from:

```
http://www.techware.com
```

Micro Focus LTD., a PC-based COBOL language tool developer with U.S. headquarters in Palo Alto, California:

```
http://www.microfocus.com
```

The site developed by Netscape Communications that provides a brief introduction to JavaScript and a number of examples and pointers to other relevant JavaScript sites:

```
http://home.netscape.com/comprod/products/navigator/version_3.0/script/
index.html
```

Netscape Communication's site where you can find the official documentation and reference materials for JavaScript:

```
http://home.netscape.com/eng/mozilla/gold/handbook/javascript/index.html
```

A site where you can find a growing number of tutorials that help to learn JavaScript:

```
http://outworld.compuserve.com/homepages/vood/script.htm
```

Directory of Java-related products, objects, and sites:

```
http://www.gamelan.com/
```

A couple of newsgroups devoted to Java and JavaScript:

```
news:comp.lang.java
news:comp.lang.javascript
```

The home page for Microsoft Access 97:

```
http://www.microsoft.com/msaccess.
```

The home page for Information Analytics and its 4W Publisher and 4W Publisher Pro products:

```
http://www.4w.com/4wpublisher/
```

The home page for the Amazon product that is sold by Intelligent Environments:

```
http://www.ieinc.com/
```

The home page for the Speedware product that is sold by Speedware Toronto:

`http://www.speedware.com/`

The home page for the Centura Web Data Publisher product that is sold by Centura Software:

`http://www.centurasoft.com/`

The home page for the Delphi product that is sold and supported by Borland International:

`http://www.borland.com/delphi/`

The home page for the Foxweb product that is sold and supported by Eon Technologies.

`http://www.foxweb.com/`

To find out about the cgic programming language:

`http://www.boutell.com/cgic/`

A great place to try out and get resource information about CGI++ is:

`http://sweetbay.will.uiuc.edu/cgi++`

A great resource if you are planning on using Visual Basic as a CGI language is:

`http://website.ora.com/devcorner/db-src/index.html`

The home page for HAHT Software, the company that has developed and sells the HAHTsite IDE product:

`http://www.haht.com/`

Oracle Corporation's web page devoted to Oracle Power Objects, which is its development tool that is targeted to facilitate Web application development:

`http://www.oracle.com/products/tools/power_objects/`

The home page for PowerBuilder, the product offering of Sybase Incorporated that is a programming language to build Web applications:

`http://www.powersoft.com/products/devtools/pb50/`

Ventana's software archive that contains a slew of information you should be interested in if you are using PowerBuilder:

`http://www.vmedia.com/alternate/vvc/onlcomp/powerbuilder/software.html`

Newsgroup devoted to writing CGI scripts for the Web:

`news:comp.infosystems.www.authoring.cgi`

Newsgroup devoted to writing HTML:

`news:comp.infosystems.www.authoring.html`

Newsgroup devoted to using images and image maps on the Web:

`news:comp.infosystems.www.authoring.images`

The web page for Software Engine, the flagship product from Software Engines, Inc.:

`http://www.engine.com/`

Reference Material

The Web developer's virtual library:

`http://www.stars.com/`

A site maintained by Jeff Rowe that deals with Web database tools and techniques:

`http://cscsun1.larc.nasa.gov/~beowulf/db/existing_products.html`

A listing of the Internet Service Providers (ISPs) located around the world can be found at:

`http://www.thelist.com/`

Billed as the largest online source of books, both technical and non-technical, this is an URL that you'll want to bookmark:

`http://www.amazon.com`

This site gives information on how to register a domain name:

`http://www.internic.net`

The JAVA White paper that describes the underlying principles of its development and intended use:

`http://www.javasoft.com/nav/read/whitepapers.`

For those of you who are highly interested in the underpinnings of the Java language specification, you can find this at:

`http://www.javasoft.com/nav/read/index.html`

A site developed by Interface Technologies Corporation that is devoted to providing a series of articles and tutorials to help with the design and development of a Web site:

`http://www.iftech.com/classes/webdev/webdev0.htm`

A site devoted to image maps and how to create and use them in Web applications:

`http://hoohoo.ncsa.uiuc.edu/docs/tutorials/imagemapping.html.`

A Yahoo site developed and maintained exclusively for CGI programmers:

```
http://www.yahoo.com/computers_and_internet/internet/world_wide_web/cgi_
common_gateway_interface/index.html
```

The URL for Web Techniques magazine:

```
http://webtechniques.com/
```

An electronic magazine for the Java community published by IDG Communications:

```
http://www.javaworld.com/
```

A site that gives information about how to develop a searchable database site and also includes references to a number of other sites focused on providing information specific to Web database application development:

```
http://www2.ncsu.edu/bae/people/faculty/walker/hotlist/isindex.html
```

This is a tutorial made available by the same people who sell WebSite, a Web server product that is very popular in small to medium sized installations:

```
http://solo.dc3.com/db-src/index.html
```

A newsgroup devoted to the Perl CGI programming language:

```
news:comp.lang.perl
```

The Web Manual of Style, written by Patrick Lynch, can be found at:

```
http://info.med.yale.edu/caim/StyleManual_Top.html
```

A Web site sponsored by Ohio State University and dedicated to espousing information about MIME:

```
http://www.cis.ohio.state.edu/hypertext/faq/usenet/mail/mime-faq/top.html
```

A Web site developed by Indiana State University and dedicated to MIME:

```
http://www.cs.indiana.edu/docproject/mail/mime.html
```

A couple of areas on the Netscape Communications Corporation Web site devoted to MIME:

```
http://www.netscape.com/assist/helper_apps/media-types.html
http://www.netscape.com/assist/helper_apps/what-is-mime.html
```

Security

A site sponsored by Netscape Communications that deals specifically with Secure Sockets Layer (SSL):

```
http://www.netscape.com/newsref/std/ssl.html
```

Take a look at this URL if you're interested in Web security:

`http://www.nortel.com/entrust/certificates/primer.html`

A site that is specific to CGI security is:

`http://www.primus.com/staff/paulp/cgi_security`

A Web site with a substantial amount of information on the subject of CGI security is available at:

`http://www.cerf.net/~paulp/cgi_security/`

A FAQ presented by Oxford University on firewalls and their use in Internet security:

`http://www.lib.ox.ac.uk/internet/news/faq/archive/firewalls-faq.html`

A WWW security FAQ presented by Compuserv:

`http://ourworld.compuserve.com/homepages/perthes/wwwsecur.htm`

Final Quarterly Report of the UKERNA Secure Email Project:

`http://www.tech.ukerna.ac.uk/pgp/secemail/q4.html`

Internet Firewalls Frequently Asked Questions from the V-One Company:

`http://www.v-one.com/pubs/fw-faq/faq.html`

One of the places where hackers meet that contains a huge collection of hacking and related links.

`http://incyberspace.com/woodstok/hack/`

Web Servers

The NCSA HTTP Server:

`http://hoohoo.ncsa.uiuc.edu/`

The home page for the A-XOrion Database Server product offered by Clark Internet Services:

`http://www.clark.net/infouser/`

The home page for the dbWeb product that is now sold and supported by Microsoft Corporation:

`http://www.microsoft.com/intdev/dbweb/`

Microsoft Corporation includes a copy of its Internet Information Server (IIS) in its Windows NT version 4.0. If you have an earlier version of Windows NT, you can download a copy of IIS from:

`http://www.microsoft.com/infoserv`

The home page for the DynaWeb product that is sold and supported by Inso Corporation:

`http://dynabase.ebt.com/dbproduct/index.htm`

The home page for the Personal Web Site Toolbox, a tool offered by W3.Com Incorporated:

`http://www.w3.com/`

The web page for Sapphire Web, the product offering from Bluestone Software that facilitates the creation and management of a Web site:

`http://www.bluestone.com/`

The following URLs list places where you can find out more about and possibly download demoware versions of server logging tools:

`http://www.eit.com/software/getstats/getstats.html`
`http://www.boutell.com/wusage`
`http://www.openmarket.com/products/webreport.html`

Newsgroup devoted to issues specific to Web servers:

`news:comp.infosystems.www.servers.misc`

The web page for SiteBase, the Web server product offering from Cykic Software:

`http://www.cykic.com/`

Index

LICENSE AGREEMENT AND LIMITED WARRANTY

READ THE FOLLOWING TERMS AND CONDITIONS CAREFULLY BEFORE OPENING THIS DISK PACKAGE. THIS LEGAL DOCUMENT IS AN AGREEMENT BETWEEN YOU AND PRENTICE-HALL, INC. (THE "COMPANY"). BY OPENING THIS SEALED DISK PACKAGE, YOU ARE AGREEING TO BE BOUND BY THESE TERMS AND CONDITIONS. IF YOU DO NOT AGREE WITH THESE TERMS AND CONDITIONS, DO NOT OPEN THE DISK PACKAGE. PROMPTLY RETURN THE UNOPENED DISK PACKAGE AND ALL ACCOMPANYING ITEMS TO THE PLACE YOU OBTAINED THEM FOR A FULL REFUND OF ANY SUMS YOU HAVE PAID.

1. **GRANT OF LICENSE:** In consideration of your payment of the license fee, which is part of the price you paid for this product, and your agreement to abide by the terms and conditions of this Agreement, the Company grants to you a nonexclusive right to use and display the copy of the enclosed software program (hereinafter the "SOFTWARE") on a single computer (i.e., with a single CPU) at a single location so long as you comply with the terms of this Agreement. The Company reserves all rights not expressly granted to you under this Agreement.

2. **OWNERSHIP OF SOFTWARE:** You own only the magnetic or physical media (the enclosed disks) on which the SOFTWARE is recorded or fixed, but the Company retains all the rights, title, and ownership to the SOFTWARE recorded on the original disk copy(ies) and all subsequent copies of the SOFTWARE, regardless of the form or media on which the original or other copies may exist. This license is not a sale of the original SOFTWARE or any copy to you.

3. **COPY RESTRICTIONS:** This SOFTWARE and the accompanying printed materials and user manual (the "Documentation") are the subject of copyright. You may not copy the Documentation or the SOFTWARE, except that you may make a single copy of the SOFTWARE for backup or archival purposes only. You may be held legally responsible for any copying or copyright infringement which is caused or encouraged by your failure to abide by the terms of this restriction.

4. **USE RESTRICTIONS:** You may not network the SOFTWARE or otherwise use it on more than one computer or computer terminal at the same time. You may physically transfer the SOFTWARE from one computer to another provided that the SOFTWARE is used on only one computer at a time. You may not distribute copies of the SOFTWARE or Documentation to others. You may not reverse engineer, disassemble, decompile, modify, adapt, translate, or create derivative works based on the SOFTWARE or the Documentation without the prior written consent of the Company.

5. **TRANSFER RESTRICTIONS:** The enclosed SOFTWARE is licensed only to you and may not be transferred to any one else without the prior written consent of the Company. Any unauthorized transfer of the SOFTWARE shall result in the immediate termination of this Agreement.

6. **TERMINATION:** This license is effective until terminated. This license will terminate automatically without notice from the Company and become null and void if you fail to comply with any provisions or limitations of this license. Upon termination, you shall destroy the Documentation and all copies of the SOFTWARE. All provisions of this Agreement as to warranties, limitation of liability, remedies or damages, and our ownership rights shall survive termination.

7. **MISCELLANEOUS:** This Agreement shall be construed in accordance with the laws of the United States of America and the State of New York and shall benefit the Company, its affiliates, and assignees.

8. **LIMITED WARRANTY AND DISCLAIMER OF WARRANTY:** The Company warrants that the SOFTWARE, when properly used in accordance with the Documentation, will operate in substantial conformity with the description of the SOFTWARE set forth in the Documentation. The Company does not warrant that the SOFTWARE will meet your requirements or that the operation of the SOFTWARE will be uninterrupted or error-free. The Company warrants that the media on which the

SOFTWARE is delivered shall be free from defects in materials and workmanship under normal use for a period of thirty (30) days from the date of your purchase. Your only remedy and the Company's only obligation under these limited warranties is, at the Company's option, return of the warranted item for a refund of any amounts paid by you or replacement of the item. Any replacement of SOFTWARE or media under the warranties shall not extend the original warranty period. The limited warranty set forth above shall not apply to any SOFTWARE which the Company determines in good faith has been subject to misuse, neglect, improper installation, repair, alteration, or damage by you. EXCEPT FOR THE EXPRESSED WARRANTIES SET FORTH ABOVE, THE COMPANY DISCLAIMS ALL WARRANTIES, EXPRESS OR IMPLIED, INCLUDING WITHOUT LIMITATION, THE IMPLIED WARRANTIES OF MERCHANTABILITY AND FITNESS FOR A PARTICULAR PURPOSE. EXCEPT FOR THE EXPRESS WARRANTY SET FORTH ABOVE, THE COMPANY DOES NOT WARRANT, GUARANTEE, OR MAKE ANY REPRESENTATION REGARDING THE USE OR THE RESULTS OF THE USE OF THE SOFTWARE IN TERMS OF ITS CORRECTNESS, ACCURACY, RELIABILITY, CURRENTNESS, OR OTHERWISE.

IN NO EVENT, SHALL THE COMPANY OR ITS EMPLOYEES, AGENTS, SUPPLIERS, OR CONTRACTORS BE LIABLE FOR ANY INCIDENTAL, INDIRECT, SPECIAL, OR CONSEQUENTIAL DAMAGES ARISING OUT OF OR IN CONNECTION WITH THE LICENSE GRANTED UNDER THIS AGREEMENT, OR FOR LOSS OF USE, LOSS OF DATA, LOSS OF INCOME OR PROFIT, OR OTHER LOSSES, SUSTAINED AS A RESULT OF INJURY TO ANY PERSON, OR LOSS OF OR DAMAGE TO PROPERTY, OR CLAIMS OF THIRD PARTIES, EVEN IF THE COMPANY OR AN AUTHORIZED REPRESENTATIVE OF THE COMPANY HAS BEEN ADVISED OF THE POSSIBILITY OF SUCH DAMAGES. IN NO EVENT SHALL LIABILITY OF THE COMPANY FOR DAMAGES WITH RESPECT TO THE SOFTWARE EXCEED THE AMOUNTS ACTUALLY PAID BY YOU, IF ANY, FOR THE SOFTWARE.

SOME JURISDICTIONS DO NOT ALLOW THE LIMITATION OF IMPLIED WARRANTIES OR LIABILITY FOR INCIDENTAL, INDIRECT, SPECIAL, OR CONSEQUENTIAL DAMAGES, SO THE ABOVE LIMITATIONS MAY NOT ALWAYS APPLY. THE WARRANTIES IN THIS AGREEMENT GIVE YOU SPECIFIC LEGAL RIGHTS AND YOU MAY ALSO HAVE OTHER RIGHTS WHICH VARY IN ACCORDANCE WITH LOCAL LAW.

ACKNOWLEDGMENT

YOU ACKNOWLEDGE THAT YOU HAVE READ THIS AGREEMENT, UNDERSTAND IT, AND AGREE TO BE BOUND BY ITS TERMS AND CONDITIONS. YOU ALSO AGREE THAT THIS AGREEMENT IS THE COMPLETE AND EXCLUSIVE STATEMENT OF THE AGREEMENT BETWEEN YOU AND THE COMPANY AND SUPERSEDES ALL PROPOSALS OR PRIOR AGREEMENTS, ORAL, OR WRITTEN, AND ANY OTHER COMMUNICATIONS BETWEEN YOU AND THE COMPANY OR ANY REPRESENTATIVE OF THE COMPANY RELATING TO THE SUBJECT MATTER OF THIS AGREEMENT.

TECHNICAL SUPPORT

PRENTICE HALL DOES NOT OFFER TECHNICAL SUPPORT FOR THIS SOFTWARE. HOWEVER, IF THERE IS A PROBLEM WITH THE MEDIA, YOU MAY OBTAIN A REPLACEMENT COPY BY EMAILING US WITH YOUR PROBLEM AT: discexchange@phptr.com

Should you have any questions concerning this Agreement or if you wish to contact the Company for any reason, please contact in writing at the address below.

Robin Short
Prentice Hall PTR
One Lake Street
Upper Saddle River, New Jersey 07458